SLAVERY
SABBATH
WAR &
WOMEN

Case Issues in Biblical Interpretation

Charles C. Glidewell

Willard M. Swartley

Foreword by Albert J. Meyer

= important points

___ = I disagree

___ = Emphasis

HERALD PRESS
Scottdale, Pennsylvania
Waterloo, Ontario

Library of Congress Cataloging-in-Publication Data
Swartley, Willard M., 1936-
    Slavery, Sabbath, war, and women.
    (The Conrad Grebel lectures ; 1982)
    Includes bibliographical references and index.
    1. Slavery—Biblical teaching—Addresses, essays,
lectures. 2. Sabbath—Biblical teaching—Addresses,
essays, lectures. 3. War—Biblical teaching—Addresses,
essays, lectures. 4. Women in the Bible—Addresses,
essays, lectures. 5. Bible—Criticism, interpretation, etc.—
Addresses, essays, lectures.
    I. Title. II. Series.
BS670.S93 1983   220.6'01   82-23417
ISBN 0-8361-3330-7 (pbk.)

Acknowledgments: Quotations from *Christology at the Crossroads: A Latin American Approach* by Jon Sobrino (trans. by John Drury), *The Gospel in Solentiname,* vol. I, by Ernesto Cardenal (trans. by Donald D. Walsh), *The Liberation of Theology* by Juan Luise Segundo (trans. by John Drury), and *Third-Eye Theology: Theology in Formation in Asian Settings* by Choan-Seng Song—all are reprinted by permission of Orbis Books, Maryknoll, New York. Quotations from *The Sabbath and the Lord's Day* by H. M. Riggle are reprinted by permission of Warner Press, Anderson, Indiana. The material from *The New Testament Teaching on the Role Relationship of Men and Women* by George W. Knight III, copyright 1977 by Baker Book House, is used by permission. The references from *This Is the Day: The Biblical Doctrine of the Christian Sunday in Its Jewish and Early Church Setting* by Roger T. Beckwith and Wilfrid Stott are reprinted by permission of Marshall, Morgan & Scott Publications, Ltd., London. The extracts from *The Christian Attitude Toward War* by Loraine Boettner are reprinted by permission of Wm. B. Eerdmans Publishing Co., Grand Rapids, Michigan. The quotation from *Why I'm an Adventist* by Dan Day is reprinted by permission of Pacific Press Publishing Association, Mountain View, California. Quotations from *Woman in the World of Jesus* by Evelyn and Frank Stagg, copyright ©1978 The Westminster Press, are by permission. Material from *Sunday: The History of the Day of Rest and Worship in the Earliest Centuries of the Christian Church* by Willy Rordorf (trans. by A. A. K. Graham), © SCM Press Ltd. 1968, are used by permission of The Westminster Press, Philadelphia. For copyright clearance information, see page 6.

The paper used in this publication is recycled and meets the mini-
mum requirements of American National Standard for Information
Sciences—Permanence of Paper for Printed Library Materials, ANSI
Z39.48-1984.

03 02 01   17 16 15

To order or request information, please call
1-800-759-4447 (individuals); 1-800-245-7894 (trade).
Website: www.mph.org

"Although the scope of the book allows but a limited selection of witnesses, they are fairly chosen, and allowed to speak their own minds. Comparative hermeneutical insights are drawn from the interpretations observed. In effect, the cases provide models for understandings which will keep future interpreters from abusing the text and allow them to '*listen* carefully *within* the text, *learn* helpfully from *behind* the text, and *live* freely from *in front of* the text.' Given the proliferation of books on these issues, and some of the thorny questions raised by them, Christians who wish to deal earnestly and honestly with the relevant biblical texts will surely be helped by this book to understand the nature of the debate and to discern more adequately the way in which God addresses us today. I heartily recommend this good study for church and seminary use alike."—Robert P. Meye, Dean of the Fuller Theological Seminary School of Theology.

"Among the numerous merits of the book, some of those which stand out are: the readable style, the clear organization and presentation of the material, the ample documentation of each position presented, the perceptive diagnosis of factors which have contributed to develop certain views, the excellent synthesis of and interaction with the various views presented. The clarity of the presentation and organization makes this book ideal for didactical use in a classroom or in a study group."—Samuele Bacchiocchi, Professor of Religion, Andrews University.

"Swartley's interpretive perspective reflects informed scholarship and . . . develops a rather full range of interpretive principles through four masterful case studies. The book will provide an excellent pedagogical aid for teaching exegesis and hermeneutics. It should also be a most useful, practical point of reference for bringing a fresh perspective and a renewed sense of responsibility into the current discussions of the interplay of biblical authority and biblical interpretation. The book utilizes the lessons gained in hermeneutical perspective from the cases on slavery, Sabbath, and war to illumine the urgent discussion on women's place in church leadership. I want my students, colleagues, and friends in the church representing the whole spectrum on biblical interpretation to read it." —David M. Scholer, Dean of the Seminary and Professor of New Testament, Northern Baptist Theological Seminary.

"This book consists of four case issues in biblical interpretation: slavery, Sabbath, war, and women. In a highly readable style the author shows how opposite sides of each issue can be supported through the use of biblical texts. Through each chapter and issue, the reader is confronted with the question of how cultural setting and traditional teaching determine biblical understanding. This is an excellent resource for those who assume they accept the whole Bible and follow its teaching on these issues. Highly recommended."—Emma Richards, copastor, Lombard (Ill.) Mennonite Church.

"This book admirably demonstrates the importance of hermeneutical issues by grounding them concretely in four practical areas of biblical interpretation. Willard Swartley convincingly demonstrates the need for interpretation as a consciously critical and self-critical process, showing that it is not at all obvious how we are to understand the variety of biblical material which relates to these four issues of slavery, Sabbath, war, and women. In particular he underlines the part played by an interpreter's own self-identity and his or her own social content. This book contributes positively to the ongoing hermeneutical discussion."—Dr. Anthony C. Thiselton, Senior Lecturer in Biblical Studies, University of Sheffield, England.

"The questions raised are not only questions of how individual scholars interpret the Bible, the methods they follow, but also about the basis of the authority of the Bible itself and about its major theological witness versus its more historical/cultural/situational conventions and practices. Underlying the scope of this book are an array of questions about the nature of Scripture itself and its uses and misuses, the wide variety of contexts in which the texts are set, the contexts in which they are interpreted, the views of the interpreters, the questions of reinterpretation within the canon of Scripture, the theoretical tools used in attempting to overcome the distance between the text, its context and the meaning of the text for our time, places, and positions. . . . Swartley's research is another step in furthering the essential task of opening up the Word of God for today, embedded in Scripture's written texts and their variants for centuries. Through the method of comparative interpretation, Swartley proposes guidelines about how to free the message that sets us free—women and men, warrior and pacifist, 'slave and free.' "—Constance F. Parvey, Visiting Professor, Vancouver School of Theology.

"In a fair and judicious manner the author presents the problems of the role of the Bible in the dispute over important theological questions. Presenting the arguments of the contending parties themselves, he then proceeds to identify and analyze the hermeneutical problems which emerge. The reader is drawn into the author's concern through the recognition that precisely the problems emerging in these test cases are the ones he or she faces in interpreting Scripture. The serious student of the Bible, whether formally trained or not, will find here an intriguing mine of questions and insights and a powerful stimulus toward clarification and critical examination of the principles and methods of interpretation he or she uses."—Paul D. Hanson, Bussey Professor of Divinity, Harvard University.

"When the Bible is used to support opposite views on contemporary social issues, one can despair of ever finding an objective evaluator. Everyone seems to begin from his or her own presuppositions. Willard Swartley's book, *Slavery, Sabbath, War, and Women*, is as objective as any book I have read on the topic of biblical interpretation. At the same time, Swartley has cut through dull abstractions and plunged into topics that have aroused strong emotions historically and in the present. Being especially interested in women's issues, I was impressed by Swartley's ability to critique the hermeneutical principles behind both the hierarchical and feminist views. I find that the interpretative methods Swartley proposes have raised my confidence in using the Bible to tackle knotty social issues."—Reta Finger, Editorial Coordinator, *Daughters of Sarah*.

To
Mary,
Louisa,
and
Kenton

from and with whom
I continue to learn
that understanding
—the art of interpretation—
is sometimes painful,
unpretentiously profound,
surprisingly practical,
and co-creatively joyful

Contents

Foreword by Albert J. Meyer 17
Author's Preface 19
Introduction 21

Chapter 1: The Bible and Slavery

Preview of the Debate
I. The Pro-Slavery Case 31
Meet the Debaters
Position in Brief

Thesis 1: Slavery was divinely sanctioned among the
patriarchs.
Thesis 2: Slavery was incorporated into Israel's national
constitution.
Thesis 3: Slavery was recognized and approved by Jesus
Christ and the apostles.
Thesis 4: Slavery is a merciful institution.

II. The Anti-Slavery Case 37
Meet the Debaters
Position in Brief

Thesis 1: The so-called slavery of the patriarchs in no way
justifies the system of slavery in the USA.
Thesis 2: God's deliverance of Israel from slavery in Egypt
shows, once and for all, that God hates and
condemns slavery.
Thesis 3: Hebrew servitude in the time of Moses was
voluntary, merciful, and of benefit to the
servant; it was not slavery.

Thesis 4: Israel's history and the prophetic oracles
confirm that oppressive slavery did not exist
in Israel; God would have roundly condemned
it, had it existed.
Thesis 5: Neither Jesus nor the apostles approved of or
condoned slavery.

III. The Pro-Slavery Rebuttal 46

IV. The Anti-Slavery Rebuttal 50

V. Supplement to Slavery Debate: Hermeneutical
Alternatives 53
1. The Bible says both yes and no.
2. Biblical teaching is to be applied to believers.
3. The slaves' use of the Bible shows distinctive
emphases.

VI. Hermeneutical Commentary 58
1. "Literal" interpretation (a vice or a virtue?) needs
clarification.
2. The entire biblical witness must be considered with
willingness to recognize diversity.
3. Specific passages should not be used for "attendant
features," but for their main emphases.
4. Theological principles and basic moral imperatives
should be given priority.
5. Self-serving interests in biblical interpretation must
be recognized and resisted.
6. Interpreters must use a method that allows the text to
speak its message.
7. Interpreters must ask whom the text addresses and
holds accountable.

**Chapter 2: The Bible and the Sabbath: Sabbath, Sabbath-Sunday,
or Lord's Day?**

Overview of the Problem

I. The Sabbath Position: The Seventh Day Holy 67
1. God ordained the Sabbath in creation.
2. The Sabbath is an essential part of the moral law.
3. Sabbath observance was important through Israel's
history B.C.
4. Jesus observed the Sabbath.
5. The apostles practiced Sabbath observance.
6. Rome changed the day.

II. The Sabbath-Sunday Position: One Day in Seven Holy 73
   1. God ordained the Sabbath in creation.
   2. The moral law commands Sabbath observance.
   3. The New Testament changed the day of the Sabbath.
   4. Patristic writings show the early church's observance
     of Sabbath-Sunday.

III. The Lord's Day Position: Seven-Days-in-One Holy 78
Resumé of Position
   1. The Sabbath originated with Moses.
   2. The Sabbath's original purpose was ethical and hu-
     manitarian.
   3. Sabbath-keeping in Judaism deteriorated into
     legalism.
   4. Jesus broke Sabbath laws and fulfilled its moral pur-
     pose.
   5. Early Christians celebrated Jesus' work on the day of
     his victory, the first day of the week.
   6. Sabbath observance and first-day resurrection cele-
     brations continued side by side in the early church.
   7. The promised rest of the Sabbath has begun in
     Christ; unbelief prevents entering.
   8. In later church history (mostly fourth century), Sab-
     bath rest became part of Lord's day celebrations.

Position Represented by
  A. H. M. Riggle 80
  B. Willy Rordorf 82
  C. Paul K. Jewett 87
  D. D. A. Carson, ed. 89

IV. Hermeneutical Commentary 90
  A. Minor observations on the debate
  B. Major hermeneutical issues
   1. Tradition (church belief and practice) plays an im-
     portant role in understanding Scripture.
   2. The historical method of Bible study is essential.

Chapter 3: The Bible and War

I. Positions Supporting/Allowing Christian Participation
  in War 97
A. Traditional Position A 97
   1. God commanded to fight and kill.
   2. God honored military leaders.
   3. Many New Testament sayings endorse war.
   4. The apostolic writings teach subjection to authority.

5. Pacifists misinterpret the Scripture.
6. The change from theocracy to church does not invalidate this position.

B. Traditional Position B 102

1. God as warrior is basic to Jewish and Christian theology.
2. Christians must fulfill both kingdom and state obligations.
3. Kingdom ethics cannot be absolutes in this fallen world.

C. Theologies of Revolution and Liberation 106

1. Exodus: liberation from oppression is central to biblical thought.
2. Justice: God's justice requires tearing down in order to build up (Jeremiah 1:10).
3. Messianism: the messianic hope is defined chiefly as liberation and justice.
4. Incarnation: Jesus' coming means liberation, justice, and humanization.
5. Death/Resurrection: this paradigm, central to the Christian faith, stands for radical change and revolution.

II. Pacifist/Nonresistant Position(s) 112

A. The Old Testament Witness 113

1. Warfare has its roots in humanity's fall 113
   a (variant). Old Testament warfare expressed God's will for the people when kingdom and state were combined.
   b (variant). God allowed war as a concession to Israel's sin.
   c (variant). Israel's military warfare resulted from its failure to trust God *as warrior.*
2. The Old Testament criticizes warfare and prepares for the New Testament teaching of nonresistant love and pacifism 115
   a. OT shows examples of nonresistance.
   b. Patriarchal narratives are pacifist.
   c. The Reed Sea paradigm called Israel to "not fight".
   d. God fought *for*, not with, Israel.
   e. God fought also against Israel.
   f. Israel did not honor the death of "war heroes."
   g. The prophets criticized kingship and military power.

h. Past victories were not used for war, but trust.

i. The prophetic hope calls to peace.

j. OT contains pacifist, universalist strands.

k. Holy war culminated in "reverse fighting."

l. OT contains the roots of the NT ethic.

3. Since it prepares for the New, the Old Testament
cannot be used for normative Christian ethics 117

B. The New Testament Evidence........................118

1. Jesus' teachings (reflected in the apostles) are
clearly pacifist.....................................118

a. Nonresistance: overcome evil with good.

b. Love the neighbor and the enemy.

c. Jesus taught against the use of the sword.

2. The nature of God's kingdom and Jesus' messiahship supports the pacifist/nonresistant position 122

a. Jesus' proclamation of the kingdom of God in the
context of first-century politics shows Jesus' pacifist commitment.

b. Jesus' temptations were political in nature.

c. Peter's confession, a political manifesto, prompted
Jesus' teaching on the pacifist way of the cross.

d. The suffering servant-Son of Man-Messiah introduced a bold new pacifist picture for messianic
thought.

e. Jesus as conquering lamb demonstrated the new
way.

3. Christ's atonement calls for pacifist discipleship 127

a. Atonement means victory over the powers.

b. Atonement means reconciling justification.

c. Discipleship means identifying with/following/
imitating Jesus Christ.

4. The nature and mission of the church leads to
pacifism 131

a. The church is the body of Christ's peace.

b. The church's mission is peace.

c. The church is separate from the state, but subordinate to it and called to witness to it.

—Variants on the nature of witness

5. Peace is the heart of the gospel 136

a. Peace permeates the New Testament.

b. Peace is rooted in eschatology.

III. Hermeneutical Commentary 138

A. Minor observations on the debate

B. Major hermeneutical issues

1. The relationship of the Old and New Testaments
poses a difficult hermeneutical problem.

2. Both diversity and unity in Scripture must be acknowledged.
3. A view of biblical authority must incorporate these hermeneutical problems.
4. The application of Jesus' ethic raises certain hermeneutical problems.

Chapter 4: The Bible and Women: Male and Female Role Relationships

I. The Genesis Narratives 152
  A. Genesis 1:26-27; 5:1 152
    1. Hierarchical interpreters speak.
    2. Liberationist interpreters speak.
  B. Genesis 2:18-25 154
    1. Hierarchical interpreters speak.
    2. Liberationist interpreters speak.
  C. Genesis 3:16 156
    1. Hierarchical interpreters speak.
    2. Liberationist interpreters speak.

II. Women in Old Testament History 157
    1. Hierarchical interpreters speak.
    2. Liberationist interpreters speak.

III. Jesus and Women 160
    1. Hierarchical interpreters speak.
    2. Liberationist interpreters speak.

IV. Pauline Teaching and Practice 164
  A. Galatians 3:28 164
    1. Hierarchical interpreters speak.
    2. Liberationist interpreters speak.
  B. 1 Corinthians 11:2-16; 14:34-36 166
    1. Hierarchical interpreters speak.
    2. Liberationist interpreters speak.
  C. Romans 16 174
    1. Hierarchical interpreters speak.
    2. Liberationist interpreters speak.
  D. Teaching in the Pastoral Epistles 178
    1. Hierarchical interpreters speak.
    2. Liberationist interpreters speak.

V. The Witness of the Gospels 182
  Liberationist interpreters

VI. Hermeneutical Commentary 183

1. The influence of the interpreter's bias must be acknowledged and assessed.
2. The text holds the interpreter accountable for his/her bias.
3. How shall the diversity of Scripture be evaluated?
4. How shall the divine and human dimensions of Scripture be understood?

Chapter 5: How Then Shall We Use and Interpret the Bible?

I. Hermeneutical Comparisons Between Case Issues 192
  A. Slavery and Sabbath
  B. Slavery and War
  C. Sabbath and War
  D. Women and War
  E. Women and Sabbath
  F. Women and Slavery
  G. Hermeneutical Reflections

II. The Use of the Bible for Social Issues 204
  A. Six Alternative Views
    1. Jack T. Sanders: the New Testament has no useful social ethic for us.
    2. Rudolf Schnackenburg: the Bible has clear social ethical teachings but neither Jesus nor Paul changed social structures.
    3. John H. Yoder: biblical teaching speaks to social ethical issues and calls the church to prophetic witness.
    4. Birch and Rasmussen: the Bible influences social ethics through God's people in numerous ways.
    5. "FEST": the Bible stresses God's action and the church as the locus of the new order.
    6. Juan Luis Segundo: analysis of the social situation is a prerequisite for understanding the Bible's social ethic.
  B. Evaluative Response

III. Model of Understandings for Biblical Interpretation 211
  A. Sample Models 211
    1. Pro-slavery model (1820): stresses the veracity and equal authority of all parts of Scripture.
    2. Grant R. Osborne: distinguishes between the cultural and the normative.
    3. William E. Hull: one must assess the distance between the text and the interpreter.

    4. Elisabeth Schüssler Fiorenza: calls for assessment of
       the interpreter's biases and values.
    5. Peter Stuhlmacher: calls for consent to the text in the
       light of theological tradition and critical reflection.

  B. Proposed Components for a Model of Understand-
    ings 215
    1. The community of faith is the proper context in
       which Scripture is to be understood.
    2. The view of biblical authority recognizes the signifi-
       cance of both *historical* revelation and historical
       revelation.
    3. The method of study must enable the interpreter to
       grasp and respond to the text's distinctive message.
    4. The method must include the assessment of the in-
       fluences upon the interpreter.
    5. Interpretation includes reflection upon the signifi-
       cance of the distance between the text and the in-
       terpreter.
    6. The purpose of biblical interpretation is the edifica-
       tion of believers and the discovery of God's Word to
       humanity.
    7. Interpretation is validated through several important
       processes.
    8. God's Spirit plays a creative, illuminative role in bib-
       lical interpretation.

IV. Proposed Method for Bible Study 224

  A. *Listen* carefully from *within* the text 225
    1. Hear; read the text, observing its distinctive struc-
       ture.
    2. Become aware of the text's literary form, its type of
       literature, and its distinctive images.
    3. Read the text in several translations (or in its
       original language).

  B. *Learn* helpfully from *behind* the text 226
    4. Define key words and assess the significance of the
       grammatical structure.
    5. Discover the literary context of the text and the
       text's function in the larger narrative.
    6. Identify the historical setting of the text, noting dis-
       tinctive cultural, social, economic, and political
       perspectives.
    7. Put the message of the text into dialogue with or cri-
       tique of (by) other biblical texts, considering the di-
       rection of biblical teaching, Old to New Testament,

and the witness of Scripture to Jesus Christ, God's
clearest revelation.
8. Learn how the text has been understood by other
people in diverse cultural and historical settings.

C. *Live* freely from *in front of* the text.....................227
9. Engage in self-examination, assessing the influence
of "Who am I?"
10. Reflect upon the significance of the distance
between the world of the text and your world.
11. Meditate upon the text, opening yourself to its word
and allowing it to dialogue with and critique your
entire life/world—past, present, and future.
12. Test the co-creative interpretive experience with
other believers for confirmation, correction, and
mutual edification.

Conclusion: Summary of Learnings 229

Appendices... 235
    1. Biblical Interpretation in the Life of the
      Church (MC 1977 Statement)................... 235
    2. Pacifist Answers to New Testament Problem
      Texts... 250
    3. Interpretive Commentary on Marriage Texts 256
    4. The Wider Use of the Bible: Ephesians as a Model .. 270

Notes... 277
Bibliography 334
Index of Scriptures... 349
Index of Persons 357
The Conrad Grebel Lectures.................................. 365
The Author 367

Foreword

How do we as Christians today obtain reliable information and perspective from the witness and experience of the Christ whose name we bear? How do we test our lives and words against the life and witness of our Predecessor and Lord? And how do we comprehend authentically the larger context of God's action in history within which we are to engage in our mission as God's contemporary representatives?

The textbook response to these questions is that we turn to the written testimony of those who knew Jesus personally and of prophets in other times who spoke for the Lord. Children may experience something of the Good News incarnated in family and community life. Young people may hear stories of the past from their parents and teachers. But the principal means most serious Christians have of testing the authenticity of contemporary words and actions is through facts and understandings gained in a study of the writings of the apostles who knew Jesus and of others who walked with God years ago.

The problem is that Christians sometimes arrive at very different understandings from these writings. The problem is not new. At one point in his growing conflict with the scholars and interpreters of his day, Jesus exclaimed, "You study the scriptures diligently, ... and yet"—to put it in a contemporary paraphrase—"you miss the whole point!" (John 5:39-40).

17

In this book Willard Swartley brings to our attention four case problems in biblical interpretation in modern times. Some of his comments and citations are painful. Will future generations find us as blind and misguided as some of our forebears in the faith? Swartley's reporting elicits humility, almost despair. What is truth? How can we ever be sure we are hearing the Lord, not just echoes of our own voices and cultures?

There is no hope for us in today's church if we cannot be honest about the weaknesses of our forebears and our own doubts and insecurities. The biblical call to repentance includes identifying dead-end paths of the recent and more distant pasts and turning from them. We cannot hear what God is trying to tell us if we cannot listen and are not teachable. If we are to hear aright we need to allow the communal structures of our hearing and obedience to be themselves shaped as voluntary and missionary communities of discernment distinct from the larger societies in which we find ourselves. And having done all, we still need to recognize that the truth we incarnate in our lives and communities is in earthen vessels.

Throughout this work, the author wrestles with the question of how the Bible can speak to us in our prejudice and cultural provincialism. He wants to let the Lord break through to us with the unexpected—with what we cannot just deduce from the laboratory or common life experience, but need to be told. He wants us to be able to hear God speaking through the Bible.

The contemporary Christian church is living in times of serious challenge, as is evident in the case studies of this book and their updating in today's headlines. The Conrad Grebel Projects Committee contributes this work to today's church, commending it to Mennonites and Christians of many communions with a prayer that it may contribute to the faithfulness of us all to our common Lord.

Albert J. Meyer
Mennonite Board of Education
February 15, 1983

Author's Preface

I express appreciation to the Conrad Grebel Projects Committee and to Albert Meyer, executive secretary of the Mennonite Board of Education, for sponsoring this project as a Conrad Grebel Lectureship. The procedure of the committee, both the appointment of four consultants and the arranging for three oral presentations of the lectures, has been most helpful. I thank especially the consultants appointed by the committee—Richard Detweiler, John Lederach, Millard Lind, and Marilyn Miller—for taking time to read the entire manuscript in two separate drafts and to prepare helpful written responses.

I am grateful also for the comments and counsel I received from various people through giving the lectures at Eastern Mennonite College, Conrad Grebel College's School of Adult Studies, the Associated Mennonite Biblical Seminaries, the Denver Mennonite Winter Seminar (especially to Peter Ediger for suggesting that the slaves' use of the Bible be included in chapter 1), and the Pacific Coast Ministers and Spouses Retreat. The presentation of chapter 3 in two lectures at the Amsterdam Doopsgezinde (Mennonite) Seminary also provided helpful perspectives for the final form and emphasis of this chapter. The sharpening of insights received from students in my biblical hermeneutics class at the Associated Mennonite Biblical Seminaries has also been significant.

Special thanks go to Mark Wenger, who in two independent

studies did a significant amount of research for chapters 1 and 2; to Robert Peters for primary research in Philadelphia on the slaves' use of the Bible; to Willard Roth for counsel on editorial matters as well as points of substance; to Paul Hanson and Alan Kreider for helpful comments on chapter 3; to Jacob P. Jacobszoon for counsel on the hermeneutical sections; to Mary Jean Kraybill for both counsel on the project and proofreading; to Charmaine Jeschke for proofreading and editorial counsel; to Priscilla Stuckey Kauffman for proofreading, editorial work, counsel, and completing the extensive index; to the able typists for their perseverance in seeing this manuscript through many drafts and their willingness to work in some cases under the pressure of deadlines and with sacrifice of personal convenience: Carolyn Albrecht, Lila Collins, Jean Kelly, Louisa Swartley, and Sue Yoder; to Rachel Stoltzfus for both typing and managing the circulation of the manuscript to the consultants; to Mary Swartley for typing chapters 3 and 5 of the final draft, preparing a first draft of the index, and giving both moral support and counsel to the project; and to Herald Press book editor, Paul M. Schrock and copy editor Mary Ellen Martin. Without the help of many people, this publication would not have been possible.

                                    Willard M. Swartley
                                    Thanksgiving 1981 and
                                    Easter 1982

INTRODUCTION

The Bible appears to give mixed signals on these four case issues. This study of opposing interpretations of Scripture on these four case issues, therefore, seeks to serve the goal of identifying difficulties and clarifying basic learnings in biblical interpretation. The hermeneutical disputes of the church over the first three issues are intended also to stand in the service of illuminating our contemporary agenda: how should we understand the scriptural teaching(s) on the role relationships of women and men?

Together, these four case issues raise basic questions in biblical interpretation:

1. How are the two Testaments related?

2. How is the authority of Jesus related to all of Scripture?

3. What is the relationship between divine revelation and the culture in which the revelation is given and perceived?

4. Does Scripture mandate, regulate, or challenge practices associated with these four case issues?

5. Does the Bible say only one thing on a given subject, or does it sometimes show differing, even contradictory points of view?

6. What does it mean to take the Bible literally? Is that a vice or a virtue? Does "literal" signify the intended meaning of the author or a meaning that seems natural to us?

7. To what extent do the interpreter's predetermined positions, even ideologies, affect the interpretive task?

During the last decade this last question has emerged into central focus within hermeneutical discussion. Numerous writings have called attention to the influence of the interpreter upon the process and outcome of interpretation. The interpretation of the text, we are told, is determined to a great extent by the glasses of the interpreter. Liberation and feminist theologies have done much to bring this point into focus.[1] In his study of the contemporary philosophy of hermeneutics, Anthony Thiselton has ably documented the fact that interpretation has two horizons, the text and the interpreter.[2]

While granting these factors, we must not overlook the primary position of the text in the interpretive process. Interpreters, issues, and ideologies come and go, but the word of the text stands from generation to generation. All serious interpretation must seek to let the text speak and call the interpreter into its service, both in thought and action. When this happens, a co-creative event occurs in time and space—an event derivative from and imaging God's own creative activity in which the world came into being through the Spirit and the Word (Gen. 1; Ps. 33:6).

The meaning of this suggested imagery, interpretation as co-creative event, is that the word of the text acts with power through the interpreter.[3] Interpretation influences patterns of thought and shapes behavior as well. Indeed, the interpretive event casts a vote for the future shape of the world.

In the study of these four case issues—slavery, Sabbath, war, and the role relationship of men and women—I became poignantly aware that the text through the interpreter became a resource of power. Likewise, the viewpoint of the interpreter influenced how the text was understood. Hence, while the glasses of the interpreter influenced his/her use of the Bible, the text as understood by the interpreter exercised power upon the shape of the life-world of the interpreter and his/her community.

I live with the conviction, supported by the biblical text in my judgment, that there is a "wrong or right" in this interpretive process; otherwise this study could be of little benefit. Further and more important, the text itself would be only an object, a thing to be used by interpreters however they wish. Its position as subject, with power to shape the interpreter, would be given over to the interpreter, who as subject would shape the text. Such is neither exegesis nor interpretation, but a fashioning of the text into a puppet of the interpreter's own design.

To be sure, no interpreter comes to the text value free. Biblical hermeneutics is not hermetically sealed off from how the interpreter views his/her world, whether in total or in part—the function of the police officer in the local town, the meaning of sex, healing, national defense, or the welfare check. But it is one thing to acknowledge such influences upon the interpreter and still another to reduce the text to the status of an ideological victim of the interpreter, thus depriving it of its power over the interpreter. To gain a proper angle of vision for dealing with differences in biblical interpretation, it is essential in my judgment to hold the text in the position of subject, believing that the power of its word can change the viewpoint of the interpreter.

For this reason, this study intends to contribute to an understanding of biblical interpretation that regards both the text and the method of interpretation to be important. A hypothesis, guiding my work in this study is that the appropriate (God-intended) biblical word is more likely heard on controversial issues when:

1. The historical and cultural contexts of specific texts are considered seriously.
2. Diversity within Scripture is acknowledged, thus leading to a recognition that (a) intracanonical dialogue must be heard and assessed, and (b) the Gospels in their direct witness to Jesus Christ are to be taken as final authority.
3. The basic moral and theological principles of the entire Scripture are given priority over specific statements which stand in tension either with these principles or with other specific texts on the subject.

Conversely stated, the appropriate (God-intended) biblical word is least likely heard when:

1. Numerous texts, occurring here and there throughout the Bible, are sewn together into a patchwork quilt with disregard for the different cultural fabrics and historical textures of each patch.
2. The interpreter assumes a "flat view" of biblical authority; i.e., all texts are of equal significance to us and must be harmonized into one, rational, propositional truth.
3. Specific texts on a given subject are used legalistically—for example, 1 Timothy 6:1-6 on slavery—to silence the spirit of pervasive moral emphases, such as "Love your neighbor as yourself."

In my judgment, these case studies confirm the hypothesis. But the reader will need to judge whether the interaction between

the hypothesis, the handling of the case issues, and the hermeneutical conclusions has been validly undertaken and whether the
findings are helpful to communities of Christian faith as they seek
to be good stewards of the Word of God.

Purposes of This Study

This case-issue approach to biblical interpretation then has
several specific goals:

1. This approach attempts to provide a descriptive statement
of how the Bible has been interpreted differently on four separate
issues. While these cases are intended primarily to illumine hermeneutical issues, the statement of each case will contribute also to
historical research on these topics.

2. The primary goal in setting forth alternative positions on
these four issues is to provide case illustrations that both show the
necessity of careful biblical interpretation and raise methodological
issues which hermeneutics must address. The hermeneutical commentary at the end of each chapter identifies and discusses the
major problems in biblical interpretation which each case occasions. This discussion will suggest ways to resolve these problems
and, in some cases, refocus the "problem" so that it becomes a positive resource in the church's use of the Bible.

Many readers will wish for a definitive position statement on
each issue, but this goes beyond the purposes of the study. The objective of this contribution is to learn something about biblical interpretation by listening to how different interpreters use the Bible.

3. The study of these four case issues will set the context then
for comparative hermeneutical insights (part A of chapter 5). By
thinking analogically from one case to another, some new insights
and resources for evaluating differing interpretations will emerge.
Such comparative perspectives should help to illumine current debates, showing which uses of the text are more appropriate, valid,
and useful and which should be given up. Especially in forming a
position on the role relationship of men and women, the reader
should ask how the method of interpretation for her/his own position correlates with both the method for, and the position on, the
other case issues. Put simply, if I as interpreter extend my method
of interpretation for one issue (choose any one) to the other three
issues, do I see consistency or inconsistency in my method? Or,
with which interpretation do I identify on all four issues? Does the
interpretive method I follow support me in that position?

4. Because the Bible is used in such contradictory ways on

these issues, the question of whether the Bible should be used at all for dealing with social issues must be addressed. Even though such use is hermeneutically difficult, as these four case issues show, the discussion will argue for the appropriateness and necessity of the church's use of the Bible for socio-ethical issues. A thematic study of the biblical book of Ephesians will illustrate, however, that the church's appropriate use of the Bible is much broader than its use for social issues (see Appendix 4).

5. This study will then propose a model of appropriate understandings for believers who desire to use the Bible as a significant resource for shaping values and forming convictions on social issues. Such a model of understandings is intended to help interpreters avoid common misuses of the Bible and to create conscious pre-understandings that will make study of the Bible fruitful, allowing it to encounter us with its message.

6. I will attempt to translate this model of understandings into a hermeneutical method, consisting of three major components of responsibility: *listen* carefully from *within* the text, *learn* helpfully from *behind* the text, and *live* freely from *in front of* the text.

7. Finally, I present a summary of hermeneutical learnings to serve both as an index and a systematic statement of the various hermeneutical insights gained from the study of these four case issues and the learnings in chapter 5. These learnings together with the model of understanding and the method of interpretation (chapter 5) are intended to aid the Bible reader *to listen to the text,* and while aware of his/her own situation in life, experience the surprise that *the text reads us.*

Limitations of This Study

Certain limitations are clearly manifest in these endeavors:

1. Each of the four issues competes for full book space in itself. All the chapters have been shortened in the final draft in order to allow the main topic of biblical interpretation to remain the subject of the book. Hence none of the four issues is treated as fully as it might be; not all relevant sources, even within the time period selected, are reported. Those used are intended to represent the major interpretive options. The pacifist position, however, in chapter 3 has been given more space than the purposes of this study alone allow. Here the bias of the author shows itself in the effort to represent the full range of today's major biblical arguments for pacifism (unfortunately, not all variant positions could be as fully presented). In the long view of history and the consequences

for the church, the cosmos, and even for the role of women, this issue in my judgment is of supreme importance.[4]

2. The style of writing may be disconcerting to some readers, especially on two accounts. The regular use of the present tense to introduce quotations has seemed to be necessary since various writers are cited in support of a position presented in the present tense; thus this study is not historical research for its own sake. Moreover, I am aware that writers change their minds; I apologize therefore if a given citation no longer represents the position of the writer. Readers should keep this limitation in mind especially as they read statements of authors who wrote more than a decade or two ago.

Further, some readers may find the extensive quoting cumbersome, especially in chapters 1 and 2. Even though a more even style of writing could have been achieved by casting these quotations into my own words, I have considered the style of the language, especially in the slavery debate, an important part of the argument. Some of these quotations, from a historical point of view, are gems to be treasured.

3. Some readers may consider this work to be deficient because it does not deal extensively with the nature of divine revelation and biblical authority. While I discuss these topics in the hermeneutical commentaries at the end of chapters 3 and 4 and again in the model of understandings (chapter 5), I put the discussion within the context of the hermeneutical process. Some may argue that these topics must be settled first before interpretation begins (for example, one must affirm the inerrancy and infallibility of Scripture). The plea of this study, which may be a strength as well as a limitation, is that statements on these topics must be shaped by awareness of the difficulties in Scripture that a study like this brings to our attention. No statement on inspiration, inerrancy, and infallibility is of itself able to resolve these hermeneutical issues.[5] Hence the reader should view this study as one addressed primarily to interpretation and only indirectly to the nature of Scripture.

4. As with all efforts in biblical interpretation, a limiting circle of relationship exists between the text and the interpreter. Since I selected these four topics and arranged the arguments, which were, however, assessed and affirmed by numerous people, my interests and the variety of influences upon my life affect and limit this contribution from beginning to end. But this is the way it must be for all of us; it makes the role of the hermeneutical community (see chapter 5) not only helpful but vitally essential.

With these limitations and others, this study intends to contribute, nonetheless, to the conformity of our lives to the image of Jesus Christ. This image beckons us toward a life-world hospitable to Jesus of Nazareth, whom many of us call Messiah, liberator-judge of humanity, and re-creator of all things.

Use of This Book

Seldom can a book be used profitably by reading first the end and then working backward through the book. But for some purposes, especially study by small groups, I recommend such an approach for this book.

For such a group study, especially in the congregational context for a quarter of study (13 sessions), I recommend beginning with Appendix 4, following with Appendix 1, and then devoting one session to every two points in the summary of 22 learnings (pp. 229-233). These learnings are indexed so that the reader can readily find the relevant discussion of each point in the preceding five chapters. The arguments for the opposing positions on these case issues can then be read to the extent that they helpfully illustrate the need for the respective hermeneutical learnings. Two or three members of the study group may be asked to study in advance and present orally the opposing positions on a given case issue. At some point in the study process, perhaps toward the end, each person should be encouraged to read as many of the four cases as possible and especially chapter 5 completely.

For the classroom—whether in college, university, or seminary, where more time is allocated for the student's study—I recommend using the book in its order of presentation, except that Appendices 4 and 1 might also be profitably read first in order to set the contribution of the case issues within a broader context.

Finally I call attention to several matters to assist the reader's understanding of the material. The time periods of the quoted sources differ from case to case. Chapter 1 on slavery utilizes sources from 1815 to 1865, with the exception of John Woolman who lived in the previous century. The sources for chapter 2 on the Sabbath and Lord's day are mostly from the twentieth century, with a few earlier ones representing the Puritan position. Chapters 3 and 4 utilize sources from the present generation of writers (extending back into the 1940s), except as earlier sources (such as Reformation writers) have been quoted by contemporary writers.

Further, I have arranged chapter 1 in the form of a debate. Because the slavery issue is removed from us today, I felt it was possible to present it in this more dramatic form of communication, but I apologize to blacks—and women—for some of the language used in the quotations and in my restatement of then perspectives. I trust that such historical perspective will sensitize all readers to the ugly roots of racism and sexism wherever they continue. On the other hand and at the other end, I did not arrange the biblical commentary on the male-female issue into a systematic position statement as I did for the other issues. The purpose of this chapter is to provide the interpretive material that can assist readers, both personally and corporately as believing communities, to find their way to a position of belief and practice.

Above all, I hope that this study will help every reader to a more aware and responsible use of the Bible in today's world.

SLAVERY
SABBATH
WAR &
WOMEN

CHAPTER 1

The Bible and Slavery

Preview of the Debate

For

The Bible's defense of slavery is very plain. St. Paul was inspired, and knew the will of the Lord Jesus Christ, and was only intent on obeying it. And who are we, that in our modern wisdom presume to set aside the Word of God ... and invent for ourselves a "higher law: than those holy Scriptures which are given to us as 'a light to our feet and a lamp to our paths,' in the darkness of a sinful and a polluted world?"

—John Henry Hopkins (1864)[1]

Against

Slavery seeks refuge in the Bible only in its last extremity.... Goaded to frenzy in its conflicts with conscience and common sense, ... it courses up and down the Bible, "seeking rest, and finding none." The law of love, glowing on every page, flashes through its anguish and despair.

—Theodore Dwight Weld (1837)[2]

The Pro-Slavery Case

Meet the Debaters

1. John Henry Hopkins, DD, LLD, bishop of the Episcopal diocese of Vermont and author of *A Scriptural, Ecclesiastical, and Historical View of Slavery, from the Days of the Patriarch Abra-*

ham, to the Nineteenth Century, published in 1864.[3] Hopkins also wrote a tract in 1861 on the "Bible View of Slavery" and circulated it to Episcopal bishops and ministers in the New England and middle eastern states.[4] Earlier, in 1850, Hopkins presented his views in lectures at Buffalo and Lockport, New York; these lectures were published in *The American Citizen* in 1857.[5]

2. Albert Taylor Bledsoe, LLD, professor of mathematics at the University of Virginia. Writing for the important volume *Cotton Is King,* published first in 1860, Bledsoe addressed his extensive treatise to the moral, political, and philosophical issues involved in slavery; it includes a lengthy section on "The Argument from the Scriptures."[6]

3. Thornton Stringfellow, DD, from Richmond, Virginia. Stringfellow's sixty-page treatise, published also in *Cotton Is King* and elsewhere,[7] is notable for its lucid, eloquent, and relatively brief statement. In presenting the case of the slavery advocates, I employ his four theses as the outline. His essay is entitled "The Bible Argument: or, Slavery in the Light of Divine Revelation."[8]

4. Charles B. Hodge, DD, distinguished Princeton professor. Hodge's forty-page essay, appearing also in *Cotton Is King,* is entitled "The Bible Argument on Slavery."[9]

5. George D. Armstrong, DD, pastor of the Presbyterian church of Norfolk, Virginia. His book *The Christian Doctrine of Slavery,* published first in 1857,[10] devotes its 148 pages almost exclusively to the exposition of pertinent New Testament texts.

6. Of lesser voice in the debate are Governor Hammond of South Carolina and Professor Dew of Virginia. "Hammond's Letters on Slavery" and Professor Dew's arguments presented to the Virginia legislature in 1831-32 appear in the book *The Pro-Slavery Argument.*[11]

Position in Brief

We, theologians and Christian statesmen from 1815 to 1865, hold that the Bible says nothing to condemn slavery as sinful, and some of us maintain that the Bible in fact commands slavery. Rooted in Noah's prophetic cursing of Ham-Canaan's descendants, slavery has been and should be practiced by God's people. Abraham, champion of faith, had many slaves. God told the Israelites to buy slaves and gave specific instructions pertaining to their service. Jesus never spoke against slavery, but used the slave image as a model for Christian conduct. Paul and Peter instructed masters and slaves in how to conduct themselves as Christians, and Paul obeyed the fugitive slave law in sending the runaway slave Onesimus back to Philemon, his master. Nowhere does the Bible condemn slavery. Either believe the Bible and support slavery, or oppose slavery and throw out the Bible as God's authoritative Word.

We now present our use of Scripture which clearly supports our position that slavery accords with God's will.

Thesis 1: *Slavery was divinely sanctioned among the patriarchs.*

First, consider Noah's curse upon Canaan (Gen. 9:24-27). The "first appearance of slavery in the Bible" is, as Hopkins says, "the wonderful prediction of the patriarch Noah."[12] Stringfellow comments similarly, "May it not be said in truth, that God decreed this institution before it existed."[13] Noah's curse upon Canaan prophesied the black African's destiny. As S. A. Cartwright said in his 1843 essays, when Japheth became enlarged by the discovery of America (foretold 3,800 years before), Canaan appeared on the African beach to get passage to America, "drawn thither by an impulse of his nature to fulfill his destiny of becoming Japheth's servant."[14]

Second, Abraham is our godly example. Abraham—champion of faith for all Christians—received, possessed, and willed slaves to his children as property. Slavery is not like divorce. It cannot be said that before Moses the situation was different. No, Abraham was a great slaveowner; he brought slaves from Haran (Gen. 12:5), armed 318 slaves born in his own house (Gen. 14:14), included them in his property list (Gen. 12:16; 24:35-36), received slaves as a gift from Abimelech (Gen. 20:14), and willed them as part of his estate to his son Isaac (Gen. 26:13-14). The Scripture says that the Lord blessed Abraham by multiplying his slaves (Gen. 24:35). And did not the angel command the slave Hagar to return to her mistress (Gen. 16:1-9)? This clearly supports the fugitive slave law.[15]

Third, in the time of Joseph, God approved slavery. How did Joseph save many Egyptians from famine? God commanded that Joseph buy the people and the land, making them slaves to Pharoah (Gen. 47:15-25).[16]

Thesis 2: *Slavery was incorporated into Israel's national constitution.*

God authorized two types of slavery for Israel's national life: (1) Israel was allowed to take foreigners as slaves. God commanded the

Israelites to "go into the slave markets of the surrounding nations" to buy slaves, to hold them as property, and to will them to their descendants as an inheritance in perpetuity (Lev. 25:44-46).[17] Based on this text, Stringfellow says, "God ingrafted hereditary slavery upon the constitution of government."[18] After quoting this text, Bledsoe says, "Now these words are so perfectly explicit that there is no getting around them."[19] (2) God provided that the Hebrews might "sell themselves and their families for limited periods, with the privilege of extending the time at the end of the sixth year to the fiftieth year or jubilee, if they prefer[red] bondage to freedom."[20] This practice is described in detail in both Exodus 21 and Leviticus 25.

For this second type of slavery, two specific regulations merit our attention: (1) In Exodus 21 certain "conduct is punishable by death, when done to a freeman, which is not punishable at all, when done by a master to a slave, for the express reason, that the slave is the master's money" (verses 20-21, 26-27);[21] and (2) the institution of slavery takes priority over the institution of marriage (Ex. 21:2-4). If a slave leaves his master after seven years, having married the master's daughter, both wife and children stay with the master. The slave is required to leave his family and go out alone. As Stringfellow has said, "The preference is given of God to enslaving the father rather than freeing the mother and children."[22]

Thesis 3: *Slavery was recognized and approved by Jesus Christ and the apostles.*

Jesus and the apostles saw the cruel slavery practices of the Roman empire but never said one word against them. The apostles, who represent Jesus Christ, fully agree with Jesus, even appealing to his words on this subject (1 Tim. 6:1-6). As Governor Hammond of South Carolina has put it:

> It is vain to look to Christ or any of his Apostles to justify such blasphemous perversions of the word of God. Although Slavery in its most revolting form was everywhere visible around them, no visionary notions of piety or philanthropy ever tempted them to gainsay the LAW, even to mitigate the cruel severity of the existing system. On the contrary, regarding Slavery as an established, as well as an inevitable human condition of human society, they never hinted at such a thing as its termination on earth, any more than that "the poor may cease out of the land," which God affirms to Moses shall never be.
>
> It is impossible, therefore, to suppose that Slavery is contrary to the

will of God. It is equally absurd to say that American Slavery differs in form or principle from that of the chosen people. We accept the Bible terms as the definition of our Slavery, and its precepts as the guide of our conduct.[23]

Hopkins comments similarly:

... while [Jesus] rebukes the sins of all around him, and speaks with divine authority, ... he lived in the midst of slavery, ... and uttered not one word against it![24]

The apostolic writings teach us seven points on slavery:

1. The apostles approved of slavery but disapproved of its abuses (Eph. 6:5-9; Col. 3:22-25; 4:1; 1 Tim. 6:1-2; Tit. 2:9-10; 1 Pet. 2:18-19.)

... they [the apostles] did not shut their eyes to the abuses of these several institutions—civil government, marriage, the family, slavery; nor did they affect an ignorance of them, but carefully distinguishing between the institutions themselves and the abuses which had become attached to them, they set themselves to work with zeal and faithfulness ... to correct the abuses.[25]

2. The apostles teach that the church has no authority to interfere with slavery as a political system; the church's task does not interfere with the political and economic systems. Professor Dew says of both Jesus and the apostles:

When we turn to the New Testament, we find not one single passage at all calculated to disturb the conscience of an honest slaveholder. No one can read it without seeing and admiring that the meek and humble Savior of the world in no instance meddled with the established institutions of mankind; he came to save the fallen world, and not to excite the black passions of men.[26]

3. The distinctions made between master and slave are not an impediment to faith and are thus insignificant (Gal. 3:28; 1 Cor. 12:13; Col. 3:11). Whether he be slave or master, a man can be equally good as a Christian.

These external relations ... are of little importance, for every Christian is a freeman in the highest and best sense of the word, and at the same time is under the strongest bonds to Christ (1 Cor. 7:20-22).[27]

Master and slave are, alike, the creatures of God, the objects of his care, the subjects of his government: and, alike, responsible to him for the discharge of the duties to their several stations.[28]

Paul treats the distinctions which slavery creates as matters of very little importance in so far as the interests of the Christian life are concerned.[29]

4. Slaveholders were accepted and affirmed not only as church members, but also as church leaders. Bledsoe says:

As nothing can be plainer than that slaveholders are admitted to the Christian church by the inspired apostles, the advocates of this doctrine are brought into direct collision with the Scriptures. This leads to one of the most dangerous evils connected with the whole system, viz., a disregard of the authority of the word of God, a setting up a different and higher standard of truth and duty, and a proud and confident wrestling of Scripture to suit their own purposes.[30]

5. The apostles gave no exhortation that Christian masters should free their slaves, but said rather that slaves should remain in their existing state, for masters have a right to their slaves' labor. 1 Corinthians 7:20-24 speaks clearly to this point, says Stringfellow:

Under the direction of the Holy Ghost, Paul instructs the church, that, on this particular subject, *one general principle* was ordained of God, applicable alike in all countries and at all stages of the church's future history, and that it was this: *"as the Lord has called every one so let him walk."*

Paul has thus ordained the pattern for the church that slaves should be content "with their *state*, or relation, unless they could be *made free*, in a lawful way."[31]

6. Of great importance to our pro-slavery argument is 1 Timothy 6:1-6, in which Paul declares that his doctrine of slavery is based on "the words of our Lord Jesus Christ himself." Although it is generally held that Jesus was silent on this subject, Paul backs up his comment to believing slaves to honor unbelieving masters by saying that these are "the words of our Lord Jesus Christ." Therefore, Stringfellow says, Christ did speak on this subject. ". . . if our Lord Jesus Christ uttered such words, how dare we say he has been silent? If he [was] silent, how dare the Apostle say these are the words of our Lord Jesus Christ. . . ?" Stringfellow argues that Jesus Christ revealed to Paul this doctrine of slavery;[32] abolitionists who teach that godliness abolishes slavery are sharply rebuked by this text.

Such men, the Apostle says, are "proud, (just as they are now,) know-ing nothing," (that is, on this subject,) but "doting about ques-tions,... and destitute of the truth, supposing that gain is godliness: from such withdraw thyself."—1 Tim. vi: 4, 5.

Such were the bitter fruits which abolition sentiments produced in the Apostolic day, and such precisely are the fruits they produce now.[33]

7. Finally, and most important, Paul's own example indicates that the biblical apostolic writings fully support slavery. As Armstrong puts it:

Paul sent back a fugitive slave, after the slave's hopeful conversion, to his Christian master again, and assigns as his reason for so doing that master's right to the services of his slave.[34]

Hopkins concurs:

He [Paul] finds a fugitive slave, and converts him to the Gospel, and then sends him back again to his old home with a letter of kind rec-ommendation. Why does St. Paul act thus? Why does he not counsel the fugitive to claim his right to freedom, and defend that right...."?

The answer is very plain. St. Paul was inspired, and knew the will of the Lord Jesus Christ, and was only intent on obeying it. And who are we, that in our modern wisdom presume to set aside the Word of God,....[35]

Thesis 4: *Slavery is a merciful institution.*

Through the practice of slavery prisoners taken in war through the centuries have been spared death, and through slavery "millions of Ham's descendants" who otherwise "would have sunk down to eternal ruin" have been "brought within the range of the gospel influence." The role of biblical morality is to ameliorate the conditions of slavery; any attempt to meddle with the institution may lead to the extermination of the race.[36]

To conclude our case that the Bible is for slavery, Professor Hodge says:

If the present course of abolitionists is right, then the course of Christ and the apostles were [sic] wrong. For the circumstances of the two cases are, ... in all essential particulars, the same.[37]

The Anti-Slavery Case

Meet the Debaters

1. Albert Barnes, prolific Bible expositor and ardent social

reformer, a Princeton graduate and Presbyterian minister in Philadelphia (1830-67). Barnes's 384-page book entitled *An Inquiry into the Scriptural Views of Slavery*, published first in 1857, leaves virtually no stone unturned in the argument.[38]

2. Theodore Dwight Weld, evangelist, social reformer, and author of a widely disseminated pamphlet entitled *The Bible and Slavery*, published in 1837.[39] The essay appeared also in the *Anti-Slavery Quarterly Magazine* that same year and was later published in 1864 by the Board of Publication of the United Presbyterian Church under the title *The Bible Against Slavery*.[40]

3. George Bourne, outspoken Presbyterian minister in Port Republic, Virginia, and courageous anti-slavery pioneer. Bourne wrote a fiery treatise condemning slaveholders, especially ministers of the gospel, as oppressors and thieves. The work was entitled *The Book and Slavery Irreconcilable*.[41] Published already in 1816, it crucially influenced abolitionist leaders Theodore Dwight Weld and William Lloyd Garrison, publisher of the famed *Liberator* in the 1830s and 40s.[42] In part for his anti-slavery stand, Bourne was defrocked in 1819. A later publication, in 1845, entitled *A Condensed Anti-Slavery Bible Argument* (1845), was Bourne's most important contribution from a hermeneutical point of view,[43] although it lacks the prophetic invective of his 1816 manifesto, bursting like a bombshell upon his Virginian ministerial colleagues.[44]

4. Lesser voices in the following debate are William Hosmer, author of *The Church and Slavery* (1853);[45] James Freeman Clarke, preacher of an anti-slavery sermon in Boston on Thanksgiving Day, 1842;[46] William Ellery Channing, whose persuasive moral discourses on anti-slavery were published under the title *Slavery* in 1836;[47] and Francis Wayland, president of Brown University, who formulated the moral and scriptural case against slavery in his masterful book *The Elements of Moral Science* (1835).[48]

Position in Brief

A fire burns within our bones. We declare: (1) slavery is man-stealing, a lawless, godless criminal sin (Ex. 21:16; 1 Tim. 1:8-10); (2) slavery is an institution of oppression, which is roundly condemned by the Old Testament prophets; and (3) the injustices and cruelties of slavery fly squarely in the face of Jesus' command to love others as yourself.[49] We denounce slavery because (1) slavery reduces human life to property, mere property; people are bought and sold as things, mere things—a practice which denies human beings their God-given rights, liberties, and intelligence; and (2) the cruel and unjust evils of slavery cannot be countenanced as in any way compatible with Christian moral teaching and conduct.[50]

Further, in our biblical and evangelical opposition to slavery we hold that (1) slavery violates the eighth and tenth commandments—don't steal and don't covet; (2) Hebrew servitude was voluntary, altogether different from American slavery; and (3) the beastly conditions and brutal treatment of slaves cannot be reconciled with the biblical, Christian ethic of love.[51]

Before we pursue the biblical defense of the anti-slavery position, we remind you "why the appeal on the subject of slavery should be made to the Bible."

1. The Bible is the acknowledged standard of morals in this nation.

2. The subject of slavery is one on which the Bible has legislated, and there is, therefore, a propriety that we should ascertain its decisions.

3. The question whether slavery is right or wrong can only be settled by an appeal to the Scriptures.

4. Great reforms, on moral subjects, do not occur except under the influence of religious principle.

5. Because it is by such appeal that the advocates of slavery endeavor to defend the system.[52]

Thesis 1: *The so-called slavery of the patriarchs in no way justifies the system of slavery in the USA.*

1. Regarding the curse on Canaan (Gen. 9:25), Weld rightly says: (1) prediction of crime does not justify it; (2) national subjection, not individual bondage, is prophesied;[53] and (3) Africans are not Canaan's descendants, whose boundaries are clearly designated in Genesis 10:15-19; nowhere do we learn that descendants of Canaan moved into Africa. If Canaan includes all of Ham's posterity, then Assyrians, some Persians, and all Grecians and Romans should be slaves.[54]

Bourne has also pointed out that (1) "Canaan's posterity was to become subject to those of Shem—the Jews" (Americans, descendants of Japheth, therefore, have no claim whatsoever granted by this text), and (2) the prophecy was fulfilled in Canaan's subjection to Israel (Deut. 20:10-18, etc.).[55]

Wayland's comments also merit our consideration: (1) Noah, not God, uttered these words; (2) the words are not prophecy, for Noah is nowhere designated a prophet; and (3) this malediction was "uttered by a man just awaking out of a drunken sleep. The Holy Spirit in no other case has made use of a mind in this condition for the purpose of revealing to us the will of God."[56]

2. Regarding the patriarchs' so-called holding of slaves, the servitude of the patriarchal period under Abraham was not slavish. It was a condition of privilege, including circumcision and the benefits of the community, both religious and social. Hagar's dismissal meant denial of privilege.[57]

As Bourne has pointed out, the Hebrew word *kana* means that Abraham "acquired" or "got" servants, but they were not slaves, as you pro-slavery writers argue; otherwise Abraham's wife, Sarah, and his nephew Lot were also his slaves, since the property lists in Genesis 13 mention them also. Further, all wives were therefore slaves (see Ex. 20:17, 21). No, Abraham did not own slaves. Abraham was a man of great godly virtue; it is unthinkable to regard him as a slaveholder.[58]

Against the claim that the patriarchs were slaveholders, it must be noted, as Barnes has argued, that *kana* does not necessarily mean "to buy"; nor does *ebed* necessarily mean "slave" in the sense used today. After examining the numerous Greek words used to distinguish various forms of service-slavery, Barnes has observed that the Hebrew does not have such linguistic variety. Its main word, *ebed*, similar to the Greek *doulos*, can designate a variety of types of service. It is "never rendered *slaves*, but commonly *servants*, and *serve*" (KJV).[59] It is "not a correct method of interpretation to infer that because this word is used, that therefore slavery existed . . . [for] the kind of servitude then existing may have had none of the essential elements of slavery."[60] Although servitude of various kinds existed in the ancient world, the patriarchial practice was not slavery as we know it today.[61] And if Abraham had practiced slavery, we must remember that (1) neither God nor Israel originated such servitude, and (2) the patriarchal morality is not necessarily an example for us today (e.g., Abraham's lying about Sarah, taking Hagar as a concubine and practicing polygamy).[62]

Thesis 2: *God's deliverance of Israel from slavery in Egypt shows, once and for all, that God hates and condemns slavery.*

You ask, what was God's attitude toward the Egyptian enslavement of Israel? Let us follow Barnes' argument on this matter:

> ... if we can find a case in history concerning which God has declared his sentiments, we may draw a safe conclusion in regard to the estimate which he forms of a similar institution now.[63]

Barnes has recognized some nonessential differences between Egypt's enslavement of Israel and the United States' enslavement of the Negro, most of which show Israel's condition in Egypt as better (they had their own community, their own land, permanent dwellings, cattle, etc.). With Barnes, we enunciate also six essential similarities: (1) in both cases one people enslaves a foreign race; (2) in both, slavery originated in kidnapping and was involuntary; (3) in both, slave labor is unrequited; (4) in both, harsh and oppressive rules and punishments are employed; (5) in both, effort is put forth to retard the growth of the slave population, lest they become too powerful; and (6) in both, the number of slaves is between 2.5 to 3 million.

In view of these striking similarities and the many ways in which the Hebrew's bondage was more humane and merciful than the Negro's bondage, God's decisive action to deliver the Hebrews, including plagues against animals and people, shows God's unequivocal judgment upon all slavery. The Lord who heard the cry of the oppressed and delivered them "with a mighty hand, and with an outstretched arm, and with great terribleness" (Deut. 26:6-8), certainly deplores and hates the oppression and slavery of the Negro today.[64]

Thesis 3: *Hebrew servitude in the time of Moses was voluntary, merciful, and of benefit to the servant; it was not slavery.*

Weld, Bourne, Barnes, and Hosmer agree:[65]

1. Hebrew servitude was voluntary; a person offered himself to become a servant as a security against poverty (Ex. 21:2-6; Lev. 25:39-43; Deut. 15:12).[66]

2. Hebrew servitude, therefore, was basically a benevolent institution, a kindness to the poor or oppressed (Ex. 21:20-21, 26-27; 22:21; 23:9; Lev. 19:18, 34; 25:42-43; Deut. 27:19).

3. A servant could be redeemed at any time by a next of kin who put up money for him (Lev. 25:47-52).

4. In the seventh year, the sabbatical, and in the jubilee year all

servants were automatically freed. But a servant could compel his master to retain him permanently if he (the servant) so desired (Ex. 21:2-6; Lev. 25:10).

5. Servants took full part in religious ceremonies, all of which awarded vacation days, which in a 50-year period totaled 23 years and 64 days of time off (Ex. 20:10; 23:12; 12:44; Lev. 25:4-6; Deut. 12:11-12).[67]

6. Servants were instructed in morality and religion with full and equal membership in the covenant (Gen. 17:12; Deut. 16:9-14; 31:10-13).

7. Servants were entitled to the same civil and religious rights as masters (Lev. 24:22; Num. 15:15-16, 29; 9:14; Deut. 1:16-17) and had equal legal protection (Lev. 19:15; 24:22).

8. Strangers who came into Israel in the role of servants were to be circumcised, become members of the covenant, and thus be eligible for all the above humanitarian benefits (Gen. 17:9-14, 23, 27; Deut. 29:10-13).

9. The law required that runaway servants not be returned to their masters; they were thus legally protected from oppressive masters (Deut. 23:15-16). This law in itself would "put an end to the practice of human slavery in a week."[68]

10. Last and most important of all, Israel was a theocracy, in which God was ruler and owner of all. Under such a national constitution, slavery was both theoretically and practically excluded.[69]

How could slavery have existed among the Hebrews when the law of Moses repeatedly required kindness to the stranger, the widow, and the orphan? Indeed, the Mosiac law commanded love for one's neighbor as oneself (Lev. 19:18).

Thesis 4: *Israel's history and the prophetic oracles confirm that oppressive slavery did not exist in Israel; God would have roundly condemned it, had it existed.*

As Bourne and Barnes show in their writings, (1) throughout Israel's history there is no record of buying, selling, or holding foreign slaves, and (2) in view of the extensive prophetic condemnation of oppression and injustice with only a few denunciations of violations in Hebrew servitude and no condemnation of foreign slavery in Israel, it is clear that Israel had no such institution.[70]

Not only did God prohibit Israel from making slaves of captives as was customarily done by the heathen nations (Deut. 20:10-20), but even the Gibeonites (Josh. 9), who volunteered themselves to become Israel's servants in order to avoid extermination, were not reduced to slavery, properly so called.[71] And Solomon's forced labor was of a temporary nature for the building of the temple. "There is no evidence, that they were held as property, or that they were in any case sold, or that they were held in perpetual servitude of any kind."[72]

We assert without exception, "There was no foreign traffic in slaves."[73] Even though Israel's foreign commerce was extensive and described in detail (1 Kings 10:22; 2 Chron. 9:21), no evidence exists that Israel ever bought, sold, or held foreigners as slaves.[74] Other nations were condemned for their slave trade (like Tyre in Ezek. 27:13).

Consider also that the prophetic oracles condemning all oppression nowhere mention slavery. But we do read that King Ahaz was roundly condemned when he tried to enslave captives from Judah (2 Chron. 28:8-15). Further, the prophet Jeremiah gave a specific reason for Israel's exile—failure to give the sabbatical liberty to its servants (Jer. 34:8-20).[75] Hence if Israel had practiced actual slavery, they would have been unequivocally condemned for doing so.

> Yet multitudes of pro-slavery Christians at the present time contend, that these oppressive violations, which overthrew and destroyed ancient Israel, are strong evidence that God sanctions the most oppressive practice in the world!!![76]

Do you not know that the prophet Isaiah called for a fast to (1) "loose the bands of wickedness," (2) "undo heavy burdens," (3) "let the oppressed go free," and (4) "break every yoke." Such language would mean freeing slaves, if there were slaves in Israel; but in plain fact, there were none. To whatever extent slavery did exist in Palestine, it existed as a transgression of God's law—as sin—and was in no way justified by the prophets.[77]

It is clear, therefore, that servitude as practiced in the Old Testament is not a "true natural analogy" to present-day slavery in the United States.[78]

Thesis 5: *Neither Jesus nor the apostles approved of or condoned slavery.*

As Barnes has said, "in Jesus' discourses, there is not a sentiment which can be tortured by any ingenuity of exegesis into an approval of the system [of slavery].... He [Jesus] never uttered a word which can be construed in favour of slavery."[79] We maintain that not one word from Jesus can be used to defend slavery, but that everything Jesus said and did runs counter to the practice of slavery.

Further, there is no evidence that Jesus ever came into contact with slavery, for "there is every probability that slavery (even Hebrew servitude) had ceased in the Hebrew commonwealth long before the advent of the Savior."[80] Hence one cannot argue that Jesus condoned slavery, unless one similarly argues "that he was favourable to the sports of the amphitheatre at Rome, or to the orgies which were celebrated in honour of Bacchus, or to the claims of inspiration of the oracles of Dodona or Delphi,"[81] all of which he never contacted directly.[82]

The pro-slavery argument that Jesus' silence in condemning slavery shows his support for slavery is absurd.

> ... as we have no account whatever of any public preaching by Christ and the apostles against forgery, arson, piracy, counterfeiting, and twenty other heinous ancient as well as modern crimes, we are to presume from this supposed approving silence and acquiescence of theirs, that the whole of those crimes are morally approbated and licensed in the New Testament, by the special example of Christ and the Apostles, so that we have no moral right whatever to disturb others in the commission of them!!![83]

Let us acknowledge and accept the moral precepts of the gospels and the apostles: (1) "the doctrine of universal humanity," in which all are "equal in the sight of God"; (2) the command to imitate God's love and to love your neighbor as yourself, for the way you treat "the least of these my brethren" is the way you treat Christ; (3) the precept that every person is directly accountable to God, and no one may "impose restrictions on another" in lordship or ultimate accountability; and (4) the teaching that all domestic relationships, which included servants in the first century, are made directly accountable "to the Lord" (e.g., Eph. 5:21—6:9).[84]

While Weld and Bourne argue that the New Testament Greek word *doulos* does not designate a slave but a servant in the broad sense,[85] Barnes says that because of the prevalence of slavery in the Roman world[86] we must accept the certainty that slaves were baptized and admitted into church membership while retaining the slave status and role:

> I am persuaded that nothing can be gained to the cause of antislavery by attempting to deny that the apostles found slavery in the regions where they founded churches and that slaves were admitted into the church, together with slave-owners.[87]

The evidence is that (1) "slaveholders were admitted by the apostles to the Christian church, and were not subjected to immediate discipline for holding slaves," (2) "the apostles did not deny that those who were the holders of slaves might be true Christians," (3) "the apostles did not openly and publicly proclaim that slavery was an evil,"[88] and (4) "the apostles gave instructions to those who sustained the relation of master and slave, respecting their duties while in that relation."[89]

The apostles neither "*legislated* for slavery" nor did they approve it. Rather, they "made laws for the master—as responsible to God—not for slavery: for the slave—as a redeemed man and a sufferer—not for the perpetuity of the system which oppressed him."[90] "The principles laid down by the Saviour and his Apostles are such as are opposed to Slavery, and if carried out would secure its universal abolition."[91]

This means that: (1) "The Saviour and his apostles inculcated such views of man as amount to a prohibition of slavery, or as if acted on would abolish it." (2) "The gospel regards every human being as invested with such rights as are inconsistent with his being held as a slave."[92] (3) "The gospel, and the Bible generally, prohibits, in the most positive manner, many things which are always found in slavery" (stealing persons, oppression, depriving of lawful wages, and withholding instruction in religion and morality). (4) "It is conceded that the gospel, if fairly applied, would remove slavery from the world; it is therefore wrong."[93]

> The considerations seem to be conclusive proof that Christianity was not designed to extend and perpetuate slavery, but that the spirit of the Christian religion is against it; and that the fair application of the Christian religion would remove it from the world, BECAUSE it is an evil, and is displeasing to God.[94]

Wayland says:

> ... the Christian religion not only forbids slavery, but ... it provides the only method in which, after it has been once established, it may be abolished with entire safety and benefit to both parties.[95]

Hosmer further contends that slaves and slaveholders who defend such a system cannot be Christians; slavery cannot exist in the church. Slavery makes impossible the impartial administration of church discipline and prevents peace and unity in the church. It works against the evangelization of the world, and therefore must be extirpated from both the church and the world now.[96]

In the case of Philemon and Onesimus, Barnes says:

> The principles laid down in the epistle to Philemon . . . would lead to
> the universal abolition of slavery. If all those who are now slaves were
> to become Christians, and their masters were to treat them "not as
> slaves, but as brethren," the period would not be far distant when
> slavery would cease.[97]

Finally, we say that slavery is never an act of benevolence.[98]
The testimony of a thousand witnesses presented in *American
Slavery As It Is* shows that slavery is one of the basest, most op-
pressive, cruel, and inhumane institutions known to humanity.[99]
As Bourne says, "slavery, however supported by use of 'isolated
passages,' is against the spirit of the Scriptures."[100]

The Pro-Slavery Rebuttal

In seven areas, and certainly more, the abolitionists' views of
Scripture are wrong:

1. The divine prophecy given to Noah after the flood certainly
intended to place the curse upon Ham since he was the one who
looked upon Noah's nakedness. In Genesis 9:25 the Arabic reads
"Cursed be the father of Canaan" instead of "Cursed be Canaan,"
and some copies of the Septuagint read "Ham" instead of "Canaan."
Indeed we might suppose that the present reading arose from the
mistake of a copyist, who "wrote only *Canaan* instead of *Ham the
father of Canaan*."[101]
And further,

> . . . whether that curse included the whole of his [Ham's] posterity or
> a portion of them only, does not make the slightest difference in the
> main fact, which remains uncontroverted, namely that God *did* au-
> thorize slavery for a race, whom he foresaw as being *utterly de-
> graded*.[102]

2. To hold that Hebrew servitude was *free* and *voluntary* goes
against both the sense of the text and common sense. The Israelites
were servants or slaves in Egypt, and the same word was used to
designate the Hebrew slaves. Was Israel in Egypt voluntarily? Were
they free? God delivered Israel because they were his chosen people,
whom he determined to bring to the Promised Land; the deliverance says nothing about slavery per se.
Further, Exodus 12:44-45 clearly distinguishes between two
states of servitude: (1) the circumcised servant in "a state of *bond-*

age ... serving without his consent," and (2) the foreigner or hired servant in "a state of *freedom* ... serving with his consent for wages." Clearly, Israel had servants in *both* states: involuntary slavery and voluntary hire.[103]

In another passage and context, God clearly directed Israel to buy servants from foreign nations and to hold them as property in perpetuity (Lev. 25:44-46). Such practice is certainly akin to slavery as we have it in the South today.[104] Hence:

> You cannot deny that there were among the Hebrews "bondmen forever." You cannot deny that God especially authorized his chosen people to purchase "bondmen forever" from the heathen, as recorded in the twenty-fifth chapter of Leviticus, and that they are there designated by the very Hebrew word used in the tenth commandment. Nor can you deny that a "BONDMAN FOREVER" is a "SLAVE," yet you endeavor to hang an argument of immortal consequences upon the wretched subterfuge, that the precise word "slave" is not to be found in the translation of the Bible.[105]

3. Abolitionists say that slavery is kidnapping, a crime which the Mosaic law punished by death (Ex. 21:16) and which is ranked among those "of the deepest dye" by Paul in 1 Timothy 1:9-10. With this we agree. But kidnapping means *stealing* free persons and *selling* them into slavery, or stealing another's slaves. "The distinction between slave-holding and kidnapping is one always made, as far as we know, in laws of slave-holding states. Under Moses' law *slave-holding* was expressly authorized."[106]

4. Abolitionists claim that slavery is immoral, and that by supporting it we must then also support polygamy and divorce, since they too were allowed under Moses. But Jesus revised the moral law on polygamy and divorce (Mt. 19:7-9), but never spoke against slavery. Further, the church has always unanimously agreed that polygamy and divorce are wrong and sinful.[107] "All three, polygamy, divorce and slavery, were sanctioned by the law of Moses. But under the gospel, slavery has been *sanctioned* in the church, while polygamy and divorce have been *excluded* from the church."[108]

> All I can say is, truth is mighty, and I hope it will bring us all to say, let God be true, in settling the true principles of humanity, and every man a liar who says slavery was inconsistent with it, in the days of the Mosaic law.[109]

5. Abolitionists argue that Jesus never encountered slavery and that everything he said and did flies in the face of slavery. Let it be said again that support of slavery is not support of all its abuses,

just as support of Nero is not support of oppression and torture. We must not confuse the theory and practice *in itself* with a *particular expression of it.* Jesus' teaching does condemn oppression, robbery, and violence, but not slaveholding as an institution, for indeed slaveholding may be merciful. This point stands logically, for, as Hodge says, "when masters became members of the church under the apostles, then either (a) the church admitted oppressors or murderers, or (b) slave-holding was and is not inherently sinful."[110]

Further, Jesus' teaching to "love your neighbor as yourself" does not contradict slavery, for that moral commandment was given already under Moses (Lev. 19:18) in the same book in which God through Moses directed purchase of slaves (Lev. 25:44-46). If it is held (and such is assumed by all) that the golden rule is not incompatible with the husband's headship and the wife's subordination, then why is it not compatible with the slave-master relationship?[111]

Moreover, Jesus implicitly approved slavery by referring to servants or slaves in the parables (Lk. 17:7-10; 20:9-16). Jesus did not condemn servants for being servants, but rather praised him who served well. All Christians are represented as "servants *[douloi]* of Christ" (Rom. 1:1; 2 Pet. 1:1; Jude, verse 1), who have been bought with a price (1 Cor. 6:20; 7:23).[112] Explicitly, Jesus approved slavery in his word spoken by Paul which enjoins slaves to "regard their masters as worthy of all honor," to "not be disrespectful on the ground that they are brethren," and to be content in their state of servitude (1 Tim. 6:1-6).[113]

In view of such clear teaching, how can it be said that Jesus condemned slavery?

6. Paul's teaching on slavery, as Barnes concedes, accepts masters and slaves as members of the church and as true Christians. But the argument that the apostles could not have openly denounced slavery because the church would have "armed against itself the whole power of the State" and, therefore, it rather implanted principles that would lead to the end of the system, Hodge rightly replies: "The very statement of the argument, in its naked form, is its refutation. These holy men did not refrain from a regard to consequences."[114] One can hardly imagine such "expediency" on the part of the apostles.

Similarly, it is a false analogy for abolitionists to claim that supporting slavery by the Scripture justifies using the Scriptures to endorse also political despotism. The two cases are *not* analogous in that Nero was not a Christian, and hence his actions cannot be said to be sanctioned by Scripture. But the two issues are analogous in that Paul's counsel to be subject to the despotic power indicates he did not consider "possession of despotic power a crime." Hence "both political despotism and domestic slavery belong in morals to the *adiaphora*, to things indifferent to the gospel."[115]

Based on this point of analogy, "civil government, marriage, the family, and slavery" are dealt with "in the same way." Each requires *subjects* who subordinate themselves to these several institutions of authority.[116] Political, economic, and social institutions function for the common good when "the rights of the individual are subordinate to those of the community."[117] For example:

> In this country we believe that the general good requires us to deprive the whole female sex of the right of self government. They have no voice in the formation of the laws which dispose of their persons and property.[118]

Similarly, as Paul enjoins, slaves who are content in their station in life promote the common good and welfare of society.

7. Let the abolitionists' perverse method of interpreting the Bible be clearly and fully observed.

THE HISTORY OF INTERPRETATION FURNISHES NO EXAMPLES OF MORE WILLFUL AND VIOLENT PERVERSIONS OF THE SACRED TEXT THAN ARE TO BE FOUND IN THE WRITINGS OF THE ABOLITIONISTS. THEY SEEM TO CONSIDER THEMSELVES ABOVE THE SCRIPTURES; AND WHEN THEY PUT THEMSELVES ABOVE THE LAW OF GOD, IT IS NOT WONDERFUL THAT THEY SHOULD DISREGARD THE LAWS OF MEN. Significant manifestations of the result of this disposition to consider their own light a surer guide than the word of God, are visible in the anarchical opinions about human governments, civil and ecclesiastical, and on the rights of women, which have found appropriate advocates in the abolition publications. Let these principles be carried out, and there is an end to all social subordination, to all security for life and property, to all guarantee for public or domestic virtue. If our women are to be emancipated from subjection to the law which God has imposed upon them, if they are to quit the retirement of domestic life, where they preside in stillness over the character and destiny of society; if they are to come forth in the liberty of men, to be our agents, our public lecturers, our committee-men, our rulers, if, in studied insult to the authority of God, we are to renounce in the marriage contract all claim to obedience, we shall soon have a country . . . from which all order and all virtue would speedily be banished. There is no form of human excellence before which we bow with profounder deference than that which appears in a delicate woman, adorned with the inward graces and devoted to the peculiar duties of her sex; and there is no deformity of human character from which we turn with deeper loathing than from a woman forgetful of her nature, and clamorous for the

vocation and rights of men. It would not be fair to object to the abolitionists [in this way] . . . were not these opinions the legitimate consequences of their own principles. Their women do but apply their own
method of dealing with Scripture to another case.[119]

As Governor Hammond has said:

> But when I show them that to hold "bondmen forever" is ordained by
> God, they deny the Bible, and set up in its place a law of their own
> making. I must then cease to reason with them on this branch of the
> question. Our religion differs as widely as our manners. The great
> judge in our day of final account must decide between us.[120]

The Anti-Slavery Rebuttal

In seven areas, and certainly more, the slavery advocates' use
of the Scripture is wrong:

1. All Hebrew manuscripts known to us read "Canaan" and not
"Ham, the father of Canaan" in Genesis 9:25. Let those who so
highly honor the Bible take what the text says. Only by "a singular
perseverance in . . . perverseness of interpretation. . . , notwithstanding the plainest rules of exegesis," do slavery supporters
continue to use the text "to justify the reduction of the *African* to
slavery."[121]

Further, does not verse 26 assign Canaan's servitude directly
to *Shem's* descendants? By what right do you then, only a smaller
part of *Japheth's* descendants living in the southern states, reduce
the Negro to property, depriving him of every normal human right?
If the text assigns the right of slavery to anyone at all, the right was
given to the Hebrews to enslave the Canaanites, whom the Lord
later instructed the Israelites to exterminate, lest Israel be cor-
rupted by their paganism (Deut. 20:10-18).[122]

2. Did Israel make slaves of their fellow Hebrews as the South
makes slaves of Negroes today? No, surely not. For although the
word *ebed* (servant) is used to denote both Israel's servitude in
Egypt and a Hebrew's voluntary service to another Hebrew (Lev.
25:39), all the regulations given by Moses for such service stress benevolent and humane treatment of the servant. And why? "Because
they were once servants in Egypt, and therefore should know well
how to treat servants."[123] ". . . it may well be supposed, that He who
led a nation of bondmen to liberty, would teach them to be protec-
tors of all other bondmen."[124]

As shown earlier, the Hebrew term *ebed* (translated "servant")
embraces a wide range of meaning. "We can ascertain the meaning

of *the word* from *the facts* in the case; not the nature of *the facts* from the use of *the word.*"[125]

3. You who argue for slavery from the Bible admit that God's command through Moses not to return the runaway servant (Deut. 23:15-16) cannot be applied to our situation today, or the institution would soon come to ruin. You explain away the truth of the text by saying it relates "to those slaves only who should escape from heathen masters, and seek an asylum among the people of God."[126]

We ask: why would God ordain such benevolence for foreigners but not for his chosen ones, the Hebrews? We also answer: "the terms of the command are unlimited."[127] In this command God provided every servant a recourse against a master's oppression. God commanded, "Thou shalt not oppress him [the servant]," and this regulation is "as though God had said, 'If ye restrain him from exercising his *own choice,* as to the place and condition of his residence, it is *oppression,* and shall not be tolerated.' "[128]

This regulation clearly indicates that all servitude in Israel was *voluntary* and the free choice of the servant was never to be violated.[129]

4. Slavery advocates dare to say that the prophets and Jesus never spoke against slavery, thereby condoning it. We have already shown the absurdity of that argument in that piracy, arson, and twenty other heinous sins are thereby condoned.

But let it be said that slavery is one of the most violent and oppressive practices in the world. "There is not another book extant half so condemnatory and denunciatory of this terrible sin, as the Scriptures, as a thousand extracts from all parts of them will testify."[130]

> Another most decisive fact is, that there is not only no account in the Scriptures of any kind of slavery in the Jewish nation, but there is no Jewish or other tradition of any such slavery. Every other ancient slaveholding nation has left distinct historical traditions of its slaveholding practice. If ever, therefore, the Jews had practised human slavery, even in violation of the Levitical law, they would have left an historical tradition of it, the same as the Greeks and Romans have of their history ... the entire absence of any such history is the strongest negative testimony that can exist that the Jews never had any such practice or custom among them.[131]

Neither under Jesus nor under Moses did obeying the command to love your neighbor and living by the golden rule allow the practice of slavery.[132]

5. Advocates of slavery misuse the Bible. Three principles of in-

terpretation, "approved and universally adopted by critical commentators," are to be followed:

> I. That the letter of a statute or other law be so construed, whenever it has different meanings in the different uses and connections, as to harmonize with the spirit or general and collective meaning of the whole connection to which it belongs.
>
> II. Where a double or different construction of the letter is admissible, that shall always be preferred which is most consistent with natural liberty, justice and righteousness, provided the general spirit of the law permit such constructions.
>
> III. All parts of every code or collection of laws or system of ethics are to be thus harmonized by construction, unless the express letter as well as the general spirit of the same prevent such harmony by such construction, in which case alone we are to allow that there is a conflict of laws in such code or collection. It is to be presumed that no fault will be found with these just and equitable rules, nor with their just and equitable application to the present important subject matter *now under consideration.*[133]

6. To answer those who say that the expediency of the apostolic method of eradicating slavery[134] discredits the apostles' moral honesty, we reply:

> There are two kinds of *expediency,* one of which is consistent with moral honesty, and the other of which is not. Expediency may be employed in a good cause to accomplish good ends; or it may be employed in a bad cause and to accomplish evil purposes.[135]

The apostle's method of laying down principles which if *"fairly followed"* would eradicate slavery was one of both expediency and moral honesty.[136]

Further, the apostolic teaching on slavery is not parallel to that regarding husbands and wives, and parents and children. The teaching on slavery differs in four ways: (1) servitude is "uniformly represented ... as a *hard* condition"; (2) submission of slaves is spoken of as a *hard* condition, "one in which they were constantly liable to suffer wrong (1 Pet. 2:18-19)"; (3) hence slaves were to cultivate the virtue of *"patience under wrong";* and (4) Paul advised escape from servitude, if possible (1 Cor. 7:21).[137]

> ... it is clear [then] that the apostles did *not* "legislate" for slavery in any such sense as they did for the relation of husband and wife, and parent and child. They never regarded the relations as similar. Everything that they said in the way of *legislation* is entirely consistent

with the supposition that they disapproved of the system, and desired that it might cease as soon as possible.[138]

7. Lastly, slavery is sinful and wrong because of what it does to the slave. The "profit of [the] master is made the END of his [the slave's] being."[139]

> Reducing a *person* to a *thing*—a *man* to an *animal.* Such is "a system of incurable injustice, the complication of every species of iniquity, the greatest practical evil that ever has inflicted the human race, and the severest and most extensive calamity recorded in the history of the world."
>
> ... when Expositors and Disciples contend for "injustice and inhumanity" by the Book; what blasphemy! and slavery, with its abettors, is "a mill-stone hanged about the neck" of the church, from which she must be loosened, or she will "be drowned in the depth of the sea."[140]

Debate Ended

Supplement to Slavery Debate: Hermeneutical Alternatives

Were there alternatives to the polarized positions here represented? The question itself needs clarification. For if one asks whether there was an alternative to being either for or against slavery, the answer is both yes and no. Voices from either side of the debate would speak against injustices in slavery, but ensuing discussion would soon disclose support for, or opposition to, the practice of slavery. If the question, however, is examined strictly at the hermeneutical level, then one can find other alternatives to the positions presented in the debate.

1. The Bible says *both* yes and no on slavery. Dr. Fisk, president of Wesleyan University, wrote in 1837 to the esteemed Professor Moses Stuart of Andover Theological Seminary, hoping to get Professor Stuart to publicly oppose slavery. But Professor Stuart responded with both *sic* and *non,* yes and no, saying that "the theory of slavery" stands opposed to the commandment "Love thy neighbor as thyself" but that Paul did not forbid slavery. When slaves and masters became Christians, Paul did not prescribe terminating the relationship, but urged the slaves to give due respect to their masters (1 Tim. 6:2). Hence "the relation once constituted and continued is not such a *malum in se* [evil in itself] as calls for immediate and violent disrupture, at all hazards."[141]

But abolitionist William Goodell, writing in 1852, abhorred Professor Stuart's exegesis, commenting sarcastically that "learned men are not always wise."[142] According to Stuart, Goodell says, "the theory of slavery is not, in itself, right;" but the practice of slavery is not, in itself, wrong.

The law of love and the golden rule decide the question of slavery *one* way, but Paul's advice to servants and masters, and his sending back Onesimus, decide it *the other* way. . . .

The relation, though not founded in moral *right*, when *"once constituted"* is not a moral wrong.[143]

The hermeneutical alternative toward which Stuart pointed, but which Goodell would not accept, holds that the Bible itself gives mixed signals on the issue. Its statements cannot be fully harmonized into consistent support of one position against the other. Further, to examine the hermeneutical alternative more adequately, the distance between the circumstances of the world(s) of the Bible and the nineteenth-century USA world prevents an immediate straight-line use of the text to support one position against another. Other factors also enter, such as the Christian community's culpability in the origin of the respective systems of slavery as well as the extent to which Christian rationale and practice enable the system to survive.

Troubling though such suggestions may be, they represent a hermeneutical alternative that should not be too readily dismissed. This alternative asks the interpreter to consider the possibility that diverse viewpoints not fully compatible with each other appear within the biblical teaching (a point to be discussed in the hermeneutical commentary on "The Bible and War") and to take seriously the distance between the world of the text and the world of the interpreter.

2. Another hermeneutical alternative is represented in part at least* by the Quaker and Mennonite approach to the problem. Rather than using the Bible to speak directly to slavery, the basic biblical value structure had so informed their thinking and practice so as to put slavery at odds with their way of life.

John Woolman's efforts to rid slavery from among the Friends represent this approach. When refusing to write wills which involved passing on slaves to children, Woolman would state his convictions:

They who know the only true God, and Jesus Christ whom he hath sent, and are thus acquainted with the merciful, benevolent, gospel spirit, will therein perceive that the indignation of God is kindled against oppression and cruelty.[144]

Once when a slaveholding Friend sought to justify slavery by appeal to biblical texts, Woolman said:

> The love of ease and gain are the motives in general of keeping slaves, and men are wont to take hold of weak arguments to support a cause which is unreasonable.[145]

Similarly, the 1688 anti-slavery petition to the Philadelphia Congress, authored mostly by the Friends with some Mennonite influence, does not specifically cite Scripture but appeals to such principles as liberty of conscience, the barbarous actions of slaveholders, the spirit of Christianity (Quakers should know better), and fair play (how would you feel if the slaves revolted, put the whites into servitude, and treated them the same way?).[146]

Though slavery was common in Pennsylvania during the revolutionary period, Mennonites did not own slaves; and little discussion on the issue appeared in their literature.[147] In 1837 a significant comment did appear in *Confession, Faith and Practice* by Peter Burkholder of the Virginia Mennonite Conference: "And, moreover, as all are free in Christ, they must take no part in slave-holding, or in trafficking with them in any wise."[148] At the March 1863 meeting of the Virginia Conference, a statement on "Hiring Slaves" was introduced.

> Hiring Slaves.—The subject of hiring slaves was introduced by Bishop Geil. Decided that inasmuch as it is against our creed and discipline to own or traffic in slaves; so it is also forbidden for a brother to hire a slave unless such slave be entitled to receive the pay for such labor by the consent of his owner. But where neighbors exchange labor, the labor of slaves may be received.[149]

In 1861 Johannes Risser wrote two articles in the *Christliche Volksblatt* arguing that the Old Testament provides at most only a remote basis for slavery; it does not contain teaching in support of slavery.[150]

Since the Mennonites would have nothing to do with slavery,[151] regarding it as against their "creed and discipline,"[152] one might ask whether their overall method of using the Bible influenced their position. Did their understanding that the Bible forbade participation in war (see chapter 3) determine their position on slavery? While it appears impossible to substantiate any such point in view of the sparsity of material on the subject, a 1773 letter from the Franconia Mennonites to the Dutch Mennonites may shed some hermeneutical light. In answering questions from the Dutch on how they determined their rule for faith and practice, the Franconia Mennonites said they appealed especially to the "Evangelists" (i.e., the Gospels) for their authority.[153] This hermeneutical statement indicates that judgments were made regarding the intracanonical dialogue; a canon within the canon had emerged.

Any proposal, however, that such an intracanonical critique was articulated by Mennonites or Quakers on the topic of slavery must await further research, and evidence beyond this author's awareness. However, it is clear that the distinctive hermeneutical alternative represented above is one in which believers focused upon obedience to Christ, upon living the way of Christ, *within their own membership.* Both Woolman's approach and the Virginia Mennonite Conference statement illustrate this alternative. The chief concern was not to resolve the issue for society but to practice the way of Christ among believers. Biblical teaching as understood in their practice was authoritative for the church.

3. A third hermeneutical alternative may be found within the slave community. Four distinctive biblical emphases appear in the slaves' use of the Bible, found frequently in the spirituals, which expressed the slaves' religious experience.

First, the slaves identified with Israel's bondage in Egypt and expressed their yearning to be free, often in the form of release from this world.

The music of the slaves "can only be understood when it is seen as the record of the thought of an oppressed people."[154] Or as another writer puts it: "The slave had a genius for phrase-making and dramatic situations, the Biblical lore was a gold mine for him, he needed it to make a social point."[155] Consider, then, phrases from the spirituals:

> Go down, Moses, into Egypt land.
> And say, "Let my people go."
>
> Good Lord, shall I ever be de one
> To get over in de Promised Land?
>
> Swing low, sweet chariot,
> Comin' for to carry me home.
>
> Deep River, my home is over Jordan . . .
> That Promised Land where all is Peace.
> Deep River, I want to cross over into Camp Ground.[156]

Frederick Douglass, exslave, said of these spirituals:

... they were tones, loud, long and deep, breathing the prayer and complaint of souls boiling over with bitterest anguish. Every tone was a testimony against slavery, and a prayer to God for deliverance from chains.[157]

Second, often associated with this cry for freedom was another note, the justice and judgment of God. Whether in "When de Stars Begin to Fall" or "In Dat Great Gettin-up Morning" or "Judgment Day is A-rollin Around," this "whole race of Lazaruses" longed for the judgment day, when "de work of Satan" (referring often to slavery) will be punished and ended—the falling rocks and mountains will hit the slave's enemies.[158]

God's judgment will also vindicate the oppressed; it will bring the jubilee, a frequent motif in the spirituals:

> There's a better day a coming
> Go sound the Jubilee.
>
> O gracious Lord! When shall it be,
> Lord, break them slavery powers—
> Will you go along with me?
> Lord, break them slavery powers,
> Go sound the Jubilee![159]

Third, just as the slaves saw their plight and hope in the central events of the Old Testament—bondage and liberation—so they identified with the suffering Jesus. "The slave could easily see the suffering Christ as someone whose predicament was somewhat as his own, yet infinitely more tragic."[160] Thus the slaves sang:

> Were you there when they crucified my Lord?
> Were you there when they crucified my Lord?
> Oh, sometimes it causes me to tremble, tremble, tremble,
> Were you there when they crucified my Lord?
>
> Did you ever see a man as God,
> A little more faith in Jesus.
> A preaching the Gospel to the poor,
> A little more faith in Jesus.[161]

The suffering Jesus was also "King Jesus," a common name for Christ in the spirituals. King Jesus had the power to intercept and defeat Satan and save the individual from hell.[162]

Fourth, when the Bible was used to argue directly against slavery, favorite verses were Acts 17:26 (KJV)—"[God] hath made of one blood all nations"—and 1 Corinthians 12:13—"For by one

Spirit are we all baptized into one body, whether we be Jews or
Gentiles, whether we be bond or free."[163] Austin Steward in his
Twenty-two Years a Slave says, "Does not the Bible inform us that
God hath created of one blood all the nations of the earth?"[164] Ex-
slave William Wells Brown expressed the same plea:

> Am I not a man and brother?
> Ought I not then to be free?
> Sell me not one to another.
> Take not thus my liberty.
> Christ, our Savior,
> died for me as well as thee.[165]

As exslaves received more education, their biblical arguments
against slavery were similar to those presented in the anti-slavery
case above.[166] One special insight though, prominent in the slave's
experience, was that

> slavery interfered with the natural right which a father has over his
> children since slavery assumes that the child is *owned* by the master,
> not that he is placed under the control and authority of his father.
> The father is displaced from the position where God has assigned
> him, and the master is substituted in his place.[167]

It is impossible for children to honor mother and father and "obey
their parents in *all* things" under slavery (Ex. 20:12; Col. 3:20).

The significant hermeneutical alternative represented by the
slaves' use of the Bible is their clear identification with a strong biblical emphasis, the cry for freedom and justice from the underside of
history. As a cry for help from the mighty God, it was a cry of hope.
The slaves saw in their own plight the story of God's people in the
Old Testament. They saw "themselves as a people of destiny, partici-
pating in God's working in history."[168] This distinctive hermeneutic cannot be practiced by everyone, as liberation theologians
currently say, since it is the hermeneutical privilege of the oppressed and poor. But to see clearly how this perspective affects the
appeal to biblical teaching is to see a genuine hermeneutical alternative. It forces upon every biblical interpreter an awesome question: With whom do I identify when I interpret the Bible? What
glasses do I wear?

Hermeneutical Commentary

1. Appeal to the Bible does not in itself guarantee correctness
of position. The Bible says—Yes, indeed, it does say, but how do we

interpret what it says? Both sides in the slavery debate used the Bible to support their positions. But both sides were hardly equally correct.

This raises the question of whether the literal interpretation of Scripture, as commonly understood, may not be misleading and inadequate. David Ewert has written:

> It may be a confession of piety to say: "I take the Bible literally." "I take it just the way it is written!"—but such affirmations do not guarantee a perfect understanding of the Bible.[169]

This use of the term "literal" usually means the understanding of texts in a mechanical way, using one here and one there in disregard of the historical and literary contexts, the meaning intended by the author, and the overall message of the Bible.

The word "literal," however, may be used in almost an opposite way, as it was in the time of the Reformation, to mean the text's historical meaning, or the plain sense of the text. From the time of the early church to the Reformation period, literal interpretation denoted the plain (usually historical) meaning intended by the writer in contrast to the allegorical interpretation, which sought for spiritual meanings having little or no relationship to the plain sense of the text.[170] Partly in reaction to the abuse of allegorical interpretation and partly because of the need for Christian experience to rest firmly on historical bases, Martin Luther rejected other types of interpretation, accepting only the literal interpretation which sought for the plain historical meaning and the clear grammatical sense of the text. Although this principle has been criticized and supplemented by historical-critical and linguistic methods of interpretation,[171] its basic concern for ascertaining the plain meaning of the text remains central in the interpretive work of most current biblical scholarship.

It might be noted that the slavery debate took place before the widespread use of the historical-critical method in America. Although neither side paid attention to the historical and cultural contexts of Scripture as much as current commentators do, the abolitionists did show aspects of historical-critical thinking in their statements, for example, that (1) Abraham's morality cannot simply be copied by us today (otherwise we should practice polygamy and concubinage) and (2) neither God nor Israel originated slavery—it was practiced by the pagan cultures of the time. From these basic insights, it would be natural for us today to argue that we must emphasize the way God regulated those practices in the direction of justice and mercy. Hence the Sabbath, sabbatical, and jubilee policies emerged to guarantee mercy and loving care for the servants, so that Hebrew servitude was different from the slavery experienced in Egypt and that practiced in America at the time of this debate. The principles for interpretation set forth by Bourne (see point 5 in the abolitionist rebuttal) also point in the direction of critical thinking; they enunciate some of the main points to be made below.

2. One of these considerations is that the full testimony of Scripture should be heard; all scriptural evidence is to be considered. Obscure parts are to be explained by the clear parts with the overall spirit of the teaching serving as final arbiter of meaning. In the slavery debate, both sides used the whole Bible remarkably well, and the *whole* Bible was perceived to support opposing positions!

This raises some difficult issues which will need further commentary in the course of these studies: the need for a more careful method of using Scripture (chapter 2), the problem of Scripture's diversity such as Moses Stuart's comments illustrate (chapter 3), the need to identify how Scripture in its diversity functions normatively for our thought and practice, and the extent to which the interpreter's biases affect interpretation (these last two issues will be discussed immediately below).

3. Another appropriate learning from this study is that a particular text or section of the Bible should be used for its main emphasis, not for "the attendant features." Is it right to use the life of Abraham to argue for slavery? If so, then perhaps his life can also be used to argue for concubinage and shading the truth out of self-interest. Instead of using the Abraham narrative for these points, it should be used for its main purpose and emphasis, to show the testing of Abraham's faith in God's promises.[172] If this principle had been followed in the slavery debate, then the texts in Exodus, Leviticus, and Deuteronomy would have been used in such a way to show that Israel's practice of slavery/servitude (whatever it be called)[173] accented mercy and humanitarian concern for the servants; the texts then could not be used to support a contemporary institution of slavery which legitimated cruelty and oppression. Similarly, if the Pauline texts had been used in accord with this principle, they would have supported the gospel's new ethic of impartial love for all, mutual service, and equal accountability of master and slave to God, rather than justifying the existence and continuation of slavery as a social institution.

4. Abolitionist writers gave priority to theological principles and basic moral imperatives, which in turn put slavery under moral judgment. The point we should learn from this is that theological principles and basic moral imperatives should be primary biblical resources for addressing social issues today. These should carry greater weight than specific statements on a given topic even though the statements speak expressly to the topic under discussion.

To illustrate from the slavery debate: 1 Timothy 6:1-6 does indeed contain specific directives on the topic of slavery. Jesus' command to love one's neighbor, however, doesn't mention slavery, but has direct bearing upon any evaluation of the moral character of slavery as an institution. From which set of scriptural resources do we then derive our moral guidance today? Or, to construct the question in a complementary way: how do we distinguish between that which we should regard as descriptive and that which we should cling to as prescriptive from within the vast amount of biblical literature? Certainly, grammatical construction alone offers little help in formulating an answer. Some practices which Christian believers today regard as most irrelevant to faith are written in clear, even terse, prescriptive language (e.g., the case laws of Ex. 21-23); on the other hand, many of Jesus' teachings, which all Christians regard as authoritative, appear in descriptive narrative in the Gospels. Hence linguistic construction itself tells us little about how Scripture should provide the community of faith with normative teaching for faith and life.

One of the purposes of these four studies is to provide hermeneutical perspectives, which when compared with each other (see chapter 5) might illumine this most difficult question: What aspects of biblical teaching are authoritative, or *how* are all aspects of biblical teaching authoritative, for us as God's people? How do we use biblical teaching so that we do not end up using it against itself, i.e., using some specific biblical texts to argue against and even silence some basic and very essential aspects of biblical truth?

Another way of framing the same hermeneutical concern is to ask how to be saved from the hermeneutics of the Pharisees portrayed in the Gospels. They took care to observe every specific command but directly opposed God's will, intention, and revelation in Jesus Christ. This Pharisaic use of the Old Testament should teach us that there is a wrong way of religiously and ardently using Scripture. The teaching calls us away from "letter-use" to "spirit-use," hearing its main intentions and not using specific verses—even clear directives (e.g., Lev. 25:44-45)—to mitigate and silence the clear moral and theological imperatives of biblical faith.

5. The slavery debate should alert us to self-justifying tendencies and/or self-serving interests at work in the use of Scripture. Self-serving interests hindered the discovery of the intended meaning in various scriptural texts. One can argue that every person's use is self-serving. To some extent this is true. If, however, such self-serving interest leads to injustice, oppression, or structural violence, then the very heart of biblical truth and concern is repudiated. In that case, the position is anti-biblical, despite citation of supporting texts.

It is common nowadays to recognize the enormous influence that one's situation in life has upon the interpreter of Scripture.[174] A major emphasis, spurred especially by the Latin American and feminist theologies of liberation, has emerged in biblical studies. The interpreter's religious, social, political, and (most significant) economic situation affects, even determines, what one sees in the Bible. The perspectives that the interpreter brings from his/her tradition are a constellation of influences—religious, social, political, and economic. These influences are intertwined with other factors as well—sexual identity (male or female), nationality, urban or rural orientation, and psychological factors—all of which affect one's interpretation of the Bible.

As noted previously, the slaves' use of the Bible clearly shows that their distinctive situation in life led them to perceive and use the Bible differently from either the white pro-slavery or anti-slavery writers. Experience shapes perception and understanding. This point is important first as a fact to be recognized for all interpretation. Then discussion of its negative and positive features may be considered.

Since so many different factors influence the way we understand the Bible, we might ask how people (we) come to new understandings. How do we change from one perception to another, e.g., from a pro-slavery position to an anti-slavery position? Does this happen because Scripture "objectively," over and above us, commands such response? Perhaps, and perhaps not. Quite likely the constellation of influences upon our lives is significantly altered. Whether one lived in the North or the South, came from English or German background, was black or white affected one's view on slavery. Today, moving into the city, serving in an economically poor country, or changing one's circle of friends may indeed alter one's understanding of Scripture.

Behind these visible changes in life are powerful psychic forces forging the development of a new "I" with changing likes, loves, values. How does a young person feel about her/his relatives and congregation before and after a development experience in Bolivia or Haiti? Let no one think that the interpretation of Scripture is not affected, nor that the sense of who one's *real* family and congregation are has not undergone profound assessment, evolving out of deep psychological struggles and involving the very core of one's being, i.e., whom I love and who loves me.

Social forces and psychological identity are both powerful determinants in scriptural interpretation. The answers to the questions "To what community do I belong?" and "Who am I?" immediately disclose much about how one interprets the Bible on specific, key issues. If a person is Quaker or Mennonite, we can expect certain perspectives on war and peace; if one is Seventh-Day Adventist, we can expect an interpretation of the Bible which supports that position; if the interpreter is a U.S. slaveowner in 1850, we can expect an understanding of the Bible that allows slavery; and if one is a slave or otherwise oppressed, we can expect identity with the bondage-liberation and suffering-vindication themes of the Bible.

6. Although sociological and psychological influences powerfully affect interpretation, it must also be said that the reality and power of the biblical text, standing over against and addressing the interpreter as God's Word, can change the mind and views of the interpreter, so that the interpreter's presuppositions and conscious understandings are changed by the text. This in turn may lead the interpreter to seek to change her/his social world, specifically those influences previously affecting interpretation.

For this to happen, the interpreter must use a method of Bible study that allows the text to speak on its own terms. The comments at the end of the next chapter will describe further such a method; the last chapter will propose a model of understanding and a method to be used in interpretation.

7. The Quaker and Mennonite approaches to slavery raise another issue in biblical interpretation (one which Bourne and Hosmer also addressed): To whom does one direct the biblical teaching? While divine revelation is intended for everyone to heed, whom does the interpreter hold accountable? The lesson we receive from the approach of Woolman and the Mennonite Church, reflected in the Virginia Conference statement, is that the patterns of kingdom morality taught in Scripture should be applied first to

Christian believers, the members of the church community.

Biblical morality calls the church to obedience while the biblical vision of mission calls all people to belief and life in the redeemed community. The key point is that the interpreter thinks not first for the whole society but about the way life is to be lived by members of the community of faith. This learning speaks also to the question raised above: how do people change and gain new perspectives for interpretation? From diligently studying the text? Yes. But also by becoming part of a community of faith which seeks to live out the moral teaching of the text. In this way, both through study of the text and living the truth of the text, interpretation consists not only of knowledge, but includes faith, hope, and love as well, expressed in visible structures of human community.

Chapter 2

THE BIBLE AND THE SABBATH

Sabbath, Sabbath-Sunday, or Lord's Day?

The historic meeting of Anwar Sadat, Menachem Begin, and Jimmy Carter to search for a Middle East peace settlement occurred on a long holy-day weekend. Each man held to a different weekly holy day: Sadat to Friday, the Islamic Day of Congregational Prayer; Begin to Saturday, the Jewish Sabbath; and Carter to Sunday, the Christian day of rest. These three national leaders agreed to work right through the weekend, giving their agendas greater priority than observance of each one's weekly holy day.

This event occasions three fundamental questions: Which is the correct day for special observance? What is the significance of that observance? Is it morally acceptable to forgo observance of the weekly holy day in order to continue one's work, especially when that work is pursuit of peace in the Middle East?

This chapter focuses on three different *Christian* ways of reading the Judeo-Christian Scriptures on this issue: (1) the Sabbath position, the seventh day holy; (2) the Sabbath-Sunday position, one day in seven holy; and (3) the Lord's day position, all-days-in-one holy.

Overview of the Problem

To introduce the three different Christian understandings in the Sabbath controversy, I begin with brief quotations representing the respective positions:

1. The Sabbath Position

... the sabbath is the memorial of an immutable historical fact—a finished creation and the Creator's rest on the specific seventh day at the close of creation week. We ... believe that nothing—no person or group, or power on earth—can change the commemorative, historical fact that God rested on the seventh day of creation week and gave His rest day to mankind as the perpetual memorial-reminder of a finished work—never repealed, and never to be repealed.[1]

Those who hold to Saturday as the holy Sabbath day are primarily the Jewish people and, within Christianity, the Seventh-Day Adventists and the Seventh-Day Baptists. A small group of Sabbatarian Anabaptists in the sixteenth century also held this view.[2]

2. The Sabbath-Sunday Position

The sabbath as an institution is perpetual ... it existed before and survives the Jewish sabbath, and ... it appears in its most perfect form in the Lord's day (Sunday).[3]

Or to quote from the *Westminster Larger Catechism* (Question 117):

The Sabbath or Lord's Day is to be sanctified by an holy resting day, not only from such works as are at all times sinful, but even from such worldly employments and recreations as are on other days lawful; [we make] it our delight to spend the whole time ... in the public and private exercises of God's worship.[4]

Most representative of this position were the Puritans, in England, the United States, and Canada. Many Protestants, Catholics, and Mennonites have to greater or lesser extents followed this view in which the Sabbath theology and restrictions have been transposed onto Sunday.

3. The Lord's Day Position

The sabbath began at the time of Moses; it was and is a Jewish institution. Jesus transcends the sabbath, declaring himself to be Lord of the sabbath. The sabbath's true intentions are expressed in Jesus' ministry. Hence, the sabbath has been *fulfilled* in Jesus Christ, who has begun the reign of God's rest in which the sabbatical vision of justice, freedom, and love are *everyday* mandates.

The Lord's Day is connected to the sabbath only through analogy: just as the sabbath celebrates God's deliverance of Israel from the Egyptian bondage, so the Lord's Day (Sunday) celebrates God's resurrection of Jesus Christ, offering to all people deliverance from sin and oppression. As the sabbath is uniquely rooted in the exodus; so the Lord's Day is uniquely rooted in the resurrection.[5]

This position, held by many Christians and found in writings of Christian scholars, has never been articulated as an official position of a denominational group, as far as I know. Certain sixteenth-century Anabaptists, however, advanced views similar to this.[6]

Since each of these three positions uses the Bible for support, the following questions arise: How does each position use the Bible? Can we observe certain patterns or principles of interpretation which influence adherents of these different positions toward their respective understandings? To answer these questions we will examine the scriptural support adduced by each position and then offer some hermeneutical observations and guidelines for proper interpretation.

The Sabbath Position: The Seventh Day Holy

The Sabbath position appeals to the following biblical teaching:

1. God ordained the Sabbath in creation.

> And on the seventh day God finished his work which he had done, and he rested on the seventh day from all his work which he had done. So God blessed the seventh day and hallowed it, because on it God rested from all his work which he had done in creation. Genesis 2:2-3.

Sabbath, rest, and *seventh* day are permanently and unalterably linked together by God for all creation for all time. God both *created* the seventh-day Sabbath and *commanded* its holy observance for all time. Adventist M. L. Andreasen says:

> Two institutions have come to us from the Garden of Eden: marriage and the Sabbath. Only one of these, the Sabbath, carries over into the earth made new. . . . "As the new heavens and the new earth, which I will make, shall remain before Me, saith the Lord, so shall your seed and your name remain. And it shall come to pass, that from one new moon to another, and from one Sabbath to another, shall all flesh come to worship before Me, saith the Lord." Isaiah 66:22, 23.

> This makes the Sabbath unique. Throughout changing customs and varying dispensations, amid the passing of empires and the crash of nations, surviving floods, famines, and even "the end of all things,"

the Sabbath stands unmoved and supreme. It, of all institutions, alone abides. Made by God and given to man for an everlasting possession, it endures as eternity itself.[7]

The divine origin of the Sabbath in creation means that:

a. The Sabbath institution was part of God's original plan for humanity, a provision made before sin entered the world. Correlatively, "if sin had not entered [the world], all [persons] would have kept the original sabbath day."[8] The Sabbath expresses God's holiness.[9]

b. Seventh-day Sabbath observance is intended for everyone. God instituted the Sabbath long before Israel ever existed. It is not merely a Jewish ceremony, but a universal institution. This is supported both by Genesis 2:2-3 and God's giving a double portion of manna to the Israelites on the sixth day, *before* God gave them the Decalogue (Ex. 16:4-5, 20-30 precedes Ex. 20:1-17).[10] Evidence also exists that other ancient nations knew of the Sabbath as a legacy of creation.[11]

c. The Sabbath is not an institution but a specific day, so ordained for all time.

> The Sabbath is not something apart from the day, which can be shifted about and perhaps placed on another day. It is the day itself, the seventh day.

> We hear much today about a Sabbath institution. But the Bible never speaks of a Sabbath institution. It talks about the Sabbath day. There is no such thing as a Sabbath institution that was blessed and made holy for the benefit of humanity, apart from a day. . . .

> The day that God blessed can never be taken from the Sabbath. The Sabbath can never be taken from the day that God blessed. These cannot be separated. They are inseparable because they are one.

> The seventh day is the Sabbath; the Sabbath is the seventh day.[12]

Or, as another writer says:

> God did not bless the Sabbath in general, nor did He bless a Sabbath, nor even the Sabbath, but the Sabbath day, and this Sabbath day is the seventh day.[13]

This identification of the seventh day as the day for Sabbath observance is not to be compromised. Any change in the day would require that the "whole work of creation would have to be done over again."[14]

2. The Sabbath is an essential part of the moral law.

Remember the sabbath day, to keep it holy. Six days you shall labor, and do all your work; but the seventh day is a sabbath to the Lord your God; in it you shall not do any work [Ex. 20:8-11; see also Ex. 31:16-17 and Deut. 5:12-15].

As a part of the Decalogue, the commandment to keep the Sabbath day holy sets forth God's moral law for all people for all time. Since Christians readily accept the validity and applicability of the other nine commandments, why should not the fourth commandment also be so regarded? It is not a commandment for Israel only, but applies to all people. The question of the Decalogue's universality likely would not have ever been raised had Christians continued to observe the Sabbath. The Sabbath underlies all the commands. "It would be easier to dispose of some of the other commandments than to dispose of the Sabbath commandment."[15]

Placed between the three commandments of obligation to God and the six commandments of obligation to fellow humans, the Sabbath commandment occupies a strategic place in the Decalogue. It "belongs to both tables of the law, and partakes of the nature of both. It has a Godward and a manward aspect. It is God's Sabbath, but we, men, are to keep it."[16]

3. Sabbath observance was important through Israel's history B.C.

Breaking the Sabbath commandment, like the breaking of any of the moral commands, was a serious offense before God. The violator was stoned to death (Num. 15:32-35).[17]

Two major prophets traced the cause of Israel's exile to God's punishment for breaking and polluting the Sabbath. Four times Ezekiel mentioned Israel's pollution of God's Sabbaths (20:13, 16, 21, 24).[18] Similarly Jeremiah pointed to Israel's failure to hallow the Sabbath as the cause for the kindling of God's wrath against Jerusalem (Jer. 17:21-27). And one of the last messages that God sent to Israel before Nebuchadnezzar destroyed the city and took the people captive was the warning that they would "become servants of a heathen people until they should have learned not to profane God's holy Sabbath."[19]

Upon return from exile, Israel again broke the Sabbath observance. Not only did Nehemiah condemn these violations— reminding the people that because of such conduct God brought the exile upon Israel—but the Jewish leader also commanded that

the city's gates be shut on the Sabbath, in order to prevent violations. Violators were to be arrested (Neh. 13:15-22).[20]

4. Jesus observed the Sabbath.

Jesus Christ, God's Son, participated in the creation of the
world: "all things were made through him" (Jn. 1:3); "for in him all
things were created" (Col. 1:16; cf. 1 Cor. 8:6; Heb. 1:1-2). "In other
words, He [Jesus Christ] is its [the Sabbath's] author and its maker
. . . and its protector."[21]

Jesus did not break the Sabbath; he broke only the human
traditions surrounding the Sabbath.

> Christ did His best to restore to Israel the Sabbath as God originally
> had given it to them, to be a blessing rather than a burden. He did not
> need to stress strictness in the minutiae of Sabbathkeeping, for Israel
> had already gone too far in that direction. With their new viewpoint,
> the people, and especially the Pharisees, believed Christ to be slack in
> the observance of the Sabbath. They did not understand that He was
> attempting to show them its real purpose; that doing good, healing
> the sick, and committing acts of mercy on the Sabbath were pleasing
> in the sight of God, rather than merely mechanically observing the
> day.[22]

In his careful analysis of Jesus' purported violations of the
Sabbath,[23] Samuele Bacchiocchi holds that Jesus' acts celebrated
the true intentions of the Sabbath—"redemption, joy, and service;"[24] the keeping of the Sabbath, therefore, is a "permanent fitting memorial of the reality" of Jesus' own redemptive mission.[25]

Further, Jesus faithfully observed the Sabbath, attending the
synagogue (Mk. 6:1-2; Lk. 4:16, 31) and teaching with authority
(Mk. 1:27-28). He "risked his life to free the Sabbath from the
wicked traditions surrounding it" (Mt. 12:9-14).[26] At no time did
Jesus undermine the moral law of the Decalogue. His summation of
the whole law—"love God" and "love your neighbor as yourself"—
provides the perspective in which the entire law, including Sabbath
observance, is to be obeyed and fulfilled (Mt. 22:37-39; 5:17-20; Jn.
15:10, etc.).[27]

In condemning the elders and the Pharisees for their slavish
pursuit of "traditions" (Mk. 7:1-13), Jesus distinguished between
the moral law and the traditions. Ignoring the multitudinous rules
which the leaders said Moses commanded, Jesus revered and kept
the Sabbath, declaring that "the Sabbath was made for man, not
man for the Sabbath." Freeing the Sabbath from all extraneous
regulations, he presented it to the people once again, as "God had

originally intended it, a blessing to mankind and to all creation."[28]

That Jesus envisioned the continuation of Sabbath observance by his followers is clear from a prophetic statement he made two days before his death: "Pray that your flight may not be ... on a sabbath" (Mt. 24:20).[29]

Jesus' rest in the tomb on the Sabbath further underscores the Sabbath command, especially since the rest came after his work on Good Friday, climaxed by the word "It is finished." After recalling that Jesus announced his mission to be "the fulfillment of the sabbatical time of redemption (Luke 4:18-19)" and that he intensified his works of salvation on the Sabbath (Jn. 5:17; 9:4) to free "souls whom 'Satan bound' (Luke 13:16)," Bacchiocchi says:

> ... it was on a Friday afternoon that Christ completed His redemptive mission on this earth and having said "it is finished" (John 19:30), He hallowed the Sabbath by resting in the tomb (Luke 23:53-54; Matt. 27:57-60; Mark 15:42, 46).

Just as the Sabbath rest culminated God's work of creation (Gen. 2:2-3), "so the Sabbath rest now at the end of Christ's earthly mission expresses the rejoicing of Deity over the complete and perfect redemption restored to man."[30]

5. The apostles practiced Sabbath observance.

As Butler points out, Sabbatarians hold that the apostles continued Sabbath observance.

> For some thirty years after Christ's death we have an inspired history of the apostolic church, in which we learn of the exceeding bitterness and hatred of the Jews against the disciples, taking every possible occasion to persecute and destroy them. But in not a single instance is there the slightest hint that they ever found them breaking the Sabbath. This negative argument affords the strongest proof that the disciples continued to observe that day as they always had before.[31]

Conversely, as Bacchiocchi argues, the first-day meetings and the reference to the Lord's day in Revelation do not indicate a transfer of the Sabbath to Sunday.

> In both 1 Corinthians 16:1-3 and Acts 20:7-12, we found that the first day of the week is mentioned to describe respectively a private fundraising plan and an extraordinary gathering of the Troas believers with Paul. Similarly we noticed that the expression "Lord's day" of Revelation 1:10, in the light of its immediate and wider context, can be best interpreted as a designation for the day of judgment and of the *parousia*.[32]

Through his analysis of the history of Christianity in Jerusalem prior to the fall of the temple (AD 70), Bacchiocchi argues that Sunday observance (replacing the Sabbath) did not arise from a weekly Lord's supper celebrating the resurrection, nor is there any evidence from this period indicating "the place, time, and causes of the origin of Sunday keeping."[33] Christians continued to observe the seventh-day Sabbath during the New Testament period.

6. Rome changed the day.

How then did the change from Sabbath to Lord's day come about?

> We ... believe there has been a wholly unauthorized, unwarranted, and presumptuous change in the sabbath by the Catholic, or great Roman, apostasy, as prophesied by Daniel (Dan. 7).[34]

This apostasy—foretold in Daniel 7:24-25; 2 Timothy 4:3-4; and 2 Thessalonians 2:3-8—"was introduced at Rome about the middle of the second century."[35]

Bacchiocchi undergirds this traditional Adventist position with his masterful research on the developments of the second and third centuries. Three factors contributed to the change from Sabbath to Sunday observance:

> The first, anti-Judaism, which appears to have caused a widespread devaluation and repudiation of the Sabbath, thereby creating the exigency of a new day of worship. The second, the development of Sun-cults with the consequent enhancement of the day of the Sun over that of Saturn, a contingency which apparently oriented Christians toward such a day, since it provided an adequate symbolism to commemorate significant divine acts [e.g., the Day of the Son (Sun), for] "it is on this day that the Sun of Justice has risen" (Jerome). . . .[36]

> [And third, the] role that the Church of Rome played in causing the abandonment of the Sabbath and the adoption of Sunday.[37]

To conclude, I present the summary that Gerhard F. Hasel (like Bacchiocchi, a professor at Andrews University) made of the Anabaptist Sabbatarian Oswald Glait's reasons for Sabbath observance:

> (1) The Sabbath is a memorial of creation and an eternal covenant. (2) The Sabbath is not a Jewish ceremonial institution but was kept from the beginning of the world by Adam, Abraham, and the children of Israel, even before the giving of the law on Mt. Sinai. (3) The Sabbath as one of the commandments of the Decalogue is still binding for

Christians. (4) The Sabbath was not changed, annulled, or broken by Christ, but he himself founded, established, confirmed, and adorned it. (5) The Sabbath was observed by the apostles and by Paul. (6) The Sabbath must be observed on the seventh day of the week which is Saturday. (7) The Sabbath is a sign of the eternal Sabbath and must be kept literally as long as the world stands, until we enter the eternal rest at the Parousia. (8) The keeping of the Sabbath is a necessity for the Christian who wants to enter the heavenly paradise. (9) Those who do not observe the literal Sabbath will be punished by God. (10) The pope invented Sunday observance.[38]

The Sabbath-Sunday Position: One Day in Seven Holy

> A well-spent Sabbath we feel to be
> a day of heaven upon earth.
> —from a Puritan[39]

When the falling dust of the world has clogged the wheels of our affections, that they can scarce move towards God, the Sabbath comes, and oils the wheels of our affections, and they move swiftly on. God has appointed the Sabbath for this end. On this day the thoughts rise to heaven, the tongue speaks of God, the eyes drop tears, and the soul burns in love. The heart, which all the week was frozen, on the Sabbath melts with the word. The Sabbath is a friend to religion; it files off the rust of our graces; it is a spiritual jubilee, wherein the soul is set to converse with its Maker.[40]

This position's understanding of the Bible follows closely the same use of the Bible as found in the previous position, except that the principle of one day in seven—but not the seventh day precisely—is the basis for Sabbath-Sunday observance. The New Testament texts mentioning Christian gatherings on "the first day of the week" and the reference to "the Lord's day" (Rev. 1:10) are considered as evidence that Sunday observance replaced Sabbath observance in the apostolic period (AD 30-100).

1. God ordained the Sabbath in creation.

> The sabbath is a creation ordinance and does not derive its validity or its necessity or its sanction . . . from any exigencies arising from sin, nor from any of the provisions of redemptive grace.[41]

God rested on and sanctified the Sabbath; we must recognize that our Sabbath observance answers to God's act and word.

> . . . sabbath observance soon becomes obsolete if it does not spring from the sense of sanctity generated and nourished in us by the recognition that God has set apart one day in seven.[42]

This portrait of God as Sabbath-keeper, standing at the portal of revelation has these four elements: rest, a septenary rest, a blessed rest, a holy rest. As a Biblical basis for Sabbath-keeping we have first the example of God and, by implication, his appointment of the Day for man.[43]

In an extensive study, *This Is The Day*, Roger T. Beckwith appeals to traces of evidence in ancient calendars, the pre-Abraham Semitic and the Babylonian, of periods of seven or eight days. From this investigation Beckwith seeks to substantiate Genesis 2, asserting that the Sabbath began with creation, that the patriarchs kept some form of the Sabbath, that the ancient calendars reveal degenerated forms of the original Sabbath, and that Exodus 16—20, therefore, renews an earlier practice.[44] Beckwith also cites texts from Jewish Hellenistic writers, Aristobulus and Philo (third and first centuries BC), which state that God "gave the sabbath to all men (not just to Israel)."[45]

Frances Nigel Lee develops a covenantal theology that connects work, protection, the promise of eternal life, etc., to God's Sabbath covenant with the first Adam.[46] He finds the first-day Sabbath already in creation: "The sabbath was the first day of the unfallen Adam's week" since he was created on the sixth day and rested on his first day.[47] *Seventh*-day observance results from the fall and the curse; Cain murdered Abel on the seventh day and his curse was sevenfold vengeance.[48] Lee thus connects the *first*-day Sabbath with the pre-fall Adam and the second Adam, Christ, and links the *seventh*-day Sabbath with humanity's fall which embraces the history of Israel.[49]

2. The moral law commands Sabbath observance.

The inclusion of the Sabbath commandment in the moral law requires Christians to keep the Sabbath, since the moral law, unlike ceremonial law, enunciates principles for all time.

Moral law is in the last analysis but the reflection or expression of the moral nature of God. God is holy, just, and good, and the law which is also holy, just, and good is simply the correlate of the holiness and justice and goodness of God. . . . Moral law is the moral perfection of God coming to expression for the regulation of life and conduct.

It would require conclusive evidence to establish the thesis that the fourth command is in a different category from the other nine.[50]

That there are moral elements in the fourth commandment pertaining to rest, worship, spiritual culture, and holiness, it would seem that no thoughtful person can deny. Its *company* in the Decalogue is a guarantee for its moral nature in part.[51]

Precisely because the command is in the moral code, the essence of the Sabbath is the moral principle, not the specific day.

The morality or substance of the fourth commandment does not lie in keeping the seventh day precisely, but keeping one day in seven is what God has appointed.[52]

... the spirit of the law regards the proportion [of time] rather than the portion absolute.[53]

Or, as Lee puts it:

... it may be said that there is in the sabbath of Sinai a contemporary form and a moral essence. The contemporary form was the rigid rest every seventh day of the week (Saturday) imposed especially on the Jewish people. The moral element lies in the fact that a certain definite day must be dedicated each week for religion, and that as much rest as is needful for religion and its hallowed contemplation is demanded. The (Saturday) sabbath of the Jews having been abolished in the New Testament, Sunday or the Lord's day must now be solemnly hallowed by all Christians.[54]

Beckwith identifies the Sabbath as a "memorial of Israel's redemption," noting that it was a "restored institution" and thus "relatively new even to" Israel. As the rainbow was the sign of God's covenant with Noah and circumcision the sign of God's covenant with Abraham, so the Sabbath became the sign of the covenant with Moses. Placed within the Decalogue—the "very heart of the Mosaic Law" and spoken by God from heaven—it is of permanent significance.[55]

Examining the Palestinian Jewish literature of the late centuries BC and early centuries AD, Beckwith notes that here, in contrast to Hellenistic Judaism, the Sabbath was given not to the nations, but to Israel alone.[56] Strict regulations governed the Sabbath in this literature, and as in Jewish Hellenistic literature it was called "the day of light." The Sabbath thus played a major role in Jewish life and community.[57]

3. The New Testament changed the day of the Sabbath.

How then did the first day replace the seventh? Seventeenth-century writer Thomas Watson answers: "Not by ecclesiastical authority. 'The church ... has no power to ordain a Sabbath.' "

Watson then presents three major points of argument.

First, he says, Christ himself changed "the Sabbath from the last of the week to the first." Psalm 118:24—"This is the day which the Lord has made"—refers to this act of Christ, as many expositors understand the verse. Also, "the Lord's day" in Revelation 1:10 is so designated because the Lord instituted it, in the same way he instituted the Lord's supper. Further, Christ arose on the first day, appearing twice on that day to his disciples (Jn. 20:19, 26). As both Augustine and Athanasius say, he thereby "transferred the Jewish Sabbath to the Lord's Day."

Second, the apostles practiced the keeping of the first day: "Upon the first day of the week, when the disciples came together to break bread, Paul preached to them" (Acts 20:7; 1 Cor. 16:2). Leading church fathers—Augustine, Innocentius, and Isidore—regard this practice of meeting on the first day to be authorized by God, sanctioned by the apostles, and inspired by the Holy Ghost.

Third, the primitive church observed the Lord's-day Sabbath, as Ignatius, living in the time of the apostle John, testifies: "Let every one that loveth Christ keep holy the first day of the week, the Lord's-day."

Just as the Jewish Sabbath, therefore, was a memorial of creation, so the first-day Sabbath "puts us in mind of the 'mystery of our redemption by Christ.' "[58] Jesus' resurrection on "the first day of the week" provides, therefore, the historical and theological foundation for the change from the seventh-day Jewish Sabbath to the first-day Christian Sabbath (Mt. 28:1; Mk. 16:2, 9; Lk. 24:1; Jn. 20:1).

This position, while emphasizing the significance of the resurrection, also maintains that Jesus did not abolish the Sabbath. The Lord's day does not replace the Sabbath; the Lord's day continues the Sabbath.

[He] uttered no word that can properly be construed as lacking in deep reverence ... he expected that his followers would continue to hold and inculcate the spirit of the historic sabbath.[59]

Christ never intended to abolish the sabbath. His efforts to correct [sabbath notions prevalent in his time] furnish the best evidence that he was desirous of preserving the true sabbath.[60]

The way in which Christ defends his actions on the sabbath never suggests that he is rescinding the sabbath, and often suggests the contrary.[61]

Whether Jesus himself specifically commanded the change to

the first day, or whether the apostles changed it, is not clear. Those who hold that Jesus changed the day say:

> ... further and definite instruction was given by the Savior in person before his ascension or by his Spirit afterwards, concerning the continued observance of the day.[62]

In either event, the New Testament indicates that the apostles met on the first day (1 Cor. 16:2; Acts 20:7; Rev. 1:10). Numerous texts show that Christians met separately from the synagogue (1 Cor. 5:4; 11:17-18, 20; 14:19, 26, 28). Further, the churches appointed their own elders (Acts 14:23).

> We have in these various citations from Scripture incontestable evidence that the first day of the week was at least one of special observance to the apostles, and to Christians contemporary with them.[63]

1 Corinthians 16:2 especially supports the view that the early Christians kept their Sabbath on Sunday.

> ... it seems fair to judge ... that the first day of the week ... reserved in a particular manner for worship and service, was the day appointed for the additional spiritual exercise of setting funds aside in systematic fashion for the relief of the Christian poor.[64]

If pressed by the Adventist position for a specific statement in which Jesus or the apostles commanded Sunday observance, one should respond (according to this position):

> Can they find a direct command to substitute baptism for circumcision, the Lord's Supper for Passover, and the church for the synagogue? Christianity did not supplant Judaism by direct command and immediately, but gradually, by growth and through example and use.[65]

Francis Nigel Lee connects the Christian Sabbath (Sunday) also to the end-time Sabbath age already begun (Heb. 3-4). He speaks of the eighth day as the day after the end of time, the day of *always Sabbath.* God's seventh day is rest from creating the world, but God's eighth day is eternal rest. Christians have begun to enter that rest; hence on the first day Sabbath they both anticipate their eternal rest in God's eighth day and experience rest from physical labor (God's seventh day).[66]

This position uses Colossians 2:14-16 and Romans 14:2-3 cautiously, however. These references are ascribed to ceremonial

days, even the ceremonial Sabbaths,[67] or the emphasis falls on
Christ as the one to whom the "shadow" points, but one who also
reinforces the Sabbath institution.[68]

*4. Patristic writings show the early church's observance of
Sabbath-Sunday.*

By analyzing patristic writings from the second to fourth
centuries, Wilfrid Stott seeks to show that the practice of the
church in these early centuries confirms Sunday-Sabbath
observance. His conclusions are:

> . . . we have argued that in Jewish Christianity the Lord's Day was
> originally observed side by side with the sabbath. . . .

> . . . we have argued that the name "Lord's Day" does not allude to the
> Lord's Supper but to the Resurrection, . . . that the festival of the
> Resurrection, like the sabbath, is a day of worship wholly devoted to
> the Lord.

> . . . we have argued that, though the ante-Nicene Fathers are often
> very critical of the Jewish sabbath, this is because . . . of the way they
> believed the Jews to observe it, not because they were fundamentally
> opposed to such an institution.

> . . . we have argued that they thought of the Lord's Day in very similar
> terms to the sabbath, as a whole day, set apart to be a holy festival and
> a rest day. On Sunday Christians deliberately laid their daily work
> aside, and spent most of the day (not just a small part of it) in corpo-
> rate worship.

> . . . we have argued, especially from the evidence of Eusebius, that the
> decree of Constantine was influenced by the church, rather than the
> reverse, and introduced nothing fundamentally new into Christian
> thought or practice regarding the Lord's Day.

> . . . we have argued that, though the early Fathers deny that the pa-
> triarchs kept the sabbath, and do not directly link the Lord's Day with
> the fourth commandment, yet they link it indirectly, and always insist
> that the Decalogue is binding upon Christians.[69]

The Lord's Day Position: Seven-Days-in-One Holy

Jesus' priestly work of salvation . . . fulfilled and replaced the sabbath
for those who believe: this salvation brought them release from sin,
joy, liberty, and true rest.[70]

Much of the Christian interpretation of the sabbath is simply going
out into the junkyards of the Pharisees and bringing back stuff that
Jesus swept out two millenniums ago.[71]

Though writers representing this position reflect different uses of Scripture, their combined emphases produce the following theses:

1. The biblical Sabbath originated not with creation but at the time of Moses as a Jewish institution.
2. The original purposes of the Sabbath were ethical and humanitarian, ensuring social equality and rest from endless work in bondage, from which God liberated Israel. The Sabbath was the foundation of the sabbatical and jubilee years, institutions providing social equality.
3. Sabbath practices in later Judaism deteriorated into legalistic restrictions, making fulfillment of the original purposes impossible.
4. Jesus broke Sabbath laws and identified his own mission with the fulfillment of the original purposes of the Sabbath. This fulfillment continues in the life of Jesus' messianic community.
5. The early church regarded Jesus' resurrection as the culmination of his salvific work; they began to meet regularly on the first day of the week to celebrate Jesus' death and resurrection through the Lord's supper. The celebration of the Lord's supper on the first day led the church to call the first day the Lord's day.
6. Though Jewish Christians continued to observe the Sabbath, Christian theology, as it developed in the context of the Gentile mission, held Sabbath-keeping to be unnecessary. The holy Sabbath of the old covenant was only a shadow of Christ; Jesus, the substance to whom the shadow pointed, has made all days holy.
7. The promised rest of the messianic age had begun now, in Christ. As in the past, so now unbelief keeps people from entering into this Sabbath rest, which God has provided through Jesus Christ.
8. Only in later church history, mostly in the fourth century, did Sabbath observance get connected to the Lord's day, producing Sabbath-Sunday observance.

In order to show the different uses of Scripture among the proponents of this third position, I will treat each of four sources separately. H. M. Riggle (writing in 1918) appeals mostly to points one and five above; Willy Rordorf's scholarly study (1962) contains all eight points, although the first is only implicit in his argument; Paul Jewett (1971) develops mostly points two, four, and five; the essays in the Carson volume reflect all points, but with modified emphases on four and five.

A. **H. M. Riggle,** *The Sabbath and the Lord's Day*

> We shall now prove that the seventh-day sabbath was created wholly
> by legislation; belonged to the monumental and shadowy rites of the
> Jews' religion; was for a temporary purpose, and was therefore
> repealable and actually was abolished (by Christ).[72]

Arguing that the Sabbath originated with Moses, is exclusively
Jewish, and has been so recognized by Christian writers through
the centuries, Riggle writes of Genesis 2:2-3:

> The Book of Genesis, including these words, was not written at the
> time of the creation of man, but twenty-five hundred years later, by
> Moses himself. In fact, this statement of Moses' in Gen. 2:2, 3 was not
> written until after the covenant enjoining the seventh-day Sabbath
> upon the Jews had been delivered upon Sinai.

> The language clearly proves that God did not bless and sanctify the
> day back at Eden when he rested, but at a later date.[73]

Noting the language of Exodus 12:2, in which God gave a new
year and a new beginning of months, Riggle locates the origin of the
Sabbath in the exodus, arguing that there "is not one command in
. . . Genesis to keep the seventh day as a sabbath." There is no indication that "the patriarchs kept the Sabbath or knew anything
about it." When Sabbatarians argue that such command was
omitted because the record is so brief, their only proof then is
"what was left out!" It is clear, says Riggle, that the Sabbath was
first commanded in Exodus 16:23-30, twenty-five hundred years
after creation. God gave the Sabbath to the Jews as a new command, together with a new year and a new beginning of months, to
indicate that their "deliverance from Egypt marked a new era in
their history."[74]

Riggle notes that in Ezekiel 20:10, 12 God's giving Israel the
Sabbath is explicitly connected to the exodus: "This text is conclusive. It simply states that God gave them the Sabbath when he
brought them out of Egypt."[75] Citing Deuteronomy 5:15, Riggle
notes again the connection between the Sabbath and the exodus;
the Sabbath is a memorial of the exodus.[76]

Having argued for the Mosaic origin of the Sabbath, Riggle
contends that the work of Jesus Christ annulled the Sabbath.

> . . . sabbath was an exact parallel of the Passover. Both were signs
> between God and the Jews; both were memorials of the deliverance
> out of Egypt; both pointed forward to Christ; and both have met their
> anti-type and passed away.[77]

We leave it [sabbath] classified just where the Bible places it, among the signs and rites of Jews, and as such it has passed away.[78]

Moses and his law are ruled out of this dispensation, and Christ and his superior law now rule in its stead. To go back to Moses is to reject Christ. To go under the law is to ignore the gospel.[79]

Using Matthew 5:17-18, Romans 10:4, and Galatians 3:23, Riggle holds that Jesus, having fulfilled the old law, was free to violate the Sabbath laws (as in Mk. 2:28—3:6). Appealing to numerous Scriptures, Riggle develops a typological relationship between the two covenants, in which the old one-day rest is replaced by an "every-day rest":

(1) The shadowy Sabbath was the observance of every seventh day. "The seventh day is the Sabbath" (Exod. 20:10). The new-covenant Sabbath is not the observance of this particular day. "One man [the Jew] esteemeth one day above another: another [the Gentile Christian] esteemeth every day alike. Let every man be fully persuaded in his own mind. . . . He that regardeth not the day, to the Lord he doth not regard it" (Rom. 14:5, 6). "Ye observe days. . . . I am afraid of you" (Gal. 4:10, 11). "Let no man therefore judge you in respect . . . of the sabbath-days" (Col. 2:16). These texts refer particularly to law days.

(2) The old was a rest of the body but one day in seven. The new is a rest of our souls every day. "For he that is entered into his rest, he also hath ceased from his own works, as God did from his" (Heb. 4:10). After God finished creation's work, he rested the seventh day. But his rest did not stop there. He rested the eighth, ninth, tenth, eleventh, twelfth day, and he has been resting from creation's work ever since. So we who have entered his rest cease from our works—self-efforts— and enjoy a perpetual soulrest.

(3) The old was a bodily rest, a temporal rest. The new is a spiritual rest that we enter by faith (Matt. 11:28, 29; Heb. 4:1-11), and is eternal.

(4) The old was enjoined in the law, and was binding upon Israel as a nation (Exod. 16:29; 31:13). The new is found in Christ under the covenant and is to be enjoyed by all nations.

(5) Under the law but one day in seven was kept holy (Exod. 20:8, 10). Under the gospel we keep *every day* holy (Luke 1:74, 75).

(6) Total abstinence from manual labor constituted a holy day—Sabbath—to the Jews (Deut. 5:14). Abstinence from manual work does not make a day holy or unholy to us under the gospel (Rom. 14:5, 6; Gal. 4:10, 11; Col. 2:16). By totally abstaining, ceasing, from our self-works, and living a righteous life, we keep every day holy (Heb. 4:10; Luke 1:74, 75). In the former the people totally abstained from manual

work; while in the latter we cease from self-strivings, and enter the glorious rest of a perfect salvation.

(7) By performing the least amount of manual work on the seventh day, the Jews broke their Sabbath, and were stoned to death (Num. 15:32-36). By indulging in the least amount of sin, we now lose our sweet Sabbath rest, and spiritual death is the result (1 John 3:8; Jas. 1:15).

(8) The old was a "shadow" or type of the new (Col. 2:14-16; Heb. 4:1-11).[80]

Riggle ends his treatise by noting the lack of evidence that Christians ever had an exclusively Christian meeting on the Sabbath, but from AD 30 to the time of Eusebius (AD 324) there is abundant evidence that Christians met as Christians on the first day of the week, the day of Christ's resurrection (Jn. 20:19, 26; Acts 2:1; 20:6-7; 1 Cor. 16:1-2; Rev. 1:10; Pliny's Letter, AD 107; Epistle of Barnabas, AD 120; etc.).[81] Further, the Lord's day

was [never] regarded [as a sabbath day, but simply] as a day of rejoicing, convocation, and religious devotion in honor of the resurrection. The idea of total abstinence from manual labor was not connected with it till centuries later.[82]

B. **Willy Rordorf,** *Sunday: The History of the Day of Rest and Worship in the Earliest Centuries of the Christian Church*

Rordorf's extensive study begins by analyzing the historical origin of Sabbath theology. After correlating the various Sabbath commands in the Pentateuch with the dates of the literary sources, Rordorf says:

'In the oldest stratum of the Pentateuch the sabbath is, therefore, to be understood as a *social institution*. After every six days of work a day of rest is inserted for the sake of the cattle and of the slaves and employees (see Ex. 23:12; 34:21).[83]

The *original,* social basis of the seventh-day rest (originally it was not called Sabbath) was soon supplemented by the priestly emphasis which specified the seventh day as "a sabbath to the Lord your God" (Ex. 20:9-10a; Deut. 5:13-14a).[84] This emphasis forms the background for the later composition of Genesis 2:2-3, in which Sabbath observance is God's own practice.[85]

A third emphasis associated with the Sabbath draws on "the character of the covenant God as protector of all the afflicted and oppressed."[86] The Deuteronomist links the social basis of the Sabbath to Yahweh's redemption of the Israelite slaves from Egyptian bondage (Deut. 5:14c-15).

Against the background of this analysis, the significance of the sabbatical year and the jubilee, both originating from the Sabbath, is readily perceived:

> The sabbath year ... naturally originated by analogy with the seven-day week and its day of rest. The *social* aim of this institution is again unmistakable: 1. The poor of the land, slaves and animals, should be able to support themselves free of charge from the produce of the land (Ex. 23.11; Lev. 25.6f.; similarly Deut. 24.19-22; Lev. 19.9-10). 2. The sabbath year is at the same time a year of remission of all debts owed by fellow citizens (Deut. 15.1ff.). 3. Hebrew slaves are released if they so desire (Ex. 21:2-6; Deut. 15:12-18). The fiftieth year which came after every seven sabbath years was regarded as an intensified sabbath year when the release of all citizens and the restitution of their patrimony were required (Lev. 25.8ff.).[87]

While these socio-moral emphases characterized the original intentions and function of the Sabbath, the domination of both priestly and legal emphases after the exile turned the Sabbath into an institution of "perpetual obligation"; disobeying Sabbath rules was punished by the death penalty. These later emphases permeated the exilic and postexilic writings.[88]

Having developed this Old Testament background for the origin and meaning of the Sabbath, Rordorf interprets Jesus' Sabbath actions and sayings as attacking both the postexilic interpretation of the Sabbath and the Sabbath itself. "It is a misunderstanding to hold that Jesus did not attack the sabbath commandment itself," Rordorf says. If Jesus had wanted to attack the casuistic laws of the Pharisees, he could have readily joined forces with scribes who were already trying "to avoid inhuman severity in the interpretation of the law." Jesus went behind all the casuistry because he saw that "this commandment enslaved human beings." He was not afraid to call into "question the commandment contained in the priestly tradition of the Old Testament."[89]

After noting the frequency of Jesus' Sabbath violations (Mk. 3:1ff.; Lk. 13:10ff.; 14:1ff.; Jn. 5:1ff.; 9:1ff.). Rordorf says:

> It is easy to understand the indignant statement made by the ruler of the synagogue, "There are six days on which work ought to be done; come on those days and be healed, and not on the sabbath day" (Luke 13.14). All these people who were healed could certainly have waited for their cure until the next day (cf. Mark 1.32ff.). Why, then, did Jesus

heal them on the sabbath of all days? Surely, not *only* because of his
compassionate love, but also with the express intention of showing
that for him the sabbath commandment had no binding force.

It is only logical that after the sabbath conflicts the opponents of
Jesus should have decided to kill him, as we read in Mark 3.6 par. (cf.
John 5.18; 7.25). This would have been the natural reaction of every
pious Jew to Jesus' attitude towards the sabbath.[90]

Rordorf also investigates the significance of Jesus' Sabbath
sayings in the Gospels. After examining Mark 3:4—"Is it lawful on
the sabbath to do good or to do harm, to save life or to kill?"—and
the three versions of the parabolic saying which gives the life of an
animal priority over the Sabbath commandment (Mt. 12:11f.; Lk.
14:5; 13:15), Rordorf notes, "The sabbath commandment was not
merely pushed into the background by the healing activity of Jesus;
it was simply annulled."[91] Rordorf understands the Gospel of John
to make precisely this claim when it links Jesus' actions on the Sabbath with the continuing work of the Father (Jn. 9:4; 5:17) and the
divine necessity *(dei)* that motivates Jesus' acts.[92]

Jesus' claim of doing the work of the one who sent him and declaring himself to be Lord of the Sabbath (Mk. 2:28)[93] show a
messianic interpretation of Jesus' relationship to the Sabbath (cf.
also Mt. 12:6 and Mk. 2:25ff. par.). As Rordorf puts it:

Jesus knew himself to be lord of the sabbath day. Jesus' infringe-
ments of the sabbath ... were therefore ... *in their outward appearance* inexcusable provocations but in their inner significance
veiled proclamations of Jesus' messiahship.[94]

Furthermore, Rordorf argues, one cannot use the texts which
record Jesus' visits to the synagogue on the Sabbath as a basis for
proposing that Jesus dutifully observed the Sabbath.

It stands to reason that Jesus used the opportunity to deliver his
message in the synagogues where people were assembled on the sabbath. On every occasion preaching was the purpose of his visit to the
synagogue. The fact that Jesus taught in the synagogue sheds no
light on his attitude to the sabbath itself. Similarly, we may not
deduce that Paul kept the sabbath like a Jew from the fact that he employed the obvious evangelistic method of preaching the gospel to the
Jews on the sabbath day.[95]

Rordorf's discussion of Hebrews 3:7—4:11 concludes that this
homily, rooted in the Jewish traditions of an eschatological Sabbath, differs little from widespread contemporary Jewish belief that

"the weekly day of rest would find its proper fulfillment in the last days ... which with its rest from toil would be like a great sabbath."[96] The passage in Hebrews does view the present period, however, as God's *today,* when opportunity continues for preparing to enter into his rest.[97]

If Jesus virtually annulled the Sabbath commandment, as Rordorf argues, how then did the early church understand the Sabbath? Rordorf regards Colossians 2:16f. as "the key to this new understanding: ... 'let no one pass judgment on you in questions of food or drink or with regard to a festival or a new moon or a sabbath.' " The next verse calls all these traditions the *shadow* (cf. Heb. 8:5), but the *substance (sōma)* is Christ. Thus all the festivals, the food laws, and the Jewish Sabbath were fulfilled in Christ. "It is a bold picture," says Rordorf, in which all these practices were "like silhouettes cast by that which was to come." But now that "the reality,... 'the substance' which cast these shadows," has come, we no longer look at the silhouettes. "This picture requires no explanation; it is plain and speaks for itself: ... not only the ceremonial laws, but the whole law of Moses was, in essence, completely fulfilled in Christ."[98]

The Gospels of Matthew and Luke (written AD 65-85) accent Jesus' fulfillment of the Sabbath; Matthew places the invitation "Come to me ... and I will give you rest" (11:28-30) before the Sabbath controversies (12:1-14), and Luke announces Jesus' mission as the fulfillment of the sabbatical-jubilee (4:16-21). The book of Hebrews also declares that the perpetual Sabbath of the future age has already dawned in Jesus. Hence:

> The sabbath theology of the early Church has shown itself in all its versions to be christocentric to the core. With messianic authority Jesus had broken the sabbath without, however, formally annulling the sabbath commandment. The Church took over this tradition. Beside it there stood the Jewish expectation of the eschatological sabbath. The Church took this expectation and adapted it, and this is the novel element in the Christian interpretation: in Christ this promised sabbath had already begun, but only in a preliminary fashion, for the consummation had yet to come. The typically Christian tension between "already and not yet fulfilled" was applied to the Jewish sabbath hope. The belief that in Jesus Christ the new age had already begun marked the real dividing line between Judaism and Christianity.[99]

Rordorf proposes that early Christians understood the Sabbath commandment as another of the antitheses set forth in the Sermon on the Mount. Jesus' teaching is:

> You have heard that it was said to them of old time, "Keep holy the
> sabbath day"; but I say unto you: only he keeps the sabbath who, in
> the sight of God, keeps holy all the days of his life.[100]

In the second half of his study, Rordorf examines early Christian Sabbath practices. He considers it likely that Christians, especially in Palestine, attended the synagogue on the Sabbath;
otherwise there would be accounts of persecution for failure to do
so.[101] The controversy which occasioned Stephen's stoning,
however, indicates that "the cultic ordinances of the old covenant,
in particular the temple and the sacrificial system" (Acts 6:14; 7:42-
49), were under attack from Christian Hellenists.[102] The decision of
Acts 15 that circumcision need not be imposed upon believing
Gentiles and Paul's view that to be *under law* is to be controlled by
"the weak and beggarly elemental spirits" (*stoicheia;* Gal. 4:8-11) indicate that the Jewish customs were not of continuing mandate in
Christian practice. Ignatius' Letter to the Magnesians (9:1-3), written around AD 110, indicates specifically that while Gentile Christians were tempted to keep the Sabbath, Christians "who walked in
ancient customs came to a new hope, no longer living for (keeping)
the sabbath *(mēketi sabbatizontes)*."[103] Ignatius lauded the Christians of his day who had ceased to keep the Sabbath.[104]

Rordorf then notes that Sunday as a day of rest is closely tied
to imperial legislation,[105] but that the Christian observance of Sunday as the Lord's day is rooted in the Easter event and the celebration of the resurrection through community meals and the Lord's
supper.[106] Lord's day observance is linked to the resurrection on the
first day and the "practical necessity for a regular time of worship
in the Christian communities." Evidence points toward "a *pre*-
Pauline origin for the observance of Sunday."[107]

After examining the texts which speak of meeting together on
the first day of the week (1 Cor. 16:2; Acts 20:7) and the various
understandings of "the Lord's day" in Revelation 1:10, Rordorf concludes:

> To sum up, we can say: from the oldest [New Testament] texts con-
> cerning the Christian observance of Sunday we may conclude that
> Sunday clearly played an important role even in the Pauline churches.
> On Sunday money was put aside for the saints in Jerusalem (1 Cor.
> 16.2), and Christians assembled for the breaking of bread on Sunday
> (Acts 20.7a). Also, in Syria a new Greek name came to be used for the
> day of the week which was made distinctive by Christians in this way:
> it was ἡ κυριακὴ ἡμέρα or simply ἡ κυριακή (Rev. 1.10).[108]

C. **Paul K. Jewett,** *The Lord's Day: A Theological Guide to the Christian Day of Worship*

Basing his argument upon statements in Ezekiel 20:11-12, Nehemiah 9:12-14, and early Pentateuchal texts (Ex. 34:21; Deut. 5:15), Paul Jewett holds that the Sabbath originated *under Moses* for *social* reasons reflecting humanitarian concerns, rest for the animals and servants.[109]

Appealing to Deuteronomy 5:15 and Exodus 20:11, Jewett says that the Sabbath had both a *social*, redemptive purpose and a *cosmic*, creational significance. In its redemptive function, "the day commemorates God's giving rest to his tired people who attained the rest in the land of promise"; in its cosmic significance, "the Sabbath commemorates God's own rest from his labor in creating the world."[110]

The primary meaning of the Sabbath is evident from the Sabbath's connection to the sabbatical year and the jubilee (Lev. 25:2-7, 20-22; 26:34ff., 43).[111] During the sabbatical year the land was to lie fallow, debts were forgiven, and slaves were released. In the fiftieth year, the year of jubilee, the land was reallocated, reminding Israel that the land was not their own, but the Lord's; all, including the less fortunate neighbor, were to receive equally this gift of God's grace.[112]

Jewett then notes that when Jesus read the jubilean text of Isaiah 61:1-2 in the Nazareth synagogue (Lk. 4:16-21), he announced himself and the kingdom he inaugurated as the fulfillment of the Sabbath, sabbatical, and jubilee vision. What then, Jewett asks, is the relationship of the Christian to the Sabbath?[113]

To answer this question, Jewett examines the Gospels to determine Jesus' attitude toward the Sabbath. He finds that Jesus put human need above Sabbath observance: "To require a man to deny his own needs in order to keep the Sabbath is to pervert the institution."[114] Further, Jesus' healings on the Sabbath were "not only acts of love, compassion and mercy; but true 'sabbatical acts,'" showing "that the Messianic Sabbath ... ha[d] broken into the world."[115] Hence, Jesus' freedom regarding Sabbath observance was the ground for the disciples' later freedom regarding the Sabbath and their practice of worshiping on the first day of the week. Without the freedom of the Lord on this matter, the Lord "whose presence was the fulfillment of the Sabbath rest," the early Christians "would never have come to worship on another day."[116]

Jewett then argues that the Christian gatherings on the first day of the week (Acts 20:7; 1 Cor. 16:2) were rooted in *"Jesus' lord-*

ship over the Sabbath" and "his resurrection from the dead . . . on the first day."[117] In his discussion of Revelation 1:10, Jewett concludes:

> Since the expression "Lord's Supper" occurs earlier [1 Cor. 11:20] than "Lord's Day," it is natural to suppose that the usage "Lord's Day" derived from "Lord's Supper," as a fit designation among Christians of the day on which they gathered to celebrate this meal as the culmination of their corporate worship.[118]

After examining the biblical texts, Jewett introduces another consideration: "The Crux of the Problem: The Unity in Movement of Salvation History."[119] Jewett speaks about the Christian's unity with, and difference from, Israel as well as the eschatological tension in Jesus' fulfillment of the Sabbath, the "now" and "not yet" tension. Hence, Jewett says,

> *The whole New Testament reflects this fundamental tension between the indicative of present fulfillment and the imperative of future consummation. To this rule the law of the Sabbath is no exception. The fulfillment of the Sabbath rest which we have in Christ is not only a present reality, but also a future hope. Those who are in Christ have indeed found rest unto their souls, yet at the same time they must give all diligence to enter into God's rest. The principle of the Sabbath, then, is both an Old Testament ceremonialism which has been fulfilled and done away in Christ, and at the same time a permanent interpretive category of redemptive history, having definite eschatological implications. Christians, therefore, are both free from the Sabbath to gather on the first day, and yet stand under the sign of the Sabbath in that they gather every seventh day.*[120]

In "framing a Christian theology of the day of worship," Jewett says that we must reject both the "yes" of the Sabbatarians to the seventh day and the "no" of the Protestant reformers to the fourth commandment. For a theology of the day of worship, Christians "must work out from these two affirmations: Christian time is divided into weeks; and Christians begin each week by gathering on the first day to fellowship with the risen Lord."[121]

In appealing to his understanding of the New Testament (Jesus) for the *day* but to the Old Testament (Moses) for the *principle* of one day in seven, Jewett moves toward position two in his attempt to work for a unity in salvation history.[122] At this point Jewett moves closer to Francis Nigel Lee's "not yet" emphasis (the messianic rest is not yet realized) and away from Willy Rordorf's emphasis on the "has come/fulfillment" aspect of Jesus' Sabbath rest.

D. **D. A. Carson, ed.,** *From Sabbath to Lord's Day: A Biblical, Historical, and Theological Investigation*

This massive work, consisting of twelve illuminating essays written by biblical scholars who studied at Cambridge in 1973, presents an exhaustive exegetical and theological basis for the eight points summarizing this position (p. 79 above). Because the work appeared too late to be fully incorporated into this study, only some brief notes about its thesis and its divergence from the above positions can here be noted.

Criticizing the exegesis of those who try to anchor the Sabbath in a "creation ordinance" from Genesis 2:1-4 (e.g., Bacchiocchi), the writers point out that the moral imperative of Sabbath observance for humanity is found not in Genesis 2, but in the fourth commandment. The Sabbath commandment, like the entire Decalogue, is linked with God's covenant to Israel. Numerous rabbinic texts are cited to show that even the Jewish people themselves held that the Sabbath was given not to all people, but only to the children of Israel.[123]

Jesus' activity on the Sabbath is best understood not as a deliberate intention to break the Sabbath (contrary to what Rordorf says, Jesus in fact broke only the Halakic laws governing the Sabbath), but as acts clearly witnessing to his lordship over, and fulfillment of, the Sabbath. His deeds pointed to his messianic claims, which in turn provided the authority for a new covenant and subsequently a new day (the first day) to celebrate redemption. Only because Jesus' followers grasped the significance of his lordship over the Sabbath did they find freedom to regard the Jewish Sabbath simply as a shadow pointing to the new order established by Jesus whose consummation continues to be anticipated (Heb. 3—4).[124]

While rest is clearly associated with the Old Testament Sabbath and the New Testament reflects the continuing observance of the Sabbath by Jewish Christians,[125] the New Testament nowhere transfers the Sabbath rest to Lord's day observance. Further, Christian believers were not required to keep the Sabbath (Gal. 4:10; Rom. 14:5; Col. 2:16).[126] Writers such as Beckwith and Stott (see position 2 above) transfer Sabbath rest theology to Sunday without biblical foundations. Nor does Jewett's joining of the Sabbath rest theology with the Lord's day resurrection theology find clear biblical support. And Rordorf's basing of the emergence of the Lord's day almost solely upon celebrations of the Lord's supper also goes beyond the exegetical evidence.[127]

Stressing therefore the fundamental discontinuity between

Sabbath and Lord's day and criticizing all "Sabbath-transference theology," A. T. Lincoln points out some similarities and points of connection: both hold one day in seven to be distinctive; both celebrate redemption; both the Sabbath and the Lord's day "prefigure the future rest of consummation"; both are "linked through the notion of worship," though this became prominent for the Sabbath only later, with the rise of the synagogue in Israel; and both point to the principle of lordship (both were *Lord's* days).[128] By celebrating the resurrection, the Lord's day may be seen as a fulfillment of the Sabbath rest. God's commands to Israel about Sabbath observance, however, may "remain instructive" to us about God's concern for our physical rest. We should also recognize the "profound social and humanitarian" significance of the Sabbath. Through these learnings we will recognize God's concern for the whole person; they will influence our view of humanity, vocation, and time. As these insights are linked to our Lord's day celebrations of our rest and liberation in Jesus' resurrection, we Christians will experience "an inner liberation ... in the way [we] go about both the work and play of the week to the glory of God."[129]

Hermeneutical Commentary

This issue, the Sabbath/Lord's day controversy, is a "hornet's nest" or "gold mine" for hermeneutical observations! To begin, I will note some relatively minor points:

1. While Riggle and Rordorf essentially agree in their conclusions, they follow quite different methodologies in biblical study. Riggle assumes the Mosaic authorship of the Pentateuch and thereby assigns the Genesis 2:2-3 Sabbath instruction to the time of Moses, not to creation; Rordorf follows the historical-critical method of reconstructing Israel's tradition-history, seeking to place each part of Scripture within a specific historical and socio-religious setting. While Rordorf and Riggle diverge when describing the original purposes of the Sabbath, they agree that *it originated in the time of Moses, not at creation.*

2. Some obviously weak interpretations appear, such as Lee's argument that the Sabbath was unfallen Adam's first day (the text never makes this point) and R. H. Martin's statement that the Lord must have changed the Sabbath day from Saturday to Sunday during the forty days between his resurrection and ascension, unless Jesus' appearances to the gathered disciples on the first day are regarded as evidence for the change (Jn. 20:19, 26). Such in-

terpretations go beyond the teaching of the text and should be avoided or, at most, advanced only as suggestions and not as interpretations of the texts.

3. Positions one and two have a difficult time with certain Pauline texts: Colossians 2:16ff., Galatians 4:10, and Romans 14:5ff. While Rordorf considers Colossians 2:16 as the key to understanding the position of the apostolic Gentile churches, Lee and Beckwith seek to identify these references with special "ceremonial" practices.

4. A potential weakness in Rordorf's work is the assumption that "the earliest" is the more authoritative and normative for our practice. He assumes that the earliest meaning of the Sabbath (socio-moral) is the more authoritative and that the earlier church's celebration of the Lord's supper on the Lord's day is more authoritative than the later church's conflation of Sabbath and Lord's day practices. Is this assumption valid? An answer to this question hinges in part on our answer to one of the major issues discussed below, the relationship of the authority of the (later) church to the authority of Scripture.

Four major hermeneutical issues are inherent in this study:

1. To what extent is tradition, the later interpretation and practice of the church, authoritative in our understanding of and response to Scripture? Writers in all three positions, even those of Protestant confession, have appealed vigorously to sources from the second to fourth centuries to substantiate their interpretations of the biblical data. But while the first position regards these developments as apostasy, the second position uses them positively, to show that its tenets are correct. The third position regards them as mostly negative, especially as they led to the Constantinian mandate of Sunday-Sabbath observance in the fourth century.

What authority does the church have in relation to the authority and/or our understanding of Scripture? Significantly, both the first and third positions perceive a shift or "fall" between Scripture and the church of the second to fourth centuries. But the first position holds that the (Roman) church changed the day of rest from Saturday to Sunday; the third position holds that the church gradually changed Lord's day celebrations to a Lord's day Sabbath rest, thus conflating two different historical institutions. The second position, on the other hand, regards the practices of the church in the second to fourth centuries to be consistent with that of the apostolic church; hence it uses the later evidence to support its New Testament exegesis.

The larger scope of this hermeneutical issue, the authority of the church, includes two specific considerations: the church's role in establishing the canon and the way the church's teaching in any given period of time shapes the understanding of the interpreter.

On the first consideration, it is clear that the major trend and practice in the second and third centuries was to observe Sunday (whether for celebration or rest), and not Saturday. All three positions agree on this. But this raises a problem for the first position. Would the church canonize writings (the New Testament) if they were obviously supportive of seventh-day (Saturday) observance (as the first position holds) *when Christians were practicing differently by observing Sunday?*[130] To interpret the New Testament in such a way as to drive a wedge between the Scripture and the church of the first few centuries is in principle untenable since it is precisely *that* church which accepted those writings as authoritative.[131] Exceptions to principle may occur, but this consideration puts the burden of proof upon those who argue that the New Testament teaching differs from the practices of the church in the second and third centuries.[132]

As one moves away from the time of the church's initial acceptance of Scripture as authoritative (canonization), the potential for emerging differences between the New Testament teachings and the church's teachings increases, to be sure. But as long as the church continues to hold Scripture to be authoritative, a self-correcting resource functioning like a compass is built into the church's theological development.

The second consideration now comes into focus: to what extent does the church in any given time period shape an individual interpreter's perception of Scripture? From the four cases of this study it is clear that people use Scripture to support their points of view. Does a theological position arise out of Scripture, or is Scripture used to defend theological positions?[133]

This question is customarily answered by speaking of a hermeneutical circle. The influence goes both ways: one's position influences what one sees in Scripture, and what is to be seen in Scripture influences one's position. To dogmatically argue for either side of influence to the exclusion of the other is to bury one's head in the sand. It is essential rather to recognize the influence of both Scripture and church in the hermeneutical process.[134]

2. Complementing the first observation, a second focuses on the use of a method of Bible study that frees Scripture from the interpreter's biases to as great an extent as possible. Only in this way

can Scripture be heard on its own terms and potentially exercise its authority over us. The predominant method used by biblical scholars to accomplish this goal is called the historical-critical method,[135] illustrated best in this study by Willy Rordorf's attempt to set each Sabbath/Lord's day text within its specific historical context and *then* to inquire about the teachings' significance for us today. The historical part of the method insists that the text must be understood in its historical context; the critical aspect asks how the text is significant for us (the church) in our particular time and place.

By taking the historical context seriously, the third position (especially Rordorf and Jewett) affirms the priority of the socio-moral significance of the Sabbath, emphasizing the Sabbath's relationship to the practices of the sabbatical and the jubilee years. In contrast, the first and second positions, influenced by theological traditions reaching all the way back into the Old Testament, place emphasis on *the day of rest.* While both the first and second positions emphasize rest *from work,* the third position emphasizes rest *for all.* The emphases of positions one and two lead then to mandating and regulating what one can and cannot do *on the day,* while position three affirms and celebrates justice and equality as the meaning of the exodus and the resurrection.

Demonstrated in great detail, Rordorf's study asks the standard questions about the various texts:

1. What is the date of the composition of the text?
2. What is the historical setting of the text?
3. Does the text serve a special function—cultural, theological, priestly, etc.?
4. In what type of narrative does the text occur—liturgical, legal, prose, poetry, etc.?
5. How do the various texts on this subject with similar or differing emphases fit together?

Rordorf's reconstruction of the texts (influenced, to be sure, by his religious commitments and tradition) stresses the link between the Sabbath and the socio-moral institutions of the sabbatical and jubilee, a point missed completely by position two and blunted by position one.[136]

The value of the historical-critical method, therefore, is that by seeking to distance the text from the interpreter, the text can speak on its own terms, disclosing truth not known before by the interpreter. The text must first be taken *from us* in order that it can stand in its situation with its own message.[137] Only through this "distancing" can the text become authoritative over our prejudices and biases. But certainly the interpreter's work is not complete when the interpreter only describes what the text meant back then in that situation. The interpreter, open to and thirsting for the power of the Spirit *(ruach/pneuma)* behind and within the text, must ask: How is this significant to us (me)? And how do we (I) identify with that text?

The historical-critical method, however, fails us usually at this point. While introducing us well to the biblical world, it seldom enables the Bible to speak authoritatively to our world. Supplementary efforts are necessary for this to happen.[138] Rordorf's work, while illuminating the Sabbath traditions *via* study of their historical settings, manifests other weaknesses of the historical-critical method as well. For example, by assigning certain parts of the biblical Sabbath tradition to later priestly influence, he thereby assumes that that element of the Sabbath tradition and canonical record should exert little or no authority upon the life of the church. In making this judgment, he has failed to provide criteria for his method of intracanonical critique; i.e., how and why is one tradition, even though developed later, regarded as less authoritative? Similarly, in assigning Matthew 24:20 ("Pray that your flight may not be ... on the sabbath") to the later Matthean church community (see note 95), rather than to Jesus himself, he fails to note that by so doing he actually weakens, rather than strengthens, his case. If the church (even Palestinian) at the time when Matthew was written (around AD 85 according to Rordorf) generates such a saying, then indeed there is strong evidence for continuing Sabbath observance. This evidence would need to be assessed for its weight upon Rordorf's total argument, Colossians 2:16 and Romans 14:5 notwithstanding. These points illustrate one of the major weaknesses in many scholars' use of the historical-critical method: evidence that argues against the viewpoint of the writer will be assigned to literary strands or later dates in such a way as to relieve, at least immediately, the responsibility of the writer to take it seriously. But such maneuvers, upon careful examination, have not really solved the problem but have only pushed it into another category also demanding hermeneutical attention. To put this criticism another way, historical-critical scholars often fail to handle adequately the relationship of critical decisions to wider questions of canonical authority and the consequent significance of this consideration for the faith and practice of the church today.

Nevertheless, while the historical-critical method oftens fails to address adequately the significance of (all) biblical teaching for us today, it does serve us well by helping us to discover the meaning of the text in its own setting and world. But we must recognize that even then we cannot negate, leave aside, or even transcend completely the theological, sociological, and psychological forces upon and within us; we must put them rather under the light of the text as consciously as possible. When we as individual interpreters seek the discerning insight of the community of faith, that community also must recognize the forces impinging upon its interpretations, else the community only reinforces what was already believed.

Having heard the text first on its terms as much as possible, we must then seek to discern its significance both personally and corporately so that interpretation becomes an event, an event of understanding. When this happens, our self-in-community receives insight that may reinforce previous understandings, question our traditional perspectives, critique our social, economic, or political situations, and call for and enable major change in and among us to occur. As discernment of the text's significance leads to obedient, vital response, biblical interpretation stands in the service of the larger purpose of Scripture, to exert its authority over our lives.

An appropriate invocation for us as interpreters therefore might be: "Help us, God, not to mistake the assertion of our biases and prejudices for the authority of the Spirit-driven Word within and behind the word of Scripture." To be serious in this plea means committing ourselves to a lifelong disciplined study of the text along with disciplined scrutiny of ourselves and our biases as interpreters.

3. The relationship between the Old and New Testaments surfaces as another important topic in this case issue. All positions agree that Jesus exerted messianic authority over the Sabbath commandment. When then is the relationship between the Testaments? And what is their respective authority for the Christian church today?

4. A fourth issue, related directly to the third, focuses upon the problem of unity and diversity within Scripture. Do some texts command Sabbath observance while others prescribe Sunday observance and still others warn against all holy day observance?

These two issues, since they figure so largely in the discussion of the Bible and war, will be addressed in the next chapter.

Chapter 3

THE BIBLE AND WAR

Should Christians fight? Does the Bible allow or forbid Christians to participate in their nations' wars? In the early eighties, spurred certainly by agonies raised by the threat of nuclear war, two books (one published and one forthcoming) address this issue by placing opposing positions in dialogue: *War: Four Christian Views* (ed. Robert G. Clouse [Downers Grove, Ill.: InterVarsity Press, 1981]) and *When Christians Disagree: War and Pacifism* (ed. Oliver Barclay [London: InterVarsity Press, 1984]). In both books the writers employ Scripture to support their opposing points of view.

In 1960 I corresponded with six evangelical leaders to raise questions on their writings which used the Bible to support Christian participation in war. As a nonresistant-pacifist Christian I regarded Jesus' command to love the enemy as a clear word forbidding the killing of the enemy. When five of the six responded, I discovered that my correspondents employed a quite different use of the Bible from mine. All appealed much to the Old Testament and argued that the New Testament does not change the fact that God commanded the covenant people to fight, even wage war. One (G. Clark) said that since the Old Testament approves of war and Romans 13 commands Christians to obey the government, the Bible is absolutely clear. God expects Christians to fight in war; pacifism is unscriptural.[1]

Over the centuries the Christian church has generally allowed, if not supported, the Christian's participation in war.[2] The historic peace churches (Brethren, Mennonites, and Quakers) and numerous individual Catholic and Protestant Christians, however, have understood the biblical teaching to forbid participation in war. The purpose of this chapter is to examine how both those who allow and those who forbid Christian participation in war use the Bible. Which Scriptures are used, and how are these Scriptures interpreted by each group?

Positions Supporting/Allowing Christian Participation in War

Because the current realities of war include the awesome threat of nuclear warfare with its potential obliteration of a nation or all of humanity, many writers who would not support pacifism on biblical and theological grounds are shifting positions for pragmatic, ethical-theological, and also political reasons. Hence it may seem grossly out-of-date and hardly fair to cite writings from thirty or forty years ago. Nonetheless, in the thinking of many Christians today, the following arguments provide the basis for Christians to decide to serve in the nation's military service. This thinking therefore informs the decisions of many people who participate in military service and support the arms race even if political realities require use of nuclear weapons.

The various arguments allowing for participation in war show quite different uses of the Bible. For this reason they will be presented as three separate positions: traditional position A, traditional position B, and theologies of revolution and liberation.

Traditional Position A

This position, guiding the thinking and action of the majority of Protestant church members, supports Christian participation in war by the following appeal to the Bible.

1. God commanded to fight and kill.

George W. Knight III, New Testament professor at Covenant Seminary, St. Louis, Missouri, says:

> The God and Father of Abraham, Isaac, and Jacob, and of our Lord Jesus Christ, instructed his people of old to wage war when necessary and to slay the enemy.... these explicit instructions by God make it impossible to maintain that God prohibits the believer from engaging in war under any circumstances.[3]

Loraine Boettner, an American Reformed theologian writing in 1942, says that in "thirty-five or more references throughout the Old Testament ... God ... commanded the use of armed force in carrying out His divine purposes."[4] Boettner cites numerous stories and references documenting his point.[5]

Gordon Clark, writing in 1955 as professor of philosophy at Butler University, also cites numerous texts in which God "commanded his people to wage war." He concludes: "If the Old Testament is clear on anything, it is clear that God positively commanded war."[6]

Richard S. Taylor, professor of theology and mission at the Nazarene Theological Seminary, Kansas City, Missouri, argues that God's command to kill in war is not incompatible with God's perfect love. Although perfect love does not murder, hate, commit adultery, steal, or lie, it does not follow that perfect love opposes capital punishment and war.

> Surely it is axiomatic that nothing God ever does can be non-loving. God's retributive justice, in its own sphere, is as truly an expression of perfect love as [is] His redemptive action at Calvary.
>
> Now let me draw from this a secondary axiom. God's deputizings belong to His holy acts. That He deputizes angels to take human life has been no problem with us, but it should be if the deputizing of life-taking is inherently incompatible with perfect love. And if using angels for such work is legitimate, we have no logical ground for objecting to His similar use of man. For a deputized act, if wrong for the deputee, is equally wrong for the deputizer. Whether the deputee is man or angel does not alter this. If therefore the man who has been deputized by God to take life is necessarily guilty of murder, we must accept the obnoxious implication, even though blasphemous, that God is guilty of murder.[7]

2. God honored military leaders.

Arthur F. Holmes, professor of philosophy at Wheaton College, quotes Martin Luther on this point:

> If the waging of war and the military profession were in themselves wrong and displeasing to God, we should have to condemn Abraham, Moses, Joshua, David and all the rest of the holy fathers, kings, and princes, who served God as soldiers and are highly praised in Scriptures because of this service.[8]

Harold Snider, a minister who wrote in 1942 *Does The Bible Sanction War? (Why I Am Not a Pacifist)*, echoes the same point, arguing against pacifists who call war sin:

Now if "all war is sin, unconditionally and always" as our pacifist friends hold, then "righteous" Abraham partook of that sin; Gideon, blest of the Lord and carefully instructed in warfare, was a sinner; David and a host of others must be included in this same category, and—worst of all—we would be compelled to include the most High God and His Son Jesus Christ! But according to the Infallible Word (which we prefer to the opinion of our ambitious pacifists) ALL WAR IS NOT SIN![9]

3. Many New Testament sayings endorse war.

New Testament texts which either explicitly or implicitly endorse war are cited by numerous authors.[10] Most frequently cited are:

Luke 3:14. John the Baptist did not ask soldiers to quit their service, but said rather, "Extort from no man by violence, neither accuse any wrongfully, and be content with your wages." Compare 1 Corinthians 7:20, in which Paul counsels remaining in the state into which one has been called.[11]

Matthew 8:10 (Luke 7:9). Jesus commends the faith of the centurion, a Roman soldier, who "commanded troops which carried out the cruel and ruthless policies of the Roman legions." W. G. Corliss also notes the confession of the soldier at the cross (Lk. 23:47; Mk. 15:39).[12]

Acts 10. "Peter is sent to Cornelius, the centurion soldier. The narrative speaks of that soldier as God-fearing, as one that works righteousness, and as acceptable to God."[13]

In an earlier epoch, when intense debate raged between pacifists and war supporters, a much larger set of texts was used,[14] some of which appear in Boettner's description of Jesus' ministry as warfare:

Jesus went into the temple and with a show of physical force poured out the changers' money, overturned their tables, and drove out those who through their fraudulent dealings were making the temple a den of robbers. On numerous occasions He met His enemies, the scribes and Pharisees, face to face and denounced them as hypocrites and liars, declaring that they were of their father the Devil and doomed to perdition, Matt. 15:7; 23:33; John 8:44, 55. In the parable of the wicked husbandmen He accepts as true and justified the course of action ascribed to the lord of the vineyard (by whom He means God): "He will miserably destroy those miserable men," Matt. 21:41. At the conclusion of the parable of the pounds He repeats as belonging to the normal order of things the words of the nobleman (words which, coming from Him, must seem very strange to a pacifist): "But these mine enemies, that would not that I should reign over them, bring hither, and slay them before me," Luke 19:27. No one else in Scripture gave more frequent or sterner warnings of the punishment which God will inflict upon the wicked. In the well known judgment scene of Matt. 25 Jesus Himself sits as Judge and passes sentence upon His enemies in these stern words: "Depart from me, ye cursed, into the eternal fire which is prepared for the Devil and his angels" (Vs. 41). Those were not the words of a pacifist, nor could His enemies have looked upon Him as such.[15]

Boettner also cites the war/soldier symbolism of the Christian life (Eph. 6:10-20; 2 Tim. 2:3-4; Rev. 19:11, 15) as biblical endorsement of war, saying:

> It is hardly conceivable that the Scriptures should present the Christian life under a symbolism having to do so distinctly with soldiering and warfare and at the same time repudiate the reality for which it stands as always and everywhere wrong. We cannot imagine the different aspects of the Christian's life set forth through a symbolism borrowed from the liquor trade or the vice racket.[16]

Clark makes the point that Jesus' command to pay taxes (Mt. 17:27; 22:21) counts also, at least to some extent, in support of the view that Jesus endorsed Christian participation in war, since he knew that much of that tax went for the military functions of the empire.[17]

4. The apostolic writings teach subjection to authority.

Clark regards Romans 13 as "too definite to be misunderstood ...; Paul explains the origin and function of government." These functions are "collection of taxes" and "the power of the sword" to both execute criminals and wage war.[18]

Knight concurs with this view and then focuses on the call to subjection (cf. also 1 Pet. 2:17ff.): "We are not to resist the God-ordained powers because to do so is to withstand the ordinance of God." Furthermore:

> The state is to avenge. It is a terror to evil. . . . In using the sword or gun, the state is expressly called a minister of God. . . .
>
> Yes, the state must serve as a police force. . . . We must recognize the right of policemen to shoot to kill. . . . And when the state or policemen or soldiers are doing so, we as Christians are called on to support them in every way, with money and with service as a policeman or soldier ourselves, if called to do so.[19]

In the Old Testament, kings ruled by the decree of God (Prov. 8:15-16; 1 Sam. 24:6; 26:9; 2 Sam. 7:13; Jer. 27:6, 12). Therefore, we must not resist them.[20]

Corliss says that the "only disobedience to government that God allows ... is refusal to deny the faith (Dan. 3:12-18) and refusal to stop doing what God has specifically commanded ... (Acts 5:29)."[21]

5. Pacifists misinterpret the Scripture.

First of all, pacifists usually misinterpret the commandment "Thou shalt not kill." The Hebrew word *rasah*, translated "kill" in the sixth commandment, is only one of six words for "kill." Since God commanded taking of human life (Gen. 9:6; see also point 2 above), *rasah* really means murder.[22] Peter Craigie (see position B below) lends scholarly concurrence to this judgment, saying that the text is best translated, "You shall not kill a fellow Hebrew."[23] On this basis, Taylor therefore distinguishes between killing and murdering, allowing the former but forbidding the latter as violating God's perfect love.[24]

Further, pacifists regularly appeal to Matthew 5:38-40 for a doctrine of nonresistance with which they then repudiate war and/or the Christian's participation in war. This pacifist interpretation is wrong on the grounds of internal consistency. Jesus himself did not turn the other cheek when struck at his trial, but rather challenged the smiter, "Why do you strike me?" (Jn. 18:23). Basing his challenge on the law itself, Paul likewise resisted in saying, "God shall strike you, you whitewashed wall!" (Acts 23:3).[25] As Carl F. H. Henry, well-known former editor of *Christianity Today*, put it, the "Sermon is a guide in the immediate 'one-and-one' neighbour relationships of life";[26] it must "be supplemented by biblical ethics in the larger sense if an adequate ethics in official and social relations is to prevail."[27]

Further, the pacifist use of the golden rule to argue against military force fails to consider who the "others" are. Are they the "murderous invaders" or "our own wives and children who need our protection"?[28]

A particular theological emphasis which similarly judges the pacifist interpretation to be in error comes from the argument of dispensational theology (which most of the above writers do *not* represent). Dispensationalism regards the present time as the church age or age of grace (dispensation 6), whereas the Sermon on the Mount is considered the rule for the age of the kingdom (dispensation 7). Snider, holding this view, contends that only when the kingdom is established will "the marvelous teachings of Matthew 5, 6, 7 become the standard of conduct among the Kingdom peoples."[29]

6. The change from theocracy to church does not invalidate this position.

Knight recognizes that, because Israel was a unique theocracy, no nation or Christian group today may apply the Old Testament texts to itself directly "to warrant its initiating war." Responding then to the view that this factor renders invalid our current appeal to the Old Testament on the subject, Knight says, nonetheless, such appeal is valid

> because it still recognizes the basic principle under consideration, that war itself is not always ruled out as contrary to God's will. . . . A nation or an individual may, like Israel, defend itself or others.[30]

Supporting this interpretation is John Calvin's view, decisive for Reformed thinking on this subject:

> . . . the reason for waging war which existed in ancient times, is equally valid in the present age; . . . no express declaration on this subject [war] is to be expected in the writings of the Apostles, whose design was, not to organize civil governments, but to describe the spiritual kingdom of Christ. . . . in these very writings it is implied, that no change has been made in this respect by the coming of Christ.[31]

Traditional Position B

This position differs from position A above in that it represents both a "no" and a "yes" in the use of Scripture for its nonpacifist stance. These writers say "no" to any simplistic way of using the Bible by writers on either side of the issue. Peter C. Craigie, for example, in his book *The Problem of War in the Old Testament* says that the Old Testament war stories, *read as divine revelation,* explain why "the more orthodox a Christian group or individual may be, the more likely it is that his attitudes will be militaristic."[32] Craigie laments such use of the Old Testament and the terrible war record of Christianity. Leslie Rumble, in the arguments to follow, criticizes pacifists who, like fundamentalists, read the Bible so literally that they follow an "eye for eye" legalistic interpretation of Jesus' teachings in the Sermon on the Mount.[33]

The main arguments and lines of thinking (which usually go beyond the use of the Bible) are represented by the following emphases.

1. God as warrior is basic to Jewish and Christian theology.

Yahweh revealed himself to Israel as "a man of war," the one who had cast Pharaoh's chariots and his host into the sea (Ex. 15:3-4).

While writers in position A appeal to this point,[34] many Old Testament scholars regard this to be so foundational to biblical theology[35] that it precludes an absolutist pacifist position, even though they might agree with a vast amount of the pacifist interpretation.

George Ernest Wright, late Old Testament professor at Harvard School of Divinity, regards the image of "God the Warrior" as basic to the biblical conception of God: "God the Warrior is simply the reverse side of God the Lover or of God the Redeemer."[36] That God the warrior as well as God the lover acts to establish divine sovereignty, expressed by God the Lord, is the context of Wright's discussion of the warrior image. Wright disagrees with a "Mr. X," reared in a historic peace church, who holds that God the lover eclipses God as warrior in the unfolding biblical revelation.[37]

Craigie, professor of religious studies at the University of Calgary, begins his chapter on "God the Warrior" by quoting Psalm 24:8:

> Who is the King of Glory?
> The Lord, strong and mighty,
> The Lord, mighty in battle.[38]

Craigie notes that the Old Testament describes God as "Lord of *Hosts*" (literally *Armies*) more than two hundred times. Even the ark of the covenant taken to the battlefield symbolized God's presence as warrior.[39]

Regarding this pervasive Old Testament emphasis as a problem at three levels—God, revelation, and ethics—Craigie proposes that the problem may be understood, if not fully resolved, by remembering that this language is anthropomorphic and thus confesses that God participated in Israel's sinful history. That history of sinful human war was necessary because Israel was called to be God's kingdom people in the form of a nation-state. States survive, as Jacques Ellul notes, by violence and war, the collective expression of the evil that marks human nature. Israel's greatest learning came from its national defeat in war, which freed God's people from the state form of existence and brought the promise of a new covenant and new visions of peace.[40]

Israel's war history, therefore, should not be used today to justify war (no nation can claim Israel's place!), but rather it should teach us that God participates in sinful human history and that Israel's history as a nation-state prepared the way for the new kingdom, established by Jesus. The citizens of this kingdom "must not be bound by the necessity of violence (as is the state); they must transcend the order of necessity."[41]

2. Christians must fulfill both kingdom and state obligations.

Although Craigie's main arguments put distance between the Christian and the Old Testament war history, he affirms, when discussing practical ethical applications, that the Christian is a citizen of two kingdoms, "the Kingdom of God and the worldly state." While the Christian "cannot give up the love and non-violence of the Kingdom of God, for that would be to abandon the Gospel," he is also bound "in some sense by the laws of the state to which he belongs." And "the fundamental principle of the state is violence."[42] Holding to this traditional Lutheran position of two orders of obligation, Craigie endorses neither the pacifist nor the just war position.[43]

Roman Catholic writer Leslie Rumble, writing in 1959 as professor of theology and philosophy in Sydney, Australia, also advances a theory of double obligation, but differentiates between personal and social obligations, as did Carl Henry mentioned above. He says that the soldier also does not necessarily violate the command to "Love your enemies, . . . do good to them that hate you" (Mt. 5:44) because his military duties are not undertaken personally, but as an "obligation to keep within the rules of legitimate warfare."[44] The Christian soldier must love the person of the enemy and be ready to show that love outside the combatant role. Many are the stories "of sublime acts of charity toward enemy soldiers."[45]

Because pacifists, like fundamentalists, ignore church doctrine, they take Jesus' teachings in the Sermon on the Mount too literally and interpret Scripture wrongly. Jesus' own nonparticipation in war (or on Wall Street) is insufficient ground for us not to be involved. Jesus' command to "Put your sword back into its place" (Mt. 26:52) is not an argument against war but instruction given because Jesus knew it was the time for his passion. Similarly, the point of John 18:36 is not the "condemnation of the right to self-defense" but the truth that Jesus' kingdom is not an earthly kingdom. Further, Paul's words forbidding revenge, in Romans 12:17-21,

> are wholly irrelevant to the question of military activities undertaken by States seeking redress of serious injuries. St. Paul is dealing with the personal dispositions of individual Christians toward unfriendly or hostile people met within the ordinary course of their daily lives.[46]

3. Kingdom ethics cannot be absolutes in this fallen world.

This point, at home in the Reformed tradition, represents Wright's subsequent argument after asserting the ongoing complementary significance of God as warrior and God as lover. The ethic of nonviolence cannot be absolutized; we cannot make "the absolutes of the Kingdom-ethic . . . absolutes for the present age."[47]

Reinhold Niebuhr, influential Union Seminary (New York) professor of Christian ethics from 1928 to 1960, has articulated most forcefully this point of view. It is foolish, he says, to deny that Jesus' ethic is "absolute and uncompromising"; the ethic enjoins nonresistance and not nonviolent resistance.[48] In combining the moral ideal of love with vicarious suffering, the religion of Jesus "achieves such a purity that the possibility of its realization in history becomes remote."[49] Jesus' ethic "has only a vertical dimension between the loving will of God and the will of man"; it does not connect with the horizontal points of political and social ethics.[50]

Granting that the practice of an absolutist pacifist ethic by a few is a valuable reminder to the church, Niebuhr says that the pursuit of perfectionism for Christians generally "is bad religion, however much it may claim the authority of the Sermon on the Mount."[51] Christianity is more than a law of love; it recognizes the pervasiveness of human sin. This requires the Christian to seek justice in society and thus accept a tension between love and justice. War, though never justified, is sometimes necessary in choosing the lesser evil and preventing the triumph of humanity's evil egoism in immoral society. This ethic of impossible possibility, necessary for the Christian in society, goes with the choicest fruit of Christianity, the doctrine of forgiveness. Hence the Christian relies upon God's forgiveness for his/her failure to follow love in the pursuit of justice.[52]

Related to Niebuhr's distinctive emphases, the classical just war theory, conceived by Augustine, also argues for the legitimacy of Christian participation in war, provided the war meets certain conditions. While these criteria do not rest directly upon Scripture (and thus go beyond the scope of this study), Paul Ramsey—professor of religion at Princeton University—argues that the development of the just war doctrine was not a "fall" from the purity of New Testament and early church ethical practice. The primary motive was the same as that which earlier led Christians, out of Christlike love, to refuse to use armed force. In the new circumstances of the church's relationship to society, the church had to find a way to continue "responsible love and service of one's neighbor in the texture of common life." Nonresisting love had now sometimes to resist evil.[53]

Theologies of Revolution and Liberation

Numerous writers today argue for the primacy of liberation in the theological accent of the Bible. Some of these writers explicitly endorse violence as part of God's program to achieve liberation and justice. Other writers, while strongly emphasizing liberation and justice, do not *explicitly* approve the use of violence, though the use of violence is implied in the liberation/revolution they support. Still others explicitly commit themselves to nonviolent pacifism (e.g., L. John Topel, cited in the next section of this chapter). While similar theological emphases may be found in all three groups of writers, citations below will be limited to those who explicitly argue for revolution or the achieving of liberation through violence.

The argument in brief is as follows: The foundational components of biblical history show us that violence is a vital part of salvation history. God takes the side of the oppressed in the struggle to liberate and establish justice. God's people, because they are in history, cannot be isolated or insulated from the struggle. They are involved in the violence. Hence the question: which violence do you choose?

Five related emphases appear in the literature:[54]

1. Exodus: liberation from oppression is central to biblical thought.

James H. Cone, black liberation theologian of Union Seminary (New York), begins his discussion of "Biblical Revelation and Social Existence" by using Exodus texts (6:6; 15:1-2) which show that God, in this decisive event of Israel's history, freed an oppressed people by destroying the enslaving power of the mighty Pharaoh.[55] Cone cites numerous Old Testament texts depicting God acting for the oppressed against the oppressor and condemning oppression within Israel. His case for violence however, while standing in this stream of biblical emphasis, rests finally on a "no option" analysis. Violence, he says, is not the problem of a few black revolutionaries; it is embedded in the structure of American society. Cone quotes Rap Brown: "Violence is as American as cherry pie." To claim to be nonviolent within such a structure of violent law and order is to accept the violent oppressor's values.[56] The distinction between violence and nonviolence is an illusion. Only the victims of injustice can decide when the use of force is justified and whether the means is proportionate to the end.[57]

Rubem Alves, a Brazilian Protestant theologian, attributes revolution to God's initiative and regards it as counterviolence:

> God's politics ... is subversive of the stability created by the violence
> of the old. The false peace of unfreedom is out of balance and its walls
> of defense are made to crumble.
>
> There is violence involved in the process. God does not wait for the
> dragon to become a lamb. He knows that the dragon will rather de-
> vour the lamb. It must be opposed and defeated by the power of the
> lamb.... [God] does not wait for the master to decide freely to liberate
> the slave. He knows that the master will never do that. So, he breaks
> the yoke and the erstwhile master can no longer dominate. The power
> of God destroys what makes the world unfree. This use of power looks
> like violence because it destroys the equilibrium and peace of the
> system of domination. But ... what looks like the violence of the lion
> is really the power of counter-violence, that is power used against
> those who generate, support, and defend the violence of a world of
> masters and slaves. Violence is power that oppresses and makes man
> unfree. Counter-violence is power that breaks the old which enslaves,
> in order to make man free.[58]

Bruce Boston, writing in 1969 as a graduate student in social
ethics at Princeton Theological Seminary, makes the point that the
exodus, pivotal in God's salvation history, bound together revelation and revolution; the event was "both revelatory and politico-
social." In this act of liberation from oppression, God constituted Israel as a people.[59] Further, Richard Shaull—professor of ecumenics
at Princeton Theological Seminary—argues that humanity's growing vision of liberation finds strength and direction in biblical
symbols of revolution: *"The biblical symbols and images stress
discontinuity, judgment, the end of the world and the emergence
of the radically new."*[60]

2. Justice: God's justice requires tearing down in order to
build up (Jer. 1:10).

José Miranda, Roman Catholic professor in mathematics, law,
and biblical studies respectively and also adviser and lecturer for
worker and student groups in Mexico, has done a most extensive
study on justice in the Bible. Biblical faith calls Christians, says Miranda, to side with the oppressed in the revolutionary struggles of
history. Although in this study (1974) he does not explicitly endorse
the use of violence, a more recent writing ends with an explicit biblical rationale for the use of violence to achieve justice.

In the death penalty (Gen. 9:6; Ex. 17:4; 21:12, 15, 16, 17; Lev.
20:2, 27; 24:14, 23), God not only permitted but commanded violent
death as an act of justice. Crucial to his argument, Miranda notes
that Jesus quoted Exodus 21:12 in Mark 7:9-11 (par. Matt. 15:3-6);
therefore, says Miranda, *"Jesus explicitly approves the use of vio-*

lence." Jesus' teaching on love for the neighbor and the enemy "is not at variance with repulsion of the oppressor, even by violence." Texts such as Luke 22:36; Matthew 10:34; Matthew 23; and John 2:14-22 show that "Jesus never disapproved his Father's conduct" to execute vindictive justice against evil and oppression. The violence of the capitalistic system "physically kills millions of human beings day by day with hunger, or leaves them lifelong mental defectives;" to violently struggle against such injustice does not deny the teaching and action of Jesus, but joins us to him in the whipping of the extortioners out of the temple.[61]

George Celestin—writing in 1968 as theology teacher at St. Edwards University, Austin, Texas—cites Karl Rahner to argue that the struggle for power is inevitable and the "Christian cannot absent himself." And "violent use of power usually accompanies any revolution."[62] Celestin argues that extreme pacifists are in reality a threat to peace. He appeals to Jeremiah 1:10 and Luke 1:50-53 to show that God's purpose is to tear down oppressive powers and build new orders. He concludes, however, by noting that God is not always on the side of the revolutionaries but the Christian is faced with ambiguity when trying to discern the religious significance of revolution.[63]

Cone cites numerous biblical texts which correlate God's demand for justice with God's liberation of the people from oppression and with the threat of captivity if injustices continued (Amos 2:10; 3:2; 4:2; 6:12; 8:4-8; 9:7-8; Hos. 12:6; 13:5-8; Mic. 6:8; Jer. 5:26-28; Is. 1:16-17; 3:13-15).[64]

José Miguez Bonino, Argentinian Protestant theologian, says, "Peace is a dynamic process through which justice is established amid the tensions of history."[65] Bonino distinguishes between two views of peace. One, based on "the principle of the rationality of the universe" and derived from Babylonian myth and Greco-Roman thought, serves the preservation of the status quo, often legitimizing oppressive power. The other view of peace understands humanity to be in a "fight against the objectifications given in nature, in history, in society, in religion," those self-serving systems that reduce people to pawns. In this view violence plays the creative role of midwife to bring about a new order seeking justice.

While Bonino says that both views can find biblical support, it is important for Christians to recognize that neither concept can be viewed abstractly. The biblical notions of justice, mercy, faithfulness, truth, and peace are understood via concrete historical situations. Hence:

> ... violence appears in the Bible, not as a general form of human conduct which has to be accepted or rejected as such, but as an element of God's announcement-commandment, as concrete acts which must be carried out or avoided in view of a result....
>
> There are wars that are commanded—even against Israel—and wars that are forbidden—even on behalf of Israel.

The principle of coherence may be found in seeing violence as a "means to break out of conditions (slavery ... oppression ...) that leave a man, a group of people, or a people unable to be and act as a responsible agent ... in relation to others, to things and to God."[66] In this way violence serves the cause of justice and peace.

3. Messianism: the messianic hope is defined chiefly as liberation and justice.

The peace of the messianic vision presupposes justice (Is. 32:17; Ps. 85) and the overthrow of the oppressors. The struggle for liberation and justice form the heart of the messianic hope. Such struggle signals the coming of the kingdom.

While this biblical thought is utilized by numerous writers in support of revolutionary struggle, the commentary does not necessarily envision violence, as for example in Bruce Boston's essay:

> ... the revolutionary task in messianic perspective is not the seizure of power but its realignment, not the establishment of a new law and order, but the establishment of justice, not the ushering in of utopia but the generation of shalom.[67]

Arguing against pacifism, Celestin says:

> ... the theology of messianism focuses on what God is doing *right now* in the world to make man's life more human. In this context revolution can become the cutting edge of humanization.[68]

4. Incarnation: Jesus' coming means liberation, justice, and humanization.

a. The birth narratives are revolutionary. Cone cites Luke 1:49-53 to convey the revolutionary significance of Jesus' coming.[69] The commentary on the infancy narratives from the Solentiname discussion group led by the priest and poet Ernesto Cardenal, also minister of culture in the Nicaraguan government, shows well the revolutionary interpretation of Jesus' birth. The following comments made by group members, consisting mostly of peasants, are on Luke 1:51-52:

Laureano: That is the Revolution. The rich person or the mighty is brought down and the poor person, the one who was down, is raised up.

Still another: If God is against the mighty, then he has to be on the side of the poor.[70]

When discussing Herod's massacre of the babies and Rachel's weeping for her children, Laureano and Elvis say:

Laureano: I remember what happened in Chile, where they killed thousands of people, just because freedom was being born there; many people were taken up in airplanes and thrown out into the sea. But they can't put freedom down, just as Herod couldn't put Jesus down.

Elvis: The importance of the birth of Christ is that it was the birth of the Revolution, right? There are many people who are afraid of Christ because he was coming to change the world. From then on the Revolution has been growing. It keeps growing little by little, then, and it keeps growing, and nobody can stop it.[71]

Later, when discussing Joseph's return from Egypt to Nazareth because Archelaus was governing Judea, Fernando says:

I don't understand how you can read the Gospels and get spiritual lessons for your life out of it and not get involved in the Revolution. This Book has a very clear political position for anyone that reads it simply. . . . But there are people in Managua who read this Book, and they are friends of Herod; and they don't realize that this Book is their enemy.[72]

b. Jesus' prophetic ministry judges the old oppressive order.

Bonino, in correlating the two views of peace mentioned above, argues that in the person and work of Jesus Christ the values of order, rationality, and preservation are incorporated into "a dynamics of transformation and not the reverse."[73] He quotes Salesian priest Giulio Girardi:

"Undoubtedly the gospel commands us to love the enemy. . . . The Christian . . . love[s] the oppressed, defending and liberating him; the oppressor, accusing and combating him. Love compels us to fight for the liberation of all those who live under a condition of objective sin."[74]

Though Jesus was not a Zealot, says Bonino, he left no "doubts about whether he was on the side of the poor and oppressed or the power structures (religious and political) of his time." Within the oppressive structures of society, nonviolence is only credible if it leads us, like Jesus, unequivocally to conviction "for the subversion of the oppressive order."[75]

Juan Luis Segundo, priest and director of a pastoral center in Montevideo, notes that Jesus chose whom to be for and to be against (e.g., Mt. 10:5-6; Mk. 7:27). Segundo says that Jesus also put some people at arm's length in order to let others get close to him.[76] He "submerged some real people (the Pharisees) in[to] the anonymity of a group, a category, a prejudice, a law." Hence, living within the limitations of historical class struggle and finite human energy, "Jesus was no exception . . . to the use of this essentially violent mechanism."[77] Hence, Segundo says,

> Only idealistic oversimplification of Jesus' real attitudes can paint a picture of him as a human being dedicated to limitless love without a trace of resistance or violence. That he came to the point of taking a whip in hand to drive the merchants from the temple is of minor importance (Mark 11:15ff.; John 2:13ff.).[78]

c. The gospel calls for humanization.

Christ came to establish a new creation (2 Cor. 5:17). This new humanity, says Boston, is to be "recognized as an eschatological reality, completely revolutionizing and transforming present realities."[79] Jesus' incarnation calls us to be fully human, requiring us "to be fully open to the impingement of the new humanity on us from the future."[80] This way of thinking is at the heart of "the revelation/revolution dialectic" central to biblical thought. The coming of God's kingdom and the promise to completely transform history links together humanness and revolution.[81] Both Shaull and Celestin also connect God's kingdom work in Christ with humanization, advanced often but not always by the forces of revolution. Celestin notes that the great revolutions occurred in the Christian West, evidence of God's working through revolution to achieve the incarnational goal of humanization.[82]

5. Death/Resurrection: this paradigm, central to the Christian faith, stands for radical change and revolution.

Harking back to the keynote verse for his essay on revelation and revolution (Is. 43:18-19), Bruce Boston says:

> Death/Resurrection alludes to the power of the new beginning as do Exodus, Messianism, and Incarnation. It suggests that the powers and principalities, the institutional structures and their dynamics which man has created are not final, but may be transformed into

something new, something unprecedented, into a revolutionary new form and content.[83]

Having strongly accented God's identification with suffering and the cross in history, Choan-Seng Song, former theology professor in Taiwan and in 1979 Associate director of the Secretariat of the Faith and Order Commission of WCC, says:

> In the eyes of the rulers of this world the resurrection faith with the cross at its center can be a faith of insurrection. So be it! . . . An insurrection shaped by the faith of the resurrection differs from an insurrection that arises out of a struggle for political power and domination. It is an act of faith that endeavors to signal hope to a people who have become victims of a ruthless dictatorial power.[84]

Cone shows that the cross-resurrection is the climax of Jesus' ministry of identifying with the poor and oppressed. Because of God's vindication of Jesus in the resurrection, "we now know that Jesus' ministry with the poor and wretched was God himself effecting his will to liberate the oppressed."[85] Hence:

> The hermeneutical principle for an exegesis of the Scriptures is the revelation of God in Christ as the Liberator of the oppressed from social oppression and to political struggle, wherein the poor recognize that their fight against poverty and injustice is not only consistent with the gospel but is the gospel of Jesus Christ.[86]

Pacifist/Nonresistant Position(s)

John Howard Yoder, Mennonite theologian-ethicist and professor at the University of Notre Dame, points out that the pacifist/nonresistant position comes in many varieties, twenty-one by his count.[87] Hence it would seem appropriate to present at least several varieties to illustrate differing uses of the Bible. However, on the use of Scripture a quite consistent picture emerges, except for subpoints within the overall position. The three most critical differences are the explanation of warfare in the Old Testament (though all agree that it is not to be taken as normative for Christians), the extent to which Jesus' ministry was political in nature, and the degree to which (and how) the church should be involved today in political issues.

Even though differences emerge on this latter point, most authors cited here espouse pacifism as a moral commitment of Christians (rather than a political philosophy as such) which in turn has bearing upon politics. (The problems inherent in this interconnection will be discussed in the hermeneutical commentary).

Because these differences, however, do not affect in any appreciable way the use of Scripture in the theological construction of the pacifist/nonresistant position, the case will be presented as one position, while the divergent uses of the Bible will be presented as variants a, b, and c where major differences occur.

The Old Testament Witness

1. Warfare has its roots in humanity's fall.

Vernard Eller, Church of the Brethren religion teacher at LaVerne College (California), begins his discussion of *War and Peace from Genesis to Revelation* with humanity's fall into sin (Gen. 3—4). Humanity said "no" to God and decided to go its own warring way, refusing to "fight" or "dance" (Eller's metaphors) in God's image. With shocking speed, the warring spirit (Jas. 4:1-3) escalated—Adam to Cain to Lamech to Noah to Nimrod.[88]

Guy Hershberger, longtime Mennonite peace leader and writer and professor at Goshen College, Goshen, Indiana, says that although God created humanity with the "intention that human conduct should ... accord with ... holiness and perfection,... the fall of man ... brought an important change in man's nature with the result that human conduct descended to a lower level."[89] William Keeney, Mennonite ethicist and presently head of COPRED (Consortium on Peace Research, Education and Development), begins his study for lay people, *Lordship and Servanthood*, by discussing both James 4:1-3 and Genesis 3—4.[90]

While all biblically oriented pacifists connect warfare to humanity's fallen nature, they differ in assessing the moral nature of Israel's warfare.

(Variant a). Old Testament warfare expressed God's will for the people when kingdom and state were combined. J. Irvin Lehman, Mennonite Church leader in Pennsylvania, makes a sharp contrast between the Testaments, saying that in the old dispensation, when church and state were connected, war was God's will and way of establishing the people in the land and of driving out the enemies.[91] Numerous articles in the Virginia-based Mennonite periodical, *Sword and Trumpet*, advance the same point of view.[92]

(Variant b). God allowed war as a concession to Israel's sin. Hershberger, pioneering in this distinctive emphasis,[93] writes that Israel's wars resulted from its sin of not following God's perfect will, through which Israel could have taken the land without use of sword and bow. God's blueprint called for a peaceful penetration of

the land, whereby God would drive out enemy nations in phases through miraculous means (the hornet, terror, plague, and "my angel" [Ex. 23:20-23]). Israel's wars "were the consequence of her own sins, and contrary to the original intention of God."[94]

Because of Israel's sin, Hershberger holds, God via the permissive will incorporated war into Israel's civil law, a law based upon God's wrath principle, but God's perfect will expressed in the moral law forbade all killing. This *concession* is similar to God's allowing for kingship (1 Sam. 8:1ff.) and divorce (Mk. 10:2-9). This also explains why God forbade David to build the temple ("he shed blood abundantly") and why the prophets regarded Israel with its hardened heart in need of a "new heart and spirit." Isaiah catalogued Israel's sins as rebellion, making "haste to shed innocent blood," and not knowing the way of peace; they were forsaken of God because they were idolaters and warriors. Hershberger concludes his survey of the prophets: "Surely if the message of the prophets means anything it means that the day of warfare for God's people was over."[95]

(Variant c). Israel's military warfare resulted from its failure to trust *God as warrior.* While many pacifist writers mention this point, Vernard Eller and Millard C. Lind, professor of Old Testament at the Associated Mennonite Biblical Seminaries, Elkhart, Indiana, extensively develop this emphasis.[96] By careful comparison of Israel's warfare practices with those of Israel's neighbors, Lind identifies as unique the historical reality and ideal in which Israel did not fight. Exodus 14:14 is the prototype. Israel did not fight or even assist in God's victory as warrior; rather, the people stood still and saw the salvation of Yahweh. Kings and armies revealed Israel's *lack of faith* and failure to learn God's teachings in holy war.

Lind recognizes three types of response in Israel's history: (1) the "standing still" of Exodus 14:14 (cf. God's victories at Jericho and through Gideon), (2) the cooperative, assisting role as in the battle of Ai, and (3) full military preparation and human fighting as under the kings (David's battles). Stage 3, says Lind, was a complete failure in faith. Military armament showed Israel's spiritual weakness, the failure to trust God's power for its defense and security.[97]

Appealing to Exodus 19—20, Isaiah 2:1-4, and other texts, Lind maintains that God's justice is achieved not by the sword, but by God's Torah, God's gift to establish shalom upon the earth. Daniel's civil disobedience arose from obedience to the law of God's kingdom, which broke and replaced all the kingdoms of the earth. At the heart of the issue, says Lind, is whether we take the way of trust in God's law and miracle or put our trust in human law and then use force to secure our *legal* rights. Witness the civil disobedience of the Hebrew midwives against the law of Pharaoh! In whom do we trust?[98]

2. The Old Testament criticizes warfare and prepares for the New Testament teaching of nonresistant love and pacifism. (These emphases fit partly with variant b, but mostly with variant c above).

Twelve related emphases appear:

a. The Old Testament, says Hershberger, shows many examples of nonresistant action. Although God worked through warfare via a permissive will, God's perfect will still shines through the Old Testament narratives, such as Abraham's nonresistance to the Philistines and the commands to return an enemy's ox and to feed the hungry enemy.[99]

b. Millard Lind observes that the patriarchal narratives (J, E), written during the time of the monarchy, are almost totally pacifistic. By calling attention to the writers' criteria in choosing these stories with pacifist emphases, Lind suggests that the patriarchal materials articulate a critique of the military and the kingship patterns of the monarchial period.[100]

c. By noting that the Reed Sea miracle (Ex. 14:14; 15:1-21) became paradigmatic for Israel's warfare and that God chose prophetic rather than military figures to lead Israel (Moses and charismatic judges), Lind argues that military battles were departures from Yahweh's way.[101]

d. The Old Testament view of holy war affirms that God fights *for* Israel, not *with* Israel. This view challenges the legitimacy of all common war practices.[102]

e. Old Testament warfare includes God's fighting against Israel because of the nation's disobedience. Lind identifies three narratives of defeat (Num. 14:39-45; Josh. 7; 1 Sam. 4) and two poetic reflections on these defeats (Deut. 32; Ps. 78).[103] Eller also discusses various prophetic oracles which show Yahweh's warfare *directed against Zion* (Is. 3:1, 25-26; 28:21-22; 1:25-27; 13:3-5; 10:5-7, 12-13).[104] Additional texts are Amos 6:1-9; Jeremiah 7:13-15; 21:4-5; 44:11ff.[105] This strong Old Testament tradition underscores the point that holy war was not common warfare; God's war was not to be identified with national warfare.

f. Waldemar Janzen, Old Testament professor at Canadian Mennonite Bible College in Winnipeg, notes that the Old Testament does not glorify death in war or develop war hero stories as are found in the Homeric epics.[106]

g. The pervasive prophetic criticism of kingship with its military power indicates that the Old Testament itself points to another way, the establishment of justice through the Torah (Is. 2:1-4) and the way of the suffering servant, which refuses and judges the military way.[107]

h. Israel's experience with Yahweh's warfare was never used by Israel to justify war or as an excuse to prepare for war. It was used rather to call Israel to defenselessness and faith in Yahweh. Yoder points out that the prophets used Yahweh's past warfare victories to argue "*against* the development of a military caste, military alliances, and political designs based on the availability of military power," because the history assured them that Yahweh faithfully cared for Israel. God called them therefore "to trust His providence for the immediate future."[108] Further, Yoder notes, Israel's practice of *herem*, cultically devoting the enemy as sacrifice to God, repugnant though this be to us, was Israel's visible acknowledgment of Yahweh's victory.[109]

i. The prophetic perspective stresses, "In returning and rest you shall be saved; in quietness and in trust shall be your strength" (Is. 30:15). The prophetic vision of the coming reign of peace has swords beaten into plowshares.[110]

j. While the Old Testament undeniably contains shocking portraits of bloody massacres, says Jean Lasserre, Reformed Church pastor in France, it also contains universalist and pacific emphases. Jesus nurtured himself upon these emphases, committed himself to them, and repudiated the militaristic strands. Hence, says Lasserre, "the systematic refusal of violence was a personal contribution by Jesus of Nazareth, His original discovery."[111]

k. The holy war tradition culminates in the holy warrior's strategy of "reverse fighting," the paradigm of the suffering servant of Isaiah 40—55. As Eller puts it:

> Instead of power, the servant displays weakness; instead of glory, humiliation; instead of public acclaim, social rejection; instead of assertive thrusts against the enemy, absorption of the enemy's thrusts against him; instead of making the enemy suffer, suffering himself.

> Although it will be difficult for us to understand it so, this is a method of *fighting*, that is, it is a means by which God truly does win the victory and get his will to be done.[112]

l. The Old Testament, though affirming God as warrior and recounting numerous stories of war, contains the roots of pacifism which lead to the nonviolent love of the New Testament. Jacob Enz, professor of Old Testament at the Associated Mennonite Biblical Seminaries, identifies these roots: both Genesis 1 and John 1 show the incomparable power of God's "word-deed of love"; "Moses takes a shepherd's staff and burning heart into Egypt and leads out a band of slaves who raised not one sword against the world's greatest empire"; the word-deed of love in Ruth and Jonah critiques and transforms nationalistic aspiration (as in Ps. 2); and Yahweh's warfare finds fulfillment in Jesus' servant mission (Lk. 4:18-19 quotes Is. 61:1-2). Jesus' ministry is a "massive warfare of teaching, healing, proclamation, suffering, death, and glory."[113] The New Testament, deliberately selecting from the Old Testament, turns "Battle Songs into Hymns of Peace." Hence:

> The victory of implicit theological pacifism in the Old Testament prepares for incontrovertibly explicit pacifism in the New Testament.[114]

Similarly, Yoder's expository essay on "Thou shalt not kill" shows a trajectory of thought that culminates in Jesus' ethic:

> The sacredness of life as belonging to Yahweh alone was defended initially by blood vengeance, then defended better in the Decalogue by reservation to the judges, then progressively still better (as in Numbers 35) by various kinds of mitigation, and still more from the age of Jeremiah to that of Akiba in the abandonment by Jews of the structures of civil justice.[115]

In its canonical fruition, this development leads to the teaching of Jesus in which the sacredness of another's life (human blood belongs to Yahweh because man and woman are God's image) receives its strongest imperative from Jesus' forbidding hatred in the heart.[116]

3. Since it prepares for the New, the Old Testament cannot be used for normative Christian ethics.

Most nonresistant/pacifist Christians affirm that the New Testament (Jesus' and the apostles' teachings) is normative for Christian life and practice. Recognizing that the Old Testament presents problems, pacifists understand the Old Testament as either preparatory (even though sometimes contradictory) or supportive to the New Testament. The Mennonite Church statement in the pacifist brief to the "Discussions on War/Peace Issues Between Friends, Mennonites, Brethren and European Churches" states:

> Believing that the Scriptures of the Old Testament are likewise divine

in origin and authoritative in character, Mennonites hold that these Scriptures are a record of the progressive revelation of the nature and will of God, leading to the full and final revelation found in the New Testament. Therefore, Old Testament Scriptures which are sometimes cited in support of Christian participation in war may not be used to contradict clear New Testament teaching, but must be interpreted in the light of the teaching of Christ and the Apostles, for in Christ we find the norm for the whole of Scriptures. The national history of Israel as recorded in the Old Testament cannot have normative significance for us, for much in it contradicts Christ. It is significant to note that Israel rejected Christ, at least in part, because he refused the Messiahship in a national and therefore coercive sense.[117]

The statement "Peace Is the Will of God," representing both the historic peace churches and the International Fellowship of Reconciliation, explains that war and violence is a sub-Christian ethic embedded in the "structure of the unredeemed society," while Christians are called to live a new reality wherein

> man is restored to unity with God and made a "new creature in Christ," where "old things are passed away" and "all things are become new" (II Cor. 5:17), where he cannot "continue in sin" because he is "dead" to it (Rom. 6:1, 2). There is no provision for the Christian to revert, under force of circumstance, to the sub-Christian code of conduct.[118]

The New Testament Evidence

Pacifist uses of the New Testament fall under five main points:[119]

1. Jesus' teachings (reflected in the apostles) are clearly pacifist.

a. Nonresistance: overcome evil with good.

> But I say to you, Do not resist one who is evil. But if any one strikes you on the right cheek, turn to him the other also; and if any one would sue you and take your coat, let him have your cloak as well; and if any one forces you to go one mile, go with him two miles.
> Mt. 5:39-41.

> Repay no one evil for evil.... Never avenge yourselves.... If your enemy is hungry, feed him.... Do not be overcome by evil, but overcome evil with good. Rom. 12:17, 19-21.

> Do not return evil for evil or reviling for reviling; but on the contrary bless. 1 Pet. 3:9; cf. 1 Thes. 5:15.

These verses form the foundation for the nonresistant/pacifist view of numerous writers. John Ferguson, Quaker and president of

Selly Oakes Colleges, Birmingham, England, begins *The Politics of Love* by expositing Matthew 5:39. He notes that it is not clear how 5:39 should be translated: "Do not make a stand against (resist) the evil one" (who? the devil? this hardly fits), or "Do not make a stand against (resist) by evil means." The latter, totally faithful to the Greek text, concurs with Romans 12:21—"do not use evil means in the endeavor to overcome evil with good."[120] For Hershberger these verses are an integral part of Jesus' teaching on love and forgiveness, and provide the basis for Christian refusal to exercise power in governmental justice and for Christian refusal to participate in war. Nonresistance is an intrinsic part of the doctrine of salvation (1 Pet. 2:21-23; Phil. 2:5-11, 14-15).[121]

. Henry A. Fast, writing in 1959 and Mennonite biblical scholar at Bethel College in Kansas, holds that the Sermon on the Mount's sayings do not appear to be directed to the political and military dimensions, but they disallow "all use of violence, all desire for revenge, and all resentment and ill will."[122] Jesus regularly lifted his teaching "out of the political-national plane into the personal-religious sphere"; his "conception of the kingdom was wholly free from current dreams of political freedom and national ascendency."[123] Agreeing that the primary reference in the sermon is to the *personal* enemy, G. H. C. Macgregor, Scottish New Testament scholar, regards this new principle, however, as Jesus' alternative to "leading the Jewish patriots against the Roman legions"; this new way sets "forth in action the power of suffering and sacrificial love to vindicate the moral order and recreate a sinful world."[124]

Acknowledging that this teaching has its genius in its *maximalizing* human authenticity, *interiorizing* morality, and *converting* one to the neighbor, L. John Topel, Jesuit biblical theologian at Seattle University, calls for serious regard of this ethic in all spheres of life, observing that

> it is one thing to build from the same fundamental principles into a more adequate ethic in a new situation, and another to structure an ethic around entirely different principles so that the basis of ethics is changed . . . as happened in the history of Christian thought.[125]

After noting that Guy F. Hershberger, Reinhold Niebuhr, and Emil Brunner agree that the Sermon on the Mount "does not envisage the problem of the state," Culbert Rutenber, writing in 1958 as professor of philosophy at Eastern Baptist Seminary in Philadelphia, says:

> Yet nonviolent resistance is so much *nearer* the New Testament ideal
> of love than [is] bloodshed, war and violence that the kind of pacifism
> that advocates nonviolent resistance is at least the minimum position
> that the Christian ought to take where social groups are involved.[126]

Rutenber points out, however, that this teaching does not guarantee happy consequences; instead it links the believer to the Christ of the cross. But by obeying this calling, believers are promised an inheritance of blessing (1 Pet. 3:9).[127]

Yoder sets his discussion of this teaching within the context of Jesus' refusal of prevailing political options, and notes its place in the larger discussion of fulfilling the law. "The alternative" Jesus presents "is creative concern for the person who is bent on evil, coupled with the refusal of his goals." The old limit on vengeance "has now become a special measure of love demanded by concern for the redemption of the offender."[128]

b. Love the neighbor and the enemy.

> But I say to you, Love your enemies and pray for those who persecute
> you. Mt. 5:44.

> You shall love your neighbor as yourself. Mt. 22:39b.

These teachings of Jesus, reflected throughout the apostolic writings (Rom. 12:9, 17-21; 13:8-10; Gal. 5:14; Jas. 2:8), are considered by all pacifist writers to be the moral muscle of the pacifist position. In the dialogue with the European churches, pacifists argued that "love for the enemy" cannot be compatible with "killing the enemy," despite arguments to the contrary.[129] Hans-Werner Bartsch, German New Testament scholar at Mainz, says this teaching, together with Matthew 5:38-42, is expressive of what it means to be children of God; loving one's neighbor and enemy is a concrete way of testifying to the message of salvation. Social conduct or policy which violates this teaching violates the gospel.[130]

Citing a parallel in Luke 6:27b-36, Yoder notes that this teaching distinguishes the disciple of Jesus from people who love only those who love them. It "portrays the character of God." To be perfect in love is to be like God, undiscriminating in love.[131] Articulating similar emphases, Ronald Sider, president of Evangelicals for Social Action and theology teacher at Eastern Baptist Seminary, says:

> One fundamental aspect of the holiness and perfection of God is that
> He loves His enemies. Those who by His grace seek to reflect His holi-
> ness will likewise love their enemies—even when it involves a cross.[132]

Another pacifist emphasis stresses the positive, active aspect of love, an important complement to Jesus' teaching on nonresistance in Matthew 5:39. Sider says that Jesus was not "advocating a passive, resigned attitude toward oppressors." His command to love the enemy was a "specific political response to centuries of violence and to the contemporary Zealots' call for violent revolution."[133] Macgregor regards the sequence of Matthew 5:38-42 and 5:43-48 to be an essential connection which precludes a negative, passive nonresistance. Nonresistance is put into the service of the all-embracing, positive commandment to love. "The pacifism of Jesus . . . is never 'passivism.' "[134]

Gordon D. Kaufman, Mennonite and professor of theology at Harvard Divinity School, argues that love does not allow one to withdraw from evil but "goes into the very heart of an evil situation and attempts to rectify it. . . . It is in the midst of sinful situations that love must be found working, if it is love at all" (Mt. 11:19; Lk. 7:34). He identifies three expressions of love: witnessing to the truth, accepting the neighbor or enemy in his or her sinfulness, and not forsaking a person or society even when it decides for what we consider wrong and sinful (Rom. 5:10; 1 Jn. 4:10, 19; Mt. 5:46-47; 2 Cor. 5:21). Apparent contradictions may ensue, such as refusing to participate in war but continuing to love and accept an individual or a group of people who choose to participate in war. Loving responsibility will lead, through letter writing or voting, to responsible counsel that recommends the best alternative on political issues, even though the nonresistant/pacifist could not endorse fully, or participate in, such political or military action because of his/her religious commitment.[135]

William Klassen, Mennonite New Testament professor in Vancouver, British Columbia, has devoted several essays to Jesus' command to "Love Your Enemy." He examines the significance and novelty of the teaching against the background of Old Testament teaching, Qumran literature, Maccabean beliefs, and pre-Christian Judaism.[136] Klassen shows that Jesus' command contrasts sharply with the emphasis in Qumran literature, in which the sons of righteousness will mete out vengeance upon the sons of darkness. It contrasts also with the Maccabean patriotism that converts zeal for the law into battle against foreign political oppressors. But Jesus' command to love the enemy is not unique; it has parallels in pre-Christian Judaism.[137] Rather, what is novel about Jesus is his action to create a people of peace. Jesus' gathering together "children of peace" and designating his followers as such (Mt. 5:9;

Lk. 10:5-6) is the novel expression of the love command.[138]

Jesus' command to love the enemy is fleshed out with strategy (pray for your persecutors, do good to those who hate you), with concrete motivation (be children of the Father, be perfect in love, follow the golden rule), and with specific examples (turn the other cheek, go the second mile).[139] Klassen also shows how Paul applied this teaching in Romans 12—13 to the Christian's relationship to political power. The themes of *love* and the *good* "are intimately interwoven." "*Agape* love is transparent in its rejection of the evil, and in its alignment with *to agathon* [the good, 2: 9]." This perspective guides the argument of 13:1-7, in which the authority's function is to approve the good.[140]

c. Jesus taught against the use of the sword.

> Then Jesus said to him, "Put your sword back into its place; for all who take the sword will perish by the sword." Mt. 26:52.

> Jesus answered, "My kingship is not of this world; if my kingship were of this world, my servants would fight, that I might not be handed over to the Jews; but my kingship is not from the world." Jn. 18:36.

> ... for the weapons of our warfare are not worldly but have divine power to destroy strongholds. 2 Cor. 10:4.

To these verses Jean Lasserre joins the third temptation (Mt. 4:8-10), in which the devil offers Jesus the kingdoms of the world. Lasserre notes that Jesus refused to let the crowd make him king by force (Jn. 6:15); that Jesus chose a distinctive style of entry into Jerusalem (Mk. 11:1-10); that, though possible, Jesus refused to call twelve legions of angels to fight the Roman soldiers (Mt. 26:53); and that the crowd taunted Jesus in his defenselessness at his crucifixion (Lk. 23:35). Lasserre says that Jesus considered but rejected the use of the sword throughout his ministry and that this accords with other apostolic teaching (Mt. 15:18-19; 5:21-22; 1 Jn. 3:15).[141]

After noting numerous occasions when Jesus refused to make a sword-type response,[142] Ferguson says Jesus taught that violence breeds violence; as Messiah he stood not for war and military victory but for disarmament and peace.[143] Rutenber says that Matthew 26:52 is a "definite and unambiguous" text forbidding even the defensive sword.[144]

(See Appendix 2 for a pacifist discussion of problem texts.)

2. The nature of God's kingdom and Jesus' messiahship supports the pacifist/nonresistant position.

a. Jesus' proclamation of the kingdom of God in the context of first-century politics shows Jesus' pacifist commitment.

Most pacifist writers agree with wider New Testament scholarship that Jesus' proclamation of God's kingdom occurred within a politically revolutionary context.[145] Klassen contrasts Jesus' position with those of both the violent Zealots and the apocalyptic holy war hopes of the Essenes at Qumran. Instead of gathering sons of light to prepare for "final battle against the sons of darkness," Jesus went about gathering "children of peace," a novel ethical contribution to the contemporary political scene.[146] Yoder says that Jesus introduced a revolution that differed from, and judged inadequate, the interiorized piety of the Pharisees, the withdrawal of the Essenes, the collaborationist strategies of the Sadducees and the Herodians, and the revolutionary violence of the Zealots. He demonstrated the servant way by being a light to the Gentiles (the foreigner-enemy), and began a new, voluntary community, comprised of both Jews *and Gentiles* and offering a new way to deal with offenders.[147]

Another significant point in the portrait of Jesus' pacifist commitment is that Jesus identified his mission with both the servant mission of Isaiah 40—55 and the Sabbath-sabbatical-jubilee justice of the Old Testament. André Trocmé, French Reformed scholar, identifies the beginning of Jesus' public ministry (AD 26-27) with the actual calendar year of jubilee and argues that Jesus proclaimed the kingdom of God as a call to practice jubilee (Lk. 4:16-19).[148] Trocmé then shows how jubilee's radical socio-economic ethic permeated the message and mission of Jesus. Developing this perspective, Yoder discusses numerous aspects of Jesus' ministry (mostly from Luke's Gospel) which show socio-political import:

> The Annunciation (Lk. 1:46ff.; cf. 3:7ff.);
> The Commissioning and Testing (Lk. 3:21-4:14);
> The Platform for Jesus' Public Ministry (Lk. 4:14ff.);
> The Reaffirmation of the Platform (Lk. 6:12ff.);
> Jesus' Teaching on the Cost of Discipleship (Lk. 12:49—13:9; 14:25-26);
> Jesus' Epiphany in the Temple (Lk. 19:36-46);
> The Last Renunciation (Lk. 22:24-53); and
> Jesus' Execution and Exaltation (Lk. 23—24).[149]

Yoder concludes that Jesus in his divinely mandated mission came as "the bearer of a new possibility of human, social, and therefore, political relationships."[150]

Noting that the Jewish messianic hope anticipated a military leader, the reunion of scattered Israel in a rebuilt Jerusalem, and a kingdom of social justice, peace, and righteousness, Ferguson says, "In all this we see that the messianic hope was political, and that Jesus accepted it as such while reinterpreting it."[151] Ferguson then describes the political dimensions of Jesus' ministry: in not succumbing to the temptation to possess the kingdoms of the world, Jesus refused "worldly means of military conquest," but "asserted in a *political context* 'you shall do homage to the Lord your God and worship him alone' "; he preached God's sovereignty and gathered a new community which practiced economic sharing; his entire ministry was fraught with the political messianic question, especially when the crowd sought to make him king, expecting him to lead a political revolt; his disciples included Zealots and a Roman collaborationist; his entry into Jerusalem had political import (Lk. 19:41-44); his apocalyptic discourse foretold the overthrow of the temple; and he was "executed for a political offense."[152]

But the politics of Jesus' messiahship was different, says Ferguson, in five ways: (1) Jesus called for national repentance; (2) he called for social justice, mutual concern and sharing; (3) he called for peace, not war, as both means and end; (4) he identified with the suffering servant and called his disciples to suffer rather than retaliate; and (5) he answered Roman domination by extending the grace of the gospel to all people, even the "Roman enemy." In this ministry Jesus offered an alternative to the way of the Zealots; it validated his teaching against violence and demonstrated the redemptive power of love.[153]

b. Jesus' temptations were political in nature.

Pacifists comment extensively on Jesus' temptations since they focus the nature of both the kingdom and Jesus' messiahship. Macgregor says of the third temptation (Mt. 4:8-11): "To refuse to 'worship Satan' must then mean, not to renounce a national kingdom *simplicitur*, but to renounce 'satanic' methods of winning that kingdom."[154]

The temptation to gain the kingdoms of the world through bowing to Satan, Yoder suggests, is indicative not of "some sort of Satan cult" but of "the idolatrous character of political power hunger and nationalism."[155] Further, Yoder connects "turning stones into bread" to an economic option of messiahship: by feeding multitudes Jesus could become king (as in Jn. 6). Or, by "jumping from the temple" he could signal a religio-political freedom fight and launch the messianic mission as religious hero (cf. the Palm Sunday entrance).[156] Similarly, Donald Kraybill, Mennonite sociologist at Elizabethtown College in Pennsylvania, regards the three temptations as forms of "Right-Side-Up Kingdom[s]," which Jesus' "Upside-Down Kingdom" rejected: the mountain politics of violent revolution, the temple piety of the mainline parties, and the wilderness bread of a welfare king.[157]

c. Peter's confession "You are the Messiah" (Mk. 8:27-38), a political manifesto, prompted Jesus' teaching on pacifism and the way of the cross.

Ferguson identifies this as "a passage of vital significance."[158] He says that Jesus did not refuse Peter's affirmation of him as Messiah but immediately revealed himself to be "a Messiah of a very different color."[159] Jesus identified his messiahship with the suffering servant of Deutero-Isaiah, and the Son of man, who was to suffer and die. This led to Peter's rebuke and Jesus' counterrebuke. Jesus' answer, "Away with you, Satan," is the language Jesus used in the third temptation. Ferguson interprets:

> In trying to turn Jesus from the way of suffering to the more familiar concept of Messiah, Peter is renewing the temptation to achieve political power by the devil's means and on the devil's terms, and indeed Luke in his version of the temptation says that "the devil departed, biding his time" (Lk. 4:13). The time came at Caesarea Philippi.[160]

Ferguson notes that this episode is followed by teaching in which Jesus as the suffering servant-Son of man called his disciples "to eschew the way of violence and accept instead the way of suffering, non-violent love which took Jesus to the cross."[161]

d. The suffering servant-Son of man-Messiah introduced a bold new pacifist picture for messianic thought.

Macgregor joins the theme of God's kingdom to that of Jesus' messiahship. He proposes that Jesus redefined popular thinking on at least two basic points: "Jewish nationality alone was no guarantee of the possession of the Kingdom," and Jesus refused "to wage the messianic war" to overthrow the Gentile empire even though he did not disclaim messiahship.[162]

Topel notes that Jesus never used the title Messiah to designate himself (except in Lk. 24:26, 46—*after* his resurrection—and in Jn. 4:25-26 to a Samaritan). In Mark 8:29; 14:61; 15:2, and parallels, Jesus responded evasively to the title. Topel explains, "Probably by Jesus' own time the title 'messiah' had come to have such heavily nationalistic and political implications ... that Jesus avoided [it] because it would not serve to [describe] what he meant to do."[163] On the other hand, Topel says, the title Son of man occurs 81 times in the Gospels, in all cases on the lips of Jesus to designate himself. Jesus' most astonishing achievement is to use this title with its apocalyptic, heavenly connotations (Dan. 7:13) to designate his suffering servant work. Three times Jesus said he was "going to Jerusalem to suffer and die as the Son of man."[164] "For the Son of man . . . came not to be served but to serve, and to give his life as a ransom for many" (Mk. 10:45). Topel then describes the numerous Gospel emphases which show Jesus fulfilling the prophecies of the servant's work, including the bringing of jubilee justice to the nations (Lk. 4:16ff.). Topel regards this emphasis as the heart of New Testament theology.[165]

For Eller also, this is the heart of the matter. He cites many Gospel texts to show the intertwining of the two Isaiah traditions—the triumphal, invincible messianic Zion and the lowly suffering servant. Commenting on Jesus' Palm Sunday entrance into Jerusalem, Eller says:

> What this *entry* actually leads to is death on a cross—which in itself is a king's triumph. A *king* on a *donkey:* Isaiah's Messiah and Deutero's Suffering Servant are one and the same person.[166]

e. Jesus as conquering lamb demonstrated the new way.

Eller follows up his discussion of the Messiah-servant view of Jesus with comments on the lion-lamb image of Revelation, noting that the lamb image also comes from Deutero-Isaiah. In this lamb image of Christ, most basic to Revelation, we have

> a powerful symbol of self-giving defenselessness. That he bears the marks of slaughter indicates that he already has played through the role of innocent suffering to its bitter conclusion in martyrdom and death—and yet has gone *through* death, surmounted it, and become the Living One. And yet, the fact that, without contradiction, this Lamb *is* the Lion—surely this indicates that the Lamb's way of defenselessness is a true posture of *strength* and a means of *fighting and conquest.* John has made the Isaiah/Deutero combination, the Suffering-Servant Messiah, more graphic than has ever been done before.[167]

The lamb Jesus is God's warrior; the defenseless victory of this warrior-lamb climaxes the holy war tradition of the Old Testament. The warrior died as a conquering, atoning martyr, thus uniting the biblical strands of war and peace. Peace comes through the lamb's death, the blood of the cross. George Fox, founder of the Friends, and later Quaker writings emphasize this point. T. Canby Jones, Quaker religion professor, sums up Fox's view of *The Lamb's War:*

He who is King of kings and Lord of lords who rides at the head of this
army will slay only with the sword of the Spirit which are the words of
his mouth. Such words and weapons slay not men but wickedness.
The sword of the Spirit does not destroy men's lives. It saves their
souls. The weapons of this conflict are "not carnal but mighty
through God to the pulling down of strongholds." (2 Cor. 10:4). Those
who rely on material weapons throw away the spiritual. But the army
of the Lamb will overcome those who rely on physical force and the
Lamb shall have the victory and of his kingdom there shall be no
end.[168]

Fox identifies Jesus, says Jones, with the suffering lamb of Isaiah
53, who in Revelation makes war in righteousness, rides forth to
conquer on a white horse, slays with the sword of his mouth, and
receives blessing and honor as king of kings, Lord of lords, the Lord
omnipotent and everlasting.[169]

Yoder concludes *The Politics of Jesus* with a chapter on "The
War of the Lamb" and subtitles his book *Vicit Agnus Noster* (Our
Lamb Conquers). The conquest of the slain lamb indicates that "the
cross and not the sword, suffering and not brute power determines
the meaning of history." Further, "the meaning of meekness in history" is defined by the person of Jesus himself, who "became flesh
and dwelt among us."[170]

3. Christ's atonement calls for pacifist discipleship.

Pacifists make this point in a variety of ways. Sider argues
that only by disregarding Christ's atonement can one reject God's
peacemaking way of dealing with enemies.[171] Yoder unites discipleship with Christ's death on the cross, justification with reconciliation, and following in Jesus' footsteps with the lamb's victory.[172]
Eller tucks Jesus' teaching on discipleship between chapters on
Jesus as Messiah-servant and lamb-king so that Jesus' atoning
work is seen clearly as the basis and model for discipleship.[173]
Philippians 2:5-11 and 1 Peter 2:21-24 frequently appear, serving
almost as creedal pillars in Hershberger's work.[174]

Use of the Bible on this strategic point will be limited to several
selections each for three areas of emphasis:

a. Atonement means victory over the powers.

Paul's teaching on Christ's victory over the principalities and
powers functions as a partial parallel to John's war of the lamb.
Thomas N. Finger, Mennonite theology teacher at Northern Baptist
Seminary in Chicago, points out that the significance behind both
"the rulers ignorantly crucifying the Lord of glory" and the early
church's emphasis on Christ "tricking the devil" in the ransom
theory of the atonement have a common base in Jesus' humble

servant life. God did not deceive the devil but came in servant form, true to the divine nature. The powers, because of their arrogance and deference to the devil, didn't recognize Christ and thus unwittingly crucified him. God then vindicated the lamb-king/servant-Messiah, as well as God's own Godness, by disarming the powers and triumphing over them through resurrecting Jesus (they didn't know *whom* they crucified).[175] Jesus thus went *through* the enemy's stronghold and led out captives in his train. Hence redemption, the buying back of those enslaved by the powers, is part of the Christus Victor act.[176]

The powers *(exousia)* including both earthly rulers and spiritual powers, are dethroned in the process. Affirming the seminal contributions of H. Berkhof, G. B. Caird, and Oscar Cullmann,[177] Yoder quotes Berkhof's exegesis of the three verbs in Colossians 2:15:

> (1) He "made a public example of them." It is precisely in the crucifixion that the true nature of the Powers has come to light. Previously they were accepted as the most basic and ultimate realities, as the gods of the world.... Now that the true God appears on earth in Christ, it becomes apparent that the Powers are inimical to Him, acting not as His instruments but as His adversaries.
>
> (2) ... Christ has "triumphed over them." The unmasking is already their defeat.... The resurrection manifests what was already accomplished at the cross: that in Christ God has challenged the Powers, has penetrated their territory, and has displayed that He is stronger than they.
>
> (3) The concrete evidence of this triumph is that at the cross Christ has "disarmed" the Powers. The weapon (the power of illusion) from which they heretofore derived their strength is struck out of their hands.... No powers can separate us from God's love in Christ. Unmasked, revealed in their true nature, they have lost their mighty grip on [people]. The cross has disarmed them; wherever it is preached, the unmasking and the disarming of the Powers takes place.[178]

By submitting to these powers but "refusing to support them in their self-glorification," Jesus frees believers from all illusory power including law, order (the *stoicheia* in Gal. 4), bondage, and sin (Col. 2:13-15). Jesus' victory—effecting also the unity of Jew and Gentile, which the powers could never accomplish—thus empowers the church to witness to the principalities and powers.[179]

Having thus been saved from the power of the powers, believers testify to the peace of Christ's peace, as the Bethany Theological Seminary's brief to the dialogue between the peace churches and the European churches states:

> The Church affirms in faith that Christ has gained the victory over the powers that enslave the world and man. In his death and resurrection Christ's victory over sin, death, law, and Satan is conclusive and final. In this victory God initiates the age of the new creation in Christ. In the resurrecting power of this new age man also, by faith, dies to the old aeon of chaos and self-centeredness and is raised a new creation (Gal. 2:20; Rom. 6:1-11; 2 Cor. 5:17). He is once more restored to fellowship with God, to harmony and peace with his fellowmen and to wholeness within his new purified self (Rom. 5:10f.; 6:17f.; [7:] 22f.; 8:1-17), presaging the restoration of all fallen creation along with the sons of God (Rom. 8:19-23). Christ is Lord over Church and world, the power of governing, and all other powers of creation.[180]

This victory view of the atonement[181] argues then that to live Christ's way of peace is realistic for believers, since they are freed from the pretentious tyrannies of the powers. The necessities of self-defense, balance of power, and idolization of law are not the believers' agenda.[182]

b. Atonement means reconciling justification.

Building upon the work of Markus Barth,[183] Yoder also relates the doctrine of justification to peace, both vertically and horizontally. God's justification of the believer creates peace with God (Rom. 5:1)—yes, but also peace between those who were former enemies, hostile to one another. The great historical demonstration, the very context in which the understanding of justification emerged, was the making of peace between Jew and Gentile (Gal. 2:14ff.; Eph. 2:11f.). This is God's new creation (2 Cor. 5:17), God's new humanity (Eph. 2:15), wrought by Christ's atonement. "To proclaim divine righteousness means ... God sets things right"; God establishes relationship with sinners (Rom. 5:8) and makes peace between enemies (Eph. 2:14-17). Justification and reconciliation are not sequential, but one and the same.[184]

Marlin E. Miller, Mennonite professor of theology, critiques the traditional doctrines of the atonement for not relating "the crucifixion [to] the social reality of the messianic peace." Paul, says Miller,

> emphasizes that the work of Christ inherently means the making of peace between human enemies as well as providing their common access to God. Peacemaking between enemies thus belongs fundamentally to the death and resurrection of Jesus Christ.[185]

Sider also links atonement to the way of nonviolent love:

> That the cross is the ultimate demonstration that God deals with His enemies through suffering love receives its clearest theological expression in Paul. "God shows his love for us in that while we were yet sinners, Christ died for us. . . . While we were enemies we were reconciled to God by the death of his Son" (Romans 5:8, 10). Jesus' vicarious cross for sinners is the foundation and deepest expression of Jesus' command to love one's enemies. . . .
>
> Because Jesus commanded His followers to love their enemies and then died as the incarnate Son to demonstrate that God reconciles His enemies by suffering love, any rejection of the nonviolent way in human relations involves a heretical doctrine of the atonement. If God in Christ reconciled His enemies by suffering servanthood, then those who want to follow Christ faithfully dare not treat their enemies in any other way.[186]

Using Romans 4:25, Sider also unites nonviolence with Jesus' resurrection: "We can live nonviolently because we walk in the resurrection."[187]

c. Discipleship means identifying with/following/imitating Jesus Christ.

Virtually all pacifist writers emphasize this theme. Yoder, after relating these images of discipleship to God's nature and to Jesus' life, devotes one section to "The Disciple/Participant and the Death of Christ," including the following dimensions:

(1) "Suffering with Christ as the definition of apostolic existence" (Phil. 3:10f.; 2 Cor. 4:10; Col. 1:24; 1 Cor. 10:33f.; 1 Thes. 1:6);

(2) "Sharing in divine condescension" (Phil. 2:3-14);

(3) "Give your life as he did" (Eph. 5:1f.; 1 Jn. 3:16);

(4) "Suffering servanthood in place of dominion" (Mk. 10:42-45; Mt. 20:25-28; Jn. 13:1-13);

(5) "Accept innocent suffering without complaints as he did" (1 Pet. 2:20f.; 3:14-18; 4:12-16);

(6) "Suffer with or like Christ the hostility of the world, as bearers of the kingdom cause" (Lk. 14:27-33; Mt. 10:37ff.; Mk. 8:34ff.; Jn. 15:20f.; 2 Tim. 3:12; Phil. 1:29; 1 Pet. 4:13; Heb. 11:1—12:5);

(7) "Death is liberation from the power of sin" (1 Pet. 4:1f.; Gal. 5:24);

(8) "Death is the fate of the prophets; Jesus, whom we follow, was already following them" (Mt. 23:24; Mk. 12:1-9; Lk. 24:20; Acts 2:36; 4:10; 7:52; 23:24; 1 Thes. 2:15ff.);

(9) "Death is victory" (Col. 2:14; 1 Cor. 1:22-24; Rev. 12:10f.; cf. 5:9ff.; 17:14).[188]

Yoder identifies the one aspect of Jesus' life we are told to follow or copy—not his carpentry, his rural (camping) life, his teaching methods, or his celibacy, rather:

> There is thus but one realm in which the concept of imitation holds, but there it holds in every strand of the New Testament literature and all the more strikingly by virtue of the absence of parallels in other realms: this is at the point of the concrete social meaning of the cross and its relation to enmity and power. Servanthood replaces dominion, forgiveness absorbs hostility. Thus—and only thus—are we bound by New Testament thought to "be like Jesus."[189]

Both Eller and Topel relate discipleship to the atoning work of Christ. Quoting texts calling for identification with Christ (Col. 2:12; Rom. 6:5, 10-11; 1 Cor. 4:9-13), Eller notes that Paul's life and ours are not "to be understood as a *duplication of* Jesus but only a witness to him."[190] Eller then devotes a chapter to Gospel texts (Mt. 5-7; 10:34-39) which portray King Jesus' call, "Follow me."[191] Eller's discussion of Revelation also unites discipleship with atonement by arguing that the triumph of believers through their faithful witness-death *(marturia-martus)* is assured because of King Jesus' own triumph in his witness and death.[192]

Richard McSorley, proposing that "imitation of Christ" includes discipleship,[193] calls Christians to imitate Christ the peacemaker, the reconciler.

> His method is the cross: accepting suffering with love, not inflicting it on others. The invitation of the gospel to love is entirely contradictory to the use of military force.... Christ's way of life was not military. It was a pacifist peace-making....
>
> His life is the "way" God teaches us to live.[194]

4. The nature and mission of the church leads to pacifism.
   a. The church is the body of Christ's peace.

Marlin Miller describes the church as a "new corporate existence in which hostility and conflict give way to a new social and religious identity." This new humanity is the Messiah's "own corporate existence, the messianic community in which hostilities are overcome and former enemies live in peace."[195]

Under the title "The Family of Nations," Macgregor quotes six Pauline texts describing the solidarity and unity of diverse peoples in Christ (Eph. 3:14f.; 4:25; 1 Cor. 12:13; Rom. 10:12; Gal. 3:28; Col.

3:11). Similarly, Yoder in his call to "Let the Church Be the Church" says, *"Christian internationalism is the true unity* which the servant church must let be restored."[196] Because the church is a unique international peoplehood, its participation in war breaks the bond of unity; pits members of the body against each other; and dishonors Christ, the head of the body. When Christians of one nation take up arms to fight against, or defend themselves from, Christians of another nation, both groups deny their confession that Jesus, and not Caesar, is Lord.[197]

One of the five reasons Myron Augsburger, Mennonite theologian and evangelist, gives for "The Basis of Christian Opposition to War" is that as pacifists "we regard membership in the Kingdom of Christ as our primary loyalty."[198]

> To affirm that one is a member of the Kingdom of Christ means that loyalty to Christ and his Kingdom transcends every other loyalty. This stance transcends nationalism, and calls us to identify first of all with our fellow disciples, of whatever nation, as we serve Christ together.[199]

b. The church's mission is peace.

Augsburger regards war as opposing the church's mission: "We cannot kill a man for whom Christ died. . . . We cannot take the life of a person God purposes to redeem."[200] In writing for *Christianity Today,* Augsburger says:

> From an evangelical perspective it may be said that whenever a Christian participates in war he has abdicated his responsibility to the greater calling of missions and evangelism. . . . The way for Christians to change the world is to share the . . . good news of the Gospel rather than to think we can stop the anti-God movements by force.[201]

Jim Wallis, editor of *Sojourners,* says: "The church, as conceived in the New Testament, is commissioned to be a countersign to the world's values and the representative of a new order." It is to be "a demonstration of what human life can be in the love and power of Christ."[202] Similarly, Norman Kraus, Mennonite historical theologian and missionary, says that the church demonstrates the Spirit of God in its life of "justice, mutuality, respect, and forgiveness." As a reconciled community bearing witness to God's movement in human history, it should, like a city on a hill, be a light to the world.[203] Its peacemaking ministry, indeed its hallmark, will lead its members to "work for the vindication of God's kingdom and justice" by identifying with the poor and downtrodden, healing the sick and wounded, freeing the slaves and imprisoned, feeding the hungry, and caring for the rejected and lonely. "Peacemakers are those who 'hunger and thirst to see right prevail' " (Mt. 5:6, NEB).[204]

This same emphasis appears in Yoder's writings with explicit relevance to the principalities and powers. Utilizing Berkhof's commentary and Ephesians 3:8-11, Yoder says that Paul's mission to the Gentiles, the uniting of Jew and Gentile in the peace of the cross, is the demonstration/announcement to the powers of God's manifold wisdom. This new way, this new creation, is a sign "to the powers that their unbroken dominion has come to an end."[205] The church engages in its mission to the powers by its very existence, by its liberation from the dominion of the powers. It "does not attack the powers; this Christ has done."[206] Living and proclaiming the victory of Christ, says Yoder, is

> a social, political, *structural* fact which constitutes a challenge to the Powers. . . . It is a declaration about the nature of the cosmos and the significance of history, within which both our conscientious participation and our conscientious objection find their authority and their promise.[207]

James Metzler and Robert Ramseyer, from the context of Mennonite missionary experience, write in *Mission and the Peace Witness* that peace and peacemaking are inherent in the church's gospel mandate in the Great Commission. Pacifism is not an appendage, but "the *way of life* to which [people] are . . . called" in the missionary message (1 Pet. 2:21; 3:9). "Shalom Is the Mission."[208]

Another aspect of the church's peace mission is to witness against specific evils. The ad hoc group from the historic peace churches working with the World Council of Churches' leadership said that the "Church must be seen as witness of Christ's victory, not just in individual life, but also in society" in order to fulfill "The Christian Vision of World Community." The church must witness against violence on three levels: personal, structural, and strategic.[209] Sjouke Voolstra, Dutch Mennonite pastor and biblical scholar, says that "the struggle for peace and justice in the world" is an indispensable part of any authentic peace understanding and witness.[210]

Yoder formulates a biblical and theological basis for *The Christian Witness to the State*. Since Christ's victory and lordship over the powers is an accomplished event (Col. 2:10, 15; 1 Cor. 15:20-28), the church is called to witness in accord with its own convictions in order to encourage the good and to restrain evil. The

church witnesses "to serve peace, to preserve the social cohesion in
which the leaven of the Gospel can build the church, and also
render the old aeon more tolerable."[211]

 c. The church is separate from the state, but subordinate to it
and called to witness to it.

The separation of church and state is rooted in the Radical
Reformation's belief in what Robert Friedmann calls "The Doctrine
of Two Worlds,"[212] or, as Anabaptist scholar Walter Klaassen puts it,
"the two kingdoms doctrine."[213] Klaassen, in his introduction to
seventeen primary sources on the subject, says:

> The kingdom of Christ was characterized by peace, forgiveness, non-
> violence, and patience. The kingdom of the world, or Satan, was strife,
> vengeance, anger, and the sword which kills. Government belonged to
> this kingdom of the world.[214]

After surveying the New Testament teachings on this subject,
Archie Penner, Mennonite Bible and religion teacher at Malone
College in Ohio, says:

> [The book of] Revelation breathes the air of complete separation
> between the Christian and the state. The reason is not far to seek. The
> Christian, the saint, is in the order of grace and the church is the
> bride of Jesus Christ. The state, as here pictured, is of the order of the
> "world" *(kosmos)*—human society outside of the order of grace, and
> standing in diametric opposition to God and Christ. This view of
> human society as outside of Christ and in opposition against Christ
> is essentially the concept of Jesus, John, and Paul. The concept finds
> its concrete expression in the moral meaning of the term "world."[215]

At the same time, the state is regarded as a servant (instru-
ment) of God's wrath; Christians, therefore, are called to subordination. Using Romans 13:1-7, 1 Timothy 2:1-4, and Titus 3:1-2, Penner says that the believer is called to submission and obedience,
conditioned however by readiness to do every good work. "It is not
absolute obedience which is enjoined. Rather, it is obedience which
is active when good is to be done."[216]

Yoder discusses Romans 13:1-7 in the context of his larger discussion of "revolutionary subordination." After noting that Romans
13 is not the sole or even central source for a New Testament view of
the state and that Romans 12—13 must be studied as a unit, he
proposes that Romans 13:1-7 instructs Christians to be subordinate to whatever structure of state sovereignty exists without giving a *particular* government (or government *per se*) the halo of

divine ordination ("ordain" is better translated "order"; i.e., God orders the powers); that subjection does not mean participation in the military or police service; that the government's function of bearing the sword "does not refer to the death penalty or to war"; and that

> the Christian who accepts his subjection to government retains his moral independence and judgment. The authority of government is not self-justifying. Whatever government exists is ordered by God; but the text does not say that whatever the government does or asks of its citizens is good.[217]

Yoder understands "attending" in verse 6 as a temporal participle: "the authorities are God's servants *when they attend* to this very thing," namely, rewarding the good and punishing the evil. Verses 3, 6, and 7 contain criteria for moral discrimination, thus indicating that Christian response to particular governments or government actions must be guided by moral discernment, allowing possibly for disobedience while remaining subject to punishment.[218] This voluntary subordination, exercising judgment in moral response, carries within it revolutionary and missionary power. By renouncing patterns of domination and by following the way of Jesus Christ (Phil. 2:5-11), the church's subordination becomes a concrete witness to the world. "We subject ourselves to government because it was in so doing that Jesus revealed and achieved God's victory."[219]

Recognizing and affirming Yoder's and C.E.B. Cranfield's studies on Romans 13:1-7, Sider calls for both subjection to government and

> a vigorous nonviolent offensive against, indeed active resistance to, governmental injustice. We should resist the evils promoted or perpetuated by governments.... We can engage in political lobbying, voter power, economic boycott, political demonstration, civil disobedience, tax refusal, even total noncooperation and still be subject to our government.[220]

(Variant A). Many nonresistant Christians would object to this emphasis, because it takes government (God's ordained leadership for the realm of evil) too seriously. In the judgment of such persons the church's task is to keep separate from such evil and not pretend to know how government should run its business. Some within this variant position object also to Yoder's emphasis on the lordship of Christ over the powers. Christ is head of the church, not the state.[221]

(Variant B). On the other hand, some pacifists do not emphasize the distinction between the entities of church and government as expressed above. They freely engage in government lobbying and will also hold political positions in government, seeking to extend pacifist principles into political policy and strategy.[222]

　5. Peace is the heart of the gospel.

　　a. Peace permeates the New Testament.

John Driver, Mennonite missionary, notes that the term "peace" occurs over a hundred times in the New Testament; it describes "the fundamental work of Jesus Christ" in his creation of the new community.[223] Macgregor includes eleven of these texts under "The Way of Peace" (Lk. 2:14; Jn. 14:27; Mt. 5:9; Jas. 3:18; Rom. 10:15; Eph. 6:15; 4:1-3; Heb. 12:14; Rom. 16:20; 2 Cor. 13:11; Phil. 4:7).[224] Marlin Miller observes that the New Testament frequently refers to God as the God of peace, Jesus as the Lord of peace, and the Holy Spirit as the Spirit of peace.[225]

Viewed against the background of the Old Testament meaning of shalom, which includes human well-being and social justice, peace in the Christian gospel is not merely a personalistic, inward feeling but a new reality of social, economic, and political consequence. The New Testament extends the meaning of shalom by Christ's unique historical achievement in making peace between two hostile groups, the Jews and the Gentiles through the reconciling power of the cross, thus overcoming the most fundamental societal division.[226]

In addition to Paul's use of the word, "peace" *(eirēnē)* occurs in Luke-Acts to denote the meaning of the gospel itself (see Is. 52:7 for the Old Testament background of this insight). In Luke 1:79; 2:14, 29, "peace" is used synonymously with "salvation"; in 10:5-6 it stands as the hallmark of the gospel; and in 19:38, 42 it functions as the key word for describing acceptance of Jesus himself. In Acts 7:26 "peace" describes an act of attempted reconciliation; in 9:31; 10:36; and 15:33 peace describes the new messianic community in which Samaritans and Gentiles are united with Jewish believers into one body of faith.[227]

　　b. Peace is rooted in eschatology.

Both Eller and Yoder emphasize the connection of peace to eschatology. Using Isaiah 41:22-23a; 42:9; 43:19a and 2 Corinthians 5:17, Eller argues that the Christian position is rooted in God's new order of life. The Bible "consistently . . . defines and describes peace in *eschatological* terms. It never speaks of peace without relating it to the activity of the horizonless God."[228] This perspective to peacemaking is rooted in crossbearing, witnessing to Christ's victory over evil, and trusting in God's final vindication of the peacemaker (Matt. 5:9). Eschatological peacemaking contains dimensions of faith and hope which secular peacemaking lacks; the two should not be confused.[229]

Using 1 John 3:1-3 as his text,[230] Yoder makes Christian hope foundational to peacemaking. Noting that hope was the theme for the 1954 WCC meeting in Evanston, Illinois, Yoder says:

> There is no significance to human effort and, strictly speaking, no history unless life can be seen in terms of ultimate goals. The *eschaton,* the "Last Thing," the End-Event imparts to life a meaningfulness which it would not otherwise have. . . .
>
> "Peace" is not an accurate description of what has generally happened to nonresistant Christians throughout history, nor of the way the conscientious objector is treated in most countries today. Nor does Christian pacifism guarantee a warless world. "Peace" describes the pacifist's hope, the goal in divine certainty which makes his position make sense; it does not describe the external appearance or the observable results of his behavior. This is what we mean by eschatology: a hope which, defying present frustration, defines a present position in terms of the unseen goal which gives it meaning.[231]

Yoder's exposition of this thesis appeals to numerous New Testament teachings and texts: the nonresistant disciple's separation from this world (1 Jn. 4:17); a willingness to bear the cross as Jesus' way of living in the old aeon (Mt. 10:38; Mk. 10:34ff.; Lk. 14:27); finding our human solidarity in Christ and his way to peace (Jn. 15:20; 2 Cor. 1:5; 4:10; Heb. 12:1-4; 1 Pet. 2:21f.; Rev. 12:11); God's lordship over history claimed for Yahweh/Jesus Christ (Is. 10; 1 Cor. 15:24); and the patient endurance of suffering believers who trust in the eventual triumph of Christ (Rev. 6:9-11; 13:10; 14:12; Heb. 11:1—12:4).[232]

Finally, Sider makes the pacifist position a central perspective to New Testament thought and authority:

> In every strand of NT literature and with reference to every kind of situation (whether family, church, state, or employment), the way of the cross applies. Jesus' cross, where He practiced what He had preached about love for one's enemies, becomes the Christian norm for every area of life. Only if one holds biblical authority so irrelevant that one can ignore explicit, regularly repeated scriptural teaching; only if one so disregards Christ's atonement that one rejects God's way of dealing with enemies; only then can one forsake the cross for the sword.[233]

Hermeneutical Commentary

Before I address the major issues in this debate, some comment on the opposing arguments is appropriate. First, it is important to remember that individual authors quoted in support of a particular point within a position may not agree with all aspects of the position as presented.

Second, picking up a hermeneutical concern in chapter 1, the arguments show unevenness in the use of moral and theological principles, a method contrasted to proof-texting. Each of the positions shows use of both moral-theological principles and specific verses for support. The biblical case for revolution and liberation, however, is most distinctive in its use of basic theological emphases. But it should be noted that liberation theologians did not use some major biblical emphases, such as the people's trust in Yahweh's defense or Jesus' refusal of violent options in his messiahship.

Third, does any position as presented miss important aspects of the biblical evidence? (Here the fault may lie with the presentation as well as with position.) Strikingly, the positions allowing for war or violence screen out a considerable portion of the New Testament theology employed by the pacifists. The pacifists, however, never squarely address the theological problem of a warrior God, although both Eller's and Lind's contributions infer that God's actions as warrior belong to the divine prerogative of judgment and vengeance against evil. And the liberationists tread softly over the strong nonviolent imperatives of Jesus' message and ministry. On the other hand, the liberationists pick up most adequately the prophetic and "relationally real" dimensions of Jesus' life and teaching.

The purpose here is not to "call" one position correct and the others wrong but to underscore again the points developed at the ends of chapters 1 and 2. Both one's political-economic-social perspective and one's religious tradition play powerful roles in determining how one reads the Bible. David Lochhead's booklet on *The Liberation of the Bible* helpfully addresses this issue. Lochhead shows how "right-wing" interpretation stresses biblical teaching on authority and patriotism, puts law over liberation in the Exodus narratives, and applies much of the Bible individually. "Liberal" interpretation, he says, values liberty and equality, sees in the Bible the progress of humanity toward liberal ideals, and uses the Exodus narratives to support freedom guaranteed by democratic institutions. The "radical" interpretation accents justice and the liberation of the oppressed.[234]

While Lochhead calls for the liberation of the Bible from ideological captivity through more honest methods of interpreting, he also argues that no one can be totally free of ideological commitment.[235] This awareness is an important part of biblical interpretation.

New Major Issues Addressed

The problem most apparent in this topic lies in the opposing testimony of the Old and New Testaments. On the surface of the biblical text the New Testament appears pacifist but the Old Testament condones war. Hence the continuity and discontinuity of the Testaments becomes a major issue.

But is the issue even that simple? Pacifists also make a case for their position from the Old Testament, and those arguing for Christian support of war also make a case for their position from the New Testament. In these instances both claim to explain the *true* meaning of the text in the face of opposing understandings. These differing appeals to Scripture raise a second hermeneutical consideration which urgently beckons our attention, namely, the unity and diversity of viewpoint found within the biblical text, even within each Testament.

With these two issues and previous learnings in focus, a third question emerges: what principles guide intracanonical dialogue and critique? Does the canonical dialogue itself provide patterns for interpretation which in turn reflect particular insights into the nature of biblical authority? And then a fourth issue emerges: can the biblical teaching be applied directly to societal structures today, especially politics? Niebuhr, Ramsey, and Yoder represent different answers to this problem.

We now address these four major issues:

1. The different understandings of the relationship between the Old and New Testaments function crucially in the hermeneutical conflict between the traditional positions of both A and B and the nonresistant/pacifist positions. The respective views of the testamental relationship may even be regarded as presuppositions to the construction of each position.

Arthur Holmes has recently identified this problem as one of two key issues which determines the difference between the Anabaptist (pacifist) and Reformed-Lutheran-Catholic (just war) positions. He says:

Generally, the Christian pacifist appeals to the New, which in his view takes us beyond the precept and example of the Old to a law of love. The just war theorist, however, is apt to see the law of love in the Old as well as the New, so that the New fulfills, reinforces and interprets the Old rather than superseding it. The law of love is a reaffirmation of the underlying spirit of the Old Testament Law, at one with the spirit of justice rather than in conflict with it. Love as well as justice requires action to protect the innocent and to repel and deter aggression.[236]

Similarly, G. E. Wright regards the Old Testament as more relevant than the New to the social and political realities of life in this world.[237]

While acknowledging some moral progression in the Testaments, especially regarding divorce and polygamy, Gordon Clark wrote in 1955 that "this advance ... has little bearing on the morality of war; God never commanded polygamy ... but he did command wars."[238] The principle to follow, he says, is "that we must preserve from the Old Testament all that is not specifically abrogated in the New."[239] Loraine Boettner complements Clark's view by calling attention to the New Testament's silence on war, because apparently, he says, "the Old Testament teaching was sufficiently explicit and did not call for any addition or modification."[240]

On the other side, pacifists regard the testamental relationship differently. Richard C. Detweiler, Mennonite theologian and president of Eastern Mennonite College in Virginia, says the Anabaptist pacifist view of Scripture holds "that the coming of Christ has brought about a new situation." This puts "the Christian's relation to civil government ... now under the New Testament ethic which supersedes that of the Old Testament."[241] Myron Augsburger describes the relationship as "the process of God's unfolding revelation" and says that "some practices in the Old Testament ... were sub-Christian."[242] Hence we must see, says Jacob Enz, how "the New Testament church under the Lordship of Christ was converting" the Old Testament's "shockingly nationalistic poetry ... into militant hymns of peace." But this is no way rejects the Old Testament; while the New Testament turns its "Battle Songs into Hymns of Peace," we must also see the roots of the pacifist ethic in the Old Testament.[243]

After surveying the leading contemporary scholarly Christian views of war in the Old Testament and classifying them into one of three categories of emphasis (divine sovereignty, preparatory, OT as failure), Waldemar Janzen joins those who understand the Old Testament as preparatory for the New on this issue: "I see the roots of pacifism, though not pacifism, in the Old Testament."[244] In addition to asking the reader of the Old Testament to observe how it moved toward what was to come later (the New Testament), John H. Yoder asks the reader to consider also how Israel's warfare differed from what went *before* or prevailed at that time.[245] This approach leads Millard Lind to declare that Israel's break and distance from the Near Eastern views of power is greater than the differences that exist between the two Testaments. Hence the Old Testament, when viewed against the ancient Near Eastern background, points toward the New Testament and away from the pagan views of power and warfare.[246]

Vernard Eller even speaks of a "unified argument regarding war and peace" in both Testaments and shows how God as warrior is present in both Testaments, battling against evil and freeing humanity from bondage.[247] Similarly, Guy Hershberger says:

> The entire Scriptures correctly interpreted will show the Old and New Testaments to agree that the way of peace is God's way for His people at all times; that war and bloodshed were never intended to have a place in human conduct.[248]

One of the most insightful contributions to this problem of the relation between the Testaments comes from the pen of the Anabaptist Pilgram Marpeck. Writing extensively on this matter in the sixteenth-century Reformation context, Marpeck emphasized the time distinction between the Testaments, using the terms "yesterday and today" and *"Ordnung Gottes."* Because genuine historical difference exists between the Testaments, one cannot assign to one period what belongs to the other; the different circumstances in different times make a real difference. Nor can the difference be explained by change in God. The problem is solved, rather, by keeping in view the categorical difference between Creator and creature. God is not bound to time and space, but humanity is. When God's dealings with humanity are under discussion, one cannot ignore the different circumstances in the different time periods. All creatures are bound and limited by time and place; they can perceive morality only within the restrictions of time and place.[249]

The difference between the Testaments, therefore, must be attributed not to an essential change in God's moral will (contra Marcion), but to the essential historical difference between Old and New Testament times and places. In Old Testament time the incarnation had not yet happened; Christ had not yet died for humanity's sin; and Christ's resurrection proclaiming triumph over all foes (including the principalities and powers) had not yet taken place. Thus the historical time had not yet come when it was possible for the new humanity in Christ to exist, a people who would live according to the way of Jesus. The historical events that occurred in the New Testament time and place made, and make, a difference in salvation and morality. Marpeck used the contrasts of "summer and winter," "day and night," and "figure and essence" *(Figur/Wesen)* to describe this actual, real difference.[250]

Marpeck also described the continuity between the Testaments, using the words "preparation" and "promise." While Marpeck, following Luther, recognized a negative function in the Old Testament's preparation for the New ("Christ is the great physician who heals those who through the law have been 'crushed, pierced, and broken'—*zerschlagen, zerschnitten,* and *zerbrochen*"), the Old Testament should be seen also in a positive preparatory role, God's first grace.[251] God called a people out of paganism into covenant community; redeemed them from oppression; gave them the Torah to live by; taught them the way of holiness, steadfast love, and forgiveness even when they were disobedient and rebellious; and planted within them the messianic hope. Hence the Old Testament should be viewed as the *promise* of what was to come in fuller measure in the New. Promise and fulfillment best describe the relationship.[252]

In the cultivated soil of God-consciousness of the Old Testament, God gave promises pointing toward the time of a more perfect disclosure of divine will, a historical event that could create and shape a more faithful people of God. The promise of a new future (Is. 43:19) was fulfilled when God came to us in a Son (Heb. 1:2). With, by, and in Jesus, God's will is most perfectly disclosed; in the community that seeks to follow Jesus, God's way is most perfectly known and lived. Jesus, as we know him in the Gospels, functions as the ultimate source of hermeneutical authority. All other Scripture must be seen through these Gospel lenses of biblical authority.

2. The second issue, the diversity of viewpoint within the biblical record, is a dimension of the same problem. Here we set aside for the moment, however, the testamental contrast and ask how it is possible for a people to testify to such diverse views of the same God. Is it possible for the Bible, as God's inspired revelation, to take opposing views on the same subject—to say "yes" to war in some texts and "no" to war in others? By acknowledging that the Bible gives conflicting signals on this topic, is not God made to be fickle, relative, and nonauthoritative?

The positions allowing for war and those forbidding war for Christians offer two basically different solutions to this problem. The positions allowing war regard the two portraits as somehow compatible: at both the level of God's character and that of the people's morality, warfare is an indispensable part of God's holiness and sovereignty. God uses war and violent revolutions to accomplish his purpose, and calls his people, therefore, to participate in these dramatic acts of divine purpose. The pacifist teachings in the Bible, therefore, are true but only partial expressions of God's nature and moral prescription for humanity. The larger theological and ethical picture includes God the warrior and the moral responsibility of the covenant people to participate in God's cause. The strong pacifist strand of teaching, even in the New Testament, is in some way bracketed within the larger theological and moral perception.

An attractive hermeneutical gain of this approach lies in its resolution of the apparent contradictions within the biblical text. The pacifist element is explained as one aspect of the larger truth. Hence in practical expression the pacifist ethic may be applied to personal spheres of life while the nonpacifist is used for the social (Carl Henry). Or the pacifist ethic may be applied to kingdom citizenry while the nonpacifist is applied to national citizenry (Peter Craigie). Or the pacifist ethic lacks appropriateness for living within the realities of this yet not fully redeemed world (Wright, Niebuhr, and liberation thought). In any case, these writers affirm both the pacifist and nonpacifist dimensions of the Bible, providing a hermeneutic which accepts the whole Bible as authoritative. At the same time, they produce an overall rationally conceptual, even propositional (if desired), unity in biblical revelation on this point. The final punch of this argument, hermeneutically, is that it can be used by those who hold a most theologically reflective interpretation of moral obligation to participate in war and also by those who make a very simplistic appeal to the Bible (everything must be equally authoritative) to substantiate Christian support of war.

In contrast, the pacifist solution to the problem regards the two portraits to be incompatible, at least to some degree. It holds that the kingship and military experiences of Israel are already under critique in the Old Testament and that a definitive rejection of this "like the nations" conduct is revealed authoritatively in Jesus Christ. It requires rethinking the nature of biblical revelation, biblical authority and the authority of the community as it interprets Scripture. Although the point has never been explicitly recognized in contemporary pacifist literature, some aspects of the historical-critical method of interpreting Scripture are essential to the pacifist position. Pilgrim Marpeck's discussion of the finality of the New Testament's ethical mandate over that of the Old, revolutionary in its sixteenth-century setting, certainly shows aspects of the historical-critical method as it developed several centuries later.[253] The striking difference, however, is that the later historical-critical endeavors developed not from commitment to radical discipleship but from rationalistic presuppositions; hence apparent contradictions in the biblical text were cited as evidence against its authority.

But the Anabaptist biblical criticism was ethically revolutionary. It was guided not primarily by rationalistic logic, but by such fervent eschatological hope and disciplined obedience to biblical teaching that the pacifist teaching of Jesus seemed entirely appropriate for all realms of life in this world. They saw the reborn, transnational peoplehood as God's new creation; hence *only* the kingdom ethic was appropriate for their whole life.

Two factors then muted the hermeneutical problem regarding warfare. First, the Anabaptists' fervent commitment to the kingdom vision gave existential validity to the pacifist ethic; and second, they developed a hermeneutic which forged a new understanding of biblical authority.

3. What view of biblical authority undergirds then the positions of this study?

Writers representing traditional position A tend to make the fundamentalist view of Scripture a prerequisite for discussion of the matter.[254] Boettner prefaces his discussion of the biblical texts by saying:

> In all matters of controversy among Christians the Scriptures are accepted as the highest court of appeal. Historically they have been the common authority of Christendom. We believe that they "are given by inspiration of God, to be the rule of faith and practice"; that they contain one harmonious, consistent, and sufficiently complete system of doctrine.[255]

Similarly, Richard Taylor says:

> Now I reject out of hand the liberal view that the Old Testament writers were mistaken in thus ascribing these wars to the command of God. If any would discount these records as unreliable traditions which slanderously misrepresent God—let him do so, but between him and me there is no basis for a helpful meeting of minds.[256]

Positions B and C, however, represent quite different views of Scripture from position A. The writers of positions B and C employ freely not only the historical-critical method but also argue that considerations from beyond the text must guide one's ethical thought on this matter (see hermeneutical issue 4 below and alternative 6 in "The Use of the Bible for Social Issues" in chapter 5).

Most pacifist writers mentioned above adhere strongly to the authority of the Bible. Hershberger says that his position of nonresistance describes "the faith and life of those who accept the Scriptures as the revealed will of God, and who cannot have any part in warfare because they believe the Bible forbids it."[257]

The Mennonite Church statement in the pacifist brief to the "Discussions on War/Peace Issues Between Friends, Mennonites, Brethren and European Churches" expresses its scriptural basis as follows:

> Holding firmly to the authority of God's revelation of his nature and will as it is found in the Holy Scriptures both in the spirit, life, and redemptive work of Christ, and in the direct teachings of Jesus and the Apostles, and believing that war is altogether contrary to this revelation, Mennonites hold that all war is sin, as is all manner of carnal strife, and that it is wrong in both spirit and method.[258]

Yoder cites "biblical grounds" for objecting to war;[259] Ronald Sider says that only if one regards biblical authority irrelevant can one forsake the cross for the sword;[260] and Eller invites his reader to "let the Bible speak its piece."[261] Beyond these specific statements, the number of full-length monographs written by pacifists to ascertain biblical perspectives on this topic is important evidence of their seriousness on this point (Enz, Lind, Macgregor, Ferguson, Rutenber, Trocmé, Yoder, Eller, Topel, McSorley, Lasserre, Keeney— all cited above).

Hence, while the writers in traditional position A and the pacifist writers affirm the authority of the Bible, they interpret the Bible quite differently. The real question is: in what way is the Bible authoritative? Whereas writers in traditional position A tend to equate authority with rational coherence at the propositional and logical level (a kind of "flat Bible" view), the pacifists link authority to both the witness of Scripture to Christ (in this way it is divine Word and revelation) and then to the biblical sanctions upon belief and behavior. As noted above, the distinction between historical time periods was quite fundamental to the Anabaptist view of Scripture. Without this distinction, so crucial to Marpeck's view, the case for pacifism gains little hermeneutical support. Biblically-based pacifism identifies Jesus and the New Testament as the supreme̓authority for ethical and theological understandings. This perception then functions as the criterion for distinguishing between different emphases present in the Old Testament.[262]

Revelation in history, an axiom of biblical theology informed by the historical-critical method, stands foundational to any pacifist view of biblical authority. In biblical revelation God acts and speaks within history, within the limitations of a people's experience—geographically (Palestine and outward), linguistically (Hebrew and Greek), culturally (from the pagan background of the ancient Near East and the Greco-Roman world), and religiously (the fight against Baalism together with the faithfulness and apostasy of the people). The pacifist arguments take serious account of these factors, whether in Marpeck, Lind, Yoder, Lasserre, or McSorley.

The political and economic experience of the people is also part of God's revelation in history, as Lind's discussions on the rise of kingship and of the city-state in Israel point out. Significantly, Israel's great breakthrough of new self-understanding in Deutero-Isaiah's call to be a suffering servant came when Israel was politically exiled. Similarly, the teaching of Jesus belongs to the kingdom of God, not to Palestinian or Roman political and economic structures. While revelation in history suffers limitation from history it also creates a new history, a new economics, and a new politics; hence *this view of biblical authority requires an understanding of divine revelation as dynamically interacting with history and culture* (more will be said on this in chapter 4).[263]

4. A fourth hermeneutical issue raised by this case dispute is the problem of applying Jesus' ethic directly to all spheres of life, especially politics. This problem has several dimensions. First, on the hermeneutical level the interpreter must consider the extent and significance of the difference between the world of the text and the world of the interpreter. Second, this issue imposes a methodological problem upon Christian ethics: does one consider Christian ethics to be applicable only to some people (believers) or only to some spheres of life? And third, a problem arises for moral ontology: is it possible to allow dichotomy in the nature of morality and/or in moral accountability (i.e., some people stand under the sanction of a moral imperative but others do not)? While these issues take us beyond the scope of this study, some comments are essential since these factors affect the use of the Bible on this issue.

Regarding the extent and significance of difference (and

distance) between the worlds of the text and the interpreter, it is in my judgment not only essential but inevitable that this be acknowledged in interpretation. The pro-slavery argument that slavery in Israel and slavery in the United States are the same is not convincing. One need only ask: did the Christians in both systems have the same degree of responsibility for the institution of slavery? Further, did U.S. slavery practice the seventh-year release and institutionalize protection for fugitive slaves? Similarly, can any modern war be equated with Israel's wars? Or, can any war in history be equated with threatening nuclear war? Nor can the different Christian attitudes toward war in the first and twelfth centuries be glossed over! Church history, theological developments, and paradigmatic changes in societal structure must all be considered for their effect upon the hermeneutical task. The situation of the interpreter does and must affect the application of biblical teaching.

But, the key question is whether we use the different, new situation *to excuse us* from the demands of the Christian ethic (cf. Mk. 7:9-13) or whether we assess the new situation for the purpose of applying as fully as possible the moral intention of the biblical teaching.[264] Jesus' understanding of the significance of the new situation is clear in this regard: "You have heard that it was said, but I say ..." (Mt. 5:21-48).

In my judgment, John Ferguson is correct in evaluating the church's record on the war issue as one of forsaking the "fundamental principles" and structuring its "ethic around entirely different principles." This has been true not only in the just war theory. In Niebuhrian thought also, the concern for preserving democracy, for making sure the "better nation" wins, and condoning war as the "lesser evil" to tyranny go far beyond, and away from, New Testament ethics.[265] Many of the same nonbiblical assumptions guiding Niebuhr's thought are at work also in the reasoning of liberation hermeneutics. Even though liberation thought appeals to basic biblical theological emphases, the condoning of violence to achieve those ends brings in nonbiblical values through the door of social analysis and national self-interest. This has the effect of turning Jesus' statement of fact about the sinfulness of history—there will be wars and rumors of wars until the end comes—into a word of approval. But the context of this statement (Mk. 13:7) is clearly the preparation of his disciples for persecution and suffering as they remain faithful in the sinful world until the end comes; the statement is not a justification of war, and certainly not approval for his disciples to participate in war.

At this point, the second dimension of this hermeneutical issue comes into focus. It is clear that the New Testament addresses Jesus' ethics to believers. It is clear also that the believers are to be a light to the world. But what then is the next step by which the church relates its ethics to the larger society? The difficulty of this matter has been well illustrated in the recent writings of Martin Hengel, New Testament professor at Tübingen University. In his excellent books on Jesus' teaching on violence, set within the revolutionary ferment of first-century Zealotry,[266] Hengel says that Jesus' teaching, contrasting sharply to that of the Zealots, "demanded love of enemies and renunciation of violence."[267] This is "the heart of the proclamation of Jesus." Jesus' way "is the way of nonviolence (Gewaltlosigkeit), of personal appeal, directed primarily to the conscience of the individual, the way of patient persuasion and concrete assistance in life."[268] This is revolutionary, says Hengel, only if it is clearly seen as repudiating all violence, whether in "just war" or "just revolution" guise.[269]

Ten years later, in the context of the German Peace Movement's appeal to the Sermon on the Mount for its basis of ethical action, Hengel writes sharply against this use of Jesus' teaching: Jesus' ethic cannot be used for politics; it is "Das Ende Aller Politik"; it calls Christians to be "Die Stadt auf dem Berge" (the city on the mountain).[270] Beyond this point, Hengel gives only two clues for direction: that God forgives our inevitable falling short of the harsh and rugged ethic of Jesus, and that by reflecting upon the hard words of Jesus and his way to the cross we might find ways by which indirect positive impulses extend to society, also for politics ("auch für politisches Handeln").[271]

Hengel's contribution lacks two elements essential to the nonresistant/pacifist position described in this chapter: the choice to be faithful to the ethic of God's people (the church) in the face of nationally claimed obligations; and some position on the specific forms of the church's witness to the powers—government as well as other powers in society, such as business and education. By not accepting "hermeneutical escapes" from the Sermon on the Mount's hard teachings and in warning against a direct use of the sermon's ethics for politics, Hengel's work, however, helpfully focuses the issue under discussion. While I accept Yoder's and Sider's emphasis on the Christian's and church's witness to the powers, numerous nonresistant/pacifist Christians object to all attempts to influence politics; others promote active involvement in government in order to express as much as possible pacifist principles in politics. (See

"The Use of the Bible for Social Issues" in chapter 5 for further discussion of this point.)

The third dimension of the hermeneutical issue under
consideration (going clearly beyond the scope of this work) arises
when dichotomy between church and world enters the debate: does
God have two patterns of morality—one for the church and one for
the state? Those who answer "yes" (e.g., the pacifist "variant a" view of
war in the Old Testament) are left with a difficult problem of
explaining the nature of morality and the moral nature of God.
Hence most pacifists hold that such dichotomy results not from
God or the nature of moral ontology but from two patterns of
response, belief and unbelief, to God's moral purpose for humanity.
This dichotomy is therefore temporal, and will be resolved eschatologically, when "the kingdom of the world has become the
kingdom of our Lord and of his Christ" (Rev. 11:15).

Those positions allowing for Christian participation in war
also face the problem of a moral dichotomy in their attempted distinction between personal and social ethics: the theory of double obligation (kingdom and nation) or the two-sided existence of the
Christian, as saint and sinner (Lutheran theology). My purpose
here is not to attempt to resolve this problem, but to describe how it
becomes entangled in the hermeneutical agenda of this case issue.

The problem of war then, like the other topics of this study,
raises basic hermeneutical issues. It requires Christians to think
critically about the relationship between the Testaments, the problem of diversity within the canon, the question of biblical authority,
and the praxis dimension of Jesus' ethics—how are they lived out
in life and expressed in human history?

Chapter 4

THE BIBLE AND WOMEN
Male and Female Role Relationships

With this issue we come to a contemporary storm center in biblical interpretation. Does the Bible teach a specific hierarchy and prescribed roles for men and women? Or is the Bible itself a liberating resource for role-oppressed women and men? Does Scripture command women to be veiled and silent in public worship, thus excluding them from leadership ministry, especially ordination? Or does Scripture welcome and even commend women in an unrestricted variety of Christian ministries dependent upon gifts and calling?

On March 24, 1979, U.S. President Jimmy Carter appealed to Christ, not Paul, as the biblical basis for his support of the Equal Rights Amendment. At a town hall meeting in Elk City, Oklahoma, Carter said:

> I think if one reads different parts of the Bible you can find a good argument either way.... I know that Paul felt very strongly that there ought to be a sharp distinction between men and women and women's role ought to be minimal. But I have a feeling that Christ meant for all of us to be treated equally, and he demonstrated this in many ways.[1]

Is the problem resolved simply by choosing between Paul and Jesus (not to mention the choice between Carter and the pope)? Didn't Jesus appoint only male apostles and entrust the official leadership of the kingdom movement only to men? Conversely, wasn't it Paul who said "in Christ there is neither male nor female"? While Carter's hermeneutical hunch may be inadequate, his perception that the Bible may be used to argue either for or against women's liberation hits the nail on the head. Indeed, it is difficult to know what the Bible says and means on the role of women in relation to men and on leadership responsibilities in the church. Because the issue is undergoing intense contemporary debate, I will limit my citations to literature of the last several decades.[2]

While writers on this issue—even among those representing the same basic position—show differing emphases, the primary points at which the two opposing views differ most clearly lie in what I call "hierarchical" and "liberationist" relationships. Terms such as equality, partnership, and complementarity may be used in specific senses by both positions. The essential difference hinges upon whether Scripture teaches clearly and normatively a hierarchical relation of men over women or whether it supports the liberation of both males and females from such hierarchical patterns of relationship.

The three emphases on which the hierarchical and liberationist interpreters diverge are:

Hierarchical	**Liberationist**
1. Women are expected to be subordinate to men—in the home, church, and society.	1. Men and women are called to mutuality in relationship. Subordination for women *because they are women* falls short of the highest biblical ethic.
2. Especially in the home, husbands are to exercise headship over wives, with roles prescribed in accord with this pattern.	2. Patterns of leadership and prescribed social roles are not mandated by the biblical text. Abilities, needs, and agreements should determine leadership and roles.
3. Within the church, women are restricted from the preaching ministry and from teaching men. Other forms of leadership are to be exercised under the authority and leadership of men.	3. The gifts of women and men alike should determine who will fill various leadership roles. Women are free to participate in all the leadership ministries of the church.

These alternative positions are supported by different understandings of various biblical texts. In order to demonstrate how each position interprets the crucial texts, I cite or summarize the pertinent commentary for each position on these key texts. This will enable the reader to examine more carefully just how the biblical text is used and will also assist the reader in forming or testing his/her own understanding on this issue.

The Genesis Narratives

Genesis 1:26-27; 5:1

Hierarchical Interpreters Speak:

While the hierarchical interpreters writing in the fifties through the seventies (Ryrie, Zerbst, and Knight) do not comment directly on this text, Stephen Clark, responding to the extensive liberationist commentary, says that this passage does not speak to the topic:

> The passage is not concerned with differences between men and women.... Those who try to make the case that Genesis 1 is uphold-ing a view of man and woman that does not involve any differentia-tion in roles or subordination of woman to man are reading some-thing into the passage that is not there.[3]

Liberationist Interpreters Speak:

Liberationist interpreters emphasize the poetic parallelism between the phrases "male and female" and "the image of God."

1. Paul Jewett, after surveying different understandings of "imago Dei," accepts and paraphrases Karl Barth's exegetical com-ments on this text:

> ... now comes what may be called the first great surprise of the Bi-ble.... Genesis 1:27b ("male and female he created them") is an ex-position of 1:27a ("in the image of God created he him").... God created Man male and female. The primal form of humanity, then, is the fellowship of man and woman.[4]

To be "in the divine image" involves then "the double obligation to live as man *or* woman and as man *and* woman."[5] Describing the male-female relationship as partnership, Jewett says that Genesis 1 contains no hint of male supremacy.

2. Letha Scanzoni and Nancy Hardesty comment similarly:

> What does it mean to say that male and female are created in the image and likeness of God?...

We believe that the image of God is not only rationality but "relationality."...

Sexual differentiation does not dictate social roles. Scripture speaks of no "separate spheres" or "different functions." Both sexes were created with the biological and psychological capability for parenthood and both were also given what theologians call the "cultural mandate." Agriculture, animal husbandry, education, industry, government, commerce, the arts—every human being is equally responsible under God for all aspects of life on this earth.[6]

3. A task force of the World Council of Churches states:

Genesis, chapter 1, describes God's creative act in entrusting dominion over the creation not to man in the singular, but in the plural. The plural is used in verse 26b, even before the mention of "male and female" in verse 27. Note also that their common mission is primarily to rule (v. 26b and 28b), while their fruitfulness ... is described as God's blessing upon them.... [This fruitfulness] is placed under ... joint authority which characterizes the mission of man and woman.[7]

4. Perry Yoder comments similarly, noting that "Adam" should be translated "humanity" since both sexes are included. A plural verb is used in "let *them* have dominion" (verse 26), and a plural pronoun occurs in "male and female he created them" (verse 27). Further, both sexes share in the call to dominion; neither is given priority over the other and neither is more godlike. The fact that both are created in God's image bestows upon humanity inestimable worth.[8]

5. Phyllis Trible contributes a structural analysis of the Hebrew poetry. The phrase "in his image" of line one occurs in inverted order in line two:

a   b   c
and created God humankind in his image,
c'   b'   a'
in the image of God created he him.

In line three then, "male and female" replaces "in the image":

in the image of God created he him
male and female created he them

Trible says, "Clearly, 'male and female' correspond structurally to the 'image of God,' and this formal parallelism indicates a semantic correspondence."[9]

From a similar analysis of Genesis 5:1, Trible draws four

points of insight: (1) *hā'ādām* (humanity) is not one creature but two, male and female; (2) "male and female are not opposite but rather harmonious sexes"; (3) such "sexual differentiation does not mean hierarchy but rather equality"; and (4) in not delineating "sexual relationships, roles, characteristics, attitudes, or emotions," the text allows "freedom in the interpretation of male and female." While designating two responsibilities for humanity, procreation (1:28a) and dominion over the earth (1:26, 28b), the text "does not differentiate between the sexes in assigning this work."[10] Trible then notes that the metaphor "image of God" is the most basic way to "know humankind in its fullness, 'male and female.' "[11]

Genesis 2:18-25

The uses of this text by hierarchical and liberationist writers are also strikingly different.

Hierarchical Interpreters Speak:

1. Hierarchical interpreters generally refer to Genesis 1 and 2 as a unit, implying that what is said for Genesis 2 counts also for Genesis 1.[12] Discussion of Genesis 2 often occurs in the context of explaining 1 Corinthians 11 and 1 Timothy 2. Charles Ryrie states, "It is important to notice that the principle of silence is linked to the principles of subjection and difference between the sexes and grounded in the Genesis account of creation and the fall."[13]

2. George Knight III concurs:

> [1 Corinthians 11:9] affirms that man was not created for woman, but woman for man. This furnishes the scriptural basis for Paul's affirmation in verse 3 that the man is the head of the woman. He is saying in effect that if one human being is created to be the helper of another human being, the one who receives such a helper has certain authority over the helper. It is said in opposition to this that because sometimes in the Old Testament God is called man's "helper," . . . this argument cannot be valid. Cannot a word, however, have a different nuance when applied to God than it does when applied to humans? Certainly a different nuance or connotation of a word does not nullify the apostolic exegesis and application.[14]

3. Stephen Clark comments extensively on Genesis 2. He cites three reasons why the partnership between man and woman should be understood to include subordination of woman: (1) "Man is the center of the narrative"; (2) "it is the man who is called 'Man' or 'human' and not the woman," thus designating him as representative head of the human race; and (3) man is created first, giving him as "firstborn" a natural precedence by birth.[15] Clark also

notes other indications of woman's subordination: the man names the animals; the man also names the woman;[16] God holds the man accountable for the transgression, before and after the curse (3:9, 22); and the man gives the woman a new name (3:20).[17]

Further, Clark says, "According to Paul, woman's subordination to man is grounded in man's being created first" (1 Tim. 2:12-13; 1 Cor. 11:8-9).[18] But this subordination is a very specific kind, one "that makes one person out of two." In their oneness, woman is a helper, partner, and complement to man, the head in the relationship.[19]

Liberationist Interpreters Speak:

Various writers comment perceptively on Genesis 2:

1. The Old Testament use of the word "helper" (Hebrew, *ēzer*) does not support the notion of inferiority or subordination:

> The Hebrew word used for helper, *ēzer* is found 21 times in the Old Testament. It is used to designate Yahweh (in 9 different places). In 16 cases the word indicates a superior who "assists" us. In the other 5 verses it has no hierarchical sense.... If the word *ēzer* is to be interpreted as "an assistant of inferior status," this would contradict its constant use in the Old Testament *(WCC on Women)*.[20]

2. The other half of the King James word, "meet" in "helpmeet," comes from the Hebrew word *nēged*. The Old English word "meet" means "fit" or "suitable." The Hebrew supports this meaning:

> *Nēged* is a preposition meaning "before," "in the presence of...." "Suitable," "corresponding to," or "adequate" to meet all man's needs for physical, intellectual, and social communion might be better translations for the Old English "meet" [Scanzoni-Hardesty].[21]

3. Perry Yoder calls attention to the literary structure of this narrative, indicating that in Genesis 2 as in Genesis 1 the most important thing is created last. In Genesis 2, therefore, the narrative moves to its climax in the creation of woman, reserving for her the place of importance in the literary structure of the narrative.

4. Yoder also notes that the formula "bone of my bone" and "flesh of my flesh" binds man and woman together in both might (bone) and frailty (flesh). This formula—together with verse 24, in which man leaves father and mother and cleaves to his wife—emphasizes the interdependence of male and female.

5. Further, sexual differentiation begins only after the com-

panion is created, since *adam* simply denotes that taken from the ground *(adamah)*; *ish* (man) and *ishah* (woman) denote male and female. When the woman is created, *adam* becomes bisexual and at this point experiences humanization and socialization.[22]

6. Phyllis Trible calls attention to the difference between verses 19 and 23. In verse 19 the verb "call" is joined to a proper name to denote the naming of another person or thing, thus extending authority to one over the other. It is used twice in verse 19 and once in 20 when *adam*, the earth creature, names the animals. Verse 23, however, uses only the verb "call"; the verb lacks a proper noun object and thus is not to be understood to mean "name."

> Hence, in calling the woman, the man is not establishing power over her but rejoicing in their mutuality.

> The word *woman ('issa)* demonstrates further that the issue is not the naming of the female but rather the recognition of sexuality. *'Issa* itself is not a name; it is a common noun, not a proper noun. . . . Thus the creature's poem does not determine who the woman is, but rather delights in what God has already done in creating sexuality.[23]

7. Paul Jewett points out that 2:24 does not mesh with the practice of Jewish patriarchy, in which the husband *does not leave* mother and father. This divergence from the practice of the community which gave us the narrative is significant in the way it affirms "that a husband and wife are bound by stronger ties than parents to children." Jewett concludes:

> The argument, then, that the woman should be subject to the man as her head because, according to Genesis 2, she was created from the man, is not without its refutation in the sequel to [the] very creation narrative on which it is traditionally based.[24]

Genesis 3:16

Hierarchical Interpreters Speak:

1. In commenting on 1 Timothy 2, Fritz Zerbst interprets Genesis 3:16:

> While Adam was the first to be created, Eve was the first to be deceived; and, although Adam also became guilty, Genesis 3:16 indicates definitely that the Fall did not invalidate the regulations ordained in creation with regard to man-woman relationships. With regard to the difference in position of man and woman prior to and after the Fall, Calvin states "that now [after the Fall] the subjection is less 'free' than it had been prior" [to the Fall]. . . . The significant feature of the

Timothy passage is its appeal not only to Gen. 2, but also to Gen. 3, as a basis for its directives. These two passages in Genesis must, in our estimation, be embraced in the common view.[25]

2. George Knight argues that this order of man's rule over woman is not based on the fall and the curse alone, but on the order of creation and the fall together.[26]

3. Stephen Clark holds that the fall and curse introduce a "dominating form of subordination" into the previous partnership type of leadership/subordination.[27]

Liberationist Interpreters Speak:

Liberationist writers argue that Genesis 3:16 shows male domination to be rooted in the fall and the curse.

1. Noting that Genesis 3 declares that *"Man is a sinner"* in revolt against God, Paul Jewett says the phrase "man shall rule over woman" *describes*—"it does not *prescribe*; it protests; it does not condone." This tyranny of man over woman is a perversion of his humanity.[28]

2. Phyllis Trible points out that within the context of the fall, "the man names his wife's name Eve (v. 20) thereby asserting his rule over her."[29]

3. Perry Yoder comments:

... while chapter 3 serves as an explanation for the less than ideal state of affairs that may now exist, it does not condone or pardon it. On the contrary, concessions or inadequate realizations of God's will in terms of creation are to be challenged.[30]

Women in Old Testament History

Hierarchical Interpreters Speak:

1. Ryrie uses the word "paradox" to describe the circumstances of women in Old Testament Israel. It is a "paradoxical situation of subordination and dignity." Hence:

The major contribution of Jewish women was in their service in the home. Although their legal rights were practically non-existent, they were accorded a place of honor in carrying out the privileges of motherhood. The general principle which applied to the status of women in Judaism was, "The King's daughter within the palace is all glorious, but not outside of it."[31]

2. Zerbst regards "equality of sexes" as a pagan alternative to

God's design for Israel but observes that within Israel the oppression of women occurred as a result of deterioration into legalism. Zerbst says:

> The demand for equality of the sexes with respect to position and
> rights could not arise in the Old Testament, because there the origin
> of marriage was traced to God, the Creator and Lawgiver. Nor could it
> arise in Judaism, for there only a legalistic misconception . . . could
> take root. It remained for other religions and cultures to express the
> equality of the sexes, although only in their periods of decline.[32]

Liberationist Interpreters Speak:

1. It is difficult to determine whether John Otwell argues ultimately for the subordination or the liberation of women. In his book
And Sarah Laughed, Otwell argues that procreation and survival
were primary values in Israel, to which cultic and legal functions
played a supportive role. Within this context, motherhood was
valued most highly. Otwell says, "No higher status could be given
anyone than was given the mother in ancient Israel. Motherhood
. . . was a sacred act of great magnitude which only the woman
could perform."[33]

Unlike many writers who see discrimination against the female in the ritual law's doubling of the time of the mother's "un-
cleanness" after the birth of a female, Otwell sees it exactly the opposite way:

> . . . the woman who had just given birth to an infant may have been
> "unclean" because she had been too closely involved with the work of
> deity. She would need a period to be de-energized, so to speak; and
> that period would need to be twice as long for the birth of a [female]
> ·child which might become capable in its turn of bearing children for
> a male child.[34]

Otwell concludes his book by formulating the status of women
as a doctrine: "She was co-worker with God in the creating and
sustaining of the people of God. She also participated fully and
freely in the common life of that people."[35]

2. Most interpreters of the liberationist position, however,
regard the status of women in the Old Testament as oppressed—a
situation which Jesus condemned and corrected. Liberationists
point out that Old Testament women had no inheritance rights,
could not take vows, could not initiate a divorce, and were excluded
from many cultic activities. Women were victims of the "double

standard" in that virginity at marriage was required only of females.[36]

3. Phyllis Bird notes the variety of images and roles for women in the Old Testament. She says:

> Despite the family locus of most of the women's activity, the knowledge and abilities of women were not confined to the family circle or limited to expression in strictly female activities. The possession of special gifts and powers beneficial to the larger community was recognized and acknowledged in women as well as men.[37]

4. Dorothy Yoder Nyce also emphasizes the positive roles that many women filled in the Old Testament. She mentions various women who worked together with men: Miriam worked with Moses and Aaron; Deborah functioned like Samuel as a judge; and Huldah gave leadership in Josiah's reform program. Nyce concludes, however, "that the overall facts about men and women reveal sin: the failure to let God alone be authority and the denial of human oneness."[38]

5. Trible, having done extensive research in this area, has identified at least seven streams of evidence which argue for female liberation from within the Old Testament theological tradition.

First, she notes that numerous feminine images of God's activity counter the predominantly male image of Yahweh: supplying water for Israel, feeding the people manna, and clothing the human family. Specific maternal imagery includes "carrying the sucking child," "a woman in travail," and "bringing Israel to birth." All of this precludes any exclusively male conception of Yahweh.[39]

Second, Trible appeals to the exodus for support of female liberation, noting that the civil disobedience of the Hebrew midwives nurtured the revolution which led to Israel's release from bondage. Trible proposes that a "patriarchal religion which creates and preserves such feminist traditions contains resources for overcoming patriarchy."[40]

Third, Israel's sense of corporate personality disavows sexism. For when such solidarity marks a community, both victor and victim in sexism die and in "liberation all live equally as human beings."[41]

Trible's egalitarian exegesis of Genesis 2—3, cited above, constitutes the fourth point.

Fifth, Trible regards the Song of Solomon as a *midrash* (commentary) on Genesis 2—3, portraying love that mutually affirms the male and female. These love songs show "alternating initiative for woman and man," and no trace of male dominance. Hence, she concludes, "in Yahwist theology neither male nor female chauvinism is warranted."[42]

Sixth, Trible presents a fascinating essay on the relationship between the noun *womb (reḥem)* and the verb *to have compassion (raḥem).* Commenting on texts which join the two meanings of the root *rḥm* in motherly compassion (e.g., 1 Kgs. 3:26), especially to describe God's care for Israel (Hos. 1:6; Jer. 31:15-22; Isa. 46:3-4; 49:13-15; 63:15-16), Trible concludes,

> With persistence and power, the root *rḥm* journeys throughout the traditions of Israel to establish a major metaphor for biblical faith: semantic movement from the wombs of women to the compassion of God. For us the language has unfolded new dimensions of the image of God male *and* female.[43]

Seventh, through a literary analysis of the story of Naomi and Ruth in four scenes, Trible shows how these women manage the struggle to survive physically, culturally, and religiously, preserving their integrity in a man's world and becoming channels of blessing for both women and men. These women function

> as paradigms for radicality. . . . They are women in culture, women against culture, and women transforming culture. What they reflect, they challenge. And that challenge is a legacy of faith to this day for all who have ears to hear the stories of women in a man's world.[44]

Jesus and Women

Hierarchical Interpreters Speak:

1. Ryrie devotes four chapters to this topic. Though his purpose is to elevate womanhood through a eulogy of Mary, restrictiveness of role also emerges. He says that

> [Mary] is not only the mother *of our Lord,* she *is* the *Mother* of our Lord. The Mother could only be a woman; yet the Incarnation was in a man. . . .

> Mary is significant as a model of ideal womanhood. . . . Mary was of a retiring nature, unobtrusive, reticent, perhaps even shrinking from observation, so that the impress of her personality was confined to the sweet sanctities of the home circle. Or, as Walpole puts it, "we see in the little that is told of her what a true woman ought to be."[45]

In discussing Jesus' attitude toward women, Ryrie cites various incidents in the Gospels which illustrate his appreciation of woman's spiritual capability, woman's intellectual capability, and woman's ability to serve. Jesus' attitude toward women was revolutionary, says Ryrie.

> Their spiritual privilege was equal with that of men; definite differences, however, existed in their spiritual activity.... What is not said about women is as important as what is said. It is significant that there was no woman chosen to be among the twelve disciples. It is significant that the Lord's Supper was instituted in the presence of men only. The apostolic commissions ... were given to men only.... All these significant facts put together are proof that the activities assigned to women were different from those which our Lord assigned to men.[46]

Ryrie then says that woman's rightful role is service, denoted from the Greek word *diakoneō*, which is used to describe women's work in the Gospels:

> ... women had a very special place as ministers to Jesus in a sense in which no man was His minister.... He limited the sphere of their activity by glorifying the domestic responsibilities with which they ministered to Him.[47]

2. Zerbst holds that Jesus' relationship with women contrasts sharply with Judaism's view of women. "Woman has full share in the kingdom of God" (cf. Gal. 3:28). But "over and against this ... stands the fact that women were not received into the circle of the twelve and were not among the seventy ... sent out." Hence "Jesus does not remove or invalidate the regulations concerning the man-woman relationships ordained in creation."[48]

3. Clark also regards Jesus' relationships with women to be distinctive from both prevailing customs and the views expressed in rabbinic writings. After citing nine instances in which Jesus demonstrated new patterns of relationship,[49] Clark emphasizes, however, that Jesus did not address the topic of social roles. Though he accorded women a new spiritual status and demonstrated a brotherly-sisterly relationship, Jesus "in no way call[ed] into question the basic Old Testament pattern of roles for men and women."[50] Hence "Jesus was not revolutionary with regard to the roles of men and women."[51]

Liberationist Interpreters Speak:

1. One of the most original and sustained liberationist interpretations of Jesus is Leonard Swidler's article "Jesus Was a Feminist." Swidler calls attention to the view of current biblical scholarship that the Gospels, written thirty to fifty years after

Jesus, are colored by the faith and views of the early church. He says:

> The fact that the overwhelmingly negative attitude toward women in Palestine did not come through the Christian communal lens by itself underscores the clearly great religious importance Jesus attached to his positive attitude—his feminist attitude—toward women.[52]

Swidler notes that the Greek word *diakonoun* (Lk. 8:3; cf. Mk. 15:40f.) is the same basic word used for "deacon," which designates a specific church task in early Christianity. For Jesus to have had women disciples and for the early church to have reported it in their writings was a major cultural breakthrough.

> The significance of this phenomenon of women following Jesus about, learning from and ministering to him can be properly appreciated when it is recalled that not only were women not to read or study the Scriptures, but in the more observant settings they were not even to leave their household, whether as a daughter, a sole wife, or a member of a harem.[53]

Most significantly, the prominence of women in the story of Jesus' resurrection—this central event of the gospel narrative—says Swidler, is a strong statement about the role of women; Jesus disclosed himself first to women and entrusted to them the responsibility of telling the apostles. Thus:

> The effort of Jesus to centrally connect these two points [his resurrection and the role of women] is so obvious that it is an overwhelming tribute to man's intellectual myopia not to have discerned it effectively in two thousand years.[54]

Further, Swidler notes that women were prominent in each of the other three resurrections in the Gospels: Jairus' daughter, the widow's son of Nain, and Mary and Martha in the raising of Lazarus.

The stories of the sinful woman (Luke 7) and the woman taken in adultery (John 8) show that Jesus did not regard women as sex objects. Further, Jesus' healing of the woman with the flow of blood and his commendation of her faith show that Jesus rejected the blood taboo. And Jesus' encounter with the Samaritan woman shows that he purposely violated the common cultural code governing male-female relationships.[55]

By insisting on monogamy and forbidding divorce, Jesus denounced the view that women are "basically chattel" and condemned the "double moral standard." In visiting with Mary and Martha, Jesus approved the intellectual role for women and refused to force all women into a stereotype, the kitchen syndrome. Thus, Swidler says,

> it is difficult to imagine how Jesus could possibly have been clearer in his insistence that women were called to the intellectual, the spiritual life just as were men.[56]

Further, Jesus' reply to the woman who cried out, "Blessed is the womb that bore you, and the breasts that you sucked" (Lk. 11:27), called women to the work of the kingdom rather than to motherhood as the first priority for their lives. These distinctive words were retained in the tradition because the early Christian communities knew that Jesus put kingdom work over sexual functions.

Noting also that Jesus portrayed God in the image of a woman in the parable of the lost coin, Swidler concludes his survey:

> From this evidence it should be clear that Jesus vigorously promoted the dignity and equality of women in the midst of a very male-dominated society. Jesus was a feminist, and a very radical one. Can his followers attempt to be anything else—*De Imitatione Christi?*[57]

In a later contribution, *Biblical Affirmations of Women,* Swidler presents an exhaustive and impressive collection of texts from the Gospels which show positive views of women.[58]

2. Evelyn and Frank Stagg point out that Jesus' teaching against looking upon a woman in lust and his teaching against divorce protest male domination of women. In a cultural setting where adultery was considered transgression of a father's or husband's rights, Jesus' statement that lusting "adulterates" the woman (Mt. 5:28) "extended the understanding of adultery in two directions: it could be committed against a woman; it could be committed in the heart even if not given overt expression."[59]

The Staggs also answer the hierarchical interpretation that Jesus' appointment of male apostles only restricts official leadership to men:

> The Twelve probably served as a sign for the reconstitution of Israel which Jesus proposed to bring about....

> If the fact that the Twelve were all males excludes women from Christian ministry, it must be considered that they also were all Jews. Does this exclude all non-Jews from Christian ministry? It is sounder to

see the Twelve as a sign for reconstituted "Israel," with no necessary implication of bias in Jesus and no necessary implication for the shape of Christian ministry today.[60]

3. A special topic in this section is Jesus' address of God as Father (Abba). Robert Hamerton-Kelly argues that already in the Old Testament prophets Israel's view of God as Father challenged traditional patriarchal understandings. Extending this development, Jesus' use of the symbol, God as Father, stressed the sovereign, liberating, and compassionate dimensions of God, with "mother" elements flowing into it. "Far from being a sexist symbol, the 'father' was for Jesus a weapon chosen to combat what we call 'sexism.' It is possible," he suggests, that "Jesus chose the father symbol precisely to humanize the patriarchy."[61]

Pauline Teaching and Practice

In Paul's writings we find texts which give different signals. Some appear to prescribe specific roles for men and women; others appear to grant freedom from these roles. One set of texts (Gal. 3:28; 1 Cor. 7; and Rom. 16) appears liberationist; the other set (1 Cor. 11 and 14, the domestic codes in Ephesians and Colossians, and the teachings in the pastoral Epistles) appears more hierarchical in emphasis. Here I will present commentary on only two texts from each set in order to limit the length of the Pauline section of this chapter (see Appendix 3 for commentary on the other texts). The following discussion will adequately illustrate the strengths and weaknesses of both exegetical positions and provide the necessary background for hermeneutical observations and comments.

Galatians 3:28

Hierarchical Interpreters Speak:

1. While Ryrie affirms that this text clearly indicates that spiritual privileges come equally to men and women and shows Christianity to have advanced beyond Judaism, yet this principle of spiritual position and privilege does not mean "the obliteration of all differences between the sexes." Further, "to use these words to imply that there can be no subordination of women is to misunderstand Paul's meaning."[62]

2. Similarly, Zerbst says that Galatians 3:28 does not speak about male/female roles assigned in creation. Therefore, although it affirms equality of the sexes regarding life in Christ, it "does not an-

nul, either in marriage or in church regulations, the difference established in creation between the sexes."[63]

3. Likewise—while acknowledging the meaning of the text to be that ethnic, national, racial, social, and sexual differences do not determine spiritual standing—Knight believes the verse "does not deny the teaching of 1 Timothy 2 and 1 Corinthians 14," which forbids women to teach and exert authority.[64]

4. Clark, through 45 pages of sustained discussion, comes to the same conclusion. He makes, however, some additional exegetical points: the topical context is justification, standing before God, and not social roles; parallel Scriptures (Col. 3:9-11; 1 Cor. 12:12-13) with similar but not identical pairs of terms lead to the conclusion that both male and female are created in God's image and united to Christ through the gift of the Spirit;[65] and in saying analogically that in Christ there is neither slave nor free, Paul is not an abolitionist.[66]

But the in-Christ reality changes more than just the God-man and God-woman relationship; it does affect social relationships. Hence, Paul does teach how *Christian* masters and slaves should relate to each other, an analogical basis for declaring that in Christ men and women also relate to each other in new ways. However, at two points the analogy between slavery and sexual roles breaks down: Paul nowhere connects slavery to a decree of God, but he does appeal to a creation order for the subordination of women; and if Paul intended to teach that both slavery and sexual distinctions are to be abolished, then while slavery could be and has been abolished, *all* sexual distinctions cannot be abolished.[67] Clark also affirms Paul's coherency: what the apostle teaches in Galatians 3:28 does not contradict what he says in 1 Corinthians 11:2-16, written only several years later.[68]

Liberationist Interpreters Speak:

1. Richard and Joyce Boldrey regard this verse to be a manifesto of Christian freedom, mainly from sin and law, but also from the limitations of creation, since the phrase "male and female" follows the technical formula of Genesis 1:27. The two terms of the pair are not joined with "nor" as are the terms of the other two pairs, but with "and" *(kai)*, thus showing dependence upon the Genesis formula. Hence, Paul is saying that "in Christ, relationships between men and women should transcend the male-female division."[69]

2. Don Williams says that Paul here declares that the barriers

due to race, social status, and sex have been broken down. Paul
takes a radical step beyond the old order.

> Redemption does not merely restore God's intention in creation. Re-
> demption brings into being a whole new world, a whole new order.

> Male dominance, egotism, patriarchal power and preferential priority
> is at an end. No longer can Genesis 2-3 be employed to reduce woman
> to an inferior position or state. If redemption is real the warfare
> between the sexes is over. At the same time, female seduction,
> manipulation, and domineering is also over, "for you are all one in
> Christ Jesus."[70]

3. John Neufeld, writing in *Study Guide on Women*, urges the
church to take Paul's "breakthrough" in this verse as "our guide
and norm" and thus affirm "the full partnership of men and
women." Neufeld recognizes a tension between the kingdom vision
and the cultural reality, which in Paul's time kept him from fully
implementing the radically new vision, not only for female liberation, but also for abolition of slavery. Further, although the church
in the first century did not fully achieve female liberation, we should
not use that cultural accommodation to mandate accommodation
as a principle (cf. slavery). Rather, Galatians 3:28 calls us toward the
full liberational reality.[71]

4. In commenting on this verse, Jewett notes that whereas
Paul usually appeals to the second creation narrative, here he
alludes to Genesis 1, maintaining that Christ *redeems* the creation
vision, bringing into reality the true and full partnership of male
and female. Redemption, Jewett says, is not a rejection of creation
but a realization of its intentions. In Christ man and woman "become what God intended them to be when he created Man in his
own image." This verse in Galatians 3 together with Romans 16
shows that Paul fundamentally agrees with Jesus, even though
elsewhere he backs off from implementing the vision.[72]

5. Virginia Mollenkott similarly sees Paul here affirming that
the gospel of Christ calls for revolutionizing the rabbinic perspective, which elsewhere Paul follows. Mollenkott says:

> By insisting on the few Pauline subordination passages and stopping
> short of the many Pauline liberation passages Christians have been
> denying the full impact of the gospel of Christ as it had entered Paul's
> experience and as it was intended to modify human society.[73]

1 Corinthians 11:2-16; 14:34-36

These texts are considered together because they are

ostensibly from the same pen on the same subject in the same epistle. In chapter 11, women are instructed to be veiled when praying and prophesying; in chapter 14 they are commanded to be silent. The main issues with which commentators struggle are these: (1) How do we explain the apparent contradiction between freedom to pray and prophesy in public and the command to be silent? (2) How do we understand the dynamics of the situation in Corinth? Were women removing the veil, thus innovating against custom? Or was Paul's command to wear the veil, itself the innovation? What did the veil signify? (3) How do we understand Paul's restrictions regarding women in these texts in light of the role-freeing emphasis of Galatians 3:28 and Romans 16?

Hierarchical Interpreters Speak:

1. Ryrie takes a clear and provocative position on each of the three questions above. He holds that the norm for woman's role in public worship was and is to be silent, as clearly taught in 14:34 (and 1 Tim. 2:12), since chapter 14, not 11, addresses the subject of participation in public worship. Chapter 11 addresses the practice of veiling for women and headship for men, which implies the subordination of the women to the men. That "women prayed and prophesied at all was very extraordinary and probably limited to the Corinthian congregation," located in a city of very loose morals.[74]

2. Zerbst's exegesis of these texts centers on the phrase "it is a shame *[aischron estin]*," occurring in 11:6, 13 and 14:35. Why is it shameful for women to unveil and speak in public worship? Rejecting various suggested explanations, Zerbst argues that Greek women were usually *unveiled*. Hence in Corinthian Greek society neither removal of the veil nor speaking in public would have been considered shameful. Hence:

> Only this one interpretation remains, therefore, that Paul recognizes in the desire of women to speak in the church a desire for an equalization of men and women which would annul the Law that commands *hypotage* (subjection). The Law here confirms what already had to be said on the basis of creation, namely that man is the head of woman. The attempt of woman to achieve equality with man is declared *aischron* (shame) by Paul, because it is contrary to the will of God as revealed in creation and in the Law. The *aischron* derived its inner fullness not from contemporary custom or from Paul's environment, but only from the will of God.[75]

3. Knight identifies the crucial emphases of these texts to be "the hierarchy of headships" and "role relationships." The veiling

testifies to the woman's recognition of God's intended "chain of subordination." Christ's subordination to God is analogous to woman's subordination to man. Such subordination neither makes Christ a second-class deity nor woman a second-class person.[76]

This hierarchical and role relationship of man and woman is explained further by the way in which woman reflects man's glory since in creation she was taken from him. Man reflects God's glory; woman reflects man's glory. Paul, says Knight, is basing his views on Genesis 2:18-25, in which woman is said to be made for man in order to "help and be the helper of man." Further, the phrase "because of the angels" indicates the "desire to see God's order preserved and God's glory displayed."[77]

In 11:11-12, Paul stresses

> the equality and natural interdependence of man and woman to indicate that the order referred to in verses 8 and 9 does not glorify man but teaches that "all things originate from God" (v. 12). ... [Hence] the role relationship of man and woman and their mutual dependence can be correlated without one concept destroying the other.[78]

The command for women to keep silent in 14:34 refutes the argument, advanced by the Corinthians, that the exercise of all spiritual gifts requires women to speak in worship. No, says Paul, "such an exercise of that spiritual gift is contrary to God's order of creation and no appeal to spiritual gifts or freedom can set this aside."[79]

Knight summarizes:

> We conclude from our survey of these three key passages [also 1 Timothy 2:12] that the apostle Paul laid down a universally normative regulation which prohibits women from ruling and teaching men in the church. These passages are not illustrations but commands; these commands are grounded not in timebound, historically and culturally relative arguments that apply only to Paul's day and age, but in the way God created man and woman to relate to each other as male and female.[80]

4. While Clark recognizes the difficulty of understanding clearly some of Paul's teachings in these texts, the main point of male headship is clear to him. The difference between Jewish and Greco-Roman customs regarding the veiling of women in public does not hold much significance for the discussion, according to Clark, because Paul's stated concern is not conformity to the norms of society for missionary reasons. Even the wearing of the head

covering, an appropriate cultural expression of subordination in that culture, is important only because it expresses the principle that woman is under the authority of man. Further, Paul's reference to hair length and what nature *(phusis)* teaches is only an analogical point to the main emphasis, which is the difference between, and the order for men and women, to be respected for worship. Nor is Paul correcting an abuse, since he commends the Corinthians on their practice in this regard (see 11:1, 2ff. in contrast to 11:1, 17ff.). Rather, in 11:2-16 Paul is addressing the important point of honoring distinct male and female roles in worship, and here the emphasis falls upon male headship.[81]

Paul's argument appeals to three points: the structure of creation (Gen. 2 is important); hair length, showing male-female differences; and apostolic authority, "to establish a universal practice for all the Christian churches" (11:16).[82] The declaration on interdependence (verses 11-12) affirms that "men and women are in a complementary partnership with one partner in subordination to the other."[83] However, the main emphasis of verses 2-16 is "the order of the heads," not subordination. In 14:34-36, a supplement to the chapter 11 text, the main emphasis falls on subordination. The command to be silent, however that be understood (probably limiting certain types of speech), is not instruction about restoring order (men too are accountable for that), but an instruction to "the women to be silent because they are women, not because they are disorderly."[84] Hence the two texts complement each other in teaching headship and subordination as key principles for sexual roles in the Christian community.

5. In a recently published exegetical work [which came to my attention too late to be incorporated fully into this study], James B. Hurley holds that 1 Corinthians 11 speaks only once of the veil—in v. 15 where the hair is given to her *for* (instead of) a veil *(peribolaiou).* Elsewhere in the text the long hair itself—worn upon the head—is the covering *(katakaluptō)* that Paul commands; women were not to cut their hair short as the harlots did, because that would dishonor her head, her husband, and show disrespect for his authority *(kephalē* means both source and authority). Further, Hurley argues from study of the primary sources, based on his doctoral dissertation, that women in ancient Judaism and in the Greco-Roman culture were generally not veiled in public—the shawl/face veil for women came into Near Eastern custom later through Islam. Hurley also argues that men and women were given a cooperative social mandate in creation; women's role was

restricted only religiously in Israel. The New Testament specification of the religious restriction is the teaching of doctrine in the church and headship in the home, both positions of head-authority. The former belongs to the male *elder* in the congregation and the latter to the husband. Women may serve and lead within those parameters, even as deaconesses, as Phoebe possibly did. *Man and Woman in Biblical Perspective* (Grand Rapids, Mich.: Zondervan, 1981).

Liberationist Interpreters Speak:

1. Russell Prohl argues that all the restrictive texts in the New Testament refer to wifely submission. He holds that wives were threatening their marriages by speaking in public and unveiling. He concludes:

> The time has come to declare that since the public activity of a woman is no longer considered as a breach of the marriage vow, and since the law of the land no longer denies to the woman the right to act independently in public gatherings, women are eligible candidates for any office in the church of Christ, if, of course, they have the qualifications equal to those of the male candidates for the office.[85]

2. A second liberationist interpretation—advanced by Morna Hooker, Richard and Joyce Boldrey, C. K. Barrett, and others—holds that the veil *gave* women the authority to participate in worship freely and unhindered. Since man reflects God's glory, his head is to be bare—to let God's presence permeate the gathering. Since woman reflects man's glory, she must be veiled in order not to reflect the man's—i.e., the male's—glory. The veil thus magnifies God's glory by refusing to reflect man's glory. These interpreters understand the veil to symbolize the effacement of human glory in the presence of God and, at the same time, to serve as a sign of the *exousia*, the authority, which is given to woman through Christ. In worship, then, both men and women show God's glory and the two sexes have equal power.[86]

In three related articles, Robin Scroggs—regarding the veil as a sign of authority to pray and prophesy—argues that Paul is an unqualified supporter of female liberation (14:34-35 is non-Pauline, a later interpolation, in Scroggs's view).[87] Scroggs concludes his article in *The Christian Century:*

> Thus, far from being a symbol of subjugation, the headcovering is rather a symbol of her liberation in the new creation. In the es-

chatological community, where freedom reigns, woman no longer stands chained to the roles of the old creation. The days of Genesis 3 are gone forever!

The evidence clearly indicates that we must make a radical reversal in our interpretation of Paul's stance toward women. Far from being repressive and chauvinistic, Paul is the one clear and strong voice in the New Testament speaking for the freedom and equality of women.[88]

Scroggs then notes that the deutero-Pauline writings (1 Tim. 2:12ff.; 1 Cor. 14:33b-36; Col. 3:18; Eph. 5:22-24) "rewrote Paul to make his writings conform to the establishment church."[89]

Complementing this emphasis, many interpreters also note that the word "head" (*kephalē*) in 1 Corinthians 11:3 means "source" or "origin"; it does not connote the idea of "rule over" or "lord it over" another.[90]

3. Elaine Pagels reviews these discussions on "Paul and Women" and expresses her doubts about the Hooker-Boldrey-Scroggs interpretation. She says, "If Paul intends to affirm the new equality of man and woman, why does he select Gen. 2:18-23 as his exegetical source instead of Gen. 1:27, which suggests an equal . . . creation?"[91] Unpersuaded by the exegesis, Pagels thinks that Paul expresses "two utterly opposite views"—an affirmation of liberty and also a reversion to convention as commonly practiced within Judaism.[92]

This position accords with that of Jewett, who holds the more common view that the veil represents restrictive subordination. He says, "Perceptive women have seen in the veil all that opposes their development as authentic persons."[93] Paul considered the woman's refusal to wear the veil insubordination not only to man, but also to God.

What then should we make of Paul? Jewett notes that "all the Pauline texts" supporting "female subordination . . . appeal to the second creation narrative," which in the rabbinic thought of Paul's time was used as the basis for the doctrine of subordination and the perpetuation of restrictions upon women.[94]

Jewett also notes that Scripture is of both divine and human origin. The divine element, he says, teaches full equality and partnership of male and female. But in 1 Corinthians 11, Paul resorts to rabbinic thought, of human origin. The arguments advanced by Paul are

incompatible with (a) the biblical narratives of Man's creation, (b) the revelation which is given us in the life of Jesus, and (c) Paul's [own] fundamental statement of Christian liberty in the Epistle to the Galatians.[95]

Jewett explains:

> It is not the subordination of *some* women to some men, but the subordination of *all* women to *all* men, because they are women, that constitutes the indefensible thesis, indeed the unscriptural thesis. When one grasps the basic contour of revelation, as it begins with the creation narratives and culminates in Jesus Christ, one cannot make a case for such ontological subordination of the female to the male.[96]

The distinctive hermeneutical feature in Jewett's comments is his critical judgment that the Pauline texts commanding female subordination and silence reflect the rabbinic influence on Paul and that, therefore, they should not be accepted as normative for Christian practice. While these texts reflect the human dimension of Scripture, the many texts which regard man and woman as equal, interdependent partners are to be regarded as normative and of divine authority.

Mollenkott concurs with Jewett and calls for examining our understanding of Scripture's authority:

> Many biblical feminists fear that if they admit that some of Paul's arguments undergirding female submission reflect his rabbinical training and human limitations, the admission will undercut the authority of scripture and the doctrine of divine inspiration....
>
> It seems to me far less detrimental to the authority of scripture to recognize that some of Paul's arguments do reflect his human limitations, just as the imprecatory Psalms which express David's vindictive hatred of his enemies are reflections of David's human limitations.[97]

4. Constance Parvey proposes that Paul's teachings in the epistle to the Corinthians can be rightly understood only by recognizing that they were written within the context of a growing Gnostic heresy plaguing the Corinthian church. She says that all the difficulties which Paul addressed in the epistle "show signs that gnosticized, pneumatic believers had penetrated [the church community], disregarded established customs, and, among other problems they had created, had also influenced some of the women."[98] In chapter 11 "Paul clearly appears to be arguing against the influence of radical Gnostic ecstatics, who were said to have an aversion to women covering their heads."[99]

Paul answers the problem, she says, with arguments from

Jewish tradition. Women should keep their heads covered as a sign of subordination to men. It isn't becoming for a woman to pray with her head uncovered; it is rather shameful. The phrase "because of the angels" means that the veiling is necessary in order that women do not seduce angels into sexual pleasure as happened in Genesis 6, bringing into existence the giants.[100]

Parvey says:

> The weight of Paul's argument is determined by the cultural and religious situation in which he was brought up, but with one exception. By inserting verses 11 and 12 he points toward a new set of assumptions about how differentiations are made in the body of Christ.

> Having projected the seeds of the new vision and sketched its broad strokes, Paul remained, however, still socially a product of his time.[101]

Parvey's treatment of 14:34-35 emphasizes the contrast between the ecstatic influences of Gnosticism and the Jewish rabbinic concern for order, which Paul supported in the face of threatening Gnostic heresy.[102]

Parvey's view of the Corinthian chaos is complemented by Catherine Clark Kroeger's essay on "Pandemonium and Silence at Corinth." She describes the ecstasy and orgiastic practices that characterized worship of Bacchus, a mystery cult prevalent at Corinth in the first century. Bacchus, known also as Dionysus and popular among women, was described (according to an ancient text) as " 'him of the orgiastic cry, exciter of women, Dionysus, glorified with mad honors.' "[103]

Kroeger proposes that the Corinthian situation was influenced by the disorder, enthusiasm, and female dominance characteristic of the mystery cults. Paul's response is a stern call to order and self-control, requesting subordination of women to men and prohibiting women from participation in tongues-speaking. Kroeger agrees with the Boldreys' interpretation that the word "speak" in 14:34 *(lalein)* means "to talk nonsensically" and refers to tongues-speaking, the larger subject of the chapter.[104]

The distinctive aspect of this last perspective of liberationist interpretation is its reconstruction of what was going on in the Corinthian community. In this context of aberrant conduct, prompted by mystery cults, Paul wrote these restrictive words. Thus, because these commands were situationally motivated, they should not be considered normative for all situations throughout

all time. The interpretation opens the way for making Paul's liberationist teaching normative.[105]

Romans 16

Romans 16 mentions 27 people, 10 of whom are women if we
take verse 7 to read Junia. These women were a significant part of
the early church's ministries, with some—such as Phoebe, a
deacon, and Junia, an apostle—occupying positions of leadership.
Acts 18 indicates that Priscilla functioned with her husband,
Aquila, as a church leader, performing a teaching ministry. Other
texts might also be considered in this discussion, specifically those
citing the work of Lydia (Acts 16); Euodia and Syntyche, Paul's co-
workers (Phil. 4:2-3); Nympha, in whose house the church met (Col.
4:15); and Apphia, whom Paul addresses in the letter to Philemon.
Also, 1 Timothy 3:11 appears to speak of deaconesses in the church.
How do we understand these various ministries of women in
churches where Paul functioned as a missionary leader?[106]

Hierarchical Interpreters Speak:

1. Ryrie recognizes that Phoebe is a witness to the important
services rendered by women in the primitive church, but argues
that *diakonon* in Romans 16:1 should be understood in the
general, unofficial sense. Ryrie also recognizes that Romans 16:2
describes Phoebe as a succorer of many *(prostatis pollōn)* and that
the term *prostatis* usually denotes having authority or exercising
leadership. But as used here, Ryrie says, the term should be understood in the general sense of service.[107]

Ryrie also notes that the great majority of commentators seem
to understand the reference in 1 Timothy 3:11 to be to deaconesses.
But, holding that Paul wrote these words not many years after the
letter to the Romans, Ryrie says that the apparent fact that there
were no deaconesses in Romans "does not help the argument that
these women in Timothy were deaconesses."[108] Ryrie concludes:
"Women workers, yes; women deacons, no."[109]

2. "The activities of Priscilla, the prophesying daughters of
Philip, Phoebe, and others," Zerbst argues, do not establish the fact
that women "exercised the office of Word Proclamation in Paul's
time."[110] Zerbst says that none of these instances show women
exercising such ministries *publicly*. That Phoebe "was a deaconess
authorized to teach is very much in debate. No evidence for it can be
found in the New Testament."[111]

3. Knight addresses three aspects of this discussion. After surveying a wide range of meanings for *diakonos* in the New Testament, including the state as a servant of God, he argues that the term in its restricted denotation of "officers of the church ... is applied self-consciously to men but not to women."[112]

Second, Knight considers the meaning of *prostatis*. Although the masculine form indicates one who stands before—front-rank man, leader, or chief—the feminine form, used here of Phoebe, means "protectress, patroness or helper."[113]

Finally Knight considers the argument that Priscilla's work is evidence of women teaching in the New Testament churches. He recognizes that her name often precedes that of her husband, Aquila, that a church met in their house, that they are both designated Paul's fellow workers in Christ Jesus (Rom. 16:3), and that both explained to Apollos "the way of God more accurately" (Acts 18:26). While Priscilla's ministry is certainly important, Knight says,

> this personal and private ministry with her husband ... in no way negates the teaching of the New Testament that excludes a woman from a public ministry of teaching and ruling in the church.[114]

4. Clark considers Romans 16:1-2 and 1 Timothy 3:11 together and concludes that "there is some possibility that Phoebe was a deaconess," but the later church sources define the work of deaconesses as primarily the "care of the women"; deaconesses were "intermediaries between the women and the heads of the community."[115] Clark also acknowledges that the Greek word *Iounian* in 16:7 could be translated "Junia" and thus denote a female apostle. But it might denote "Junias," a man, or the verse could be translated so that Andronicus and Junia(s) "are people well known to the apostles." That *Iounian* denotes a female apostle is unlikely "in view of the evidence that only men were chosen to be apostles and the complete lack of evidence elsewhere for the existence of any female apostle."[116]

Liberationist Interpreters Speak:

1. Mollenkott regards the Pauline practices and teachings in Romans 16 as contradictory to those in 1 Corinthians 11 and 14. Mollenkott sees positive and cordial relationships between Paul and the many women who were leaders in the early church. In

Colossians 4:15, Paul gives warm personal greetings to Nympha, in whose home the local congregation met for services.

Mollenkott comments on Junia and Phoebe:

> In Romans 16:7 Paul salutes a woman named Junia as a kinsperson and a fellow prisoner and says she is "outstanding among the apostles"! And in Romans 16:1 he commends Phoebe, referring to her as both *diakonos* and *prostatis*. Paul seems perfectly comfortable with the fact that Phoebe was a minister or deacon *(diakonos)* of the church at Cenchreae and a ruler over many people *(prostatis)*, including no doubt many males.[117]

2. Williams comments on each woman mentioned in Romans 16.[118] Of Phoebe he says, "She holds an official function as 'deaconess' or 'minister.'" He notes that the word used is masculine *(diakonon)*, the same word Paul used to identify himself, Apollos, Tychicus, and Timothy as ministers of the gospel (1 Cor. 3:5; Eph. 6:21; Col. 4:7; 1 Tim. 4:6). "There is no reason," Williams says, "to suppose that Phoebe does not hold a ministerial office."[119]

Regarding Priscilla's ministry, he says:

> Nowhere is it suggested that Priscilla is inferior to or under the authority of Aquila in ministry. To the contrary, she shares a title and task of equality as a "fellow-worker." She is a fellow-worker in suffering and in church building and is universally recognized as such.[120]

Williams argues that the Greek accusative *Iounian* in Romans 16:7 belongs to the feminine "Junia"; it is not likely that it is a contraction of the masculine "Junianus." Williams says:

> Only an extra-Biblical assumption that a woman could not be an apostle keeps most commentators from reading Junias as Junia. The church father Chrysostom had no such bias. He writes, "And indeed to be Apostles at all is a great thing.... Oh! how great is the devotion of this woman, that she should be even counted worthy of the appellation of apostle!"[121]

3. Bernadette Brooten notes that while almost all modern versions of the Bible translate the word as "Junias" (masculine) in 16:7, early church commentators regularly understood it as "Junia" (feminine): Origen (ca. 185-253/54), Jerome (340-419), Hatto of Vercelli (924-961), Theophylact (ca. 1050-1108), and Peter Abelard (1079-1142). Aegidius of Rome (1245-1316) seems to have initiated, in general reference to "these honorable men" *(viri)*, the male understanding. Luther, leaning upon Stapulensis' commentary

(Paris, 1512), also took the name as masculine. Thereafter, the translation tradition followed the masculine "Junias" rendering. But the evidence of the first ten centuries and the text itself (with the feminine "Julia" in a manuscript variant) support "Junia," a female apostle. Brooten notes that the term "apostle" in Paul's letters refers to more than the twelve (Acts 14:4, 14), but that it does denote one with special authority (Gal. 1:1, 11f.; 1 Cor. 9:1).[122]

Brooten concludes:

> In light of Romans 16:7 then, the assertion that "Jesus did not entrust the apostolic charge to women" must be revised. The implications for women priests should be self-evident. If the first century Junia could be an apostle, it is hard to see how her twentieth century counterpart should not be allowed to become even a priest.[123]

4. In several articles on women in the pre-Pauline and Pauline churches, Elisabeth Schüssler Fiorenza holds that women played prominent roles in the early Christian missionary movement, so much so that Paul's restrictive language must be seen as a reaction to developments prior to his missionary work. Noting that "apostle" and "deacon" are interchangeable in Paul's vocabulary (2 Cor. 11:13, 15), Fiorenza holds that Phoebe was a missionary apostle of the church at Cenchreae, with her title *prostatis* connoting "leading officer, president, governor or superintendent." Fiorenza assumes that "Phoebe had a position of great authority within the community of Cenchreae" and beyond; she was respected by Paul himself.[124] Whether as missionary *co-workers* (Priscilla, Euodia, and Syntyche), leaders of house churches (Priscilla, Nympha, and likely Phoebe), fellow *apostles before Paul* (Junia and possibly Phoebe), or "those who labored hard in the Lord" (Mary, Tryphaena, Tryphosa, and Persis), these women are never portrayed in subordinate positions to Paul or to other men. Fiorenza concludes:

> Paul's letters indicate that women were among the most prominent missionaries and leaders of the early Christian communities. They were co-workers with Paul but did not stand under his authority. They were teachers, preachers, and prophets. As leaders of house-churches they had great influence and probably presided also at the worship celebrations.[125]

These various writers (more could be cited)[126] agree that women participated freely in the ministries of the church and were welcomed and approved by Paul himself. Paul's restrictive teach-

ings, therefore, must be understood as (1) occasioned by the circumstances to which they were written and (2) not binding upon
the thought and practices of God's people.

Teaching in the Pastoral Epistles

Four specific strands of teaching form the focus for commentary: (1) the command for women to be silent, prohibiting them
from teaching or having authority over men (1 Tim. 2:11-12); (2) the
rationale for this prohibition which regards woman as more easily
deceived, becoming the *first* transgressor, and the linking of her salvation to her childbearing; (3) the injunctions in 1 Timothy 3:2, 12
that bishops and deacons should be the husbands of only one wife,
taken by some to exclude women from these offices of church
ministry; and (4) the reference to women (as deaconesses?) in 1
Timothy 3:11 (with 1 Tim. 5:2 and Tit. 2:3 used as supportive texts).

Hierarchical Interpreters Speak:

1. Ryrie connects the "principle of silence" to the "principle of
subjection and difference between the sexes."[127] This, Ryrie holds, is
rooted in creation, "grounded in facts which are not altered by
geography or centuries." Since Adam was formed first, "he had first
an independent existence and could in no way be subordinate to
Eve." Then Ryrie notes that Paul

> further adds the idea that "the woman's yielding to the wiles of a
> serpent shows her to be an unsafe guide." Subordination, de-
> pendence, and difference of nature are the three reasons the early
> church assigned for the non-participation of woman in public vocal
> ministry.[128]

Ryrie admits that the great conservative commentator, J. B.
Lightfoot, held that "the female diaconate [was] as definite an institution in the Apostolic Church as the male diaconate"; he notes also
that the "great majority of commentators seem to understand [1
Timothy 3:11 to refer] to deaconesses." Nevertheless, Ryrie says, the
evidence is not decisive. The word for "deacon" can have the wider
meaning of service; 1 Timothy 3:11 does not refer to women deacons holding an official office, but to women workers.

> No one denies the necessity for having women workers, but one must
> be on guard against reading back into the New Testament sub-
> sequent development in church organization.[129]

2. Zerbst also bases the command for female silence on the principle of subordination rooted in the creation order.[130] But while accepting the existence of the female clerical office of deaconess (and of widows) in the early church, Zerbst argues that the tasks performed by the widows and deaconesses do not include teaching and administering sacraments.[131]

3. Knight says that women are

> to learn in quietness and all subjection. . . . That which is prohibited is teaching (didaskein) and having dominion (authentein). The prohibition is not that a woman may not teach anyone (cf. Titus 2:3-4) but that within the church she must not teach and have authority over a man (andros).[132]

Paul's "I do not allow" (epitrepō) is based upon the creation order: "The one formed first is to have dominion, the one formed after and from him is to be in subjection."[133] Knight says that the qualifications for bishops and deacons are given in male terms. Though women are mentioned in connection with the deacons, they "are not mentioned in the midst of the description of bishops because women are excluded from the ruling-teaching office." Further, it "would seem . . . that the office of deacon is an office for men only, but that at the same time women are to be involved in that diaconal area."[134]

4. Clark considers 1 Timothy 2:8-15 to be a key text for addressing the role relationship of men and women. Similar to Ephesians 5 and 1 Corinthians 11, it bases the discussion upon God's principle in creation. Further, this text is especially important because it alone directly addresses the "question that is central to the structure of the roles of men and women—the question of authority and teaching in the community." Hence "it clearly addresses the subject of men and women in community leadership" within the context of discussing church order.[135]

The emphasis of the text is that women should adorn themselves, not with "expensive or luxurious ways," but "in quietness and subordination."[136] This instruction parallels the call to men to exercise spiritual leadership and avoid quarreling. The key words are subordination, quietness, teach, and exercise authority. Quietness is closely related to subordination and denotes readiness to accept teaching and direction. Viewed within first-century patterns of teaching, the kind of teaching forbidden to women is that which involves personal direction and exercising authority over men. Although the word authentein could mean "domineer" (thus only a sinful usurping of authority would be proscribed), its use in this context refers to any exercise of authority which violates the principle of subordination. Nor is the instruction situationally motivated. It "gives direction to women because they are women and not because they are untrained or disorderly."[137]

As in the other key texts on this subject, the instruction is grounded in a fact from creation, in this case the greater gullibility of the woman, which is not the result but the cause of Eve's transgression. This fact of revelation is not an empirical point (suggesting we must verify it by the way women behave), but a typological teaching. The woman's easier persuadability shows up also in redemption: "she was the first to believe God in the redemption" (the resurrection account). In both fall and redemption the man holds, though, the place of responsible head (Rom. 5:12, 15, 17-19).[138] Clark does not choose decisively among the four possible meanings of the clause "the woman will be saved through childbirth,"[139] but leans toward associating it with the way woman, through childbirth, initiated the redemptive event which reversed the consequences of the fall.[140]

Liberationist Interpreters Speak:

1. In a reprint in Fuller Theological Seminary's publication for alumni, *Theology, News, and Notes,*[141] A. J. Gordon (writing in 1894 and following the exegesis of Alford and Wiesinger) interprets 1 Timothy 2:8-11 to say that women (verse 9) are "in like manner" as men (verse 8) to pray in every place (publicly). The text calls *for* the participation of women in public worship and prescribes that it be done "in modest apparel."[142]

With the change from *gunaikas* (plural) in verse 9 to *gunē* (singular) in verse 11, Gordon says, "the quietness and subjection" describes the manner in which the *wife* is to learn. But this text (together with 1 Cor. 11:5; Acts 2:17; and Acts 21:9) welcomes women's participation in public worship.

Gordon admits that the text forbids women to teach. "To teach and to govern are the functions of the presbyter." At this point Gordon speaks against ordaining women as bishops and teachers.[143]

2. Williams attributes the cause of the restriction in 1 Timothy to a local situation in which women's teaching exacerbated heretical developments. Viewing 2:11-15 within the context of the book's wider teaching, Williams holds that the congregation was threatened by various heresies (1:6-7; 4:1; 6:20) in which women

played significant roles—leading worship and even teaching—which their newfound faith, in contrast to Judaism, allowed. "The lack of past instruction among Jewish-Christian women could account for some of the theological chaos in Ephesians."[144]

Williams observes that women were *then* supposed to learn but not teach because they needed to be instructed before they were qualified to teach. The verb for "permit" (verse 12) is in the present tense: "I am not presently permitting women to teach or rule. . . ." Just as the uninstructed women were deceived by false teaching, so was Eve deceived in the fall (verses 13-14). Verses 13-14 provide rationale for the temporary situation, but verse 15 points to a redeemed situation. Williams takes "childbearing" to mean "the birth of the child," the Messiah, through whom "all women are united corporately . . . in redemption." Williams concludes:

> While Paul does not actually say it, we may rightly infer that the time will come for women to engage in the teaching task of the church once the abuses are corrected and they are properly instructed. Can she who bears the Messiah be prohibited from teaching His gospel?[145]

Williams takes "the husband of one wife" qualification in 1 Timothy 3:2, 12 as a restriction possibly against polygamy, but more likely against divorce. Verse 11 of the third chapter is best understood to mean "women who are deacons."[146]

3. Jewett's commentary focuses not so much on the local situation which occasioned restrictions upon women's teaching and ruling, but upon the rabbinic, human dimension of Paul (or the post-Pauline writer). Jewett does not regard the mandate as binding because here, as in 1 Corinthians 11, Paul's arguments are based on the *rabbinic* interpretation of Genesis 2, which

> is palpably inconsistent with the first creation narrative, with the lifestyle of Jesus, and with the apostle's own clear affirmation that in Christ there is no male and female.[147]

Though Jewett considers the Mary-Messiah interpretation of 2:13-15, he thinks it likely that most translations are correct in conveying the idea that woman, who

> was the prime mover in the fall and therefore under a curse in childbearing (Gen. 3:16), will be brought safely through the threatening experience of motherhood, if they, i.e. women, continue to live a life becoming of the Christian name.[148]

4. After asking why Paul imposed "silence on women *because*

of Eve (1 Tim. 2:12-14)," Mollenkott answers by ascribing the instruction to Paul's rabbinic training, which contradicted "his Christian vision . . . that the gospel conferred full equality on all believers."[149] Mollenkott then calls upon evangelicals to reassess their view of the authority and inspiration of Scripture so that they can accept the facts of Scripture. She asks Bible readers to stop following the rabbinic interpretation of Genesis 2 and to acknowledge contradiction within Paul.

> We are forced to recognize that the famous sections on women in the church are simply *descriptions* of first-century customs applied to specific situations in local churches.[150]

The Witness of the Gospels

Chronologically, after Jesus and after Paul came the writing of the four Gospels and Acts. While it has always been acknowledged that each of the four Gospels shows distinctive emphases, only in the last three decades have scholars grasped the extent to which a given Gospel reflects both the theological bent of the author and the developments in the Christian community he represents.

Of the writers used in this research, only several have grasped the significance of this point for the subject at hand. These several writers represent the liberationist interpretation.

1. The Staggs devote their last two chapters to "Woman in the Synoptic Gospels and Acts" and "Woman in the Johannine Writings." The Staggs' summary of the Synoptics and Acts conveys the hermeneutical significance of their findings:

> The Synoptic Gospels and Acts take us at least to around A.D. 60, the time of Paul's arrival in Rome. . . . Compared with 1 Corinthians and the five letters containing the Domestic Code (Colossians, Ephesians, 1 Peter, Titus, and 1 Timothy), woman's status as reflected in the Synoptics and Acts is amazingly free. There is no discernible disposition to place limits upon women. There are reflections of the bias of traditional language, and traditional roles play some part. There is no reference to the rib narrative of creation. There is no suggestion that woman is to be subordinate to man. The apostles, the Seven in Acts, and official leaders generally are male. On the other hand, there is no exclusion of women from teaching or preaching; there is rather an affirmation of woman's right to the study of the word and the ministry of the word. Homemaking is normative for woman, but there is no restriction of woman to this vocation. There is no hint that she is to be silent in church, and there are no directives as to her cosmetics or wardrobe.

That in the Synoptic Gospels woman occupies such a place of dignity and freedom is probably to be attributed to the Gospels' fidelity to Jesus. The view that the Gospels tell us much about the church but little about Jesus is a dogma that has little in its support. For all the freedom exercised by the Evangelists and their sources, they apparently do retain an authentic picture of Jesus. Nothing that already has developed in the churches leading to various codes for conduct obscures the strong lines that belong to Jesus of Nazareth, liberator of the human being, and in particular liberator of woman. The Evangelists not only preserve Jesus' perspective on woman, but they seem to be comfortable with it. [While] . . . Luke-Acts is seemingly beyond 1 Corinthians in date, . . . restrictions upon woman explicit in this letter are unknown to Luke-Acts.[151]

The Staggs' study of the Gospel of John notes that women play key roles in the Gospel: the Samaritan woman, Mary and Martha, Mary in anointing Jesus, the women at the cross, and Mary Magdalene in the appearances of Jesus.[152] The Staggs point out that because of "the word of the woman" many Samaritans believed (4:39); that many Jews, having come to Lazarus' sister Mary and having seen what Jesus did, believed (11:45); and that Mary Magdalene testified to the male disciples, "I have seen the Lord!" (20:18).[153]

2. Parvey ends her essay with a section on Luke-Acts, noting that writers usually focus only on Jesus' attitude in the Gospels but fail to recognize that the Gospels also "reflect the successive settings in which they were written down and finally shaped by their various editors."[154]

After noting the prominence of women in the Luke-Acts narrative, Parvey concludes: (1) Though not the only Gospel to do so, Luke addresses "itself to both a male and female audience." (2) ". . . the pedagogical structure of Luke clearly indicates that it is essential to educate both women and men." (3) ". . . women from all social levels were drawn into participation in the first-century churches. In worship, teaching, institutional and missionary life, the Spirit, indeed, was poured out on both 'sons and daughters.' "[155]

Hermeneutical Commentary

1. It is striking to note how one's position affects and even determines what one sees in the text. The emphasis on female subordination permeates the hierarchical commentary, but the word "subordination" occurs *only once* in the texts cited above,[156] and that is in a text (1 Cor. 14:34) which counts least in the hierarchical argument, precisely because its apparent call for women to be silent

in worship is an injunction that even the most thoroughgoing hierarchical interpreters cannot accept as normative policy. On the other hand, emphasis on equality permeates the liberationist commentary, but such a word occurs nowhere in the various texts cited. One may argue, however, that the concept of equality is present, but this raises an even longer agenda: What concept of equality? From what social, political, and economic world context? Precisely what does equality mean when viewed within the social world of these ancient texts? And what does it mean today?

To illustrate the above observation, let us recall the commentaries on Genesis 1:26-27 and Genesis 2. The hierarchical interpreters see nothing in 1:26-27 that speaks to the issue, as they define it; namely, subordination of women to men. But the liberationist interpreters could rest their case on these verses alone, precisely because they do not speak about subordination or prescribe difference in roles; whatever is said of the male is said equally of the female. Both are called to the tasks of procreation and dominion over the earth; both are made in God's image; and their bothness is even part of that image. To the hierarchical eye, the text says nothing on the topic; to the liberationist eye, the text says all that ever needs to be said.

The commentaries on Genesis 2 again strikingly illustrate the point. The same evidence is used to support opposing views: because man is *central* in the narrative, he is head (Clark); because woman is the *climax* of the narrative, her equal or even more important role/position is affirmed (P. Yoder). The word *ēzer*, meaning "help," denotes complement that includes subordination (Clark); the word *ēzer* means "complement" in the sense of interdependence and partnership between equals with no indication of a subordinate (or inferior) role (Yoder, Jewett, Trible). Similarly, Adam names the woman, thus showing his authority over her (Clark and Knight); Adam calls to the fellow earth creature woman, rejoicing in their mutuality (Trible).

Which side of the argument is correct? Does one side follow a better method of interpretation? Does one side listen more carefully to the text? Does one side willfully pervert the meaning of the text? The most telling question of all, would further comments about the way the texts should be understood really change either side's point of view? Perhaps yes and perhaps no. But what is clearly illustrated, however, is that the interpreter must recognize and own the ideological influence that governs the task of interpretation. Ideology, whether subordinationism or liberationism, is at work in the above commentaries. Let no one think that only a disinterested, dispassionate objective search for truth motivates these commentaries!

Ideology, however, must not only be acknowledged, but also assessed. The term itself needs clarification. On the one hand, as Robert McAfee Brown notes, the word carries "an almost neutral meaning, standing for any system of ideas expressing a particular point of view."[157] But, as Brown points out, a pejorative connotation frequently arises also in which the "rationalization of self-interest" is part of the ideology. This leads then to ideology's defense of the status quo and the screening out of those perspectives which might challenge one's ideology. The term, as used in this writing, should be understood to mean one's value perspective, shaped by a complex mixture of psychological, sociological, economic, political, sexual and religious factors. This blend of influences creates culture and personality. Ideology then carries no inherently negative connotation, but self-serving interests lie ever close to the surface of each person's ideology.

2. While the purpose of this hermeneutical commentary is not to judge one ideology superior to another, it is important to ask whether the task of biblical interpretation should hold ideology accountable. One's answer depends, of course, on the authority one allows for the biblical text. My view of the Bible (supported in turn by a set of values and commitments) leads clearly to a positive answer. Biblical interpretation, if it is worthy to be so called, will challenge the ideology of the interpreter. It can and will lead to change, because people do not come to the text thinking as God thinks, or even as the people of God thought in serving as agents of divine revelation.

For this reason, method of interpretation is important. As noted earlier, some method must be used which gives the text distance from the interpreter's ideology, a method which allows the text to speak its piece, to function as a window through which we see something besides our own thoughts. Otherwise the text becomes a mirror reflecting back what we want it to say. While both positions in this debate demonstrate both mirror and window dimensions in interpretation, the hierarchical interpreters play a mirror game, setting up the texts in positional relationships to each other so that each reflects the same image. The liberationist writers (at least some of them) concede that not all of the texts say the same thing. This vulnerability becomes a strength because it shows that the projection of the interpreters' ideology onto the text has been broken. *They see something that doesn't say exactly what they would like the text to say.* This fact, in my judgment, represents breakthrough and hope because it witnesses to the possibility that interpreters can listen to the text carefully enough *not to like it.* It powerfully demonstrates that the text's message has been heard and respected.

To illustrate the point further: The hierarchical position makes Genesis 1—2 mirror what 1 Corinthians 11 mixed with Ephesians 5:21-33 says. And then 1 Corinthians 11 is made to say exactly what Genesis 2 has been made to say. One might cite the harmonizing of Scripture with Scripture as a basic rule for interpretation, but such harmonization easily opens itself to the criticism of the mirror game, making Scripture reflect what the interpreter thinks. The rule itself functions to silence precisely that which may stand out as different, different both from what the interpreter thinks and different from other text messages. How clearly this is illustrated in the hierarchical commentary on Romans 16 and numerous related texts portraying women in leadership roles! Testimony that threatens the headship-subordination ideology is effectively silenced by the hierarchical interpreters, primarily by use of this harmonizing principle. The hermeneutical maxim then which says we should interpret Scripture by Scripture must be put into tension or tandem with another consideration: listen first for the distinctiveness of each text; distinguish its call/message from other calls/messages.

In admitting tension between various Pauline texts, liberationist interpreters therefore engage in biblical interpretation and reflection that demonstrates "getting out of our own ideological skins." Further, they seek a resolution, offered most notably by Jewett and Mollenkott, that makes a judgment about the relative authority of the different signals; the rabbinic interpretation of Genesis 2 reflected by Paul, they say, falls short of Scripture's best witness to God's will for male-female relationships. Subordinationist proponents will object, of course. But the very coherency difficulty of the position testifies to a breakthrough in overcoming the tyranny of the mirror game played by the interpreter's ideology. The interpretation represents a wounded, but not despairing, position in coherency; it represents a position of difficult honesty. For that reason alone, it merits serious attention.

3. This discussion assumes then that the interpreter must be prepared to encounter diversity of thought among biblical texts, a point developed at the end of the last chapter. How this diversity of

thought is assessed becomes an important consideration in biblical interpretation.

On the one hand, such diversity can occasion offense to the interpreter, especially if he/she holds a view of biblical revelation and inspiration which precludes any conceptual difference of perspective in the Bible.[158] In that case, an interpretation which speaks of "two utterly opposite views" in Paul (Pagels) will appear incredibly weak. It runs against precisely what cannot be allowed, according to this doctrinal view of the Bible. It is wrong because doctrinal ideology says so.

But the question these four case issues force us to ask is this: how do we honestly listen to different texts and allow them to puncture our ideologies, whether these be doctrinal, political, or sociological? If Bible study is never allowed to change our doctrine, indeed our beliefs, then why do it? As a *pretend* game? Granted, Bible study usually serves to reinforce believers in their faith and practice. This is as it should be unless the people have become totally apostate and pagan. But the principle of change must also be maintained; otherwise we impugn the claim of divine revelation and make *"biblical authority"* into a shibboleth, but deny the Bible's power. The sword is two-edged also in that the emphases of the texts require liberationists to be more cautious in attributing (likely modern) concepts of equality to the meaning of the texts.

Diversity within biblical thought may be viewed not as a liability but as a strength. It testifies to the genuineness of revelation in history, as noted in chapter 3. As Paul Hanson writes in his recent monograph on *The Diversity of Scripture*, diversity "bespeaks nothing less important than the biblical view that the God of Israel is a God who is encountered in the stuff of history and human experience."[159] In this way biblical thought differs from timeless myth and rigid religious systems; it is rooted rather in a historical community's ongoing relationship with God. Diversity in theological thought and emphases is "the natural result of the one true God's graciously relating to humans, drawing humans into a relationship inviting free response and full engagement." Containing diversity, even competing traditions, "the Bible portrays a creative, redemptive dynamic which moves at the center of all reality and guides creation toward God's goal of a kingdom wedding peace and justice."[160]

This dynamic view of Scripture witnesses then to the vitality of divine revelation. While this is evident in the various competing and complementing traditions within the Old Testament (repre-

senting over fifteen centuries of time), as Hanson ably demonstrates,[161] it is also prominent in the New Testament as the
gospel is addressed to different peoples and problems in different
geographical and cultural settings during more than half a century.
This understanding might be called the missionary principle of the
Bible, and the missionary factor for biblical interpretation. Biblical
truth is concrete, shaped usually by specific contexts, needs, and
opportunities. Interpretation should affirm and celebrate this feature of divine revelation, communicated through many different
writers in different linguistic, cultural, and political contexts. The
variety itself becomes the missionary's textbook. The biblical text
spoke God's Word in a variety of cultural, economic, political, and
social settings.

To study Paul's epistles from this point of view is most
instructive; it can function as a basic resource for missionary training. One quickly discovers, for example, that Paul's letter to the Galatians would have made little sense to the Corinthians, had they
received it by mistake. Or, if 2 Corinthians had been received by the
Philippians, what confusion would have resulted! The Gospels also
were written to specific communities and therefore contain distinctive emphases. It is important, therefore, to learn as much as possible about the communities to which the writings were addressed in
order to better understand the writings. For this reason the
contributions of Constance Parvey and Catherine Kroeger are helpful to our understanding of 1 Corinthians 11:2-16, a teaching
which all interpreters have admitted is difficult to understand.

J. Christiaan Beker's major work on Paul's theology is especially helpful in this regard. Beker proposes that Paul's letters
represent *contingent* expressions of Paul's *coherent* gospel. Beker
locates the coherent center in God's apocalyptic/eschatological
triumph, expressed decisively—but not yet finally—in Jesus
Christ's resurrection from the dead (thus Jesus' death is viewed as
liberation from the old age and its powers). Because Paul's letters
address a variety of situations, prompted by his apostolic call to proclaim the gospel to the Gentiles, Paul's theology can be grasped only
when both the contingent and coherent elements are identified and
properly interrelated.[162] Beker's contribution, as well as Hanson's,
shows us that the hermeneutical assessment of Scripture's unity
and diversity is foundational and essential to the task of construct-
ing biblical theology, the basis upon which we must build when using the Bible for current social issues.

This approach teaches us that the Bible presents models of

how to apply the gospel perspective to different situations in different cultures in different time periods of the church. It shows us also that the Bible is a living document, one in which God encounters all people and speaks a word that is comprehensible, potent, and transforming. Lines of continuity and major points of unity will also emerge in the biblical text, since ultimately the Bible testifies to the redemptive activity of one God. Some of the major points of unity and continuity are clearly the one God of the Old and New Testaments, the story of God's covenant peoplehood throughout the biblical history, the kingdom or rule of God, and the mission of God's people to be servants of justice and peace.[163] The function of the canon itself teaches us that some viewpoints did not fit into the parameters of biblical revelation; they are not to be regarded as models for our own understanding and application of biblical teaching. What was rejected, as well as what was included, is instructive to us.[164]

4. The approach of Jewett and Mollenkott to this issue, however, asks us to consider one very specific feature of diversity within the canon. Some teachings, they say, represent the divine dimension of Scripture and some, the human. The emphasis itself is not new since the recognition of the divine and human dimensions in Scripture regularly appears, even in conservatively oriented theological writings.[165] The application that Jewett and Mollenkott make of this understanding, however, represents a novel consequence of an old doctrine. For the long-standing confession that Scripture is both human and divine assumed that both elements were present in all of Scripture, similar to the presence of the human and divine in Jesus. Hence, it was said, the divine Word came in human language, was communicated in the context of a specific geography and culture, and most significantly, came through a variety of writers, whose distinctive speech patterns and cultural concerns were respected by, and evident within, the Scripture.

But to make the critical judgment that a *given biblical teaching* falls on the human side of the ledger while another falls on the divine side calls for new discussion on the meaning of the twofold nature of Scripture. Difficult problems immediately emerge: how does the Bible reader/interpreter know which Scriptures go on which side? What criteria are to be used for making those judgments? What view of the writers does this imply? Was Paul sometimes writing humanly (1 Cor. 11:2-10, 13-16) and other times writing divinely (1 Cor. 11:11-12; Gal. 3:28)?

The potential consequences of this approach are quite far-reaching. To illustrate, one might propose that the biblical texts which most clearly support the first position represented in chapters 1-4 should be arbitrarily assigned to the human side of the twofold nature of Scripture while the texts used to support the last position in each chapter should be put on the divine side. Or, holding the opposing view, one might argue that the texts that most clearly support the last positions should be put on the human side. In this approach the twofold nature of Scripture becomes the sword of ideology's armament, rendering inauthoritative those parts of Scripture which conflict with (and could potentially critique) the interpreter's ideology, and holding as authoritative those parts of Scripture which reinforce the interpreter's views.

If one thinks analogically of the early church's christological debates, one soon recognizes that this approach to Scripture might be called Nestorian hermeneutics. The two natures are present in Scripture but remain distinct from each other. Perhaps it is not fair to represent Jewett's and Mollenkott's interpretations in this.way; they likely would not fully accept the analysis. But their comments, lacking necessary qualifications, draw the hermeneutical procedure in that direction.

The proper alternative is not to back away from affirming the twofold—divine and human—nature of Scripture, nor to deny the rabbinic influence upon Paul. Rather, the unity of the divine and human dimensions in Scripture leads the interpreter to respect the divine authority of the humanly limited Word, even the call for women to be silent or the divine command to Israel to practice the *herem* (the cultic sacrifice of the enemy). This does not mean that these commands are made normative for all time or even for other situations in that time. Instead, it means that as interpreters we need to ask what these various divine-human paradigms reveal to us.

What does Scripture teach us through Paul's use of the rabbinic interpretation of Genesis 2 to speak to the Corinthian situation? In this question the human, cultural dimension is not denied, but viewed positively. When one looks at the larger literary context in the epistle (1 Cor. 11—14), it becomes clear that the Scripture as revelation is teaching that cultural patterns are to be respected and utilized, not for reifying them as ends in themselves, but for promoting the larger goals of the gospel: the orderly conduct of worship, the edification of the whole body, and the primacy of love in human relationships. However, in view of other scriptural testimonies which give women prominent roles in early church leadership (thanks to the diversity of the canon),[166] the 1 Corinthians 11 teaching on male headship should not be translated into a church policy that prohibits women from functioning in church leadership roles.

Using then the missionary factor for hermeneutics—the diversity of expression as *faithfulness* to the gospel—we must ask: what uses and criticisms of culture in our time and place enable us best to achieve goals central to the gospel, whether these be the goals of 1 Corinthians 11—14 or those articulated elsewhere in Scripture, including the unity of male and female in Christ (Gal. 3:28)? The divine-human nature of Scripture can then, like its unity in diversity, become an enriching resource for believers who live by its light.

Note: Correspondence with Virginia Mollenkott since this book was first published leads me to indicate that the larger principles which she developed in *Women, Men and the Bible* do protect her position from the liability discussed above. Her reference to some arguments reflecting Paul's human limitations (pp. 103-104) are not meant to indicate that these arguments lack scriptural authority. Rather, from these also we can derive significant learnings when we apply the principles of biblical interpretation presented in her book.

— W.M.S.

Chapter 5

HOW THEN SHALL WE USE AND INTERPRET THE BIBLE?

Having observed the varied uses of the Bible in these four cases, we must now ask: what can we learn from all this? Should, and how should, the Bible be used to address social ethical issues? And most significantly, how then should we interpret the Bible?

This chapter consists of four related parts addressing these questions. The first part consists of hermeneutical comparisons among the four case issues of this study. In the second part I take up the question of whether (and how) the Bible is to be used to address social ethical issues (see also Appendix 4 on the wider use of the Bible). In parts three and four then, I propose a model of understandings and a method for biblical interpretation.

Hermeneutical Comparisons Between Case Issues

To what extent were the arguments in these four cases hermeneutically similar? Were similar uses and misuses of the Bible present in the arguments regarding the different issues?

These comparisons seek to identify some of the hermeneutical similarities and differences in these arguments. The comparisons are on the hermeneutical level and are not intended to suggest that these case issues are similar in their moral nature. Care will be taken to distinguish between comments about the moral nature of the issues and the hermeneutical features of the arguments. Some comments will be made also about the significance of these hermeneutical observations.

Slavery and Sabbath

These two institutions are quite opposite in their moral nature. Slavery oppresses human life; the Sabbath is intended to free and celebrate life.

What then are the hermeneutical similarities?

1. For both slavery and the Sabbath, interpreters took sides on whether the two institutions were of pre-Abrahamic origin, or whether they began in the time of Moses. Pro-slavery writers went back to the so-called prophecy of Noah regarding Canaan and his descendants. Similarly, Sabbatarians argued that the Sabbath was mandated in creation and applies, therefore, to all people for all time.

The abolitionist writers, on the other hand, based their understanding of Hebrew servitude on the Mosaic laws which made grace, mercy, and benevolence the foundation of the master-servant relationship. Similarly, the Lord's day proponents traced the origin of the Sabbath to the time of Israel's deliverance from Egypt; they therefore regarded the Sabbath as the memorial day of their freedom, celebrating liberation for the captive and equality of master and slave.

The pro-slavery and Sabbatarian positions, therefore, traced the origin of these institutions to a primeval (pre-Genesis 12) divine mandate. Both were established as laws for the universe. The abolitionist and Lord's day proponents, however, held that these institutions, which originated from non-Israelite sources, were decisively regulated toward humanitarian values as a result of God's redemption and grace revealed in the exodus.[1]

An important hermeneutical issue raised by this comparison is one's view of the origin of the literature in Genesis 1—11. Does one hold that this literature originated before the beginning of Israel's history and that it predetermined Israel's beliefs, or does one regard Genesis 1—11 as arising out of and thus reflecting Israel's history, experience, and faith? While the latter appears correct, elements of oral tradition may antedate Israel's history.

The Sabbath then, which functioned as a sign of God's covenant with redeemed Israel under Moses, *later* was rooted also in creation, in Israel's testimony to God as Creator in Genesis 1—2.

The curse upon Canaan expressed Israel's later understanding of its relationship to the Canaanites, arising from God's promise of the land of Israel. This perspective then that Genesis 1—11 arises out of Israel's exodus experience and theology influences the interpretation of these chapters.

By viewing these matters in this light, the interpreter of the texts will hold that Genesis 2:1-4 cannot be disconnected from God's redemptive purpose for the Sabbath as revealed to Israel. The curse on Canaan will be seen in particular historical terms and will not be universalized to sanction slavery (not even by appealing to a textual variant to identify Ham and "his black [?] descendants" as the recipients of the curse, as Hopkins sought to do).

2. It is instructive to reflect upon the way Jesus Christ is related to both topics, slavery and the Sabbath. Jesus challenged and corrected the evils attached to both. He declared himself Lord of the Sabbath, calling people to live all of life for the well-being of others. The true purpose of the Sabbath found its clear expression in the life and death of Jesus, a man for others; Jesus extended God's jubilean grace to all people.

Similarly, Jesus modeled the life of the servant (slave). Slavery's oppression was replaced by voluntary servanthood, a model for all people in every social stratum. This prohibits one group of humanity from ruling over another group, and thus renders indefensible the pro-slavery appeal to "God's decree" that one race of people (or class) should rule over another.

By fulfilling the humanitarian purpose of the Sabbath, rest and equality for the servants, Jesus inaugurated a continuous practice of Sabbath, sabbatical, and jubilean ethics, thereby also abolishing even the Old Testament pattern of servitude. For no one can continue to have servant-slaves if one continuously practices the sabbatical year, in which servant-slaves are released.[2]

3. Though the early church apparently continued both Sabbath observance and slavery, Jesus Christ freed both institutions from their oppressive elements. Jesus violated Sabbath rules, and Paul eliminated Sabbath observance as an obligation (Col. 2:16, 20). Similarly, both master and slave were called to equal service and accountability to God. Masters were to regard their slaves as sisters and brothers. The gospel, therefore, not only regulated the practice of slavery but introduced a new master-slave relationship. The new wine, put into the old cultural wineskins, brought the judgment of the gospel's jubilean ethic upon both institutions, radically changing their nature as institutions.

Slavery and War

Many of the above comments on slavery and the Sabbath apply to war as well, but differences are also evident (see footnotes 1 and 2). On the moral level, however, both slavery and war appear intrinsically evil to me. As such they contrast to the goodness of the Sabbath. Further, both the hierarchical and liberationist interpreters consider God's intended role relationship for woman and man to be part of God's good creation.

On the hermeneutical level, both slavery and war present major difficulties:

1. Neither slavery nor war is explicitly condemned in Scripture, though we might wish them to be. Only as we apply prominent and basic biblical teachings (e.g., love for the neighbor and enemy) are slavery and war consequently condemned. But these principles are not applied *directly* against slavery and war within the text itself. Prescriptive and regulative statements on slavery and war in the biblical text are problematic since both appear intrinsically evil.

2. While the New Testament explicitly regulates the conduct of masters and slaves, it does not do so for soldiers and governments (Lk. 3:14 and Rom. 13:3 are not adequate parallels to Eph. 6:5-9). This could mean that Christian participation in war was considered either more compatible with, totally incompatible with, or irrelevant to, Christian morality. The rather consistent refusal of the early church (until AD 170) to participate in war would indicate that warfare was perceived as totally incompatible.[3] Regulating instructions, therefore, were unnecessary. The difference is to be explained also by the fact that the New Testament writings were not addressed to governments or to people in government positions. Thus, while the Old Testament appears to command warfare, the New Testament appears to forbid it. War, therefore, raises the hermeneutical issue of the relation of the Testaments, but the testamental relationship is not as hermeneutically significant in resolving the biblical teaching on slavery.

Put another way, one can argue in support of slavery from the New Testament (perhaps even more cogently so) as well as from the Old, but one cannot argue for war from the New Testament as readily as one can from the Old. For this reason, the hermeneutical issue of the relation between the Testaments was identified as the major issue for hermeneutical commentary in chapter 3.

Sabbath and War

1. The biblical testimony on both the Sabbath and war high-

lights the differences between the Testaments. Support for both appeals primarily and ultimately to the Old Testament. Reading *only* the New Testament, the Christian would likely never think that war or Sabbath-keeping could be divinely sanctioned. The Old Testament, however, contains many explicit commands readily interpreted as enjoining Sabbath observance and cultic participation in war. How does one explain the striking difference between the Testaments in this regard?

2. In attempting to answer this question, one perceives also a hermeneutical difference between the two case issues. The New Testament frequently mentions the Sabbath, but argues against the prevailing practices. The same is not true for war. It appears that Sabbath observance within the community was generally accepted, but criticized when it violated compassion for the needy or jeopardized the freedom of the gospel. But as noted above, since warfare is nowhere discussed, it must be regarded, unlike the Sabbath, as an experience that was outside the range of Christian practice.

3. The imagery of both institutions *is* used metaphorically in the New Testament to discuss new realities. Warfare imagery describes the fight of Christians against evil (Eph. 6:10-18; 2 Tim. 4:7). Attaining the promised rest describes the securing of the saving rest of Christ and of the life to come (Heb. 3—4). This freedom to use the imagery, transposed into a different sphere, indicates a basic shift in *Sitz im Leben* between the Testaments. The following similarity confirms the point from the other side.

4. Both practices arose out of God's redemptive purposes in the exodus. But the pre-exodus history of the patriarchs (Gen. 12—50) never mandated Sabbath observance or holy warfare. The patriarchal narratives gave no command to observe the Sabbath or to fight against and destroy the enemy.

In contrast, the Exodus-Joshua literature contains much instruction about both the Sabbath and warfare, prescriptive as well as descriptive. Not only do both occur in the language of command, but both also have a cultic base. The priest and the ark were as necessary for war (Deut. 20) as for the Sabbath. Similarly, both were tied directly to the land. On the seventh day the land rested; all the warfare was oriented toward God's promise of the land.

By the time of Jesus and the New Testament writings, however, God's gift of land to Israel (Josh. 24:13) had been lost through Israel's disobedience (Josh.-Kings). The many Old Testament prophecies which foresaw the regaining of the land by God's people (Israel) are transposed by the New Testament into a new key, because of the fulfillment of God's promise in Jesus. Jesus promises the land to the meek (Mt. 5:5), and Paul universalizes the land promise into a cosmic promise: all of Abraham's children of faith will inherit the cosmos (Rom. 4:13-16). By regarding the mission of Jesus as the fulfillment of God's promises to Abraham (Gen. 12:1-3), the New Testament transposes the Sabbath and warfare practices of Israel and the land promise into universal and ultimate realities. Within this new context and new historical reality, warfare becomes Jesus' and the Christian's fight against evil (Eph. 6:10-18), and the Sabbath stands in the service of God's rest given in the Messiah, now and in the time yet to come (Mt. 11:28—12:14; Heb. 3—4).

5. While warfare and the Sabbath appear to have opposite functions in the Old Testament—the one takes life and the other celebrates life—in the New Testament both affirm life. Warfare imagery is used not for fighting against people but for rescuing people from evil powers and death (Col. 2:15; 1:13; Eph. 6:11-12; 1 Cor. 15:24-26), just as Sabbath-rest imagery is employed to celebrate triumph over unbelief (Heb. 3—4). The goal of both is to attain eternal life, the rest promised to those who win the battle!

Women and War

Hermeneutical comparison of these two issues is significant because the Scriptures themselves appear to give mixed signals. Although the New Testament does not explicitly speak for or against war, numerous clear New Testament ethical teachings, if followed, render participation in war impossible. But the Old Testament clearly commands the (cultic) participation of God's people in war. Even though one accepts the Exodus 14:14 ideal as the model for Israel's role (standing still and watching Yahweh fight), other texts (however one might explain them) literally command the people to fight. Similarly, the Bible contains diverse emphases on the role relationship of men and women. Some texts explicitly teach hierarchy (1 Cor. 11), while others explicitly reflect unity, partnership, and mutuality between men and women (1 Cor. 7; Rom. 16:1-7).

These two issues face the interpreter with the dilemma of diversity and even apparent contradiction within the Bible. Regarding war, the differences lie primarily but not solely between the Testaments. Regarding the male-female role relationship, the mixed signals appear primarily within the New Testament, even in one author's writings.

One can respond to these apparent contradictions in one of

four ways: seek to harmonize differing statements; ignore some of
the evidence; claim one strand of emphases authoritative over the
other; or accept and live with the canonical tension. The purpose
here is not to resolve the problem but to point out the way these two
topics pose a common hermeneutical problem (see my commentary
on diversity of viewpoint at the ends of chapters 3 and 4).

Women and Sabbath

The similar hermeneutical function of both women and the
Sabbath in the creation narratives shows how each is regarded
supremely good. The first creation narrative reaches its climax in
humanity's acceptance of the Sabbath as God's gift, bringing
release from work. The second creation narrative reaches its climax
in *adam's* acknowledging woman as God's gift, an answer to
humanity's social need. Sabbath and home, enabled by man and
woman in marriage, were Israel's two basic institutions of religious
and social meaning.

To see the man-woman relationship and the Sabbath as intrinsically good, thus contrasting to slavery and war, sets the stage
for properly interpreting all biblical texts on these subjects. The biblical texts teach the true purpose of the Sabbath, correct abuses of
the Sabbath, and show how Jesus fulfills the purpose of the Sabbath. Similarly, the biblical texts teach that humanity, male and female, was created in God's image; they also show how redemptive
history, climaxing in Jesus, restores woman to her true worth in
God's image. In both cases, biblical revelation frees that which is intrinsically good from cultural and historical bondage, occasioned by
humanity's fall. Liberation, therefore, is an appropriate description
of the influence of biblical teaching on both these issues.

Women and Slavery

Hermeneutically, there are numerous similarities:
1. On both issues interpreters quibbled over the meaning of
key words. In the slavery debate, interpreters argued over the meaning of the Hebrew word *ebed* (slave or servant?) and the Greek word
doulos (slave or servant?). Abolitionists insisted on translating
ebed "servant" while pro-slavery writers held that *ebed* means
"slave," and argued that slavery in the United States and slavery in
the Bible were the same. Similarly, they argued over whether the Hebrew word *kana* means "buy" or "acquire."

In the current discussion about the role relationship of
women and men, the meaning of *ēzer* in Genesis 2:18 is debated.

Does it mean "a subordinate helper," "an equal helper," or "a super-ordinate helper"? The word "head" *(kephalē)* in 1 Corinthians 11 also is understood differently. Does it mean "source" or also "rule over"?

Quite likely, both sides have pushed the language beyond its intended limits in both cases. The matter should not be decided by such quibbling over terms alone. Other more decisive herme-neutical insights must be considered.

2. In both cases, the words which describe the roles of slaves and women, to serve and to submit respectively, are also words that describe basic virtues for all Christians. All Christians are to be servant-slaves; all are to be submissive or subordinate to one another.

This hermeneutical coincidence can be used to bolster both sides of the argument. If all are to be servants and subordinates, what's wrong with mandating such conduct for slaves and women? Or, arguing conversely, since all are to be slaves of Jesus Christ and submissive to one another, isn't it wrong to prescribe such roles for slaves and women only?

3. Pro-slavery writers and hierarchical interpreters both have accused "the other side" of denying the authority of the Bible. As the slavery proponents put it: "They try to set for themselves a higher law than the Bible." Paul Jewett's *Male and Female* sparked Harold Lindsell's *Battle for the Bible,* which holds that Jewett's in-terpretation undermines biblical authority, specifically the inspira-·tion of the Scripture. Both issues then, slavery and women, get tan-gled up with differing views on inspiration, inerrancy, and infalli-bility. To argue against slavery in 1850 was to disregard the inspira-tion and inerrancy of the authoritative Word of God. To argue today that Paul's teaching on male headship and female subordination should not be considered a universally applicable theological prin-ciple, opens one to the charge of denying biblical authority.[4]

We have already suggested that acknowledging diversity of viewpoint within the Bible might be viewed as positive regard for biblical authority (see pp. 187-188 above). Here we note, however, that the arguments against slavery and against the headship of man over woman (and also against the Christian's participation in war) are often regarded as disrespectful, and even a denial, of the authority of God's Word.

4. Another hermeneutical similarity between slavery and the role of women is in the distinction made between "correcting the abuses" (of slavery or male headship) and condemning the respec-

tive system as such. Pro-slavery writers would often concede that
the Bible corrects the abuses of slavery, but then argue that it
nowhere and in no way condemns slavery as an institution.

George Knight III makes the same point on male headship. He
concedes that the Bible corrects the abuses of male headship; it
does not condone oppression of women. But this in no way discards
the principle of male headship over women.[5]

The abolitionist and liberationist writers, however, have
stressed that the principles of Christian morality applied to the
situation will make both institutions—slavery and subordination
of women *as women*—crumble. The ethic of love judges both in the
same way.

5. Both pro-slavery and hierarchical writers have used Paul as
the final court of appeal. The pro-slavery writers appealed especially
to 1 Timothy 6:1-6, in which, it is said, Paul quotes Jesus Christ
himself in support of slavery.

In their understanding of 1 Corinthians 11:2-16 and 1 Timothy 2:11-15, hierarchical interpreters say that not only do the plain
words of Scripture teach male headship, but Paul appeals to the
order of creation to support his teaching. So just as Paul appealed
to Jesus Christ to authorize slavery, he appeals to creation to authorize male headship.

The point may be diagrammed as follows, showing the two
levels of appeal:

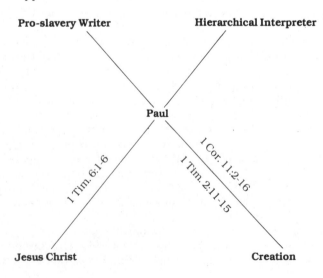

6. On the other hand, both abolitionists and liberationists have shown common hermeneutical tendencies:

    a. They give priority to Jesus and the Gospels over the Old Testament and Paul.

    b. They grant more weight to moral principles than to specific instruction given in specific texts.

    c. They hold that these basic moral teachings challenge the slavery and male headship structures.

    d. They regard Galatians 3:28 as Paul at his best, transcending both slavery and male headship.

7. Both issues are dealt with side by side in the biblical text in the Domestic Codes (the *Haustafeln*). This would indicate that both slavery and male headship were prevailing cultural practices. Paul addressed the two issues with similar ethical directive, calling each member in each pair directly to Christian morality and accountability to Jesus Christ. While the one group of interpreters understood this to be correction of abuses, the other group considered it a deathblow to the systems as such.

8. In addition to these seven areas of hermeneutical similarity between slavery and male headship over women, one significant difference merits comment. Whereas the Old Testament is more explicit in regulating slavery, the New Testament, comparatively speaking, is more explicit in regulating the male-female relationship. Further, in the New Testament one cannot find language that mandates slavery (except perhaps in 1 Tim. 6:1-6 and 1 Cor. 7:20, "Every one should remain in the state in which he was called"). As for male headship and female subordination, however, 1 Corinthians 11:2-16 and Ephesians 5:23ff. appear to mandate these particular roles.

In other words, no one is told to be a master over a slave whereas men are told to be (or are recognized as) heads over women (wives). The point is not absolutely clear since those statements could also be understood as describing the way it was. Or should they be taken prescriptively, stating the way it is to be? It appears that both are in view, since Paul appeals to creation.

Whether Paul's word, prescriptive though it be, should be interpreted as a timeless, universal mandate is another matter. This will depend upon the extent to which one regards the prescription to be conditioned by prevailing practices and specific situations. Prescriptive statements may then have a regulating rather than mandating function. This difference between regulating and mandating intention is significant for these hermeneutical comparisons. Does the Pentateuch mandate or regulate slavery? Does Paul mandate or regulate slavery? Does he mandate or regulate a hierarchical relationship between men and women? (See chapter 4, footnote 166, for an approach to an answer.)

9. One more hermeneutical similarity merits attention. Paul's conservative stance on both these issues appears motivated (at some places) by a concern that the gospel not be defamed. While this concern is explicitly stated regarding slavery (1 Tim. 6:1), it also runs through the texts speaking to the proper conduct of women. In 1 Corinthians 11, Paul's comparison of the unveiled woman with the shaven woman, his appeal to nature, and his appeal to custom indicate his sensitivity to how unbelievers will perceive and judge Christian behavior. In correcting aberrations in tongues-speaking, Paul explicitly mentions this consideration (1 Cor. 14:23; cf. 1 Thes. 4:9-12). In Titus 2:5, 9-10 the submission of both the wife and the slave is connected directly to concern for the integrity of the gospel in that cultural setting.

This raises an important point when we interpret these texts, especially if unbelievers are now more offended when Christians argue for slavery or for male headship. This observation forces us to ask how the church relates to its surrounding culture. Hearing what the text says is the starting point for hermeneutics. But the hermeneutical task requires us to speak also in our cultural settings so that the Word of God and God's own self are not defamed.

Hermeneutical Reflections

1. A contrast between the issues of the Sabbath and women, on the one hand, and those of slavery and war, on the other, has become evident. The direction of biblical thought is to liberate the Sabbath and sexual role relations from the oppressive practices in which sinful humanity imprisoned them. The direction of biblical thought on slavery and war is to regulate and critique them as institutions so that these evil practices are dissipated, or forbidden to Christians. The war of the lamb-servant renders the warfare and slavery of this world obsolete, out of order for those who live according to Jesus, the warrior true and slave supreme. The new realities turn the old practices onto their heads. In the new order, slavery and war are "out of order."

2. It is apparent that biblical teaching on each of these four issues has been understood differently. The Bible has been used to argue cogently for at least two positions on each issue, leading in all cases to opposing stands in the world of the nineteenth and

twentieth centuries. How can God's people be so divided? Why, with the Holy Spirit to guide us, do we not all see the biblical teaching on these issues in the same way?

I mention two factors (there are certainly more) that contribute to this difference.

#2.3 First, as human beings we are subject to particular influences from our culture and history. We tend to use the Bible to reinforce what we believe. While none of us can fully overcome this problem, it is possible to correct wrong notions by serious and sustained study of the biblical text and by following a method which helps us hear the text on its own terms.[6]

#2.3 Second, it must, however, be candidly noted—as these case issues illustrate—that the reason Christians disagree on these issues is because the Bible itself gives mixed signals, especially on the surface of the text. This is due not to the nature of God but to the fact that divine revelation comes into and through history and culture. The various writers of the Bible reflect the cultural practices of their times and write to and for specific situations. For this reason, any proper interpretation of a given biblical text must take into account the historical and cultural setting of both the writer and the community for which the text was written (see further comment on this in the "Model of Understandings" below).

3. Although these difficulties and persisting disagreements among interpreters may leave one pessimistic about achieving unity among God's people, several factors also introduce hope.

First, as noted above, by working seriously at good methods of Bible study, wrong understandings can be corrected. To conclude this study, I will describe in outline form a method of Bible study that can help us toward this end.

Second, the resources of the hermeneutical community and the Holy Spirit are both essential and helpful to biblical interpretation. The Holy Spirit illumines the Word and makes Bible study a vital encounter so that fresh learnings become a source of empowerment. While the community of faith sometimes limits the scope of enquiry in biblical study, it can also contribute positively by providing the resources of grace, faith, and discipleship which enable us to grasp the claims of the Bible. It can also test personal insights and thus prevent Bible study from becoming a subjective experience. These resources will be discussed further in the "Model of Understandings."

Third, as one grasps the central ethical imperative of the total Bible and then looks at these case issues and others from this vantage point, differences in interpretation may be resolved and consensus may emerge. Jesus' own example in transcending scribal arguments over which law is greatest instructs us here. By appealing to the ethical heart of the entire law (Deut. 6:4 and Lev. 19:18), Jesus taught that all moral obligation is based upon love for God and love for the neighbor. As interpreters, we need to let these eyes of Jesus discover for us our own hermeneutical path. By giving priority to this moral imperative of love,[7] we may be able to achieve consensus on the four issues of this study. For a place to begin, we might test our agreement with the following statements and direction of thought.

The biblical imperative of love forbids oppressing anyone, especially the slave. It leads one to regard the slave no longer as a slave, but as a beloved brother or sister. Christianity ends slavery by abolishing positions and roles in which some people "lord it over others." Love also calls us to use the Sabbath and all days of the week as a time to practice justice and to celebrate our salvation from bondage. Love celebrates the freedom of the Sabbath with joy. It tunes all of life into the Sabbath key. Similarly, *agape* love calls God's people away from destroying the enemy to loving the enemy, praying for the persecutor, and overcoming evil with good. War is over, for through love every person is a potential sister and brother in Christ.

So also, love—even in a patriarchal society—calls the male in his cultural power to love as Jesus loved, to forgo his cultural prerogative of power, and to recognize that women are equally God's image. Instead of prescribing rigid roles, love affirms unity, partnership, and interdependence, with each person seeking to image God in the divine fullness of Jesus Christ, the pioneer and perfecter of our faith. Only as men and women fully affirm each other do they live as God's image.

The Use of the Bible for Social Issues

This book has assumed that the Bible should be used to address contemporary social ethics. But this assumption merits some commentary and clarification. When one observes how the church has frequently misused the Bible to justify oppressive institutions such as slavery and war, one is tempted to ask whether both the church and society would not do just as well if the Bible were left out of the picture. But this I recognize as a temptation, to which I'm committed not to yield so long as the co-creative task of biblical interpretation supports me in my resistance.

To show alternative views on this topic, I will report briefly six different understandings and then comment on this important topic.

Six Alternative Views

1. Jack T. Sanders in his study of *Ethics in the New Testament* concludes that the New Testament is not at all useful for addressing contemporary social ethical issues.[8] He cites two main reasons for this judgment. After analyzing the ethical teachings and their foundations in the various parts of the New Testament (treating separately Jesus, the Gospel writers, Paul, James, and John), Sanders says that almost all the ethical teachings are influenced heavily either by eschatological hopes (especially Jesus and the Gospels) or by a restrictive ecclesiological orientation (especially John). Only at a few places does the shape of a love ethic applicable to all situations begin to emerge. But this is not worked out for societal structures.

Consequently, just as Albert Schweitzer taught us that " 'the historical knowledge of the personality and life of Jesus will not be a help, but perhaps even an offense to religion,' " so "it is with the study of New Testament ethics":

> The ethical positions of the New Testament are the children of their own times and places, alien and foreign to this day and age. Amidst the ethical dilemmas which confront us, we are now at least relieved of the need or temptation to begin with Jesus, or the early church, or the New Testament, if we wish to develop coherent ethical positions. We are freed from bondage to that tradition, and we are able to propose, with the author of the Epistle of James, that tradition and precedent must not be allowed to stand in the way of what is humane and right.[9]

2. Roman Catholic writer Rudolf Schnackenburg, in his widely used book on *The Moral Teaching of the New Testament,* presents a different point of view.[10] He acknowledges that Jesus' teaching is an eschatologically oriented kingdom ethic, but holds also that the church has and should expect believers to fulfill Jesus' moral demands "with the help of the grace of God."[11] Although Catholic moral theology has distinguished between commands (for all believers to follow) and counsels (for those with a special call to follow), the Sermon on the Mount's teachings are not so divided; they are regarded as applicable to all: "We must let the words of Jesus stand in all their severity and ruggedness. Any mitigation, however well intended, is an attack on his moral mission."[12]

Later, however, Schnackenburg says that "Jesus had no more

intended to change the social system than he did the political order." His unique contribution was to make love the supreme law and therefore point to a new way to overcome social differences. The task of the church then is "to draw concrete conclusions regarding the economic and social order."[13]

3. John H. Yoder wrote *The Politics of Jesus* to show that Jesus and biblical teaching are concerned directly with political and social ethics.[14] Noting the chasm that has existed between writers in social ethics and biblical scholars, Yoder says that his "study makes [the] claim ... that Jesus is, according to the biblical witness, a model of radical political action." This is generally visible in New Testament studies, "though the biblical scholars have not stated it in such a way that the ethicists across the way have had to notice it." Yoder then seeks to show "that Bethlehem has something to say about Rome—or Masada."[15]

After presenting Jesus' mission and message as a call to practice jubilee (the remainder of his book as well continues similar emphases), Yoder concludes:

> Jesus was not just a moralist whose teaching had some political implications: he was not primarily a teacher of spirituality whose public ministry unfortunately was seen in a political light; he was not just a sacrificial lamb preparing for his immolation, or a God-man whose divine status calls us to disregard his humanity. Jesus was in his divinely mandated prophethood, priesthood, and kingship, the bearer of a new possibility of human, social, and therefore, political relationships. His baptism is the inauguration and his cross is the culmination of that new regime in which his disciples are called to share. Men may choose to consider that kingdom as not real, or not relevant, or not possible, or not inviting; but no longer may we come to this choice in the name of systematic theology or honest hermeneutics.[16]

In two other writings, *The Original Revolution* and *The Christian Witness to the State,* Yoder develops emphases which complement his work in *The Politics of Jesus.*[17] Utilizing the themes of three assemblies of the World Council of Churches (1948, 1954, 1961), Yoder calls the church to be the church. If its life as an international body *faithfully* embodies unity, hope, and light, the kingdom ethic will witness powerfully to the world and make a difference in the political and economic structures of society.[18] After considering various church-state models in Christendom, Yoder proposes—on the basis of Christ's victory over the principalities and powers (Col. 2:15; Eph. 1:19-23, etc.)—that the church should witness to the state (Eph. 3:10) by encouraging the state in its political and economic policies to choose specific options that the church discerns to approximate most closely the ethic of the kingdom, even though the church cannot and should not expect the state to run by kingdom ethics. Yoder's model assumes an ontological difference, and thus tension, between church and state realities, thereby enabling the church to witness from the vantage point of its kingdom commitment and life in Christ.[19]

4. In a sustained discussion of this issue, Bruce Birch and Larry Rasmussen seek to understand the relationship between the *Bible and Ethics in the Christian Life*.[20] After lamenting the paucity of literature on the topic (chapter 1) and surveying several mostly unsatisfactory efforts to anchor ethics in biblical imperatives (chapter 2), the authors propose two connections between the Bible and ethics: first, the Bible develops *moral character* which informs ethical decisions (chapter 3); and second, the Bible is a resource for *the church*, which functions as a shaper of moral identity, a bearer of moral tradition, and a community of moral deliberation (chapter 4). Birch and Rasmussen also describe how the Bible may function as a primary but not exclusive resource in Christian decision-making (chapter 5); they then suggest how the biblical resources are to be made available to the church (chapter 6). The "Bible's relationship to Christian character and conduct implies that *the scattered life of the church is as fundamentally biblical in its foundation as the gathered life of the church.*"[21]

5. Within the context of contemporary concerns about violence, oppression, and poverty, four biblical scholars—Jürgen Kegler, Peter Lampe, Paul Hoffmann, and Ulrich Luz—undertook exegetical studies on the prophets, the apocalyptic writings, Jesus, and Paul respectively to ascertain whether and how the Bible concerns itself with these issues. This study, published in 1981 but begun in 1966 at Heidelberg University by the Forschungsstätte der Evangelischen Studiengemeinschaft (abbreviated as FEST), highlights the close relationship between eschatology and peace throughout the biblical writings.[22] Four of its findings are relevant to this discussion.

First, eschatology plays both a negative and a positive role in the relationship of God's people to societal conditions. Negatively, the strong eschatological orientation of biblical thought, which expects not a reform of the present order but a new order, does not of itself give concrete norms and criteria for human action. Positively, however, when the eschatological hope is connected in a special way to the experiences of God's people, specifically in Jesus' proclamation of the kingdom, eschatology does give direct content for action and norms of conduct. Hence hope and vision for the future must be christologically oriented.[23]

Second, the biblical perspective contributes another element to the project's original task of discovering whether and how biblical thought is concerned with minimizing violence, oppression, and poverty in the world. The biblical emphasis falls upon freedom from sin and *Angst* (fear and anxiety), because God's people are called to live in a new order. This produces an "inner dimension" of freedom and peace which does not, however, negate concern for the "outer dimension." All four writers agree that, even in the apocalyptic writings, the concern and hope for the outer dimension remains, so that violence, oppression, and want are to be conquered.[24]

Third, all four writers agree that the Bible accents *God's real* action in history to bring an end to this history and consummate God's kingdom. In this action, humanity is only a partner; the new order does not come about through human action alone, even with the best of human intentions.[25]

Fourth, the New Testament emphasis (especially the conclusion of the Pauline study) calls the church to a self-critical reflection upon its own nature, its commission, and its own reformation, both as a whole body and individually as members. By undertaking this task—repenting and learning how "to bear in its body the death of Christ" (cf. 2 Cor. 4:10) and thus live by God's power—the church may make its most important contribution to peace in the world.[26]

6. Another understanding of the Bible and social ethics is represented by the methodology of liberation theology's hermeneutic, specifically Anthony Tambasco's analysis of Juan Luis Segundo's use of *The Bible for Ethics*.[27] Segundo holds that both theological reflection and biblical interpretation should *begin* with concrete social analysis.[28] Further, one cannot grasp "the full message of the Bible without proper preunderstanding that should include commitment to the poor."[29] But since *this particular preunderstanding* is in the text itself, the method holds the text to be authoritative. It suggests that interpretation be viewed as an ellipse with both foci—the text and the social analysis (including the theology of the interpreter)—forming essential components of the interpretive task. From this perspective, biblical interpretation and social ethics are so firmly linked together that even the notion that the two have separate identities is called into question.

Evaluative Response

These six different sketches of how (and whether) the Bible is to be used for social issues merit some commentary. Victor Paul Furnish begins his analysis of this topic by rejecting both the "sacred cow" and the "white elephant" approaches to Scripture. The sacred cow approach regards Scripture as a sacred deposit of divine truth "valid in both general and specific ways for all times and places."[30] But "whenever one treats Paul's moral teaching as if it were a sacred cow, one runs the risk of turning it into a white elephant"[31] and viewing it as totally irrelevant. Furnish calls us instead to affirm the role of the Spirit in interpretation and to take Scripture's historical context and setting seriously.[32]

If one considers eschatological and ecclesiological perspectives as negative factors for the church's encounter with social issues, as Sanders does, then obviously the Scripture cannot help us, for the argument assumes that we must address moral issues *apart from* either the vision and power of the kingdom or the discernment and modeling of the church. Not even a partially (or, for that matter, fully) developed ethic of love will help, because love apart from eschatology and ecclesiology lacks moral muscle. Schnackenburg's good start also runs aground by abstracting Jesus and his teachings from consequential significance for his social and political world. By saying that the church "must draw concrete conclusions" about such things when Jesus didn't(!), Schnackenburg fails to see the concrete social, political, and economic effects of Jesus' teachings. Jesus, as God's prophet and Son, was killed for the way his entire ministry was a social, economic, political and religious critique upon the society of his day. Jesus was crucified by both Jews and Romans, and his death stands as a judgment upon the vested social and political interests of his society, and ours.[33]

The models of Yoder, Birch/Rasmussen, FEST, and Segundo point in helpful directions. Yoder's *Politics* makes a strong, convincing case for the New Testament's social and political character, but must be supplemented by his other writings for direction on how Jesus' teachings guide the church in its witness on social issues. His chapter on "Revolutionary Subordination" comes closest to giving such guidance, but even there the Christian's social expression of the new life within the social *structure* remains ambiguous. What is the role relationship of women to men within a patriarchal societal order? Granted, Yoder contends that the church should live its new life as confession and testimony, but the structural shape of the male-female relationship, for example—both within the church and in the larger society—needs more specific directives.[34]

Birch and Rasmussen assume a more participatory role of believers in societal structures; significantly, they speak usually of the Bible as a *resource* for social ethics. It shapes character, informs decision-making, and aids in moral judgment, but it functions typically as a resource. When discussing biblical authority in ethical matters, they recommend that the Bible "be viewed in terms of primacy rather than self-sufficiency."[35] It is a *"constant* source," "the single *necessary* reference point,"[36] and its authority must be viewed functionally, for it speaks to different issues in different ways: when addressing identity with and care for the poor, its witness is clear and consistent, but when speaking of marriage and sexuality, its instruction is more diverse.[37]

These perspectives are indeed helpful. However, I suggest that the Bible is *the essential source* for ethical reflection and moral imperative; its diversity of thought, when viewed in the context of its historical and missionary seriousness, makes it an even *more essential* source. For the church today as never before faces the realities of pluralism and global diversity. Hence the various biblical commands given in diverse specific settings light up the horizon of the church's life all over the world, both in its missionary and catechetical callings.[38]

The contributions of the FEST study are especially helpful in reminding the church of important biblical emphases that it is prone to forget when it seriously concerns itself with the social, economic, and political plight of contemporary society. The four reported conclusions need to be affirmed anew by the church. My sense, however, is that the study is incomplete. The prominent biblical elements of God's call to do justice, both in the pentateuchal and prophetic writings, and the socio-ethical significance of Christ's victory over the principalities and powers are lacking or inadequately represented in the essays.[39] Yoder's and Segundo's contributions are necessary complements.

Segundo's call for social analysis is well placed. To make it a preunderstanding or to place it in elliptical relation to Scripture, however, results in a too easy blessing upon the ideology of the social analyst. Whence come the criteria for social analysis? Granted, experience shapes perception of the text; seeing with the eyes of the poor bestows hermeneutical privilege; and *the text itself* declares this as truth. Nonetheless, it must be affirmed that the biblical revelation and not the social structure provides the insight and criteria for discerning the way life ought to be—*first in the church,* then as witness and invitation to, and judgment on, the world.

Should the church use the Bible to address social issues? Indeed it must if it aspires to fulfill in any way Jesus' call to be the salt and light of the world. Borrowing Bourne's image from chapter 1, unless it does so, it will be drowned in the depths of the sea!

Model of Understandings for Biblical Interpretation

The four case issues of this study together with these alternative views on the use of the Bible for social ethics have shown that interpretation is influenced by the theology and presuppositions of the interpreter. It is important therefore to identify our own pre-interpretive influences or understandings if we wish to advance our efforts toward fruitful dialogue and hermeneutical agreement. Although some writers refer to these as presuppositions or preunderstandings,[40] I choose the phrase "model of understandings." I use the word "model" to designate the working base, the theory with which the interpreter approaches the hermeneutical task.

Before presenting my own, it will be instructive to review other models for the sake of contrast and comparison.

Sample Models

It should be noted that the statements below are elements that contribute to a model of understanding. None of the statements was set forth as a *complete* model of understanding for the purpose of guiding the hermeneutical task. Model 1 likely comes closest to such a statement.

Model 1: In 1820 in the midst of discussing the legality of slavery as it affected the status of the proposed statehood of Missouri, the *Richmond Enquirer* set forth a model of understanding for biblical interpretation:

I
That the volume of sacred writings commonly called the Bible, comprehending the old and new Testaments, contains the decisions of the word of God.

II
That these decisions are of equal authority in both testaments, and that this authority is the essential veracity of God, who is truth itself.

III
That since there can be no prescription against the authority of God,

what ever is declared in any part of the holy Bible to be *lawful or illicit*, must be *essentially so* in its own nature, however repugnant such declaration may be to the current opinions of men during any period of time.

IV

That as the supreme lawgiver and judge of man, God is infinitely just and wise in all decisions, and is essentially irresponsible for the reasons of his conduct in the moral government of the world—so it is culpably audacious in us to question the rectitude of any of those decisions—merely because we do not apprehend the inscrutable principles of such wisdom and justice.

V

That if one, or more decisions of the written word of God, sanction the rectitude of any human acquisitions, for instance, the acquisition of a servant by inheritance or purchase, whoever believes that the written word of God is *verity itself*, must consequently believe in the absolute rectitude of slave-holding.[41]

Model 2: In an article published in the *Journal of the Evangelical Theological Society* (December 1977), Grant R. Osborne sets forth a model of general and specific principles of interpretation which will aid interpreters in deciding whether (1) all biblical commands are to be taken literally and normatively obeyed, (2) "all the command passages are cultural and can only be reinterpreted with regard to problems today," or (3) "both cultural and normative commands are found in Scripture; and we must decide which category . . . [a command] fits before we apply it" today.

Osborne then proposes three general and four specific principles for interpretation. The general principles are:

1. Didactic passages must be used to interpret historical events. . . .

2. Passages which deal with an issue systematically are used to help understand incidental references elsewhere.

3. Passages must be interpreted in the light of their context (historical and literary).

The specific principles are:

1. By using tools of redaction criticism, the interpreter can distinguish between teaching prompted by the immediate situation and that which represents earlier teaching, accepted as part of the community's faith and practice.

2. "Teaching that transcends the cultural biases of the author will be normative."

3. "If a command is wholly tied to a cultural situation that is

not timeless in itself, it will probably be a temporary application rather than an eternal norm."

4. "Those commands that have proven detrimental to the cause of Christ in later cultures must be reinterpreted."[42]

Osborne then uses these principles to discuss the key New Testament texts on male-female role relations. He concludes that "both cultural and normative commands are found in [these] Scriptures." Wearing veils and maintaining silence in church are cultural. Because of the appeal to creation, male headship and female subordination, at least in the home, are normative. This does not preclude ordination of women since teaching and speaking in the church today do not carry the same implications as in the first century. But "women should not force the issue."[43]

Model 3: In an article entitled "Woman in Her Place: Biblical Perspectives," William E. Hull begins his model of understandings by identifying the problems interpreters must face: (1) the diversity of the biblical text, (2) the upheaval of the present, and (3) the subjectivity of the interpreter. He then proposes three distinctions as essential components of the hermeneutical method:

1. The interpreter "must take seriously the similarities and differences between the ancient world and our own."

2. The interpreter "must distinguish between the empirical description of a given historical situation and a theological affirmation of the divine intention for that situation."

3. In seeking to define the unity and coherence of biblical teaching, the interpreter must distinguish between setting "human judgment above the Bible" and listening carefully to "the full-orbed witness of the entire Bible."[44]

After commenting briefly upon the wide range of biblical witness on the topic, Hull proposes a "saving history" framework for resolving the issue: (1) the old age, in which sin led to male dominance and female subordination, (2) the messianic age, which through Christ affirms male and female equality and reciprocal loyalty, and (3) the age to come, when sexuality will be abolished. The issue then, Hull says, is where the church decides to place itself on the eschatological calendar.[45]

Model 4: Elisabeth Schüssler Fiorenza identifies still other elements essential to a hermeneutical model of understanding when approaching the male-female issue:

1. Historical research, even when using the historical-critical method, has reflected patriarchal and androcentric assumptions.

Another theoretical model of early Christian history must be considered. Following is evidence of androcentric presuppositions:

a. Exegetes *assume* that men initiated the early Christian missionary movement. But it is clear that women were active very early in this movement as indicated by Paul's own references to "apostles before me" (Rom. 16:7), Phoebe's role (Rom. 16:2), the "people of Chloe," and women among the prophets and leaders (1 Cor. 11, 14).

b. Plural nouns such as "saints," "elect," and "sons" are taken to include female believers, but "apostles," "prophets," and "teachers" refer to men only, in these androcentric assumptions.[46] (Fiorenza lists two additional points, but the above are adequately illustrative.)

After commenting on a wide range of New Testament texts, Fiorenza declares that "the feminist quest for the equality of women was alive in pre-Pauline and Pauline Christianity, and that Paul for the sake of 'order' and for the sake of attracting outsiders appears to react to it."[47]

2. Historical research is not value free. Scholars do make judgments about biblical texts, both in the translations and in interpretation. This is true not only because of the value commitments of the interpreter but also because Scripture functions as inspired authority for Christian communities. The Bible "is not a document of past history"; we "cannot avoid the question of the *meaning* of NT texts for today."

3. "If the word of God is not to become a tool for the patriarchal oppression of women," biblical interpretation "in a post-patriarchal society and church . . . has to insist that solely non-sexist and non-oppressive traditions of the NT and non-androcentric models . . . do justice to divine revelation."[48]

In another article Fiorenza describes the inadequacy of both the dogmatic (traditional) and historical (scientific) methods of biblical interpretation. She calls for a new model, a "pastoral-theological paradigm."[49] This paradigm would integrate elements of both the historical and dogmatic models but would "radically question the presupposition that value-free, neutral, and uncommitted exegetical work is possible."[50] It would put the pastoral situation and our theological response to it in creative tension with the historical and dogmatic study of Scripture. And it would profit much from biblical study which, rather than viewing the Bible as a book of timeless truths, seeks to show how texts are concrete responses to specific needs within communities of faith.[51]

Model 5: Representing the wider trend toward current reassessment of hermeneutical method, Peter Stuhlmacher calls for "a hermeneutics of consent" *(Einverständis)*.[52] This means that our method will seek to conform itself in its presuppositions and outcomes to the nature of the biblical text and at the same time enable us to communicate these learnings to present scholarship and needs within the church. While utilizing elements of the historical-critical method, it will also advocate the principle of accepting the report *(Vernehmens)* and maintain accountability to theological tradition and confessional affirmation. It will seek to blend the horizons of the text and the interpreter in light of the church's tradition and confession; but it will also maintain the Protestant principle of the biblical criticism of tradition, thus respecting the primary position of Scripture. Further, such a "hermeneutics of consent" will test and verify interpretation in the praxis of faith: through personal and corporate *meditation* upon Scripture, through the witness of *preaching*, and through *living* the love, righteousness, reconciliation, and peace of the gospel.[53]

Since no model of hermeneutical principles or understandings is value free, one might question the wisdom of reflecting upon these partial models and proposing yet another one. To do so, however, is a matter of honesty and a resource for clarity. For some model of understanding (I prefer this term to "principles" because it is both more inclusive and less prescriptive in tone) influences whatever method an interpreter uses; it testifies to the interpreter's self-awareness of perspectives influencing the hermeneutical task.

Proposed Components for a Model of Understandings

The model of understandings presented here is an attempt to reflect learnings from this study as well as values and commitments arising from my own *Sitz im Leben*, church commitment, scholarly vocation, and fruitful experiences in Bible study.

1. The community of faith is the proper context in which Scripture is to be understood.

The Mennonite Church statement holds this point of view:

> The Bible is the *book of the people of God*.... The Bible is truly at home within the believing community which gave the Bible its shape.... Thus it is from the perspective of the faith and life of this community of God's people that the Bible can be interpreted and applied to today's world.[54]

Similarly, James Barr writes in "The Bible as a Document of Believing Communities":

> The Bible takes its origin from within the life of believing communities; it is interpreted within the continuing life of these communities; the standard of its religious interpretation is the structure of faith which these communities maintain; and it has the task of providing a challenge, a force for innovation and a source of purification, to the life of these communities.[55]

Several implications arise from this fundamental understanding. First is the awareness that the Bible arose out of the faith experiences of specific historical communities, from the time of Abraham to the end of the first century AD. While this means on the one hand that the Bible arose out of human historical and existential experiences, it also means that it discloses encounter with divine reality. The Bible testifies to God's initiative among, and self-disclosure to, specific groups of people who understood themselves to be the people of God. Because these testimonies to divine revelation encompass well over a thousand years in time, even in their written form, the interpreter must pay attention not only to the vertical axis of communication (God-humanity, humanity-God) but also to the horizontal, the movement from earlier to later testimony, especially because Scripture dialogues with and critiques itself.[56] Further implications of this point will be discussed in point 2 below.

Second, the usual formulation of the long-standing Catholic-Protestant debate over the relative primacy of the Bible and the church does not really fit the historical origins of the Bible. The Protestant doctrine which gives priority to the authority of the Scripture over the church does not fit the historical experience of the biblical people of faith; they did not have the complete Old and New Testaments as we have them today. Certainly they held authoritative many of the beliefs, teachings, and traditions which were incorporated into the final canonical product. But the plain fact of history is that those people gave the later church the Bible; by divine guidance they wrote it, preserved it, and disseminated it. Again, the riddle of the relationship between Bible and church is best solved not by thinking vertically (about which stands over the other) but by thinking horizontally (about which came earlier). While continuous interdependence is evident, it cannot be denied that the believers (the church) who wrote the texts and books came first; but then these texts through their authority exercised direction and sanction over people, bringing believers to birth, nurturing them, and—within the biblical period—leading them to participate again in the divine-human event of making Scripture. To set the Bible and church against each other or one over the other in authority fails to testify appropriately to the historical complexity and the divine mystery of their relationship.[57] It is more helpful to the interpretive process to recognize their inseparable relationship and relate both to the creative power of the Spirit.

A third implication of locating biblical interpretation in the church must be expressed with both negative and positive import. This emphasis does not mean placing a protective hedge around the church's use of the Bible; it is in the church's best interest for the Bible to be scrutinized, questioned, and challenged within secular critical circles, be those the critical enquiry of the university classroom, the practical demands of politics, or the hard economic realities of life. The Bible must be so exposed, because its message is not esoteric. Its own claims speak of universal accountability; no segment of life escapes its significance.

But the credibility and applicability of its claims are appropriately tested "only in the voluntary faith and obedience of the responding [obeying] community."[58] Only within communities of faith should one expect to find the variety of gifts essential to perceive fully and interpret adequately the biblical teachings. And only within such communities should one expect to find the spiritual resources essential to the motivation and empowerment for living as the biblical teachings envision.[59]

2. The view of biblical authority recognizes the significance of both *historical* revelation and historical *revelation*.

To recognize fully the significance of *historical* revelation means that we must take account of several issues already discussed in the sections of hermeneutical commentary above. This understanding will recognize that differences in thought and moral prescription occur not only between the Testaments but also within each Testament. All Scripture is *historically and culturally conditioned;* human language, customs, problems, and experiences—all expressing the arena of the *historical*—are part of the warp and woof of the biblical record. Perhaps the image of a battlefield on which different perspectives fight against each other, as James Barr suggests,[60] is too strong. But at least we must recognize that the Bible is something like an orchestra, in which there are different instruments, blending usually, to be sure, but making distinctly different sounds.

Brevard Childs has pointed the way in calling for intracanonical dialogue, listening to the way in which one part of Scripture complements another.[61] His exegetical samples, however, illustrate some conflicting signals from within the biblical text and call, therefore, for recognizing intracanonical critique, toward which Childs' concluding discussion points. As indicated in chapter 3, this diversity of expression may and should be regarded, in my judgment, as a testimony to biblical authority. The canon itself includes authoritative critique of those perspectives which play only preparatory or accommodating roles. Moreover, the variety of expression testifies to God's taking seriously the history and culture of people. Revelation comes to us not as a timeless truth, but through a historical record with many witnesses from many moments in history. When viewed in this context, the doctrine of plenary inspiration acquires new and rich meaning. The biblical testimony is full and complete in showing how God speaks to humanity, despite the limitations of history, culture, language, custom, and even prejudice.

This approach to the *historical* reality of revelation in history enables both aspects of emphasis, *historical* and *revelation*, to be compatible. This compatibility is essential for believers who take the incarnation seriously. The divine is not diminished by the human in Jesus. The two parts do not compete against each other, according to the biblical witness. Precisely when Jesus suffers and dies, testifying to his complete humanity, the Gospel of Mark declares that then, in that context, he is truly Son of God, divine (Mk. 15:37-39).[62] To hold then that Scripture is conditioned by the human element—i.e., the historical and cultural—is a confession of its glory, since it brings the divine presence and Word into the midst of *real* human situations. In its diversity, even with its mixed signals, the biblical Word is near to minister to the multitude of needs and situations in which God's people find themselves in faithfulness to their missionary calling.

Because it is *God's* Word it is authoritative. Consequently, no part of it can be relegated to a place of nonauthoritative significance. Each part plays its piece, and when heard in *relation to the whole* it accomplishes its purpose. Some parts cannot be taken as normative by themselves; they were never meant to be. But when each part is viewed in relation to the one to whom all Scripture points (Jn. 5:38-39), the authority of its testimony then becomes clear.

For this reason the authority of Scripture cannot be separated from the authority of Jesus Christ, who reveals God most fully, completely, and clearly. In Jesus also, the riddle of how the divine and human live together is resolved through demonstration.

3. The method of study must enable the interpreter to grasp and respond to the text's distinctive message.

Another understanding which the above learnings prompt and which informs the method proposed below is that we should use a method that, first, helps us grasp the meaning of the text in its distinctive historical and literary character. Such a method must be both historically critical and linguistically sensitive.[63] It must respect the "life" of each text, allowing it to speak its own distinctive word. It must insist on putting distance between the interpreter and the text so that the text is free to do more than merely mirror the beliefs and prejudices of the interpreter. It must be able to create the situation in which the interpreter occasionally may "not like" what he/she sees and learns. Not until this happens has the method provided its full worth.

Having freed the text to speak with its own power, the method must prompt the text to engage the interpreter with its life message, thus exercising its power over the interpreter. The interpreter then needs to choose whether to accept or refuse the power and message of the text. If the interpreter refuses, the task of interpretation is aborted; it is not allowed to finish its intended course. If the interpreter accepts the life message of the text, a co-creative event occurs; the text generates a new life-reality, a person-force in time and space whose thought and life will be marked by the soul force of the text.

More and more scholars are conceding that the historical-critical method, while assisting well the task of distancing the text from the biases of the interpreter, has not been able to prompt or manage the rejoining of the text's message to the life-world of the interpreter. Further, its principle of analogy, accepting as historical only that which corresponds to our human experience, has come under severe criticism also. In its most critical form and by itself, therefore, the historical-critical method is inadequate.[64] Various efforts to remedy this deficiency have been attempted, some within the framework of the method itself, and others introducing considerations which alter the method. Elsewhere I describe and evaluate these endeavors.[65]

The method proposed in the next section utilizes many helpful aspects of the historical-critical method,[66] but introduces several features which are not included in the historical-critical method in its normal scope and work.[67] For more extensive presentations of how methods similar to this one work in the study of the biblical texts, see Perry B. Yoder, *From Word to Life: A Guide to the Art of Bible Study,* and Henry A. Virkler, *Hermeneutics: Principles and Processes of Biblical Interpretation.*[68] Hans Rudi Weber has also contributed a very helpful description of Bible study method.[69]

4. The method must include assessment of the influences upon the interpreter.

This model of understanding recognizes that no interpretation is value free; every interpreter is influenced by a distinctive constellation of psychological, religious, social, economic, and political forces. For this reason the method itself must allow for an assessment of these influences in the interpretive process. This will require what Segundo has called social analysis, but even this is too limited. The assessment must include not only social, political, and economic factors, but also religious, psychological, familial, and biological (male/female) factors. But, most importantly, the assessment in my judgment, is not a precondition for understanding the text; the assessment itself is facilitated and critically controlled by the text. When we truly hear the biblical word, *we see who we are.*

An essential asset to this dialectic of hearing the text and assessing who we are is the Christian church in its global existence. As interpreters listen to and learn from other interpreters—men from women, whites from blacks, western Christians from eastern Christians, the wealthy from the poor (and vice versa)—new discoveries of truth in both the text and the self will emerge. The past reality of the church, the voices from history, are also part of this resource. The study of our own tradition of faith together with learning from other traditions will greatly aid the process of understanding who we are in the light of the biblical text. And in order not to miss what should be obvious, every interpreter must submit his/her insights to the testing of other members of the community of faith. This is important not only for validating interpretation (see 7 below) but also for assisting in the self-assessment of influences upon every interpreter.

Within every interpreter, various obstacles to the interpretive process may also be present (see Appendix 1, p. 243). These obstacles may block the interpretive process either at the point of discovering the distinctive message of the text, affirming its message once discovered, or enabling the insight to seek and gain consensual confirmation.

5. Interpretation includes reflection upon the significance of the distance between the text and the interpreter.

As the interpreter discovers the meaning of the biblical text in its setting and assesses the many influences that affect his/her grasp of the text's meaning, it is also necessary to reflect upon what has created the distance between the worlds of the Bible and the interpreter. This reflection should consist of both analytical and evaluative components.

The analytical component asks basic questions such as: how are these two worlds structurally different (religiously, socially, politically, and economically)? What (how) has the history of the Christian church contributed to this difference (in broad strokes, one considers the history of the early church, Constantinianism, Reformation history, the church's missionary history, denominational schism, and current quests for faithfulness and unity)? What have the theological and ethical traditions of the church contributed to this distance (in the rise of the just war theory, the significance of the Reformation and Counter-Reformation, Christianity's encounter with world religions, and the theological and ethical accents of one's own denomination)? In this analysis, one needs to think also of the significance of science, medicine, sociology, and psychology.

The evaluative task, quite difficult indeed, consists of assessing how societal changes, the history of the church, and theological-ethical perspectives affect the significance of the particular text. Among the many considerations that compete for attention on this agenda, two merit priority, in my judgment. How is the distance between text and interpreter, of whatever nature, to be correlated with faithfulness to the biblical teaching? And second, to what extent should the interpreter accommodate the biblical teaching to the contemporary world or situation *and/or* to what extent should the interpreter seek to change the contemporary situation and world in order to respond obediently to the biblical teaching and its values?

6. The purpose of biblical interpretation is the edification of believers and the discovery of God's Word to humanity.

Appendix 4, on the different uses of the Bible, speaks directly to the purposes of biblical interpretation. All of these functions have as their goal the edification of believers personally and corporately. These uses of Scripture proceed within the faith conviction that the Bible testifies to ultimate truth, God almighty. Hence while *interpretation* forever remains within the realm of personal and corporate confession, it confesses precisely that God's revelation of truth—the truth about God, humanity, and the cosmos—is the reason for interpretation. The struggle for correct interpretation witnesses to belief in historical transcendence: someone beyond us, objective reality, is disclosed through historical revelation in the Scripture. This one calls believers—indeed all people—to repentance, obedience, and praise of the divine name and purpose.

This understanding, making interpretation a servant to belief in God's self-disclosure, involves then the willingness to change. As our discovery of truth increases through interpretation, then our beliefs and behavior will change in accord with the interpretive insights. Behavioral change is a primary goal of interpretation in this understanding. Or as the Bible itself puts it, we are to become more and more conformed to the image of God in Jesus Christ (Rom. 8:29; 2 Cor. 3:18; 1 Jn. 3:1-3).

⋇ (7) Interpretation is validated through several important processes.

As a given interpretation seeks consensual affirmation, which I have called "objective status" on the human level, various ways of testing the interpretation occur. This testing has as its goal what may be called the validation of interpretation. Hence one often hears the question: is the interpretation valid? Does it stand up under scrutiny? Numerous processes contribute to the validating of an interpretation. I mention five important factors.

First, to verify an interpretation—i.e., to test it for its validity—one examines (possibly repeats) the study which led to that interpretation. For this to be done, the method of study leading to a given interpretation must be clearly demonstrated. The various elements of study, as described in the method below, for example, must be clearly enunciated by the interpreter so that another person can follow the logic and development of thought. The overall coherence and cogency of the interpreter's comments, as assessed by those who test the interpretation, will determine to a great extent whether the interpretation can be said to be valid.

Second, the testing of an interpretation according to one's sense of spiritual rightness is an important part of the validating process. This may be called the testimony of the Holy Spirit as it bears witness in our spirits. Granted, the content and the specifics of this criterion vary from person to person, but this factor contributes greatly to one's judgment of whether a given interpretation is valid. It is striking that the early church, in reporting its most difficult hermeneutical decision, said, "For it has seemed good to the Holy Spirit and to us ..." (Acts 15:28). The Holy Spirit, discerned within the community, played a major role in both determining and validating the decision. To be sure, many empirical historical factors contribute to a person's or community's perception of the Spirit's leading (this goes back to point 4), but the significance of this factor must not be overlooked.

Third, the discerning community of believers plays an important role in validating interpretation (see point 1 above). The community, whether the local congregation or a churchwide body, assesses an interpretation's coherence with the central tenets of its traditional beliefs, its relationship to wider Christian beliefs, or the way the interpretation accords or conflicts with how the community discerns the Spirit to be moving (see again Acts 15). Some interpretations don't win the affirmation of the community; these will be modified, wait for a more auspicious moment, or simply die. This model of understandings regards this process to be an important part of validating interpretation.

Fourth, concurring with Peter Stuhlmacher's point above, interpretation is also validated through its expression in life, the "praxis of faith." The incorporation of understanding (interpretation) into our lives through meditation, through worship, and through living accordingly functions as an empirical, validating criterion. But while this validates the claim to understanding, the incarnation of interpretation in life and praxis of itself does not validate the *rightness* of the interpretation. For this reason the call to praxis—living it out—must be put into critical and creative tension with the other aspects of the validating process.

Fifth, another important element in the validating process is how the interpretation stands up under cross-cultural testing. Because the church in its essential nature must be missionary in its thought and action, its understandings can never be, or remain, provincial. When particular insights are affirmed by people in various cultural settings, they gain validity. They stand as something more than personal insights or cultural biases. Since the Christian faith makes universal claims, this aspect of validation is important.

8. God's Spirit plays a creative, illuminative role in biblical interpretation.

The Spirit significantly influences not only the validation process, but also the interpretive process. Traditionally it has been said that the Spirit illumines the Word. The meaning of this statement in its broadest aspects merits reflection. The Hebrew and

Greek words for spirit (*ruach* and *pneuma*) have a wide range of meaning: "wind" (physical), "breath" (physiological), "good or bad spirits" (psychological), and "divine Spirit" (paranormal). The Spirit is God's mighty presence, which with the Word was the agent of creation (Gen. 1; Ps. 33:6).

Every student of Scripture knows there are times of dryness in study. But those who persevere in the task also know times of creative breakthrough, keen perception *(Erkenntnis)* in which mind and spirit *(Geist)* work together in almost a paranormal way. This, I suggest, happens because the Word and Spirit are at home with each other. Exactly opposite from the notion that one need not study but only depend on the Spirit, this model calls for a dynamic interaction between the hard discipline of study and the uplifting breakthroughs of creative insight. The Spirit works through the word and the word becomes Word through the Spirit.[70]

The significance of this understanding for the hermeneutical task is that every method provides only the structure for the study of the Bible. In the context of this framework, an encounter occurs. In the co-creative moment, text and interpreter experience life by the power of the divine Spirit. Without this experience, interpretation falls short of its ultimate potential and purpose.

Proposed Method for Bible Study

Although the scope of this project does not allow a full development of a proposed method for Bible study, it will be helpful to sketch in brief the main aspects and procedures of a recommended method. Perry Yoder's companion volume mentioned above demonstrates quite fully the linguistic and historical dimensions of Bible study, giving examples of how the method works on four different texts. Though informed by both the linguistic and historical perspectives in biblical study and various philosophical orientations,[71] my statement of method has been influenced to a major extent by an inductive method of Bible study, outlined more fully in my book on Mark's Gospel.[72]

This method reflects the conviction that there are three main tasks in the interpretive event. These are not neatly successive stages, as the proposed method might suggest, but they constantly interact and, in reality, constitute one co-creative event.

The first important task in biblical interpretation is listening to the text, *listening* carefully from *within* the text. Although I recognize the significance that ideology plays in interpretation, I nonetheless maintain that the interpreter most honors the text by seeking with all the powers of his/her being to make the encounter with the text an event of understanding generated by the text itself. Granted, there will be dialogue between the interpreter and the text in this process, but the co-creative event of interpretation should be as novel and distinctive as is each given text.

The second main task in biblical interpretation is *learning* helpfully from *behind* the text. While the first phase concentrates on the linguistic dimension of the interpretive task (see Perry Yoder's first three steps under the "conventions of language"), the second phase focuses upon the historical aspect of interpretation (which Yoder calls the "context for interpretation").[73] At this point the above emphasis on the historical and cultural cradle for biblical revelation comes sharply into focus, enabling the interpreter to better understand the message/event of the text.

Finally, the third important task in biblical interpretation consists of *living* freely from *in front of* the text. If biblical interpretation is a co-creative event, as this study proposes, then its significance lies precisely and ultimately in the text's creative power to free the interpreter for a new life in thought and action that without the text would not have become historically possible. In this view of textual significance, the task is not merely applying a learning to a given situation. To be sure, it includes that but it involves much more; the interpretive event co-creates a new human being, a new history, and a new culture. Interpretation tells history's story, and each interpreter takes the stand to give testimony before the giver of the text and the judge of history.

These three components of biblical interpretation may also be described, in somewhat weakened but more programmatic form, as *observation* of the text, ascertaining *meaning* in the text, and discovering the *significance* of the text. Each of these three main components or tasks consists of sub-tasks, outlined as follows:

A. *Listen* carefully from *within* the text *(observation).*

1. Hear, read (aloud) and reread the text, observing its world of distinctive structural relationships, contrasts, comparisons, repetitions, progression, etc.[74] Write down these observations and creatively diagram how various components of the structure, especially key words, relate to each other.

2. Become aware of the literary forms, the particular type of literature, and the distinctive images of the text. Respect the distinctiveness of each of these features in the process of listening carefully to the text.

3. Read the text in several translations, or in several languages if possible, including the original. Rather than seeking immediately to analyze differences among translations, allow yourself to respond holistically to the text. Respond to the text by asking questions and expressing feelings, even frustration with its message. At this point some attachment to the text must develop in order to sustain with spirit further investigation of its meaning.

B. *Learn* helpfully from *behind* the text *(meaning)*.

4. Define the important words or terms that occur in the text. This may require the type of work that falls into steps 6 and 8 below. Notice also the significance of the grammatical constructions, such as tense of verb or word order.

5. Study the literary context of the specific text, and identify the function of the specific text within the larger literary narrative, including the entire book. It is important to notice that texts play roles within literary narratives. Each text's personality cannot be adequately appreciated until those literary roles are identified. Imagine that the particular text is to be used within a dramatic production of the entire literary piece. What role does it play in the larger narrative and drama?

6. Identify as accurately as possible the specific historical setting in which the text was written, both of the writer and of the writing's recipients. Describe as fully as possible the religious, cultural, economic, and political factors playing significant roles in the historical milieu of the text.

7. Attempt to grasp as completely as possible the distinctive message and meaning of the specific text; after feeling its import and impact, place it in dialogue with other teachings and messages of the entire biblical text. If biblical study to date has been limited, use other resources more extensively, either oral discussion, group process or secondary literature and biblical commentaries. When placing a particular text in dialogue and perhaps even tension with other biblical texts, consider the directional factor in the unfolding drama of biblical revelation. Consider here the relationship between the Old and New Testaments and the way in which all Scripture witnesses to the authority of Jesus Christ, the supreme revelation of God.

8. Learn how the text has been understood and interpreted by other believers and scholars in various settings throughout church history. Good commentaries are useful for this task. But commitment to the lifelong endeavor of learning how others have under-

stood given texts and teachings, is also necessary. Special effort should be given to discover how believers in cultural, economic, and political situations other than that of the interpreter have understood the particular text.

C. *Live* freely from *in front of* the text *(significance)*.

9. Put the text aside momentarily, and examine yourself. As if looking in a mirror, ask yourself, "Who am I?" As interpreters, we need to think about our situations in life and identify as fully as possible our biases, prejudices, our unique strengths, and our weaknesses that we bring to the interpretation of a text. We must ask ourselves: does my situation in life enable me to identify with the message of the text—culturally, economically, politically, and religiously? We should think about people we know who are quite different from ourselves in all these respects and ask how they would hear the particular textual message.

10. Reflect upon the significance of the distance between the world of the text and your world. Identify differences in societal structure and what the history and thought of the church has contributed to these differences. Assess these changes, asking how the text speaks God's Word to you in your world, what effect you—as a result of the text—should have upon your world, and how you should bring about this effect or change.

11. Take up the text again, read it aloud, and spend time in meditation. Respect again the distinctive personality of the text, allowing for feelings of not liking it, wanting to doubt its teaching, and even weakness in adequately responding to it. As you and the text struggle together, open yourself to the creative Spirit power of the Word. Pray, sing, write, remain silent, rebel, cry, embrace, confess—whatever the text in its power calls you to do. In light of this response, assess your life values, vocational responsibility, and future goals. This should be done as a deliberate effort to correlate the impact of the text with behavioral patterns, both at the routine and intentional levels. All spheres of one's life should be opened to analysis and critique by the text.

12. Test your co-creative experience of interpretation with brothers and sisters in the believing community, and perhaps also with some unbelievers. The purpose of the testing is not merely to ascertain whether a particular understanding is correct or appropriate, but to make one's own life-world a part of a corporate life-world and thus contribute to the reality of Christian (or Jewish) community, fulfilling the edificatory function of Scripture.

Those with limited experience in Bible study may feel overwhelmed by the extensiveness of this suggested method for Bible study. But it should be remembered, as pointed out above, that these steps do not necessarily occur in neat chronological order. In many cases, these different aspects of the task proceed side by side or as part and parcel of each other. This is how it should be, for interpretation is as much an art as it is a science. Neither this nor any other suggested method should be followed in a ritualistic manner. However, discipline often stimulates creativity, and creativity in turn transforms discipline into worship.

CONCLUSION: SUMMARY OF LEARNINGS

To conclude this study, it will be useful to summarize the various hermeneutical learnings that have emerged in the hermeneutical commentaries on the various case issues and in chapter 5. These learnings may also be regarded as theses resulting from the study. In order to facilitate the correlation of these theses with the discussion in the book, I have indicated the chapter and page numbers where such discussion is found.

1. Quoting the Bible does not in itself guarantee correctness of position. The best meaning of "literal interpretation" is the effort to understand the plain meaning of the text, based upon study of both the grammatical-literary features and the historical setting of the text. Using texts out of context is a misuse of the Bible. (Chapter 1, pp. 58-60.)

2. To avoid selective use of evidence, the entire biblical witness on a given subject should be considered. This will lead to considering how biblical teaching with its variety and even apparent contradiction is authoritative; it will lead also to discerning how certain parts of the biblical witness critique other parts. (Chapter 1, p. 60, chapter 3, p. 138; see also points 12-15 on page 232).

3. Each particular text or section of the Bible should be used for its main emphasis, not for its attendant features. For this reason our study of the Bible should focus on literary units—paragraphs, chapters, sections, and entire books. (Chapter 1, p. 60, chapter 5, pp. 225-226; Appendix 1, p. 240).

4. The interpreter should give priority to theological principles and basic moral imperatives rather than to specific counsel on particular topics when these two contradict. This is part of the effort to determine how the Bible functions normatively for believing communities removed from the history and culture in which it was written. It is related also to the concern that we follow the "spirit of Scripture" and not become legalistic in interpretation. Hanging major positions on a particular—possibly even questionable meaning of a word, or on one or two texts, should be avoided. (Chapter 1, pp. 61-62; chapter 5, pp. 203-204, 212-213.)

5. The interpreter needs to examine carefully the factors that influence his/her use of Scripture. Religious, social, political, and economic factors affect our use of the Bible. Behind these are psychic forces related to our own lives, loves, values, and circles of friendship. Our communities of relationship and empathy affect our use of Scripture. Interpretations which selfishly benefit the power of the interpreter, or the group he/she represents, run counter to the basic teaching and spirit of the biblical message. The interpreter must seek by all means to become aware of the ideology guiding the interpretation and assess it by means of the Scripture and Christian communities of faith. (Chapter 1, pp. 62-63; chapter 2, pp. 81-92, chapter 4, pp. 183-186; chapter 5, p. 220).

6. Biblical interpreters must learn from the poor, the slave, the disenfranchised, the persecuted, and the oppressed. The eyes of these people have gifts of insight which bring the biblical message into clear focus. In their interpretation, prayer as cry and song as hope blend together, a "ring of truth" for all to hear. Interpretation which legitimates oppression of any kind should be avoided, because it runs counter to the central biblical teaching of justice and love. (Chapter 1, pp. 56-58; chapter 3, pp. 108-110; chapter 5, pp. 213-114.)

7. The influence of church tradition upon biblical interpretation is very significant. This influence has several dimensions. The beliefs and practices of the early church, especially in the second to fourth centuries AD, inform the interpreter's understanding of the Bible. Differences in interpreting and assessing those beliefs and practices makes understanding the Bible more difficult. The interpreter's religious tradition also exercises enormous influence upon his/her insights and judgments. The influence of church tradition functions both negatively and positively in the interpretive process. (Chapter 2, pp. 91-92; chapter 5, pp. 215-217.)

8. Sustained reading and study of the biblical text is necessary

to overcome the economic, political, sociological, psychological, and religious influences that affect our interpretation of the Bible. We should seek to become conscious of these influences upon us and use a method for the study of Scripture which gives us distance from these influences. Through sustained listening to the text, the message of the text may puncture, change, and convert the interpreter's biases and ideologies. (Chapter 1, p. 63; chapter 2, pp. 92-95; chapter 4, 185-186; chapter 5, pp. 224-227.)

9. The biblical interpreter should recognize the temporal and cultural distance that exists between the world of the Bible and the world of the believer today, especially when addressing social issues. Whether the topic be slavery, war, or the role of women, the meaning of the same word, command, or instruction may differ significantly depending upon the historical and cultural place and time in which it was and is spoken. Especially when the issue involves societal structures, the faith communities of Judaism and Christianity must consider their responsibility for those structures. It was (is) one thing for Christians to live together in Christian ways without seeking to change an oppressive societal structure such as slavery when Christians as a small minority had (have) no reins on the structure; but it is quite another thing for Christians to argue for such structures when they are created and sustained mostly by Christians. Whether we use the distance between the text and the interpreter to excuse or assist us in Christian discipleship is most significant. (Chapter 1, p. 54; chapter 3, pp. 146-147; chapter 5, pp. 213, 221).

10. The historical-critical method as employed in biblical studies is useful because it respects the distance between the interpreter and the text, making it possible for the text to speak its distinctive message. At its best the historical-critical method enables the interpreter to grasp the distinctive character of each text by placing it in its historical and cultural setting. By learning as much as possible about the situation of the writer and of the writing's recipients, the interpreter gains a clearer understanding of the text. But this method cannot perform the total task of interpretation; other perspectives and resources are necessary to supplement it. (Chapter 2, pp. 92-95; chapter 5, pp. 219-220; Appendix 1, 243-245).

11. The relationship between the Old and New Testaments is an important question in biblical interpretation, especially on issues such as Sabbath observance and participation in war. One most fruitful understanding of that relationship regards the New

Testament to be related to the Old as fulfillment is to promise. The fulfillment in Jesus, portrayed in the New Testament, provides the pattern of authority which should be considered normative. But a proper understanding of New Testament teaching frequently depends upon seeing clearly the structures of thought and life in the Old Testament which the New Testament fulfills. Hence both of the Testaments are important for serious Bible study. (Chapter 3, pp. 139-142; Appendix 1, pp. 237-238).

12. Both diversity and unity of thought are present in the Bible. Differences of perspective emerge not only between the Testaments but also within each Testament. But these differences, if viewed as God's taking history and culture seriously, can be regarded positively. Coherence amid the diversity is expected not at the level where all statements say the same thing, or where all expressions of faith are uniform, but rather at the point of seeking fidelity to the central testimony. (Chapter 3, pp. 142-144; chapter 4, pp. 186-189).

13. Diversity within the canon testifies to revelation in *history* and expresses what might be called the missionary principle. In taking the differences in history and culture seriously, biblical revelation engages in a two-way contextualization: contextualizing the gospel to people in their world and culture and at the same time contextualizing the varied cultures and experiences of people into conformity with God's will and kingdom (Chapter 3, pp. 145-146; chapter 4, pp. 186-191; chapter 5, pp. 217-219).

14. Biblical interpretation benefits greatly from keeping the missionary factor central. This is true because this emphasis lies at the heart of the fulfillment stream of biblical revelation (see point 11 above) and because it provides the appropriate perspective for us in ascertaining how diversity of expression, occasional injunctions, and cultural seriousness function positively in our use of the Bible. Only when the missionary factor is taken seriously in biblical interpretation can the church begin to assess the positive and negative features in the church's role as an agent of cultural change. (Chapter 4, pp. 188, 191).

15. Seen within the context of this missionary principle, the authority of the Bible is heightened, not diminished, by diversity of thought and expression. Even statements or teachings that appear to be contradictions on the propositional level may be understood as evidence of incarnational seriousness, God's risking of the divine message to the limitations of human history and experience. Although some expressions of the divine-human encounter may ap-

pear to be nonrevelatory to us, the relating of these events to the central stream of biblical teaching gives us illuminating, instructive, even revelatory insight. (Chapter 3, pp. 144-146; chapter 4, pp. 189-191; chapter 5, pp. 217-219).

16. The divine and human dimensions of biblical revelation are not such that they can be materially distinguished, as though some parts are divine and others human. Rather, as in the incarnation, the divine and human dwell together so that the divine is manifested in the human and the human in the divine, because of revelation *in history*. The cultural human factor is present not only in some texts but in all of the Bible. Thus, in every situation of biblical teaching the Word is near to us, sometimes instructing us to take culture more seriously and sometimes instructing us to strongly critique our culture. (Chapter 4, pp. 189-191; chapter 5, pp. 217-219).

17. The more occasional nature of some biblical teaching needs to be taken into account. When it is clear that a specific teaching was occasioned by specific problems and needs, its very specificity should be instructive to us as a model or paradigm, suggesting how we too in our settings may make specific applications of the gospel's teaching. But such applications then and now should not be regarded as timeless prescriptions. The diversity of application and expression instructs otherwise. (Chapter 4, pp. 187-191; Appendix 4, pp. 274-275).

18. Bearing in mind these various hermeneutical learnings, the church should use the Bible to address social and political issues in both its life and witness. Jesus' teachings and life have direct bearing upon social, economic, and political issues. Christian believers, both personally and corporately, should allow kingdom ethics to shape their own values to be lived out in all of life. Analysis of one's society should be made from the criteria of Christian values informed essentially by the Bible. (Chapter 3, pp. 148-149; chapter 5, pp. 204-211.)

19. The purpose of biblical interpretation is the discovery of God's purpose and will for humanity and the edification of God's people. Scripture points to Christ and to God as final authority. Interpretation, therefore, stands always in the service of obedience and worship; it calls for humbly walking with God and depends upon the vision and power of the Spirit. While the method of interpretation is indeed important, no precise set of rules can be rigidly formulated or followed in biblical interpretation. This freedom, arising from the Spirit, should not be taken, however, as

an excuse for self-justifying tendencies or laziness in study and exegesis. (Chapter 5, pp. 221-222).

20. Biblical interpretation is not a private enterprise. In the last analysis it is not the domain of either the individual or the scholar. Interpretation should be tested and validated by communities of faith. The insights and truth claims of one community should be shared with and tested by other communities of faith, especially in order to seek cross-cultural validation. Not only is interpretation to be cognitively evaluated and affirmed by communities of faith, but the value claims of the Bible are adequately perceived and tested also only by the faithful church, the people who seek to live by the power of God's salvation. (Chapter 3, p. 149; chapter 5, pp. 203, 222-223; Appendix 1, pp. 236-237.)

21. The interpreter should regard the community of faith, rather than society as a whole, to be accountable to the biblical teaching. As communities of faith live out the ethical vision and the teachings of the Bible, the patterns of biblical morality will exist in society as testimony and witness. Church members should be held accountable to the biblical standard and expected to exemplify that way of life to unbelievers. This seriousness about moral values among believers becomes then the basis for witness to the larger society (to the state, for example, on political issues). (Chapter 1, pp. 54-56, 63-64; chapter 3, pp. 148-149; chapter 5, pp. 215-217.)

22. Finally, and most importantly, biblical interpretation is co-creation with God. We should follow a method of interpretation that enables us to listen carefully to the text, to learn about the context behind the text, and to respond obediently and freely to the message of the text. The power of the past, the opportunity of the present, and the shape of the future lie awesomely in our God-given capacity to interpret, to understand and act, to co-create. (Introduction, pp. 21-24; chapter 5, pp. 222-227.)

BIBLICAL INTERPRETATION IN THE LIFE OF THE CHURCH

I. Understandings for Biblical Interpretation

A. The Origin of the Bible

The Bible is God's gift to humanity through divine revelation and inspiration. We believe that God was at work over the centuries through the process by which the books of the Bible were inspired, written, collected, and recognized as authoritative. What we call the Old Testament was accepted by Israel as the standard for faith and practice, that is, canonized, in three stages; first the law, then the prophets, and finally the writings. These three sections make up the Hebrew Bible used by Jesus and His disciples (Luke 24:44), and by the synagogue and the church today.

Additional books, known as the Apocrypha and included in the Greek Old Testament, are used by some parts of the Christian church. These books provide help for understanding the period between the Testaments.

The books in the New Testament were inspired and written basically within the first century in response to the new covenant and the fulfillment of the Old Testament in Christ. The four Gospels, the Pauline letters, and more gradually the remaining parts of the New Testament were given a place of authority equal and ulti-

Adopted by Mennonite General Assembly, June 18-24, 1977, Estes Park, Colorado; edited by Willard Swartley for use in this book.

mately superior to that of the Old Testament. By the end of the second century a book was recognized as canonical when it was commonly read in the worship services. Although certain books were "disputed" for centuries, the twenty-seven now in the New Testament were widely accepted by the church by the fourth century. These books served to preserve the gospel of Jesus Christ and the earliest apostolic witness against the distortions of legalism and heresies.

B. The Bible and the Believing Community

The Bible is *the Book of the people of God.* It is the testimony of God's people to the prophetic Word and historic events. Through this Word and these events God created a special people with a peculiar political shape among the nations. Their unique testimony finds understanding and credibility in the ongoing community of faith. The Bible is truly at home within the believing community which gave the Bible its shape. The Bible in turn has shaped the people of God. Thus, it is from the perspective of the faith and life of this community of God's people that the Bible can be interpreted and applied to today's world.

The at-homeness of the Bible in the community of faith speaks to *the issue of biblical authority.* Unfortunately, the Bible and the church are often seen as contrasting authorities. The unique authority and rule of God in Christ which is set forth in the Bible can become apparent only in the voluntary faith and obedience of the responding community.

The believing community is an *interpreting community.* This means that the community will have students who give themselves to the study and teaching of the Bible. The task of such students is not to dominate the process of interpreting the Word, but to exercise leadership in this area. It is the task of each member to participate in the interpretation of the Bible. We believe that God gives special insight to individuals as they read and study the Bible. These insights are to be tested in the community (1 Cor. 14:29; 2 Pet. 1:20, 21). This testing of interpretations ultimately needs to involve the whole people of God—individuals, study groups, congregations, conferences, denominations, and wider church.

Through interpretation of the Bible the church finds direction for its life according to God's will. The written Word points to the living Word, Jesus Christ (Jn. 5:38-40). Where Christians are committed to Christ, biblical teaching, and to each other, binding and loosing decisions can be made for obedient life together (Mt. 18:18). God's people can find their way to belief and behavior acceptable to God, thus becoming "living epistles, known and read by all men" (2 Cor. 3:2).

God's people also interpret the Bible in order to communicate its message faithfully to the world. The church is in mission. This means that the church must understand both the Bible and the modern world, and must know how to mediate the message of the Bible to that world. Examples of how this may be done are found within the Bible itself, especially in such writings as the preaching of Hosea, as he tried to reach the Baalists, and in the letters of Paul, as he reached out to the Greeks.

The believing community has more than the Bible. Jesus, our risen Lord, is with us through *the Holy Spirit.* The Bible itself is a gift of the Spirit through inspiration. The community is the temple of the Holy Spirit (1 Cor. 3:16) who enables God's people to grasp the truth of the biblical revelation. The Spirit makes the written Word active in our lives and in the world.

We deny the integrity of knowledge that is not obedient. The failure of the community in relation to interpretation is not so much that we have had the wrong methods or conclusions, but that repentance and obedience often do not follow. Knowledge without obedience is twisted and distorted, even as knowledge without love is blind and dark (1 Jn. 2:3-11; 4:6-21; Jn. 14:15-24). Love is necessary to know the mind of Jesus. *Obedience and love* open the door to interpretive insight. The one who wills to do God's will shall know the doctrine (Jn. 7:17). For the believers' church, biblical knowledge apart from the loving obedience of the community of faith is alien and idolatrous (2 Cor. 10:5).

The community which lives under the authority of the Word and Spirit is entered by *mature choice,* marked by conviction and commitment. Membership in the community of faith is not determined by accidents of birth, geography, race, or sex. The community does not depend on its children for its existence in the next generation, but introduces them to the same Lord of whom it witnesses to the world. This matter of mature commitment is the community's safeguard of the freedom to respond in radical obedience to its Lord, even at the risk of death.

C. Important Theological Perspectives (emphases from the history and tradition of the church)

1. Old and New as promise and fulfillment.

The Bible is the story of God and God's redeemed people. The covenant/testament which God made with the Israelites at Sinai was based on God's saving action and the willing response of the people. This covenant was good. It prepared for the new covenant based on God's new and decisive act in Christ (Jer. 31:31; Mk. 14:24; Heb. 7:22). The Old Testament gives to us an understanding of God, creation, sin, and redemption, which is essential for the understanding of the New Testament.

The Old Testament tells us of covenants of promise (Gen. 12:1-3; Ex. 19:5, 6; Eph. 2:12). The New Testament tells of the fulfillment of the promise (Mt. 5:17). The Bible, then, witnesses to the whole historical drama of God acting to call, save, and preserve a people. While the Old Testament provides the theological setting and is essential to the understanding of the New Testament, the New Testament explains and fulfills, but does not destroy the Old Testament. We read the Old Testament from our position as servants of a new covenant (2 Cor. 3:6), with Jesus as Lord.

The relation of the Testaments, therefore, is best understood as one of promise and fulfillment. The Old Testament, however, also challenges the worldly concept of political power, especially in its rejection of human kingship. Thanks to archaeology and progress in ancient Near Eastern studies, much more is known about the Old Testament today than in the time of the Reformation or even in the first century. These new understandings can help us see that the insights of Jesus (as he clashed with the Zealots and others of his day in the interpretation of the Old Testament in regard to his messiahship) were not arbitrary intrepretations which moved off in a new direction. Rather, Jesus shows us the true intent and direction of the Word of the Lord in the Old Testament.

Hence both a close connection and a difference exist between the Testaments. The two Testaments are more at home with each other than either is at home with the literature produced by their environments. The discontinuity of the New Testament with the Old is most evident at the points where the people of God did not live up to the best of the old covenant. Because of this disobedience, a new act of God was necessary to write a new covenant on their hearts (Jer. 31:31-34; 1 Cor. 11:25; Heb. 8:8-13). The detour into kingship "to be like the nations" is one example of the effect of environment on God's people which helped to distort their expectations of the Messiah and the kingdom of God.

2. The kingdom of God.

The people of God in the Old Testament, with God as Ruler (Judg. 3:22, 23; 1 Sam. 8:7), were experiencing something of the kingdom of God. Jesus the Messiah came to establish a new phase of God's kingdom on earth. Jesus spoke repeatedly of the kingdom of God, which he said was near at hand (Mk. 1:15), or had already broken in upon them (Lk. 11:20).

Christ's kingdom has a spiritual and a social character. Through the Word God rules the new community, begotten by the power of the Spirit. The ultimate fulfillment of the kingdom is yet to come, but Christ is Lord now in the life of believers (Acts 2:36; 1 Cor. 15:24; Rev. 11:15).

The Bible speaks of two kingdoms, the kingdom of God and the kingdom of this world. These two kingdoms are separate and distinct. The believer belongs to Christ's kingdom. Loyalty to this kingdom is absolute, making believers strangers and pilgrims in this world. The kingdom of this world is ruled by worldly wisdom and force, the kingdom of God by the Spirit of Jesus and love. The kingdom of God endures forever; the other is passing away (1 Cor. 7:31).

Positions of responsibility in Christ's kingdom are not posions of authority over others but opportunities for service (Lk. 22:25, 26). Disciples are sent into the world (Jn. 17:18) to share the knowledge of God and of Jesus Christ. This servanthood may lead to suffering and to the cross (Mk. 8:35).

Because Jesus teaches love, even for enemies, his followers cannot use weapons of force either to punish evil or defend the good (Jn. 18:36; 2 Cor. 10:4). Christians are called to be guided by the confident hope that God's kingdom will triumph through the loving words and deeds of the suffering Christ, the Lamb (Rev. 5), and believers who suffer with him (Mk. 8:34—9:1; Rom. 8:17).

3. Jesus, the Lord of Scripture.

Jesus Christ is confessed to be the Lord of Scripture. What he said and did carries divine authority. Because he revealed the will of God, Jesus opens our eyes to understand the Scriptures (Lk. 24:25). His life, obedient suffering, death, and resurrection are our guide for interpreting the Bible. All the writers of the New Testament witness to the saving event of Jesus Christ and the creation and growth of his church. The Gospels are testimonies to the ministry of Jesus and the whole New Testament is a response to this unique event. The Sermon on the Mount (Mt. 5-7) is an important summary of what it means to be disciples of our Lord. Further, the teachings of Jesus, extended into new situations through the Spirit and the apostles, are reflected throughout the New Testament.

4. Word and Spirit.

The Bible has been given to humanity through the work of the Holy Spirit. The Spirit also enables the reader to understand the Word. The Spirit gives life to the written words. Only as the Word penetrates our lives, and its message is personally appropriated, does the text become living and powerful. It is then no longer a dead letter, but a life-giving Word. When a Scripture thus becomes a living truth, is related to other texts, and then is understood within the larger framework of the biblical message, the Bible has meaning and authority.

The aid of the Spirit is necessary, therefore, for proper interpretation and appropriation. The Spirit thus witnesses to the authority of Scripture. No congregation and no prophet may claim with authority to have heard the Spirit, unless in the testing of that

Spirit, the insight is perceived to be in harmony with Scripture.

II. Interpreting the Bible

The *ultimate goal* in interpretation is to allow the Bible to speak its own message with a view to worship and obedience. In many cases what a passage says is clear. Then, the task of interpretation is concerned with discerning at what points the message touches life. However, in some cases the meaning of the passage must first be determined by careful study.

Letting the Bible speak for itself under the *guidance of the Spirit* is not all that easy. Tendencies to impose our ideas and biases need to be set aside. For example, middle-class North Americans find it easy to disregard the perspective of any other racial, cultural, or economic view of the Scriptures. Although we will always read and study the Bible from our own point of view, knowing interpretations of others will aid responsible interpretation. It is important, therefore, to both seek the guidance of the Spirit and consider insights of others. Personal Bible study will also profit greatly from following a sound method of study. We recommend the following steps:

1. *Observe carefully what the text says.*

This approach to Bible study is known as the *inductive method* of Bible study. Essentially this means paying careful attention to both the literary structure and context of a passage. This approach involves looking at words, sentences, paragraphs, and larger blocks of material, and asking questions such as who? what? where? when? and why? It means noting recurring themes, causes and effects, and relationships within the passage, as well as similarities and differences from other passages of the Bible. This approach to the Bible allows the conclusions to grow out of the text.

2. *Be sensitive to different literary forms.*

Because the Bible is made up of a variety of *literary forms,* responsible interpretation must respect the differences between narrative, parable, poetry, and discourse. Careful study will recognize the Bible's use of symbolism and imagery, striving to get the basic message without making it say more or less than it was intended to say. As various literary forms and images are understood, the puzzling features of the Bible often begin to make sense (as in the apocalyptic books of Daniel and Revelation). Thus, the Bible is seen as a living document bound up with the people of God *and, as such, it is the message of God to and through the people, of God.*

3. *Study the historical and cultural contexts of the passage.*

It is necessary for us to take seriously the historical context of any given passage and the Bible as a whole. The divine nature and will were revealed in history to a particular people over a period of many centuries. The written Word reflects this process of God's self-revelation. Hence, faithful interpretation requires careful consideration of the historical context of any given passage. Much misinterpretation has resulted from disregard for the historical context of the passage to be interpreted. A study of the Bible is always a study of a people. It is necessary therefore to enter the world of the Hebrew people and the people of the early church. This includes understanding their ways of thinking, their cultural pattern, and their distinctiveness amid the surrounding cultures and nations.

When we do that we can expect to experience a degree of cultural shock, just as we experience when we cross cultural barriers today. The ability to cross such barriers is one of the callings of the Christian, both to understand the Bible and to communicate it to other cultures of the present day. In order to understand the cultural, historical, and linguistic contexts of a given Scripture, the various *tools of biblical criticism* may be helpful. (See the discussion on biblical criticism in Part III, Section B, and on the social sciences, Part III, C.)

4. *Make wise use of various translations.*

In addition to taking seriously the cultural context of the Bible we must understand *the language itself.* Today we read the Bible in our native language. The Bible, however, was written mostly in Hebrew (Old Testament) and Greek (New Testament). In recent years many translations and paraphrases of the Bible have become available. These attempt to use contemporary English and some take account of better knowledge of ancient languages and manuscripts. A comparison of alternate renderings of a passage may lead to a clearer understanding of the biblical text. A knowledge of the biblical languages is necessary to evaluate the different translations of a verse. In general, versions made by committees (such as *KJV, ASV, RSV, NEB, NIV, NASB, JB, TEV—Good News Bible)* are more accurate and reliable than are translations and paraphrases made by individuals (such as *Weymouth, Moffatt, Phillips, The Living Bible).* Most paraphrases are so free that they are unreliable for serious Bible study. . . .

5. *Consider how the text has been interpreted by others.*

The endeavors of the early church, the medieval church, the Reformers, and contemporary Christians to understand the Bible will be instructive to us. Bible commentaries and Bible dictionaries can be valuable resources. A study of how the New Testament interpreted the Old Testament will also be helpful. By considering how other Christians throughout history have interpreted the Bible, we may be able to understand it more clearly.

6. *Consider the message of the Bible as a whole.*

One of the major errors in biblical interpretation is failure to relate a given passage of Scripture to the overall message of Scripture. It is therefore necessary to take seriously the message of the Bible as a whole and compare Scripture with Scripture. This requires acquaintance with the unfolding drama of the Bible, its major themes, and how the various themes are related and integrated into a whole. The meaning of any part cannot be arrived at apart from the message of the whole. The theological views discussed in I, C above are crucial points in understanding how the entire Bible fits together.

7. *Meditate upon the Word in the spirit of prayer.*

As we learn what the passage says and means, we should meditate upon its message. We should ask ourselves: In what way does this Scripture speak to my life and our lives? How does it instruct me and my fellow believers? How does it teach, correct, reprove, and train in righteousness (2 Tim. 3:15-17)? Some specific topics of the Bible may not apply directly to us today, although they may be pertinent to Christians in other cultures; examples are circumcision, eating meat offered to idols, and the Christian's relation to the ceremonial practices in the Old Testament. However, the manner in which God's people of the New Testament worked through these issues will be instructive to us today.

8. *Listen for the guidance of the Spirit, individually and congregationally.*

The Spirit gives life to the written Word. The Spirit uses the Word to convict of sin, righteousness, and judgment (Jn. 16:7-11). The Spirit likewise leads us into the truth, guiding our perception of the written words (Jn. 16:13). As new insights and convictions come through personal study, we should share and test them with other Christian brothers and sisters who are listening to the Spirit. The experience of the Spirit, the interpretation of the Word, and the understanding of the church should agree.

9. *Respond obediently to the Bible's message.*

Interpretation of the Bible must include our own response to its message. The response may be praise or repentance, thanksgiving or confession, examination of inner attitudes or restitution to one wronged. The Scripture speaks to us only if we are open to its message. Sin in our lives, such as malice toward other people, hinders us from wanting to know and hear the Scripture message (1 Jn. 2:4-6; Jn. 8:31ff.; cf. Mt. 5:22, 23). Lack of love and commitment to one another will also hinder believers in their effort to arrive at unity in their understanding of the Bible. Through faithful response to the Word, we discover the power of the biblical message to upbuild the interpreting community—"to break and to heal, to wound and to cure."

III. Issues for Discussion

The statements on the following issues are not intended to be definitive but a guide to discussion and further study.

A. *Obstacles to Faithful Interpretation*

Various influences from our modern life and culture hinder faithful interpretation of the Bible. These are:

1. A pace of life so fast that we do not take time to study the Bible.

2. Culture and thought so heavily influenced by Western individualism that "private interpretations" become the norm, thus making testing by the community difficult.

3. Final appeal to individual human reason or personal private experience as the judge of truth, hence resisting the role of the community in the interpreting of the Bible.

4. National allegiances and/or concern for material security that make us unwilling to freely respond to the Bible's call to faithful discipleship.

B. *Biblical Criticism*

Biblical criticism is the effort to understand as accurately as possible the historical context and the literary history of both the Bible as a whole and the specific passages of Scripture. The meaning of the word "criticism," derived from the Greek word *krisis,* means judgment, in the sense of discernment or making a decision. All Christians make judgments when they interpret the Bible. Hence, biblical criticism is itself part of the process of biblical interpretation.

Biblical scholars speak of textual criticism and literary criticism. Textual criticism is the effort to determine the better reading of the Hebrew or Greek text where the available manuscripts have different readings. Literary criticism is also important in biblical interpretation, since its concern relates to matters of authorship, literary forms, and the literary origins of the various parts of Scripture. The attempts to decide who wrote the Book of Hebrews or which of the four Gospels was written first are examples of literary criticism. In its broader meaning, literary criticism may include study of the oral traditions which preceded the writing of Scripture in its present form. It may also include noting the distinctive emphases of the separate authors of Scripture.

One could fairly say that the practice of biblical criticism goes back to the early church, since even the first Christian readers of Scripture were making judgments in the process of interpreting the Bible. The term "biblical criticism" as it is used today, however, dates largely from the Age of Reason in the eighteenth century. The term has acquired negative meaning because the biblical scholars who studied the historical and cultural backgrounds of the Bible were regarded as threats to the view that held to a God-dictated, mechanical inspiration, a common view in 17th-and 18th-century Protestantism.

Furthermore, over the past two centuries biblical critics often tended to make human reason the judge of revelation. For example, miracles were explained rationally or, lacking a rational explanation, were discounted as impossible. In order to avoid rationalistic criticism, a trend developed in the twentieth century in conjunction with existentialist theology to make biblical truth simply a matter of subjective experience. These modern tendencies to divide sharply between objective and subjective truth, thus making either rationalism or personal experience the sole judge of truth, conflict with Scripture's own assumptions and are therefore dangers to be avoided.

The positive value of biblical criticism has been its contribution in vastly expanding our knowledge of the historical, cultural, and linguistic backgrounds of the Bible. Our present knowledge of Israel's distinctiveness amidst its environment, the origin of the synoptic Gospels, and the religious environment of Paul's mission are all examples of our indebtedness to the fruits of biblical criticism. The type of contribution that biblical criticism makes to the study of a specific passage may be illustrated as follows. In Matthew 19:1-9 the Pharisees question Jesus about his position on divorce. They ask whether divorce is permitted for any cause. Study of the history and culture of that time has shown that the Pharisees were divided into two camps regarding divorce. Followers of Rabbi Shammai permitted divorce only for the cause of adultery. Followers of Rabbi Hillel permitted divorce for almost any reason at all. Hence the Pharisees were testing Jesus to see which side he would support. But, as the text indicates, Jesus pointed beyond these Pharisaic interpretations to the original purpose of God (Mt. 19:6; Gen. 2:24). This insight of historical criticism enables us to see that Jesus transcended the "party-interpretations" of the Pharisees and affirmed the will of God for marriage.

We must recognize that although the biblical commands are imbedded in the history and culture of that time, the Scripture itself provides us with criteria for evaluating how the entire Scripture should be applied to our lives and culture. Even though the Bible has been used to support differing positions on such issues as the Christians' partcipation in war, the Sabbath versus Lord's day observance, slavery, and the male/female relationship, we believe that there are principles (See I, C) which will give us helpful guidance on these issues. In this way the authority of the Bible as God's Word transcends the culture and history in which it was written.

It is important, therefore, to recognize that the function of biblical criticism is an ongoing task in which the church, by taking account of the historical, cultural, linguistic, and literary backgrounds of the Bible, seeks ever fuller knowledge of what the Scripture means for the life of the church today.

The following responses to biblical criticism may serve as guidelines for our study of the Bible.

1. We should study the Bible on its own terms as much as possible, allowing the evidence from the Bible itself to speak to issues of authorship and date of composition.

2. Because God acted through a people, Israel, and in history, the Bible reflects both God's Word and the human, historical perception of that Word. This means:

a. That the Bible both reveals God's will and also shows human disobedience to that will (as in Israel's rule by a king or permission for divorce).

b. That while the Bible enables us to know God and the divine self-revelation, we must still confess that "we see through a glass darkly" and "know in part" only (1 Cor. 13:12).

c. That the Bible points us beyond itself to Christ, the incarnate revelation of God (Jn. 5:39, 40; to God's own self, ever beyond human comprehension (Jn. 1:18; Rom. 11:33), and to the Spirit who witnesses to both God and Jesus Christ (Jn. 17:25; 15:26).

3. We should learn as much as possible about the historical, cultural, and linguistic background of the narrative of the Bible. This knowledge should not diminish but increase the authority of the Bible in guiding our lives in accord with God's will.

4. We should not box God in by making philosophies, whether ancient or modern, the judges of truth. Alert to ways in which Scripture informs our thinking and experience, we should seek for wholeness of response in our study of the Bible. We should strive for knowledge and obedience.

5. Our guide through the maze of differing interpretations of various biblical teachings must be our faith in the power of the sovereign God, our confidence in the authority and reliability of the Bible, and our openness to other sisters and brothers to check our insights. Our model shall be the community of faith around the Word, guided by the Spirit, and under the lordship of Jesus Christ—so that we might become the faithful people of God.

C. The Social Sciences

In the past few decades the social sciences have pioneered in methods of research which enable us to analyze and describe the way things are in human experience. The way things are, however, is often not the way things ought to be. Further, we believe that God's people can know God's will for human values and conduct.

While the Bible may not speak directly to given contemporary issues, we believe that honest Bible study will provide perspectives for the constructive use of the findings of the social sciences.

Psychology and sociology may also provide descriptive analyses of various aspects of religious experience, e.g., conversion. Such analyses may aid our understanding of both ourselves and the experiences of others in that they show cause-and-effect relationships within a selected range of experience. But these analyses do not and cannot ultimately explain the experience, just as the natural and historical sciences have been unable to explain the ultimate origins of nature (space) and history (time).

D. Fundamentalism and Liberalism

Much of conservative Christianity is characterized by a theology and a mood often labeled as "fundamentalistic." In biblical interpretation, the fundamentalists tend to follow a "flat book" approach to the Bible, taking all parts of the Old and New Testaments as equally binding for the Christian and often ignoring historical contexts. By reading the Bible in this way, fundamentalists often use the Old Testament to uphold participation in war. Fundamentalists are committed to "literal" interpretation. If a particular part of the New Testament is not taken seriously for our day (e.g., the Sermon on the Mount), it is usually because of prior theological consideration (i.e., these passages do not apply to the present age) and not because of a refusal to read them literally. They are often accused by others of "prooftexting," rather than basing their conclusions on the whole tenor of Scripture. From the start fundamentalists opposed most forms of biblical criticism, because they believed it threatened the authority of an inerrant Bible.

The theological liberalism of the late nineteenth and early twentieth centuries was the movement to which fundamentalism reacted. Liberalism tended to make human reason the judge of truth. Liberalism transformed biblical salvation history into intuition, symbolism, and moral action. As a result of the conflict between fundamentalism and liberalism, there has been a tendency for evangelism and social ethics to become separated from each other. "Conservative" Christianity has tended to emphasize the conversion of individuals and to ignore social problems. "Liberal" Christianity has deemphasized the conversion of individuals and has tried to reform the old structures of this world in line with a more equitable social policy.

In the Bible this is not so. The Bible emphasizes both the conversion of the individual and God's creation of a new social order with its revolutionary social ethic in Christ. Faithfulness to the Bible does not permit us to evangelize individuals without discipling them in the new order. Faithfulness does not permit us to evangelize only the individual or to stress only the reformation of the old order. We must seek divine guidance in understanding how to be faithful kingdom citizens in the midst of the economic and political-social structures of our day.

E. Dispensationalism

The attempt has often been made to divide history into a series of "dispensations," most fundamentally in the division between the Old and New Testaments, but often in other ways as well. Fundamentalism and much of evangelicalism has been characterized by a form of dispensationalism which links together the nation of Israel, the thousand-year reign of Christ, and a quite literal reading of Revelation, Daniel, and Ezekiel to describe end-time events. The Scofield Reference Bible is one example of this kind of biblical interpretation. Some of these beliefs, however, are held by nondispensationalists.

Dispensationalism emphasizes God's future activity (as well as present) on this earth, rather than in a timeless eternity. Dispensationalism tends to see the kingdom of God not as a community of love ruled by the cross, but as a kingdom in which Jesus himself becomes a state ruler, ruling by the sword. There are also other weaknesses such as considering God's purpose as twofold—the church living under grace and the Old Testament Jews and Jesus living under law—and not recognizing the reality and importance of the church's earthly existence in God's plan for the ages.

F. Family and Authority

Perhaps none of our social institutions has been subjected to more destructive forces than has the family. The revolutions in technology and transportation have largely replaced the older extended family with a smaller nuclear family. As older ethnic and communal patterns fade away, the factors which contribute to family stability are fewer and family breakdown by divorce has become more and more frequent.

Attempts are being made from within and without our brotherhood/sisterhood to prepare the family for its challenges and to strengthen its life as a basic building block of the church. For some, a part of the solution seems to be to reorient our attitudes toward male and female roles, resulting in "liberation" of both partners and negotiation of a family system suitable to them. For others, the solution seems to lie in the direction of clarifying the lines of obedience and love in the context of the more traditional authoritarian patriarchal family. For both, there is a strong appeal to the Bible as the basis for direction.

G. *View of Wealth*

If the Bible can be understood only by an obedient community, then living in an affluent society which is surrounded by a hungry world becomes a problem. Can we live on a poverty level and still function effectively in an affluent society? On the other hand, to live on a moderate level within the affluent society appears to be living in luxury by those who are in a less-advantaged economic situation. By and large, the church is not facing up to the hard sayings of Jesus in regard to increasing wealth (Lk. 12:33; 14:33; etc.) Can we understand the Bible adequately until we learn obedience?

IV. Conclusions

A. The Bible is to be interpreted within the context of the believing, obedient community, as that community seeks to communicate its message to the world. The authority of the Bible becomes evident within the covenant relationships of the believing community as it is led by the Spirit, who was sent forth by the victorious Christ.

B. The Bible should be interpreted within its historical context and in the light of the message of the Bible as a whole. This demands that we enter into the culture of the ancient world so that we might understand the gospel in its original context, and that we seek to understand the various cultures of the modern world so that we might proclaim the biblical message meaningfully to all peoples.

C. The Bible should not be interpreted as a flat book; rather, the Christ-event witnessed to in both Testaments must illumine all Scripture. For a faithful witness to that event and its meaning, both Testaments must be kept together precisely where the church has placed them. The relationship of the two Testaments is a historical one in which promise and fulfillment is emphasized by both. The Testaments belong together, with the New Testament interpreting and fulfilling the Old Testament.

D. The Bible is not to be interpreted legalistically or magically, but it should be used as an authoritative and rich resource to guide kingdom citizens in their encounters with the kingdom of this world. The kingdom of God is the rule of divine love, even toward enemies. The followers of Jesus cannot use weapons of force, but must rely upon the Word of God and obedience, which may involve suffering, to overcome the evil of this world. The gospel moves forth not by force but by the persuasive power of the Word of the Lord.

E. The same Spirit of God who inspired the writing and ruled over the making and transmission of the Bible also guides and rewards the readers and students of the Bible, and the interpreting community of faith. The Bible has the authority of Christ. It is relevant to the lives of believers individually and corporately. It must be interpreted with integrity and applied faithfully. The Scriptures are ours that we may be instructed for "salvation through faith in Christ." They are given that we may know what to believe and what not to believe, and know how not to behave and how to behave, for they are "profitable for teaching, for reproof, for correction, and for training in righteousness, that the man of God may be complete, equipped for every good work" (2 Tim. 3:15-17).

PACIFIST ANSWERS TO NEW TESTAMENT PROBLEM TEXTS

The pacifist use of the New Testament frequently contains rebuttals to nonpacifist uses of certain passages to disprove pacifism. At least eight writers consider some of these texts, giving what they regard to be explanations which show that the texts do not jeopardize the pacifist position, but in some cases even directly support it.

The eight sources cited are:

Herbert Booth, *The Saint and the Sword* (New York: George H. Doran Company, 1923).[1]

John Ferguson, *The Politics of Love: The New Testament and Non-violent Revolution* (Greenwood, S.C.: The Attic Press, n.d.).

Henry A. Fast, *Jesus and Human Conflict* (Scottdale, Pa.: Herald Press, 1959).

Guy Hershberger, *War, Peace, and Nonresistance* (Scottdale, Pa.: Herald Press, rev. ed. 1953).

G. H. C. Macgregor. *The New Testament Basis of Pacifism* (Nyack, N.Y.: Fellowship Publications, 1954).

Richard McSorley, *The New Testament Basis of Peacemaking* (Scottdale, Pa.: Herald Press, rev. ed. 1985).

Jean Lasserre, *War and the Gospel* (Scottdale, Pa.: Herald Press, 1962).

Culbert G. Rutenber, *The Dagger and the Cross: An Examination of Pacifism* (Nyack, N.Y.: Fellowship Publications, 1958).

The following table lists the passages considered and the pages where each author responds. The texts are cited in order of frequency and significance of mention among the authors; pages in parentheses indicate that brief reference only is made to the text.

Passages	Herbert Booth	John Ferguson	Henry Fast	Guy Hershberger	G.H.C. Macgregor	Richard McSorley	Jean Lasserre	Culbert Rutenber
1) Luke 22:36-38 Sell Mantle . . . Buy a Sword	24, 70-78	31-33	102-105	299-301	22-24	39-43	37-45	41-42
2) John 2:13-17 (Mk. 11:15-19; Mt. 12:12-17; Lk. 19:45-48) Violence in Cleansing the Temple	24, 332-334	28-30	119-122	301-302	17-18	33-34	45-48	40-41
3) Mark 12:13-17 (Mt. 22:15-22; Lk. 20:20-26; cf. Mt. 17:24-27) Pay Taxes to Caesar	308-309	34-36	111-114	296-297	81-82	43-45	86-97	37-38
4) Matt. 10:34-35 (Lk. 12:51) I Bring Not Peace, but a Sword	319	30-31	93-94	299	20	35-36	(43)	41
5) Rom. 13:1-7 (1 Pet. 2:13-17) Be Subject to the Powers	130-132 260-266			295-296	82-87	45-52	97-113	37-38
6) Luke 7:5-10 (Mt. 8:5-10; cf. Jn. 4:46-53) Jesus Commends Soldier's Faith	24, 79	33-34	110	298	18-20	36-38	53-55	(44-45)

Passages	Herbert Booth	John Ferguson	Henry Fast	Guy Hershberger	G.H.C. Macgregor	Richard McSorley	Jean Lasserre	Culbert Rutenber
7) Luke 11:21-22 (cf. Mk. 3:27; Mt. 12:29) Strong Man Fully Armed	300-302	39-40	105	303	25	38	55-56	
8) Eph. 6:10-17 (cf. 1 Tim. 1:18; 2 Tim. 2:3; 4:7; 1 Cor. 9:7) Martial Imagery Supports War	25, 260-265	42-43		304	26-27		56	42-43
9) Jesus' Parables Speak of Force and Violence (Mt. 22:7; Mk. 12:1-9; 13:24-27; Mt. 13:47-50; 18:32-35; 24:45-51; 25:14-30; Lk. 10:13-15)	323-325	40	116-119	303	26		57	43
10) Mark 13:7-13 (Mt. 24:6-7; Lk. 21:9-11) Jesus Predicts Wars		40-42	101-102	301	21		57	38-39
11) Luke 3:14 John the Baptist Did Not Ask Soldiers to Quit Army	82-83			298	18		53-55	44-45
12) John 15:13 Love Sacrifices Life for a Friend		36-37		305	27	38-39		
13) Luke 14:31-32 King Goes to War Prepared	298-300		108	303				
14) John 18:36 World Kingdoms Do Fight		43			25-26		142-143	(47)

Reference							
(Mt. 18:6-7; cf. Lk. 17:1-2) Cast into Sea, Millstone Around Neck			302-303	108-109			24-25	
16) Revelation 19:15 God Uses Sword and Treads Winepress of His Wrath	302-303		302-303					43
17) Mt. 23 (Lk. 11:37-52; Mk. 12:38-40) Woes Against Pharisees				95-101				
18) Acts 10-11 Cornelius Admitted to Church	24, 79-83		298					(44-45)
19) Mt. 26:52 Take Sword, Perish by Sword—Assumes Defense			(299-300)		25	34-35		
20) Rom. 1:19-21; 2:14-15 Basis for Just War		37-39						
21) Mt. 11:12 (Lk. 16:16) Violent Men Seize the Kingdom		36						
22) Rev. 12:7-9 War in Heaven		44						43
23) Mk. 8:34-35 Willing to Sacrifice Self in Death			114-116					
24) Luke 12:39-40 (Mt. 24:43-44) Guard House Against Thief			106-107					

Since four texts gain uniform prominence in these sources, I will limit comments to these four.

(1) Luke 22:36-38. Four writers—Ferguson, Fast, McSorley, and Rutenber—propose a metaphorical or figurative understanding: Jesus used the sword image to announce "the tragic spiritual battle ahead," to prepare the disciples for the bitter end. "It is enough" (verse 38) closes off any literal misunderstanding. Booth says that the text itself (in verse 37) explains the word "enough" as "fulfillment of prophecy"; it fulfills the prophecy that "he was reckoned with the transgressors." Once the prophecy was fulfilled, identifying Jesus with lawbreakers (!), Jesus prevented a literal misunderstanding by saying "It is enough." Lasserre combines these two explanations as the best solution, and with Macgregor, draws no firm conclusion except that a literal meaning makes no sense in the historical context. Twelve swords would not have been enough, let alone two, which Jesus said was enough. Hershberger hears the text as mild irony, rebuking the disciples for their lack of faith and their inability to understand the forthcoming event. All the writers emphasize that any interpretation which justifies armed defense runs counter to all that Jesus clearly taught, even on this occasion (see verses 49-53 and Mt. 26:52).

(2) John 2:13-17 (parallels). Observing that the *whip* occurs only in John, five scholars (Booth, Ferguson, Macgregor, Lasserre, and Rutenber) argue that the correct rendering of the Greek is that "he drove them all, i.e., both sheep and oxen," out of the temple. Lasserre notes that "all" *(pantas)* is masculine and refers not to the immediate masculine antecedent, the merchants, but to the oxen (the writer then adds a phrase to show he includes the sheep).[2] All eight writers say that the act demonstrated Jesus' moral authority; it was not physical violence. Fast suggests that "swinging the whip" and "turning over the tables" punctuated the authority of his word; he did not maim or kill. To use this text as a biblical basis for war, says McSorley, shows how hard it is for militarists to find biblical support for their view! Macgregor and Lasserre note the agreement among biblical scholars' that this is a messianic act: Jesus claims authority over the temple; he will purify it, even rebuild it, in accord with the messianic hope. Ferguson and Macgregor comment on the significance of the cleansing in the Gentile court. Macgregor says that, in contrast to making war on the enemy, it is an act of goodwill. Ferguson argues against Brandon's view that here the real Jesus, the violent Zealot, shines through the record: no, instead of cleansing the temple *from* the Gentiles (the Zealot aspiration), Jesus cleansed it *for* the Gentiles (see Mk. 11:17).[3]

(3) Mark 12:13-17. All eight writers concur that Jesus here gives no basis for participation in the military. Augustine's use of this text to argue for Christian support of the just war (taxes pay the

soldier's wages) is not legitimate, say Macgregor and Rutenber. McSorley points out that it makes no reference to war or to paying taxes for war. Macgregor and McSorley assert that *if* the text is applied to church-state relations, which Lasserre says is a misuse of the text, it would argue for submission to totalitarian regimes, not for military defense of one's country. Ferguson notes that the text does not address a citizen's moral obligations under democratic authority but is spoken in a context like that of Norway or France under Nazi occupation. Lasserre compares Caesar to Hitler in 1943.

All eight also agree that Jesus' reply to the "trap question" (noted by Ferguson, Macgregor, McSorley, and Lasserre) puts the claims of God over the claims of Caesar. Lasserre quotes Dibelius, who saw irony in Jesus' answer: " 'What on earth' (literally) are the things which are *not* God's, and could be reserved to Caesar?"[4] Lasserre also argues for a messianic interpretation of the text, observing (as does Ferguson) that the coin's superscription identified Caesar as god. The trap was meant to pin Jesus down as anti-Rome or pro-Rome and thus discredit his messianic claim. Jesus answered ambiguously, though some interpreted it as anti-Rome by raising the charge of teaching tax refusal (Lk. 23:2), say Ferguson and Lasserre. Fast declares that if Jesus' answer was directed to his disciples in a didactic setting, surely his broader teaching on stewardship and seeking first the kingdom (see McSorley also) would be part of the answer.

(4) Matthew 10:34-35. All eight writers agree that the "sword" symbolizes division, as the parallel in Luke 12:51 indicates; it has nothing to do with war. Macgregor, followed by Ferguson, notes that this division between children and parents is not the purpose but the result of Jesus' coming. Hershberger sees it also as a prediction of persecution, perhaps even from family members.

INTERPRETIVE COMMENTARY ON MARRIAGE TEXTS

This appendix presents the hierarchical and liberationist commentaries on the New Testament texts addressed specifically to marriage and the husband-wife relationship.

1 Corinthians 7

This chapter discusses various issues relating to marriage, addressing specifically the conjugal rights of husband and wife and the relation of marriage to one's Christian vocational calling. Note especially verses 3-4: "The husband should give to his wife her conjugal rights, and likewise the wife to her husband. For the wife does not rule over her own body, but the husband does; likewise the husband does not rule over his own body, but the wife does."

Hierarchical Interpreters

1. Charles Ryrie recognizes that the teaching of this chapter elevates the status of women. He summarizes the teaching in six points as follows:

> (1) St. Paul did not entertain any idea that marriage was in itself evil; (2) there is an equality of the rights of each partner over the other; (3) Christianity does not countenance any extra-marital relations; (4) celibacy is preferred because of the shortness of the time and because of the work to be done; (5) divorce among Christians is not allowed; and (6) virgin daughters are under the control of their parents.[1]

2. Fritz Zerbst and George Knight comment on 1 Corinthians 7 quite minimally; they simply affirm the goodness of both marriage and singleness.[2] Surprisingly, Stephen Clark in his exhaustive study has neglected completely any discussion of 1 Corinthians 7:1-6 in his treatment of New Testament family texts.[3]

Liberationist Interpreters

1. Richard and Joyce Boldrey understand the teaching of 1 Corinthians 7 to express the unity and mutuality of the revolutionary new order brought by Jesus Christ. Both husband and wife "desire" each other; they are mutually "indebted" to each other (verse 3) and refuse to "defraud" one another; each controls the other's body (verse 4), and decisions are made by mutual consent (verse 5). Such mutuality precludes any trace of male condescension and makes husband and wife interdependent and equally responsible.[4]

2. Don Williams also sees in verses 1-6 an "absolute equality of the sexes at their most intimate encounter.... No ego-trip, no will to power, no seduction or rape is tolerated.... The last thing in Paul's mind is male-dominance or egotism."[5]

3. Arguing that the "real Paul" is radically liberationist, Robin Scroggs sees in this chapter an unusual effort to show that *both* men and women have "the same freedom and the same responsibilities." He outlines the balance of emphasis as follows:

Marriage
    each man should have   each woman should have

Sexual intercourse
    the husband should give   the wife should give
    the husband does not rule   the wife does not rule

Temporary sexual abstinence
    addressed to the couple as a unit

Marriage for unmarried and widows
    parallelism not developed

General rule about divorce
    the husband should not   the wife should not

Mixed marriages
    if a brother has a wife, she is   if a woman has an unbelieving
    consecrated through husband   husband, he is consecrated
                                     through wife

Dissolution of mixed marriages
    husband, how do you know   wife, how do you know

Marital status to remain as is	
parallelism not developed	
except in the last part,	
if you marry (addressed to man)	if the virgin marries
Anxiety in and out of marriage	
unmarried man anxious about	unmarried woman anxious
Lord	about Lord
married man anxious about wife	married woman anxious
	about husband
Betrothed	
parallelism not developed	
Remarriage of widow	
parallelism not developed	

Scroggs observes that "Paul has gone out of his way to demonstrate the equality of women in all of these situations."[6]

The Domestic Codes

(Ephesians 5:21-33; Colossians 3:18—4:1; 1 Peter 2:18—3:7)

These three texts discuss in strikingly detailed ways the relationships of husbands and wives, parents and children, masters and slaves. While the texts do not speak to male-female relations generally, they are often cited to show either that (a) subordination of women to men is the biblical teaching (hierarchical) or (b) these teachings introduce liberating, egalitarian elements into an existing cultural hierarchical pattern (liberationist). For this reason, these texts contribute to the debate.

The scholarly discussion of these texts, known as the *Haustafeln* (table of household regulations), centers on (a) whether these regulations are pagan in origin, adopted by Paul (and/or the early church) as long-term ethical guidelines for cultural obligations, since the parousia had not come, or (b) whether these codes are basically Jewish in origin and substantially harmonious with the Christian ethic. Aspects of this debate appear in the description of views that follows.

Hierarchical Interpreters

1. Ryrie identifies two dominant ideas in these texts:

One is the distinctively Christian ideal that love is to be the chief ingredient of marriage.... Such a standard of love was not found in Greek society, and the comparing of the love of a Christian husband and wife with the self-sacrificing love of Christ ... surpasses the standards of Judaism.

> The other dominant idea . . . is the . . . subordination of the wife
> to the husband. Paul finds the reason for this submission in the
> headship of the husband, and Peter illustrates it by commending the
> example of Sarah who obeyed Abraham and called him lord.[7]

Ryrie then distinguishes between subordination and inferiority, arguing that Paul never viewed women as inferior, held
down by the stronger men. Rather, Christ's subordination to the
Father is the pattern for the wife's subordination to her husband.
This teaching may not be considered an "interim ethic" but is
meant for all time, "based on unalterable facts."

> In domestic relationships, then, God has appointed an order which
> includes the husband as the head and the wife in a place of honor
> though a place of subordination. . . . The early church clearly
> considered the subordination of the wife in domestic relations the
> normal and fixed status.[8]

2. Zerbst's treatment of these texts appears within a larger discussion of *hypotage* (subordination). He discusses the word's deri-
vation from *tagmata*, the arrangement of things in order. He then
notes that the New Testament writers see an order in all things—
God over all, Christ subject to God, angels and authorities subject to
Christ, the church subject to Christ, the citizen subject to government, and the three types of subjection in the *Haustafeln*. Zerbst
then seeks to distinguish the wife's subjection from other types of
subjection:

> Contrary to first expectation, the Scriptures nowhere command
> women to obey men.[9] . . . The woman is merely told that she has been
> subordinated to man, that man is her "head," and that she should
> willingly accept this divine arrangement. In these contexts the New
> Testament always addresses the woman. It never tells man to subject
> woman unto himself. It never speaks of the "power" of man. It never
> draws the deduction from woman's subjection that she should obey
> her husband in the manner in which children and servants are to
> obey their parents and masters, or in which soldiers are to obey their
> commanders.[10]

Nonetheless, however distinctive the subjection of wife to husband, Zerbst says, "the concept of . . . [and] demand for subjection
on the part of woman remains." She is therefore "not accorded full
freedom and independence."[11]

Zerbst then regards the "subordination of woman to man" to
be the basis for prohibiting women from speaking and teaching in
the churches. Since the offices of teaching and Word proclamation
connote "rule-over," the woman would violate her subjection

through their exercise. To renounce positions of rule and accept subordination is the will of God. Therefore,

> Such renunciation on the part of woman does not have dishonoring and oppressing implications for her, for she exercises it in the knowledge that the divine order is thereby being maintained. The exclusion of woman from the office can hardly be explained in any other matter, neither has it been understood in history.[12]

3. Knight's contribution regarding this specific set of Scriptures consists of three emphases. First, against those who argue that male headship is an effect of the fall from which redeemed husbands and wives should be liberated, Knight distinguishes between "a husband's oppressive rule" and the God-ordained role relationship within marriage: the husband should exercise headship, and the wife should be subject to his authority.[13]

Second, Knight holds that sin's effect ceases in the relationship because each member in the relationship is instructed to behave in a way which is difficult in that position. The husband in authority is

> to love (as Christ loves the church), not to be better, and to honor his wife. To the wife as the under-authority figure comes the vigorous admonition to respect her husband and to submit ("as to the Lord" and as the church submits to Christ) "in everything."[14]

Third, Knight notes that Paul's call to mutual submission functions as the context for the specific role relations in the home. "The setting for all role relationships is that we all belong to, need, and must submit to one another as joint-heirs of the grace of life." This applies to both husbands and elders (bishops); authority and submissive service must be combined.[15]

4. Stephen Clark extensively discusses Ephesians 5:22-33; Colossians 3:18-19; and 1 Peter 3:1-7 as the "key family texts." I summarize his commentary as follows:

First, says Clark, marriage is not the main topic of Ephesians 5:22-33; rather "the order between husband and wife in marriage" is the central focus of discussion. Marriage is viewed from that aspect.[16]

Second, "Paul directs his primary attention to the subordinates in the relationships" (the wives, the children, and the slaves). The reason for subordination is "fear of Christ" (Eph. 5:21), which is "an inner attitude of submission" and cannot be replaced by love. Fear "contains a greater note of seriousness and obligation."[17]

Third, mutual subordination is not the topic of Ephesians 5:21-33. The structure of Ephesians 5:22-6:9 shows that one party in the relationship is to be subordinate to the other; subordination means having someone under someone else. The husband's service to and love for the wife is not described as subordination. Further, the phrase "to one another" (verse 21) can be taken to mean "among you," so that there is a pattern of subordination in the group (cf. Jas. 5:16, in which sick persons are told to confess their sins "to one another," which means, of course, "to the elder").[18]

Fourth, the structure of Ephesians 5:22—6:9 illustrates the pattern of subordination for which verse 21 functions as an opening statement. The pattern is as follows (with a parallel in Col. 3:18ff.):

A. Wives to husbands
B. Children to parents
C. Slaves to masters[19]

Fifth, the basic exhortation of this core text on family role relationships "is the wife's subordination to the husband and the husband's love of his wife."[20] This role relationship serves the unity of the marriage, a point illustrated by comparison with Christ and the church. The head-body relationship of Christ and the church describes the intended role function of the marriage partners. While "head" *(kephalē)* may denote source, it also certainly means authority; no opposition exists in these two meanings of progenitor of, and head over, another.

> Both the idea of the husband as head of the wife, his body, and the idea of the wife's subordination in everything point to the same reality: the two are supposed to function as one, and consequently the wife's life must be completely under the authority of the husband as head.[21]

This close link between unity and subordination accords fully with the role relationships established for the family of Genesis 1—3.[22]

Sixth, like Ephesians 5:22-33 (par. Col. 3:18-19), 1 Peter 3:1-7 "focuses on the subordination of the wife." Here "obedience cannot be separated from subordination" (verse 6), and this stands as a general principle even in the case of unbelieving husbands (although modifications may be made as in 1 Cor. 7:12-16). Subordination is connected here also to behavioral traits—a meek and quiet spirit—and modesty of dress. The reasons for the husband's bestowing honor on the wife are three: the wife's weakness, her joint heirship to grace, and effectuality in prayer. While the first is related to difference between the sexes, the latter two "point to the spiritual equality of the man and the woman in the family."[23]

Seventh, the pattern for family household living consists of four elements for both husband and wife:

1. The husband is head and governor of the family,.... primarily responsible for the good order and discipline of the family.	The wife is subordinate to her husband, in the sense of subordinating her life and not just in the sense of taking directions.
2. The husband takes the primary concern for relations outside the family,.... community affairs and ... the relationships ... between the family and society....	The wife is the ruler of the family household under her husband and is primarily concerned with the internal order and organization of the family household.
3. The husband raises and forms his sons and sometimes other young males in the household.	The wife raises and forms the small children and ... the daughters and sometimes other younger girls in the household.
4. The husband is the protector and provider ... [with] responsibility for seeing that danger is averted ... [and] for ... the economic work,... procur[ing] food, clothing, shelter, and other necessities.[24]	The wife serves the needs of the members of the household.... She bears the main responsibility for ... housework,... preparing the food, clothing the household members, and cleaning and adorning the home.[25]

Liberationist Interpreters

Sections I and II below represent exegesis that seeks to integrate liberation and subordination, with section II extending the insights of section I. Arguing also for a liberationist position, sections III and IV regard the subordinationist teaching to represent less than the gospel's best.

I-A. In his recent commentary on Ephesians, Markus Barth contributes a lengthy and important discussion on the 5:21-33 passage. While it is impossible to reflect the richness of his 145 pages in any brief summary, I have tried to select crucial emphases which show his hermeneutical accent:

a. Barth translates verses 21-22 as follows: "Because you fear Christ subordinate yourselves to one another—e.g. wives to your husbands—as to the Lord."[26] Barth notes that all of Paul's ethical instructions are rooted in the new reality of the church, "the great result of the Messiah's mission, death, and resurrection." The latter chapters put the proclamation to the test: "does the Messiah Jesus ... in any way influence, change, and shape the life of men and women at its most intimate and perhaps crucial point?"[27]

All the exhortations of 5:21-33, except the last pair, Barth notes, are supported by a single motivation: Christ. Fear of Christ is the motive for mutual subordination (v. 21); Christ's headship over the church is the standard of a wife's subordination to her husband (22-24); the Messiah's love is the ground and measure of the husband's love (25a); His unity with His Body and His care for the church are the reason why the husband who loves his wife loves himself (28-30).[28]

The new realities of Christ and the church thus control the husband-wife relationship; headship and subordination are defined within these contexts of reality.

b. Barth considers the phrase "the husband is the head of the wife" to be original with Paul. Further,

> the fact and modality of a husband's headship is totally determined not only by the double meaning of [the] Hebrew *ros* ("head" and "chief") but above all by the event and mode of Christ's headship.[29]

The nature of Christ's *agape* love lies in his life of selfless service (Mk. 10:45); when exercised by the husband, it will mean "paying gladly whatever the appropriate price" for truly loving the wife. Such loving of the wife is the form of the husband's submission to Christ in 5:21.[30] *Love* her, love *her*, *love her*—in these three imperatives the apostle tells husbands their obligation (what they owe because they fear Christ), and "he has nothing to add beyond this."[31]

c. The wife's expression of her mutual submission in Christ is subordination to and fear of her husband. Within the context of the husband's *agape* love and the wife's fear of Christ, her wifely subordination is a confident and uplifted response.[32] Barth notes that Paul begins by addressing the wife, but at the end reverses the order. The wife's fear of her husband, softly spoken in the phrase "May she fear her husband" (5:33), is expected as a response to her husband's love. Only the husband's love as it matches Christ's *agape* love can elicit the wife's fear so that it is *not* like fear of the wrath of the authorities as in Romans 13. Likewise the subordination of the wife is "characterized as her response to the husband's love."[33]

d. Christian subordination, whether the husband's through love or the wife's through fear, is consistently *voluntary,* says Barth. The verb "subordinate" (*hypotasso*) occurs 23 times in the Pauline epistles. When used in the active, God is the subject who subjugates principalities and powers. But when applied to "members of the church, saints with prophetic gifts, or wives, or children, and slaves," Paul uses the "middle or passive indicatives, participles, or imperatives." Such subordination "describes a voluntary attitude of giving in, cooperating, assuming responsibility, and carrying a burden." It concords with the virtues of Ephesians 4:1-3: "total humility, gentleness, mutual bearing, love, unity, peace."[34]

e. Paul nowhere speaks "of a 'marriage order' or 'marriage principle' which has claim upon husband and wife." For the "powers" in God's eschatological timetable (1 Cor. 15:24-28) and for worship (1 Cor. 14:40), an order is appropriate; but in marriage

> the Bridegroom-Bride relationship between Christ and the church is Paul's substitute for a law, a prescription, a fixed custom of conduct in marriage. The spouses are responsible only to God's Messiah who "loved" them and whom they fear (5:25, 21), to one another in their unique and ever new bond of fidelity, and to the church's missionary task in its environment. Therefore, it is exclusively to the order of God's kingdom that the wife subordinates herself in her subordination to her husband. She does it voluntarily, as a dignified and respected member of the elite chosen for the festival procession and the struggle in which all of God's free children are engaged.[35]

I-B. In an article appearing in the alumni bulletin of Fuller Theological Seminary, David and Elouise Fraser follow Barth's emphases and attempt to demythologize the common "sexegesis" of this Ephesians text:

> Careful study of these verses has a shattering effect on many popular notions thought to be based on this text. The dramatic element in Paul's words is the concentration of attention on instructing and guiding the husband into a new model of marriage that transforms the patriarchalism of the first century. . . . Paul directs three words to Christian husbands. First, the husband is asked to subordinate himself to his wife as she has to him: "Be subject to one another out of reverence for Christ" (5:21). Paul makes the marriage relationship reciprocal.[36]

Second, the Frasers comment on the meaning of the husband's headship:

> When a husband understand(s) his role in a Christological way he is impelled to become the first servant of his wife. "Head" is defined in a way that concentrates solely on love. The husband is not encouraged to think of his task in terms of leadership. This is not the development of an organizational chart for the family, indicating who makes decisions and who follows them. . . . Paul does not make the husband lord in every way that Christ is Lord of the church merely by comparing them. It is only at the point of sacrificial love that the two are compared.[37]

The Frasers' third point emphasizes the oneness of the marriage union (based upon the Eph. 5:31-33 appeal to Gen. 2:24):

What was lost in the fall, expressed in Genesis 3:16 as the wife's loss of equality in a functional subordination to her husband, Jesus intends to restore. The curse is rescinded by grace, and she is placed on the same level as her husband that she might be joint-heir with him in the responsibilities and grace of life (1 Peter 3:7).... The husband and wife are to be one in love and in mutual subjection to each other. It would be difficult to find any norm for marriage as permanently threatening to all traditional marriage structures as that![38]

I-C. Other writers echo the above emphases. Letha Scanzoni and Nancy Hardesty emphasize mutual submission and note that the major focus is not on the wife's subjection, but on the husband's conduct. What is new in Ephesians 5 is not the dominant-submissive relation of husband and wife, a pattern of the pagan society, but in the way both are to relate to each other—as to the Lord.[39]

I-D. The Boldreys also emphasize mutual submission, noting that submission is the opposite of self-assertion. A husband's and wife's total concern for each other was radical in Paul's day and continues so in the present day.[40]

I-E. Don Williams summarizes the teaching in seven points,[41] concluding that "while Paul maintains the traditional hierarchical structure of the submission of wives to their husbands he modifies it by mutual submission and changes the content. Christ is the standard and model."[42]

II-A. John Howard Yoder discusses the subordination of the *Haustafeln* texts within the context of the wider New Testament teaching on subordination. For translating the Greek *hypotasses-thai* he prefers the English word "subordination" to "submission," for submission connotes passivity or subjection—"being thrown down and run over."

> Subordination means the acceptance of an *order*, as it exists, but with the new meaning given to it by the fact that one's acceptance of it is willing and meaningfully motivated.[43]

Yoder describes this subordination as *revolutionary* because, first, unlike the prevailing Stoic ethic which appealed to the dignity of the dominant partner, Paul regularly addresses first the *subordinate* partner: "The *subordinate* person in the social order is *addressed as a moral agent*."[44]

Second, it is revolutionary because the subjects, having experienced liberation from the old order and the "temptation to insubordination" freely subordinate themselves because of the example of Christ.[45] They need not smash the old structures because they know that in and through Christ they are doomed to pass away.[46]

Third, the revolutionary character of subordination "as to Christ" is evident also in "calling the *dominant* partner ... to a kind of subordination."[47] The call to *agape* love makes the dominant partner the servant of the lesser partner. Such reciprocal subordination is indeed revolutionary and cannot be equated with the Lutheran emphasis which roots the present social order in the order of creation.

> ... the *Haustafeln* do not consecrate the existing order when they call for the acceptance of subordination by the subordinate person; far more they relativize and undercut this order by then immediately turning the imperative around.[48]

Yoder's interpretation appeals directly to Jesus' model of servanthood, the theological basis for Christian subordination.

> [Jesus'] motto of revolutionary subordination, of willing servanthood in the place of domination, enables the person in a subordinate position in society to accept and live within that status without resentment, at the same time that it calls upon the person in the superordinate position to forsake or renounce all domineering use of his status. This call is then precisely not a simple ratification of the stratified society into which the gospel has come. The subordinate person becomes a free ethical agent when he voluntarily accedes to his subordination in the power of Christ instead of bowing to it either fatalistically or resentfully. The claim is not that there is immediately a new world regime which violently replaces the old: but rather the old and the new order exist concurrently on different levels. It is because she knows that in Christ there is no male or female that the Christian wife can freely accept that subordination to her unbelieving husband which is her present lot. It is because Christ has made all men free and the freed man is on the same level with his slave, that their relationship may continue as a humane and honest one within the framework of the present economy, the structure of which is passing away (1 Cor. 7:31).[49]

In relating Paul's teaching on subordination to Galatians 3:28, Yoder disagrees with those interpreters (e.g., Krister Stendahl)[50] who play off Paul's teaching on subordination against his supposedly more advanced egalitarian insight that "in Christ there is neither male nor female." Yoder argues against the modernizing of Galatians 3:28 that makes it support a twentieth-century egalitarianism which "denies all differences between 'Jew and Greek, slave and freeman, male and female.' " The point of this text, Yoder says, is unity despite the differences, *not equality*. Further, this popular exegesis fails to grasp the liberating power of the Christological basis of subordination.[51]

II-B. Dennis Kuhns follows Yoder's emphasis in his comments

on the subordinationist teaching: "Subjection and headship in Christ's kingdom have to do with serving others in self-sacrificing love."[52] Kuhns notes that voluntary subjection "was a matter of nonresistance for the Christian wives," implying that they had a right to respond differently but forwent that right because of their subjection to Christ.[53]

III-A. Paul Jewett, following Stendahl's lead, regards Paul's teaching on slavery and on the subordination of women as part of his historical limitation; it does not express the ideal found in Galatians 3:28 or 1 Corinthians 11:10-11. These teachings should not be taken as prescriptions for our social order today. The "fact that Paul ... teaches slaves to obey their masters in the same unqualified way that he teaches children to obey their parents surely reflects the historical limitations of his Christian insight."[54] Similarly the same factor of historical limitation applies to "his view of the male/female relationship whereby women as such, by the Creator's intent, are subordinate to men."[55] Jewett's assessment is that Paul "went all the way in living out the truth that in Christ there is neither Jew nor Greek" but that Paul only *began* to work this out for slave and free, and male and female. His limitations here should not restrict us; "it is high time that the church press on to the full implementation of the apostle's vision concerning the equality of the sexes in Christ."[56]

III-B. Virginia Mollenkott concurs with Jewett:

> By insisting on the few Pauline subordination passages and stopping short of the many Pauline liberation passages, Christians have been denying the full impact of the gospel of Christ as it had entered Paul's experience and as it was intended to modify human society.[57]

III-C. John Neufeld's brief commentary on Pauline teachings regarding male-female relationships also follows the Stendahl/Jewett/Mollenkott emphasis. Though Paul sought to implement the unity and equality of Jew and Greek, he

> exhibited the most caution in reference to the third pair, "male nor female." His deepest insight was that male and female were equal before God and as persons. And yet he spoke of subordination and inequality. But even as he preaches subordination his new conviction shines through: the subjection of the wife to her husband is ameliorated by the husband's love for his wife. And even as he speaks about being silent in church, his insight shines through ... when he allows women to prophesy in the church if their heads are covered.
>
> We see from this that Paul made a beginning in implementing his conviction regarding the equality of the sexes. We dare not freeze the implementation of that insight at the level the early church achieved. As with the slave-free question, so with the male-female

question, we must take the insight of Paul and implement it in our time. The achievement of the early church in this or any other area may not be considered normative for our action.[58]

III-D. The Frasers also enunciate this view in their conclusion:

There is a clear thread in the Bible of functional subordination in the differentiation of male and female roles. But that thread is woven into a very specific pattern: (1) It is the result of the fall and does not grow out of God's intention in creation. (2) It is not a permanent reality, but is part of sin's curse which is ultimately abolished in the work of Christ. (3) Its retention by the early church was due to the necessity of continuing first-century cultural standards of decency and order so that the gospel might not be hindered. (4) Paul set the church permanently in tension with all forms of functional subordination of female to male by calling for mutual subordination in the family and the church, as well as by pointing to the eschatological reality that there is neither male nor female in Christ. The church can never be content until the full personal and social implications of that eschatological reality are established and practiced in this age.[59]

IV. Frank and Evelyn Stagg devote an entire chapter to the domestic codes, including not only Colossians 3:18—4:1; Ephesians 5:22—6:9; and 1 Peter 2:13—3:7 but also 1 Timothy 2:1ff., 8ff.; 3:1ff., 8ff.; 5:17ff.; 6:1f. (which means that a major part of 1 Timothy reflects a domestic code type concern). They draw heavily upon the recent doctoral study of James E. Crouch,[60] who holds that "the early Christians found in Hellenistic Judaism a code which they adapted and Christianized for their purpose."[61]

The Staggs, in comparing Colossians 3:11 with Galatians 3:28 (likely written ten years earlier), note that "neither male nor female" is absent from Colossians. Paul's earlier vision of freedom was now eclipsed by concerns for order. Liberationism, evidenced at Corinth, greatly motivated Paul and the later church to incorporate the society's household codes into the ethics of the church.[62]

The Staggs recognize Christianizing perspectives (the points made in the exegetical contributions above) and defend a necessary tension between freedom and order (some hierarchy and subordination is inevitable in societal functioning). But after surveying the developing trend from redemptive freedom to an ever greater emphasis on social order in the chronological sequence of the above texts, they conclude:

The Domestic Code seems clearly to represent the direction in which the church was moving from the fifties or sixties onward, from a rather fluid life-style to a more structured and ordered one, from a great excitement about its freedom "in Christ" to an increasing concern for what appeared to be abuse of freedom in two directions:

in the moral threat of permissiveness and in the threat to structures within and outside the church. For much of its history the church has imposed rather strict limits upon women, and this disposition seems best understood in terms of factors that gave rise to the Domestic Code. Paul himself was a great exponent of freedom, and his fight for freedom reached its highest expression known to us in Galatians. As early as 1 Corinthians and Romans, in the middle fifties, we see strong indications of antinomianism and also resistance to authority. Paul turns to this new problem in these letters. From Colossians onward the problem of order somewhat overshadows the concern for freedom in the Pauline churches. Despite the unparalleled impulse in Jesus toward dignity and liberation for all persons, including women, and despite Paul's own early commitment to the overcoming in Christ of all partialities, various ones have come out on the short end of freedom, even within the church. In part, the roots of this are found early in the concern for order, and they have continued to bear their fruits.[63]

Hermeneutical Commentary

The commentary at the end of chapter 4 should be consulted for the major issues. What is striking about the opposing interpretations of Ephesians (Clark and Barth, e.g.) is that both appear convincing, though Clark's deficiency in adequately discussing Ephesians 5:21 must be noted (see note 18). Yoder's comments, which accord with Barth's exegetical insights but differ from Jewett's assessment of the finality of Paul's word, merit serious consideration. Further, the Staggs' analysis of the trend in the early church after AD 50-60 is not fully convincing since the Gospels were written after this date. As indicated earlier, the Gospels report not only the position of Jesus but also reflect to some degree the theology of the church at the time of their writing. Their testimony to the new status and freedom of women is enduring evidence that on this point also, as well as on others, Jesus' new wine could not be contained by the old wineskins of cultural and religious repression of women.

THE WIDER USE OF THE BIBLE: EPHESIANS AS A MODEL

One of the limitations of this study has been a narrow focus on the use of the Bible. The study has illustrated the use of the Bible to address social issues which affect the structural order of a total society as well as the church's faith and practice within that order. It will be helpful, therefore, to sketch, even if in briefest form, a wider dimension of the church's use of the Bible. Such a sketch can be made by looking directly at Scripture, especially the book of Ephesians, since it was written for the purpose of addressing holistically the concerns of several churches in Asia Minor.[1]

By following the thought structure of the Ephesians text, I identify twelve different uses of Scripture. This analysis assumes that the functions Scripture performed at the time of its writing are those it should perform today. Ephesians thus presents us with a model for the uses of Scripture.

1. Scripture describes and celebrates God's redemptive work in Christ (chapter 1). This of course has been and should be one of the church's primary uses of Scripture. The church reads the Scripture to learn what God has done and what salvation means. Ephesians 1 may well function as one of the best models in the New Testament for review of God's salvific work (cf. Deut. 26:5-9; Josh. 24; Pss. 105, 135, 136; and Neh. 9 in the Old Testament as well as Acts 7 and 13:13ff. in the New). Scripture assists and even forms the memory of God's people.

Such a recital of God's saving acts frequently occurs in the form of praise and blessing, as is the case in Ephesians 1 (compare the

Psalms and Neh. 9 mentioned above). Congregations of faith are called by Scripture to celebrate God's marvelous blessings of salvation. Read Ephesians 1:3-14 and list each blessing the text mentions, noting also the sphere or person through whom it comes and the ultimate purpose of these mighty deeds of God.

2. Scripture leads us in prayer, placing the individual needs of believers within the context of God's sovereign purposes (1:15-23; 3:14-21; 6:18-20). This too is one of the church's most essential uses of Scripture. Many prayers appear in Scripture (e.g., the Psalms and doxologies at the ends of Paul's letters). These prayers, addressing both individual and corporate needs, regularly include petition and praise. Petitions often focus on our need as believers to grow in faith, to be filled with love, and to know the hope to which we have been called. Prayer, informed by Scripture, functions for the edification of each believer and for the upbuilding of the whole body.

Prayer may also be seen as a response of praise for what God has done. Even some of the complaints of the psalmist move finally toward a heart cry of praise and thanks (e.g., Pss. 42—43). From the writer's perspective these prayers in Ephesians are cries to God for the believers; from our perspective as believers the prayers intercede on our behalf. This double edge of prayer is instructive for us: we cry our concerns to God, and we are held up to God by the cries of our brothers and sisters. With its variety of prayers—confession, petition, and praise—Scripture is indeed an important resource for the church in its prayer; one of Scripture's functions therefore is to provide prayers for the church, leading and shaping the church's expression of prayer.

3. A third function of Scripture is to help us as believers to "tell our story." It is indeed a corporate story, as Ephesians 2 and 1:11-14 indicate. The outline of the story as presented in 2:1-10 and 2:11-22 moves from who we were, to what God did, to who we are now in Christ Jesus. The story in its broadest strokes reflects upon the time when we had no identity as a people and no salvation before God. It then moves to the pivotal event in which God took initiative to change the situation, granting us salvation, hope, and identity. Its third and final phase focuses upon and celebrates this new identity which God's people come to experience within the community of salvation. The images are rich indeed: God's handiwork, one new humanity, fellow citizens with God's people, members of God's household, a holy temple in which God dwells through the Spirit. This particular recital of the corporate story stresses the riches of God's grace (2:5-7) and the new reality of peace between former enemies (2:14-17).

Using Scripture to help us "tell our stories" is important for the continuing life of the Christian community. Especially in a pluralistic world, where many social forces compete for influencing our

identity, the telling of the common Christian story plays a very significant role in the formation and development of the Christian
congregation, the conference, the denominational group, and the
Christian body as a whole. Without the experience of the story
relived again and again in the act of telling and claiming it as our
own, the survival of the congregation as a genuinely Christian congregation is in jeopardy amid the competing forces of the modern
world. The resources of Scripture to help us recover and maintain
our Christian identity are not only important but absolutely
essential for the life of the Christian community.

4. Scripture provides us with models for comprehending and
telling our own personal role in God's salvation purpose (3:2-13). In
this text Paul reminds his readers of the special function given to
him through his call to be an apostle to the Gentiles. On the one
hand, his call is set firmly within the initiative of God; on the other
hand, his mission contributes directly to God's kingdom purposes—uniting Jew and Gentile—which in turn serves as a
testimony of God's manifold wisdom to the principalities and powers.

While none of us in today's church can recite personal vocational callings as distinctive and marvelous as Paul's, with the
resources of Scripture we can understand the contribution of our
lives as rooted in God's initiative and reflecting God's purpose. We
should remember that the apostle Paul spent three years discerning his vocational mission; no doubt much of that time was spent
reflecting upon the Scriptures and God's purposes revealed
through the prophets. By spending more time in serious study of
the Bible and thus seeking to understand God's salvific purposes,
we can gain clearer insights into the meaning of our own commitment and call to service.

5. Scripture helps us to correlate our moral life with our Christian identity. A major part of the second half of Ephesians focuses
upon the Christian walk: walk worthy of your calling (4:1-16); walk
as new people, not as the pagans (4:17-32); walk in love (5:1-2); walk
in light (5:3-14); and walk wisely or circumspectly (5:15-20). This
major section merits detailed analysis which, however, lies beyond
the scope of this brief sketch. But the main point here is the way in
which specific attention is given by Scripture to the moral life of the
Christian community. The "therefore" of 4:1 indicates that the
realities of God's salvific work and the creation of corporate Christian identity function as the foundation of "responsibility" for the
Christian moral life.

The Scriptures frequently connect the ethical imperative
directly to the experiential indicative, as in 4:24. The call to put on
new conduct is rooted in the experience of having been recreated in
God's image. Often the Scriptures first describe and celebrate who
God's people are; then they call the people to live accordingly, or as

Ephesians 5:4 puts it, "as is fitting for God's people." In this way the Scriptures speak crucially to the important issue of motivation for the ethical and moral life.

6. The Scriptures help believers identify the gifts which equip various members for ministry that leads to the growth and maturity of all the members (4:7-16). In its various lists of gifts (cf. Rom. 12:3-8; 1 Cor. 12:17ff.) the Scriptures provide us with patterns for identifying gifts within the Christian congregation. These lists need not be viewed as exhaustive but illustrative of the way in which every person's contribution plays a significant role in the life of the body. The Scriptures teach us that these gifts are not self-serving but are given for use in ministry. The purpose of this ministry is to complete and perfect the body of Christ.

Few tasks are more urgent in the church's life today than the prayerful and deliberate discernment of the gifts of its members. Too often, however, within the current psychological trend of self-fulfillment, the quest to discern gifts is oriented too one-sidedly toward personalistic questions such as "What can I do well?" or "What will give me the greatest sense of self-fulfillment?" Conversely, the needs of the church body should not stifle the development of personal gifts nor thwart human growth. Rather, the discernment and use of each person's gifts should stand in the service of the body's corporate fulfillment.

7. Scripture is an important resource for the formation of our values and patterns of conduct (4:17—5:18). Scripture teaches us that this process of spiritual formation, as it is often called today, is rooted in the resource of God's power. It is connected directly to the decision of the human will (note the call to put off and to put on), and it manifests itself in specific traits of Christian character (4:31-32). Even within this one biblical text the agenda for spiritual formation is extensive enough to occupy any one person for most of a lifetime. Reflection upon a text then becomes a powerful resource for developing the character of the new life first within our own spirits and then in behavioral patterns that mirror the presence of the holy.

While all of the biblical resources for use in the life of the church mentioned so far require time and commitment, this one in particular demands the dedication of one's entire being. The disciplines of prayer, meditation, self-examination, and "binding and loosing" (Mt. 18:15-18) are some of the necessary ingredients for the lifelong task of conforming ourselves more and more to the image of God.

8. The Bible contains a variety of images which provides us with both vision and motivation for the formation of our Christian identity and our Christian behavorial patterns (4:4-6; 5:1-2). Examples of such images, found in these Ephesians texts, are "one body

and one Spirit ... one hope ... one Lord, one faith, one baptism, one God and Father of us all"; believers as imitators of God; and Christ giving himself for us as a fragrant offering and sacrifice to God. Such images, and the Bible is full of them, can provide us with the identity and motivational structure that assist us in the life of faith and enable us to contribute more fully and meaningfully to congregational life and kingdom work.

The importance of such images influencing specific ethical behavior cannot be easily overestimated. As various writers have pointed out, ethical decisions are not made simply within the context of given situations. Rather, patterns of character formation, intentions of the will, and self-identity resources greatly affect the way a person makes specific decisions in given situations. The biblical model is not that of situation ethics; it is rather the formation of character and conviction, inspired by biblical images and motifs, which enables one to make decisions with Christian values.[2]

9. Scripture guides us in worship by instructing us to be filled with the Spirit, to speak to one another with psalms, hymns, and spiritual songs, and to give thanks for everything (5:18b-20). While these verses mention the basic ingredients of the worship experience, other Scriptures give us extensive texts for singing and giving thanks (especially the Psalms and the book of Revelation).

Certainly the church has recognized this use of Scripture quite clearly throughout the ages. But the worship of the church is broader than the activity that takes place on a Sunday morning. While the Scriptures are indeed useful for corporate worship, the elements of worship as described in this text should characterize the believer's spontaneous expression of worship to God on the job, in the home, and on vacation.

10. Scripture teaches us how to correlate the gospel perspectives of new life in Christ with the prevailing social structures and patterns existing within the world (5:21—6:9). In this text Paul addresses the relationship between wives and husbands, children and parents, and slaves and masters. A most distinctive feature of the way the gospel encounters these cultural patterns is the priority and worth it places upon the person in the subordinate position in the social structure. Wives, children, and slaves are addressed directly, indicating that the gospel recognizes them as real persons and is concerned specifically about their plight. The dominant partner in the social structure is addressed on the issue of power. The specific counsel given to that partner turns the power position onto its head. Mutuality frames the instruction to wives and husbands, since the Greek text does not even contain a verb in 5:22, but has 5:22 dependent upon 5:21. Thus the perspective of the gospel moves clearly toward mutuality.

Further, both partners in the social structural pair are called to direct accountability to Christ, clearly making Christ the source of authority for the believer's conduct in social structures. Not the structures, but the Spirit of Christ himself informs the moral life.

This text is most significant for assisting the church in its use of Scripture regarding social issues. While many pages of this study have been given to the churches' endeavors in this area, the churches' fidelity to the will of God on social issues could be greatly enhanced and strengthened by careful and sustained reflection upon this one text.[3] Other texts, to be sure, will offer the same kind of insight; what is important is the commitment to listen carefully and humbly to the accent of the text and the direction in which it calls the people of God.

11. Scripture helps us prepare for warfare against evil. (6:10-17). This Scripture along with many others from the beginning to the end of the canon reminds us that the Christian life is a battle. The Bible takes evil seriously and calls Christians to be vigilant in resisting temptation and refusing to do evil. Scripture also sounds an optimistic note for this task. The resources of the Christian, illustrated here by the many parts of effective and powerful armor, are adequate not only to resist the evil one, but also to conquer evil and advance the gospel of peace.

Even though the warfare reality of the Old Testament has proved difficult for the church, the structural perception it gives for the Christian life is not at all at odds with the spirit of Jesus. The Gospels clearly present Jesus in battle against evil; the Epistles call believers to fight against evil; and the book of Revelation promises believers victory in the battle as they follow the faithful martyr and slain lamb, Jesus Christ. Pacifist believers especially can learn much from Scripture's warfare imagery. Not only will it save them from passivism, but it will anchor pacifist belief and action firmly within the biblical witness.[4]

12. Scripture gives us new content for our greetings and our goodbyes (1:2; 6:23-24). Paul's greeting of grace and peace (charista and shalom)[5] expresses not only the warmness and resource of his own person but links this resource to the grace and peace from God the Father and the Lord Jesus Christ. In his goodbye, shalom is linked to love and faith which come from God and Jesus Christ. God's grace is extended specifically to those linked to the Lord Jesus Christ with an undying love. These ordinary greetings, filled with the reality of divine resource, testify powerfully to the way in which personal self-consciousness has been shaped by Christian identity, values, and commitments. Even the injunction to "greet one another with a holy kiss," occurring in some of Paul's other letters, should not be brushed aside too lightly. The instruction is a tender sign that old things have passed away; a whole new creation has begun.

NOTES

Introduction

1. This emphasis from liberation theology is reported in ch. 3, pp. 106-112, and ch. 5 p. 208. Elisabeth Schüssler Fiorenza makes this point from the standpoint of feminist theology; see my ch. 5 pp. 213-214. For a nmon base to these perspectives, see Rosemary Radford Ruether, *Liberation Theology: Human Hope Confronts Christian History and American Power* (New York: Paulist Press, 1972), and Letty M. Russell, *Human Liberation in a Feminist Perspective—A Theology* (Philadelphia: Westminster Press, 1974).

2. Anthony C. Thiselton, *The Two Horizons: New Testament Hermeneutics and Philosophical Description with Special Reference to Heidegger, Bultmann, Gadamer, and Wittgenstein* (Grand Rapids, Mich.: Eerdmans, 1980); see especially pp. 17-24.

3. For contemporary emphases on this point, the "new hermeneutic" provides a helpful perspective. See Paul J. Achtemeier, *An Introduction to the New Hermeneutic* (Philadelphia: Westminster Press, 1969). The thought of Paul Ricoeur also supports this point; see Lewis S. Mudge's introduction to Ricoeur's thought in Paul Ricoeur, *Essays on Biblical Interpretation* (Philadelphia: Fortress Press, 1980), pp. 1-40. The exegetical work of Robert C. Tannehill on various sayings of Jesus illustrates the same point *(The Sword of His Mouth* [Missoula, Mont.: Scholars Press; Philadelphia: Fortress Press, 1975]).

4. One hypothesis which my research and reflection upon the male-female issue has suggested is that the two world wars effectively silenced the women's movement of 1860-1925. Even though the history of the women's movement looks to the post-WWI period for the movement's decline and death (e.g., William O'Neill, *Everyone Was Brave: A History of Feminism in America* [Chicago: Quadrangle Books, 1969], pp. 214-263), the war itself had devastating effects upon the movement. Besides its disruptive effects, especially to the movement's pacifist orientation, the war glorified the males *as male* war heroes, after the war, and automatically forced women *as women* to the domestic circle and to procreation—for producing more males to fight more wars. For additional points of correlation between war/peacemaking and the male/female issue see the November/December 1982 issue of

Daughters of Sarah.
    5. One useful attempt to propose a contemporary statement on the na-
ture and method of the inspiration of Scripture is Paul J. Achtemeier's
recent book, *The Inspiration of Scripture: Problems and Proposals*
(Philadelphia: Westminster Press, 1980).

CHAPTER 1
    1. John Henry Hopkins, *A Scriptural, Ecclesiastical, and Historical
View of Slavery, from the Days of the Patriarch Abraham, to the Nineteenth
Century* (New York: W. I. Pooley & Co., 1864), pp. 16-17.
    2. Theodore Dwight Weld, *The Bible Against Slavery: or, An Inquiry
into the Genius of the Mosiac System, and the Teachings of the Old Testa-
ment on the Subject of Human Rights* (Pittsburgh: United Presbyterian
Board of Publication, 1865; republished by Negro History Press, 1970), p. 13.
    3. See note 1 above.
    4. The tract drew a letter of protest from Bishop Potter of Pennsyl-
vania with approximately 160 signatures of ministers in Potter's diocese.
The tract and signatures are printed at the front of Hopkins' book. The book
then is his defense and is addressed to the Right Reverend Alonzo Potter,
DD, bishop of the Protestant Episcopal Church in the diocese of Pennsyl-
vania.
    5. To be fair to Hopkins, it should be noted that he included with
these lectures a plan for the gradual abolition of slavery.
    6. Bledsoe's treatise is entitled "Liberty and Slavery: or, Slavery in the
Light of Moral and Political Philosophy" in *Cotton Is King, and Pro-Slavery
Arguments Comprising the Writings of Hammond, Harper, Christy,
Stringfellow, Hodge, Bledsoe, and Cartwright on This Important Subject,*
ed. E. N. Elliot (1860; rpt. New York: Negro Universities Press, 1969).
    7. Stringfellow's essay has been published in condensed form in
Slavery Defended: The Views of the Old South, ed. Eric L. McKitrick (Englewood Cliffs, N.J.: Prentice-Hall, 1963). However, citations from Stringfellow
will be from *Cotton Is King.*
    8. *Cotton Is King,* pp. 457-521.
    9. *Ibid.,* pp. 841-77. Since *Cotton Is King* was published first in 1860,
the three treatises by Bledsoe, Stringfellow, and Hodge were written in the
late fifties, several years before the Civil War. For another important biblical
exposition on slavery (but one whose date comes after the 1815-65 time period of this study), see Prof. Robert L. Dabney, *A Defence of Virginia [and
through her, of the South]: Recent and Pending Contests Against the Sectional Party* (E. J. Hale and Son, 1867; republished by Negro Universities
Press, 1969), especially pp. 94-208.
    10. George D. Armstrong, *The Christian Doctrine of Slavery* (1857;
rpt. New York: Negro Universities Press, 1969).
    11. Originally published by Walker, Richards & Co., 1852, and re-
printed by Negro Universities Press, 1968. An excellent secondary source
presenting the nineteenth century's pro-slavery arguments from the Bible
can be found in ch. 5 of William Sumner Jenkins' *Pro-slavery Thought in
the Old South* (Chapel Hill: University of North Carolina Press, 1935).
    12. Hopkins, *Scriptural View,* p. 7.
    13. Stringfellow, p. 463.

14. Jenkins, p. 205.

15. Hopkins, *Scriptural View*, pp. 76-77. See also p. 8, where Hopkins says, "If the Philanthropists of our age, who profess to believe the Bible, had been willing to take the counsel of that angel for their guide, it would have preserved the peace and welfare of the Union."

16. Stringfellow, p. 472. Stringfellow sums up his argument for his first proposition with ten cogent points:

I have been tedious on this first proposition, but I hope the importance of the subject to Christians as well as to statesmen will be my apology. I have written it, not for victory over an adversary, or to support error or falsehood, but to gather up God's will in reference to holding men and women in *bondage, in the patriarchal age.* And it is clear, in the first place, that God decreed this state before it existed. Second. It is clear that the highest manifestation of good-will which he ever gave to mortal man, was given to Abraham, in that covenant in which he required him to circumcise all his *male servants, which he had bought with his money,* and that *were born of them* in his house. Third. It is certain that he gave these servants as property to Isaac. Fourth. It is certain that, as the owner of *these slaves,* Isaac received similar tokens of God's favor. Fifth. It is certain that Jacob, who inherited from Isaac his father, received like tokens of divine favor. Sixth. It is certain, from a fair construction of language, that Job, who is held up by God himself as a model of human perfection, was a great slaveholder. Seventh. It is certain when God showed honor, and came down to bless Jacob's posterity, in taking them by the hand to lead them out of Egypt, *they were the owners of the slaves that were bought with money, and treated as property;* which slaves were allowed of God to unite in celebrating the divine goodness to their *masters,* while *hired servants* were excluded. Eighth. It is certain that God interposed to give Joseph the power in Egypt, which he used, to create a state, or condition, among the Egyptians, *which substantially agrees with patriarchal and modern slavery.* Ninth. It is certain, that in reference to this institution in Abraham's family, and the surrounding nations, for five hundred years, it is never censured in any communication made from God to men. Tenth. It is certain, when God put a *period to that dispensation, he recognized slaves as property on Mount Sinai.* If, therefore, it has become sinful since, it cannot be from the *nature of the thing, but from the sovereign pleasure of God in its prohibition.*

17. *Ibid.,* p. 474; Bledsoe, pp. 341-342.

18. Stringfellow, p. 474;.

19. Bledsoe, p. 340.

20. Stringfellow, p. 475.

21. *Ibid.,* p. 476.

22. *Ibid.,* p. 477; Hopkins, *Scriptural View,* p. 9.

23. *The Pro-Slavery Argument,* pp. 107-08.

24. Hopkins, *Scriptural View,* p.15; *The Pro-Slavery Argument,* p. 452.

25. Armstrong, p. 57. See also Hodge, in *Cotton Is King,* p. 852.

26. *The Pro-Slavery Argument,* p. 452. When discussing Onesimus' case, Armstrong notes that "Christianity makes no alteration in men's

political state" (p. 42). See also Hodge, p. 853.

27. Hodge, p. 848.

28. Armstrong, p. 64.

29. *Ibid.*, pp. 65, 103.

30. Bledsoe, p. 379. See also Armstrong, pp. 21-27.

31. Stringfellow, pp. 481-482. See also Bledsoe, pp. 374-375.

32. Stringfellow, pp. 488-489.

33. *Ibid.*, p. 487. Other pro-slavery authors also make much of this text: Armstrong, who suggests that opposing slavery is ranked with the sin of blasphemy of verse 4 (pp. 23-24, 28-30, 75-79), and Hopkins (*Scriptural View*, pp. 13-14).

34. Armstrong, p. 33.

35. Hopkins, *Scriptural View*, p. 16. The entire New Testament argument is summed up by Armstrong in twelve theses, condensed into seven as follows:

> In our examination of what the New Testament teaches on the subject of Slavery, we have found—1. That slave-holding does not appear in any catalogue of sins or "offences" given us by inspired men, (§ 2-5.) 2. That the Apostles received slave-holders into the Christian Church, and continued them therein, without giving any intimation, either at the time of their reception or afterwards, that slave-holding was a sin or an "offence," (§ 6, 7.) 3. That Paul sent back a fugitive-slave to his own master again, and assigned as his reason for so doing, that master's right to the services of his slave, (§ 8.) 4. That the Apostles frequently enjoin the relative duties of master and slave, and enforce these injunctions upon both alike, as Christian men by Christian motives; uniformly treating certain evils which they sought to correct, as incidental evils, and not "part and parcel" of slavery itself, (§ 9.) 5. That Paul treated the distinctions which slavery creates as matters of very little importance, in so far as the interests of the Christian life are concerned, (§ 11.) 6. That he declares that this, his doctrine respecting the relation of slave and master, is wholesome doctrine, and according to godliness, and the doctrine of the Lord Jesus Christ (§10.) and, 7. [He] directs Christian ministers to teach it in the Church, and prohibits the teaching of any doctrine at variance with it under the most solemn sanctions known to the Church, (§ 12.)

36. Stringfellow, pp. 491-92.

37. Hodge, p. 849.

38. Originally published by Parry & McMillan, 1857, and reprinted by Negro Universities Press, 1969. Barnes is the author of the well-known commentary *Barnes' Notes*, in which he also addresses the subject of slavery in comments on Ephesians 6:5-9 and Isaiah 58:6.

39. Gilbert Hobbs Barnes, *The Antislavery Impulse: 1830-1844* (New York: Harcourt, Brace, 1933), p. 249, n. 12; see also pp. 104 and 138 for background events leading up to the publication.

40. For the full title of Weld's book see note 2 above. Page iii indicates that it was previously published in the *Anti-Slavery Quarterly*; the book passed through four editions, the last in 1838. Gilbert Barnes, Weld's biographer, tells the stirring story of Weld's influence on the anti-slavery

movement. Weld was revivalist Finney's persuasive co-worker in the early 1830s; as evangelist, Weld called converts to abolitionism. He was invited to teach at Lane Seminary because of his evangelical influence, but soon left because of anti-Negro policies. With several others, he founded Oberlin College, admitted Negroes, and trained "The Seventy" to go out as abolitionist missionaries. Invited to Washington, D.C., by a handful of anti-slavery congressmen (including John Quincy Adams), he held a position as lobbyist against slavery for several years (G. H. Barnes, pp. 104-249; see especially pp. 79-87, 105).

41. (Philadelphia: J. M. Sanderson & Co., 1816); now available in *George Bourne and The Book and Slavery Irreconcilable* by John W. Christie and Dwight L. Dumond (Wilmington, Del.: The Historical Society of Delaware and Philadelphia; The Presbyterian Historical Society, 1969), pp. 103-196.

42. Numerous anonymous articles in the *Liberator* were written by Bourne, according to his biographer, John W. Christie (p. 95).

43. The full title of Bourne's book is *A Condensed Anti-Slavery Bible Argument: By a Citizen of Virginia* (New York: S. W. Benedict, 1845). The book contained 91 pages; the text is now available in *Essays and Pamphlets on Antislavery*, Essay No. 2 (Westport, Conn.: Negro Universities Press, 1970). In 1834, Bourne wrote *Man-Stealing and Slavery Denounced by the Presbyterian and Methodist Churches. Together with an Address to All the Churches* (Boston: Garrison & Knapp, 1834). This essay was incorporated into his 238-page *Picture of Slavery in the United States of America* (Middletown, Conn.: Edwin Hunt, 1834). See Christie, pp. 100-101.

44. Excerpts from the "Introduction" illustrate the point:

> The most obdurate adherents of Slavery are Preachers of the Gospel and Officers and Members of the church. A son of Belial is easily convinced; he offers no palliative; he denounces, although he perpetuates the evil; but conceiving himself absolved from all moral obligation, he is desirous to participate in the gain as long as it can be grasped: but Christians defend *Negro-stealing;* they marshal the examples of men who lived not under the moral code dispensed by Moses; they misinterpret varied regulations of his law, and thereby transform truth into error, and the dictates of justice into the vilest improbity; they claim the silence of our Lord and his Apostles and Evangelists, as a proof that Slave-holders then were *innocent;* and they affirm that no New Testament command or denunciation is directed against involuntary servitude. *These wrest the scriptures unto their own destruction; being led away with the error of the wicked.* To tolerate Slavery or to join in its practice is an insufferable crime which tarnishes every other good quality. *For whosoever shall keep the law, and yet offend in one point, he is guilty of all:* and it is duplicate malignity; the word of God is transmuted into indulgence for sin; infidels and worldlings are encouraged to believe that Christianity is a mere deception, when its Expositors and Disciples contend for "injustice and inhumanity" by the Book; what blasphemy! and slavery, with its abettors, is "a mill-stone hanged about the neck" of the church, from which she must be loosened, or she will "be drowned in the depth of the sea." . . .

A criticism upon this volume, will not be heard, either from a *Thief,
or from him who consents with him*. The permission would
transform a *Flesh-Merchant* into Legislator, Judge, Juryman,
Testimony and Delinquent; and his opinion, especially if he be a
pretended Believer, will not be even listened to; because a *Kidnap-
per* or his Defender, is neither a Christian, nor a Presbyterian, not
a Baptist, nor a Methodist, nor a Republican; but a Despot, whose
"traffic in slaves is totally irreconcilable with the principles of justice and humanity."

O that this essay may remove the obloquy under which Religion
groans, and teach us the just estimate which we should form of a
Slave-holder's character! O, that Preachers, Officers, and Members
of the Church, may take the alarm, and contemplate the result of
their silence and example! O, that Nominal Disciples of Jesus may
strive to maintain consistency, that it may no longer be an infidel
reproach, "he is a Christian Slave-holder," *alias* Manstealer! and
O, that others may confederate for the contest, and cease not to
combat, until LEGION is exterminated from the Temple of God!
(The Book and Slavery Irreconcilable, pp. 108-109, 111-112).

45. Published in New York by W. J. Moses. Available on microfiche
cards from Bridgewater College, Bridgewater, Va.
46. Clarke's sermon was published in Boston in 1843. It is now
available in *Essays and Pamphlets on Antislavery* (see n. 43).
47. Originally published by James Monroe & Company; reprinted by
Negro Universities Press, 1968.
48. Ed. Joseph L. Blau (Cambridge, Mass.: The Belknap Press of Harvard University Press, 1963). In his "Introduction" (pp. xiv-xlv) Blau points
out that Stephen Taylor, professor of ecclesiastical history and church
government at Union Theological Seminary, Richmond, Virginia, wrote a
book-length reply to Wayland entitled *Relation of Master and Servant, as
Exhibited in the New Testament: Together with a Review of Dr. Wayland's
Elements of Moral Science on the Subject of Slavery* (Richmond, Va.: 1836).
49. These points represent Bourne's main declarations in *The Book
and Slavery Irreconcilable*.
50. These assertions represent Channing's argument in *Slavery*.
51. Summary of Weld's points in *The Bible Against Slavery*. In 1839,
Weld published a book entitled *American Slavery as It Is: Testimony of a
Thousand Witnesses* (New York: The American Anti-Slavery Society), which
recounts in eyewitness, testimonial form the inhumane, even torturous
treatment of slaves. The general editor of the 1968 reprint (New York: Arno
Press and The New York Times), William Loren Katz, quotes abolitionist authority Dwight Lowell Dumond that this book is "the greatest of the anti-
slavery pamphlets; in all probability the most crushing indictment of any institution ever written" (cover preface).
52. A. Barnes, *Inquiry*, pp. 3, 19-37.
53. With this point Weld also says that Noah prophesies *service*, not
slavery, a distinction that will come into focus later.
54. Weld, pp. 95-96.
55. Bourne, *Condensed Anti-Slavery Argument*, pp. 24-25.
56. Wayland, pp. 95-96.

57. Weld, pp. 40-41.
58. Bourne, *Condensed Anti-Slavery Argument*, pp. 31-37.
59. A. Barnes, *Inquiry*, p. 67.
60. *Ibid.*, p. 70. Bledsoe says of Albert Barnes' argument that it is like saying "no such meaning [of slavery] belongs to the English term *slave*" (p. 360). Bledsoe argues against Barnes by noting that no lexicon he knows of gives "hired servant" or "apprentice" for the Greek *doulos* (p. 362). Unfortunately, Bledsoe's rebuttal focuses on the Greek *doulos* instead of on Barnes' Hebrew *ebed*, although the logic of the argument is largely but not altogether transferable (pp. 361-63).
61. Governor Hammond says, however:

> It is absurd to say that American slavery differs in form or principle from that of the chosen people. *We accept the Bible terms as the definition of our Slavery. (The Pro-Slavery Argument*, pp. 107-108.

62. A. Barnes, *Inquiry*, pp. 60-64, 69-70, 78-80.
63. *Ibid.*, p. 83.
64. *Ibid.*, pp. 83-104.
65. Weld, pp. 40-62; Bourne, *Condensed Anti-Slavery Argument*, pp. 37-43; A. Barnes, *Inquiry*, pp. 112-160; Hosmer, pp. 45-51.
66. Bourne also cites as examples of voluntary servitude Genesis 47:19-23; 2 Kings 4:1; Nehemiah 5:5-13; and Jeremiah 34:8-17 (a prophetic reproof for "violations of the Levitical statutes regulating free and voluntary service" [Condensed Anti-Slavery Argument, p. 52]). In contrast Bourne cites instances of *involuntary* servitude, properly called slavery. These are Exodus 21:16; Leviticus 24:17; Numbers 35:30-31; Deuteronomy 24:7; and Genesis 37:27-28, 36; 42:21-22; 40:15 (p. 53). Weld also lists numerous cases of clearly voluntary servitude (pp. 60-62).
67. This calculation of time off is found in Weld pp. 43-44.
68. Bourne, *Condensed Anti-Slavery Argument*, p. 59. This contrasts with the U.S. fugitive-slave law, which required that persons finding runaway slaves return them to their owners.
69. Hosmer, pp. 45-46. Also, based on Leviticus 19:20, Hosmer says, "servants were permitted to live together as families and their domestic relations were held sacred" (p. 47). But the separation law of Exodus 21:4 certainly qualifies this.
70. Bourne, *Condensed Anti-Slavery Argument*, pp. 49-53; A. Barnes, *Inquiry*, pp. 206-226.
71. A. Barnes, *Inquiry*, p. 208.
72. *Ibid.*, p. 209.
73. *Ibid.*, p. 210.
74. *Ibid.*, pp. 211-212.
75. *Ibid.*, pp. 214-216; Bourne, *Condensed Anti-Slavery Argument*, pp. 50-52.
76. Bourne, *Condensed Anti-Slavery Argument*, p. 51.
77. A. Barnes, *Inquiry*, pp. 220-225.
78. Bourne, *Condensed Anti-Slavery Argument*, p. 54. Although concurring with this sentiment, Wayland puts more emphasis upon the nonnormative character of the Old Testament: the laws of Moses and the practices of the Old Testament are not authoritative for us today (or if they

are, we should obey *them all,* including passover, sacrifice, etc.!). Further, he says, Jesus teaches moral precepts that in some instances are opposed to the Old Testament law (pp. 390-391).

79. A. Barnes, *Inquiry,* p. 245.

80. *Ibid.,* p. 242. The *Encyclopaedia Judaica* (1972) concurs that Hebrew slavery as practiced in the Old Testament likely ceased with the second temple period since the jubilee practices also ceased then, but it does allow for the probability that the Jews had servants of non-Hebrew background (vol. 14, p. 1657). The existence and status of slaves in Israel during the second temple period continues to be disputed among scholars, with Joachim Jeremias, E. E. Urbach, and Solomon Zeitlin holding that an institution of slavery, albeit with humane practices, did exist. See S. Scott Bartchy for a brief survey of the scholarly discussion and literature: ΜΑΛΛΟΝ ΧΡΗΣΑΙ *First-Century Slavery and the Interpretation of 1 Corinthians 7:21* (Missoula, Mont.: Scholars Press, 1973), pp. 29-34.

81. A. Barnes, *Inquiry,* p. 242.

82. While the servant *(pais)* of the Roman centurion (Matthew 8:5ff.) may have been a slave, evidence is not conclusive since the term may also mean "child" or "boy" (A. Barnes, *Inquiry,* p. 243).

83. Bourne, *Condensed Anti-Slavery Argument,* pp. 70-71.

84. This is Wayland's four-point approach (pp. 391-392) found in various forms in other writers as well (A. Barnes, *Inquiry,* pp. 247-248; Channing, ch. 5).

85. Weld, p. 151. The broad word *doulos* was used for servants because it included *free* master-servant relationships; see Bourne, *Condensed Anti-Slavery Argument,* p. 77.

86. A. Barnes, *Inquiry,* pp. 251-260.

87. *Ibid.,* pp. 259-260.

88. In this context Albert Barnes denounces abolitionists who use violent denunciations in their preaching. Barnes concurs with Channing that vituperative exaggeration of slavery's evils and fanatic opposition have done the abolitionist cause much harm *(ibid.,* pp. 266-268). Quoting Channing, he concludes:

> One great principle which we should lay down as immovably true, is, that if a good work cannot be carried on by the calm, self-controlled, benevolent spirit of Christianity, then the time for doing it has not come. God asks not the aid of our vices. He can overcome them for good, but they are not the chosen instruments of human happiness (pp. 267-268).

89. *Ibid.,* pp. 260ff.

90. *Ibid.,* p. 273.

91. *Ibid.,* pp. 274ff., 340.

92. Rights likely to be violated in slavery are (1) marriage rights, (2) fatherhood relations to the children, (3) freedom of worship, and (4) property rights (A. Barnes, *Inquiry,* pp. 346-353).

93. *Ibid.,* pp. 341-365.

94. *Ibid.,* p. 375.

95. Wayland, p. 396.

96. Hosmer, pp. 53-55, 83-155.

97. A. Barnes, *Inquiry,* p. 330.

98. Hosmer, pp. 61-73.

99. See note 51 above.

100. Bourne, *Condensed Anti-Slavery Argument*, pp. 54-55. See also pp. 50, 53.

101. Hopkins, *Scriptural View*, p. 70.

102. *Ibid.*, p. 67.

103. Stringfellow, pp. 468-469.

104. *Ibid.*, p. 475; also Bledsoe, p. 340.

105. *The Pro-Slavery Argument*, pp. 106-107.

106. Armstrong, pp. 16-17.

107. Hodge, p. 860.

108. Stringfellow, pp. 515.

109. *Ibid.*, p. 477.

110. Hodge, pp. 856-857.

111. Stringfellow, p. 480.

112. Armstrong, pp. 13-15.

113. Stringfellow, pp. 488-489.

114. Hodge, p. 855.

115. *Ibid.*, pp. 857-858.

116. Armstrong, p. 57.

117. Hodge, p. 864; Bledsoe, p. 288.

118. Hodge, p. 863.

119. Bledsoe, pp. 379-380.

120. *The Pro-Slavery Argument*, p. 109.

121. A. Barnes, *Inquiry*, p. 207.

122. Bourne, *Condensed Anti-Slavery Argument*, p. 25.

123. Hosmer, p. 47-48.

124. *Ibid.*, p. 50.

125. A. Barnes, *Inquiry*, p. 70.

126. Quotation from Bledsoe, p. 345. See also Hopkins, *Scriptural View*, pp. 125-126.

127. Weld, p. 49.

128. *Ibid.*, p. 51.

129. *Ibid.*

130. Bourne, *Condensed Anti-Slavery Argument*, pp. 54-55. Bourne cites Genesis 6:11; Exodus 3:9; 12:29; 14:28; Job 20:19; 27:13, 23; Proverbs 1:11; Isaiah 1:15-24; 10:1-4; 14:2; 16:4; 19:20; 58:6-7; Ezekiel 7:23, 27; 9:9; 18:10-13; 22:29, 31; Amos 4:1; 8:4-8; Zephaniah 3:1-8; Zechariah 7:9, 14; Matthew 23:14; James 5:4.

131. *Ibid.*, pp. 61-62. Bourne then says: Josephus relates no such custom, though the word "slave" is made to appear in the English translation of his history, which is most likely to be a false rendering, because the Hebrew language, which contains no such word, was his native tongue.

132. *Ibid.*, p. 66. While this is Bourne's position, not all abolitionists would hold this view. For example, in his sermon in Armory Hall, Clarke said that both those who claim that slaveholding is sin, demanding it to be banned from the churches, and those who use the Bible to support slavery, are wrong. He rather says:

> Now the true doctrine I think, is, that slavery as a system is thoroughly sinful and bad,—but it does not follow that every slaveholder commits sin in holding slaves. That the whole spirit of the gospel is opposed to slavery, and that the tendency of Christianity was

to break every yoke, is perfectly plain. But the fact, which always remains a fact, that Jesus and his Apostles did not attempt violently to overthrow and uproot this institution, did not denounce all slaveholders, and that while we have catalogues of sins which are to be repented and forsaken, slaveholding is not among them, shows that, under all circumstances, it is not sinful [p. 14].

Compare also Moses Stuart's statement to be cited in the "Supplement to the Debate."

133. Bourne, *Condensed Anti-Slavery Argument*, pp. 25-26.

134. A view held by A. Barnes, Wayland, Channing, and Clarke, but not by Bourne and Weld. Note that arguments 4-5 come from Bourne, whereas this one comes from Barnes.

135. A. Barnes, *Inquiry*, pp. 283-384. Barnes profusely illustrates his point, devoting over a dozen pages to the topic.

136. *Ibid.*, pp. 292-293.

137. *Ibid.*, pp. 276-277. Biblical scholars from Origen to contemporary commentators have disagreed on whether the inferred ending of 1 Corinthians 7:21 μᾶλλον χρῆσαι should be "take freedom" or "use slavery" (see Bartchy's summary of positions, pp. 6-7). In his careful study of this text (1 Cor. 7:17-24) and the specific nature of the institution of slavery in ancient Greece, Bartchy has proposed another interpretation, based largely upon the structure of the Pauline argument (parallel to 1 Cor. 12-14). Just as 1 Corinthians 13 introduces a theological consideration that controls and transcends the specific problems addressed in chapters 12 and 14, so verses 17-24 control and transcend the problems of chapter 7. The problems of sexuality, in marriage or in celibacy, are set within "the theology of calling," the key point in these verses. "Circumcision or uncircumcision" (verse 19) and "slave or free" (verse 21) are introduced as parallel examples for discussing the problem of sexuality (cf. Gal. 3:28), the main topic of the chapter. The theological control is "the calling" (p. 134). Because the thought structure of verse 21 is parallel to verses 19 and 24, Bartchy proposes that μᾶλλον χρῆσαι should be translated and completed by the phrase "live according to God's call" (of Josephus' 530 uses of χράομαι, 27 bear the meaning "to live according to" [pp. 156-159]). With this interpretation Paul commands neither to remain in slavery or to take freedom; he exhorts rather to remain in "the call" and live accordingly, whether one remains a slave or is manumitted (and Bartchy argues that manumission was quite customary after twenty years of work [pp.113-120]). He translates the entire verse this way: "Were you a slave when you were called? Don't worry about it. But if, indeed, your owner should manumit you, by all means (now as a freedman) live according to God's call" (p. 159).

138. *Ibid.*, p. 278.

139. Weld, p. 17.

140. Bourne, *Book and Slavery*, pp. 111, 109; quoted from William Pitt. See also Weld for similar emphases (pp. 12-19).

141. William Goodell, *Slavery and Antislavery; A History of the Great Struggle in Both Hemispheres; with a View of The Slavery Question in United States* (New York: Negro Universities Press, 1968), p. 167. Goodell's writings were originally published by William Harned in 1852.

142. *Ibid.*, p. 168.

143. *Ibid.*, p. 169.

144. *The Journal of John Woolman* (New York: Corinth Books, 1961), p. 60.
145. *Ibid.*, p. 56.
146. See John C. Wenger's statement on this in his *History of the Franconia Mennonites* (Scottdale, Pa.: Herald Press, 1937), p. 26, and Herbert Fretz's article "The Germantown Anti-Slavery Petition of 1688," *Mennonite Quarterly Review*, 23 (Jan. 1959), 50-51. See also the article by Christian Neff, "Die erste Ansiedlung unserer Glaubensbrüder in Amerika und ihr Protest gegen die Sklaverei," *Christliche Gemeinde Kalendar*, 12 (1903), 86-94; reprinted in *Mennonitische Volkswarte* (1935), pp. 299-304.
147. J. C. Wenger, *Mennonites of the Franconia Conference* (Telford, Pa.: Franconia Mennonite Historical Society, 1937), p. 26.
148. This *Confession* was published as part of a larger work entitled *The Confession of Faith of the Christians known by the names of Mennonites*, in *Thirty-three Articles, with a Short Extract from Their Catechism....* Also, *Nine Reflections ... Illustrative of Their Confession, Faith & Practice* by Peter Burkholder then follows, translated by Joseph Funk (Winchester, Va.: Robinson & Hollis, 1837), p. 419.
149. *Minutes of the Virginia Mennonite Conference* (Virginia Mennonite Conference, 1st ed., 1939; 2nd ed., 1950), p. 6.
150. Johannes Risser, "Enthält das alte Testament, das heilige Wort Gottes eine Lehre oder nur einen entfernten Grund, welcher zu Gunsten unserer Sklaverei im Süden spricht?" *Christliche Volksblatt*, 6, No. 3 (Sept. 4, 1861), 12, 16: "Abschaffung der sklaverei," *ChrVolks*, 6, No. 5 (Oct. 2, 1861), 20. Note also the following Mennonite writings on the subject (the latter two represent research on slavery and do not speak to the Mennonite position or practice):

Vos, Willem de. *Over den slaaven-stand. Door Philalethes Eleutherus. Met eenige aanteekeningen en een voorbericht van den uitgever J. van Geuns.* Leyden: van Geuns, 1797.
Mannhardt, Hermann G. "Die Sklaverei in Afrika und die Nothwendigkeit ihrer Beseitigung." *Mennonitische Blätter*, 36 (1889), 27-29.
Harshberger, Emmett Leroy. "African Slave Trade in Anglo-American Diplomacy." Diss. Ohio State University 1933.
Hertzler, James R. "Slavery in the Yearly Sermons Before the Georgia Trustees." *The Georgia Historical Quarterly*, 59 (Supplement, 1975), 118-125.
151. Some possible exceptions to prevailing practice have been discovered. James O. Lehman, historical researcher and librarian of Eastern Mennonite College, has reported graves of nine slaves in a Mennonite church graveyard near Hagerstown, Maryland. These slaves may have been acquired with a farm purchase and kept by a Mennonite member on a semi-free basis until their death. Grace I. Showalter, Mennonite historical librarian, in her research on Joseph Funk of Singers Glen, Virginia, has located in Funk's correspondence to his children a note about his son-in-law Jacob Bear's purchase of a slave, who revolted, struck and beat Bear, and ran off, leaving Bear for dead. It is not clear that Funk's son-in-law was a member of the Mennonite Church, however. In any event, Funk says of Jacob's purchase in the letter: it is "a thing which I am very opposed to—O the unhappy Negro traffick! ... How much better it is never to meddle with

Slavery" (from Showalter's edited manuscript of Funk's March 22, 26, 1841, letter, in Menno Simons Historical Library, Harrisonburg, Va.).

152. A more recent sample of the Mennonite Church's position on slavery appeared in Guy F. Hershberger's *War, Peace, and Nonresistance,* rev. ed. (Scottdale, Pa.: Herald Press, 1953):

> A good illustration of the Christian attitude toward social injustice is found in Paul's epistle to Philemon. In this letter Paul says he is sending home the runaway slave, Onesimus, admonishing him to be faithful to his master and to serve him in the spirit of Christian love. At the same time Paul admonishes the master to deal with his slave in the same Christian spirit. The relation of Philemon and Onesimus, therefore, was no longer one of master to slave, but rather that of Christian brotherhood. Certainly human slavery is incompatible with social justice, and yet Paul does not demand the abolition of slavery. Instead, he places the whole matter on a different basis by reminding both master and slave that they are brethren and that their relations, one with the other, must be on the basis of Christian love. Certainly, where this relationship actually exists, the institution of human slavery cannot continue; and it would seem that Paul's approach in this case is the Christian solution for every form of injustice [pp. 185-186].

153. "The 1773 Letter to the Holland Mennonites," in Wenger, *History,* p. 400.

154. David McD. Simms, "The Negro Spiritual: Origin and Themes," *The Journal of Negro Education,* 35 (Winter, 1966), 36.

155. John Lovell, Jr., "The Social Implications of the Negro Spiritual," *The Journal of Negro Education,* 18 (Oct. 1939), 640.

156. Taken mostly from Simms, pp. 37-38.

157. Quoted in Lovell, pp. 640-641. See also Douglass' own writing, *My Bondage and Freedom* (New York: Miller, Orton & Mulligan, 1855).

158. H. H. Proctor, "The Theology of the Songs of the Southern Slave," *Southern Workman,* 15 (Dec. 1907), 654. Lovell comments on this point:

> And the falling rocks and mountains hit the slave's enemies. You would never get the communities all over the South which tasted slave revolts, especially in 1831, 1856, and 1860, to believe that these rocks and mountains were ethereal or that they couldn't fall at any time. You would never get post-Sherman Georgia to believe that there was no fire in hell for sinners. The slave song was an awesome prophecy, rooted in the knowledge of what was going on and of human nature, and not in mystical lore. Its deadly edge threatened; and struck [p. 641].

159. John W. Blassingame, *The Slave Community* (New York: Oxford University Press, 1975), pp. 71, 73. See the exslave Henry Bibb's testimony that most slaveholders were oppressive, in *The Narrative of Henry Bibb* (New York: privately printed, 1849), pp. 21-25.

160. Simms, p. 39.

161. *Ibid.*

162. *Ibid.*

163. Charles L. Coleman, "The Emergence of Black Religion in Pennsylvania, 1776-1850," *Pennsylvania Heritage*, 4, No. 1 (Dec. 1977), 27. Coleman cites Ezekiel 37:22 for the Acts text. 1 Corinthians 12:13 (as well as Jn. 13:34-35; Gal. 3:26-28; Col. 3:11) is cited by Isaac Allen, *Is Slavery Sanctioned by the Bible?* (Boston: American Tract Society, 1860), p. 20.

164. Austin Steward, *Twenty-two Years a Slave* (Rochester, N.Y.: William Alling, 1857), p. 21.

165. *The Anti-Slavery Harp* (Boston: Bela Marsh, 1848), p. 10.

166. See, for example, Joseph P. Thompson, who with his membership in the black Tabernacle Church must have been black—at least he articulated black sentiment in *Teachings of the New Testament on Slavery* (New York: Joseph H. Ladd, 1856); Rev. LaRoy Sunderland, *The Testimony of God Against Slavery* (New York: American Anti-Slavery Society, 1939); and Allen, *Is Slavery Sanctioned by the Bible?* Allen's writing received an award of $100 from the Church Anti-Slavery Society as the best tract on Bible teachings respecting slavery. Allen, possibly an exslave, was likely influenced by Weld since he wrote from Oberlin College.

167. In Harriet Beecher Stowe's *Uncle Tom's Cabin* (Boston: J. P. Jewett & Co., 1852), p. 84, which reflects in turn a discussion between Rev. Joel Parker (pro-slavery) and Rev. A. Rood (anti-slavery) in the *Philadelphia Christian Observer* (1846), reprinted in *The Discussion Between Rev. Joel Parker and Rev. A. Rood on the Question of Slavery* (New York: S. W. Benedict, 1852).

168. Simms, p. 38.

169. Quoted from a study paper entitled "The Christian Woman in the Church and Conference," presented July 8, 1974, at the Canadian Conference of Mennonite Brethren, Vancouver, B.C.

170. For the history of interpretation and the role of *literal* interpretation compared to other methods, see Robert Grant, *A Short History of the Interpretation of the Bible*, rev. ed. (New York: Macmillan, 1963), pp. 80ff. For a sympathetic appraisal of allegorical interpretation, see Beryl Smalley, *The Bible in the Middle Ages* (Oxford: Clarendon Press, 1941).

171. These methods are described and utilized in Bible study method in the helpful book by Perry B. Yoder, *From Word to Life: A Guide to the Art of Bible Study* (Scottdale, Pa.: Herald Press, 1982), pp. 24-40. See also George Eldon Ladd, *The New Testament and Criticism* (Grand Rapids, Mich.: Eerdmans, 1967); I. Howard Marshall, *New Testament Interpretation: Essays on Principles and Methods* (Grand Rapids, Mich.: Eerdmans, 1977); William A. Beardslee, *Literary Criticism of the New Testament* (Philadelphia: Fortress Press, 1970); Edgar Krentz, *The Historical-Critical Method* (Philadelphia: Fortress Press, 1975); and Norman R. Petersen, *Literary Criticism for the New Testament Critic* (Philadelphia: Fortress Press, 1978), pp. 9-48.

172. See P. Yoder's discussion of Genesis 12:10-20, the lead story in the Abraham narrative (pp. 62-64, 184-189).

173. Strikingly, modern versions, even Clarence Jordan's *Cotton Patch* translation, are free to translate *ebed* and *doulos* as "slave" because we are no longer in the debate! If Jordan, with his convictions against racism, had done his translation in 1850, the word *doulos* could not have been rendered "slave"!

174. Jordan's *Cotton Patch* translation vividly illustrates that one's set-

ting in life affects basic perception, even the choice of words for a Bible translation.

CHAPTER 2

1. *Seventh-day Adventists Answer Questions on Doctrine* (Washington, D.C.: Review and Herald Publishing Co., 1957), p. 176; hereafter cited as *SAAQD*.

2. See Gerhard F. Hasel, "Capito, Schwenkfeld, and Crautwald on Sabbatarian Anabaptist Theology," *Mennonite Quarterly Review (MQR)*. 46 (Jan. 1972), 41-57, and "Sabbatarian Anabaptists" in the *Mennonite Encyclopedia*, Vol. 4, p. 396.

3. A. E. Waffle, *The Lord's Day: Its Universal and Perpetual Obligation* (Philadelphia: American Sunday-School Union, 1885), p. 358.

4. Quoted from Francis Nigel Lee, *The Covenantal Sabbath* (London: The Lord's Day Observance Society, 1966), p. 260.

5. My own summary of the position to be described in the third section of this chapter.

6. E.g., Pilgram Marpeck. See William Klassen, *Covenant and Community: The Life, Writings, and Hermeneutics of Pilgram Marpeck* (Grand Rapids, Mich.: Eerdmans, 1968), pp. 105-106: "Pilgram Marpeck's Theology," *MQR*. 40, No. 2 (Apr. 1966), 100.

7. M. L. Andreasen, *The Sabbath: Which Day and Why?* (Washington, D.C.: Review and Herald Publishing Association, 1942), p. 9.

8. *SAAQD*, p. 158.

9. Jewish scholarship supports this position, as reflected in Abraham Joshua Heschel's exposition on the meaning of the Sabbath:

> "The world to come is characterized by the kind of holiness possessed by the Sabbath in this world...."
> The essence of the world to come is Sabbath eternal, and the seventh day in time is an example of eternity.

Heschel quotes the first statement from the rabbinic commentary, *Mekilta to Exodus (The Sabbath: Its Meaning for Modern Man* [New York: Farrar, Straus and Giroux, 1951], pp. 73, 74).

10. M. L. Andreasen, pp. 67-68.

11. This claim arises from references to the Babylonian week, or the Babylonian monthly *sabattu* celebration connected with the full moon, or seven-day festivals. See Niels-Erik A. Andreasen, *The Old Testament Sabbath: A Tradition-Historical Investigation* (Society of Biblical Literature, Dissertation Series, No. 7, 1972), pp. 1-3, 94-97. Though Andreasen recognizes that most scholars today have given up attempts to locate extrabiblical origins of the Sabbath and agree that it originated with Moses (p. 8), he concludes, after surveying various theories:

> The Old Testament understands the reason for the seventh-day Sabbath to rest in a divine fiat. It does not remember when the Sabbath began and where it originated. Perhaps we should take this to mean that the Sabbath is older than the Old Testament literature and that its origin was as obscure to it as it is to us [p. 120].

12. Carlyle B. Haynes, *From Sabbath to Sunday* (Washington, D.C.:

Review and Herald Publishing Association, 1942), p. 14; Dan Day, *Why I'm an Adventist: A Christian Invites You to Examine His Faith* (Mountain View, Calif.: Pacific Press Publishing Association, 1974), pp. 18-21.

13. M. L. Andreasen, p. 53.

14. George Ide Butler, *The Change of the Sabbath: Was It by Divine or Human Authority?* (title page missing), p. 25.

15. *Ibid.*, pp. 79-81.

16. *Ibid.*, pp. 31-32.

17. *Ibid.*, pp. 86-89.

18. *Ibid.*, p. 96.

19. *Ibid.*, pp. 97-98.

20. *Ibid.*, pp. 99-101.

21. *SAAQD*, p. 149.

22. M. L. Andreasen, p. 103.

23. Samuele Bacchiocchi, *From Sabbath to Sunday: A Historical Investigation of the Rise of Sunday Observance in Early Christianity* (Rome: The Pontifical Gregorian University Press, 1977), p. 32. Bacchiocchi, a Seventh-Day Adventist on the faculty of Andrews University, was the first non-Catholic to graduate with a doctorate from the Pontifical Gregorian University. This book, an outgrowth of his dissertation, is a masterful scholarly study, which seeks to show the nonbiblical origin of Sunday observance and attributes its origin primarily to the Roman Church.

24. *Ibid.*, p. 30.

25. *Ibid.*, p. 38.

26. Haynes, pp. 19-21.

27. M. L. Andreasen, pp. 117-131.

28. *Ibid.*, p. 143.

29. Butler, p. 209; Bacchiocchi, pp. 69-71.

30. Bacchiocchi, pp. 62-63.

31. Butler, pp. 210-212.

32. Bacchiocchi, p. 131.

33. *Ibid.*, pp. 132-164, especially 164.

34. *SAAQD*, p. 169.

35. *Ibid.*, pp. 166-167.

36. Bacchiocchi, pp. 268-269.

37. *Ibid.*, p. 211. See also pp. 310-312, which quote Thomas Aquinas, among others, in support of Rome's authority for the change.

38. Hasel, pp. 49-50.

39. Andrew A. Bonar, *Memoir and Remains of Robert Murray M'Cheyne* (1844; rpt. London: Cox and Wyman, Ltd., 1966), p. 597.

40. Thomas Watson, *The Ten Commandments* (Guildford, England: Billings and Sons, Ltd., rev. ed., 1965; orig., 1692), pp. 94-95.

41. John Murray, *The Claims of Truth*, Vol. I of *Collected Writings of John Murray* (Chatham, England: W. and J. Mackay, Ltd., 1976), p. 206.

42. *Ibid.*, p. 210.

43. R. H. Martin, *The Day: A Manual for the Christian Sabbath* (Pittsburgh: Office of the National Reform Association, 1933), pp. 2-3.

44. Roger T. Beckwith and Wilfrid Stott, *This Is The Day: The Biblical Doctrine of the Christian Sunday in Its Jewish and Early Church Setting* (London: Marshall, Morgan & Scott, 1978), p. 206.

45. *Ibid.*, pp. 8-10.

46. Francis Nigel Lee, *The Covenantal Sabbath* (London: The Lord's Day Observance Society, 1969), pp. 17-23.

47. *Ibid.*, p. 71.

48. *Ibid.*, pp. 85-86. See also p. 33, where Lee says, "But when Adam broke the covenant of works (perhaps by desecrating the then sabbath day?!!—thus Tostatus, Luther, etc.), he lost his sabbath rest in God."

49. *Ibid.*, pp. 105-109.

50. Murray, pp. 196-207.

51. William DeLoss Love, *Sabbath and Sunday* (New York: Fleming H. Revell Co., 1896), p. 144.

52. Watson, p. 95.

53. George Junkin, *Sabbatismos; a Discussion and Defense of the Lord's Day of Sacred Rest* (Philadelphia: James B. Rodgers, 1866), p. 108.

54. Lee, p. 31.

55. Beckwith, pp. 13-14.

56. *Ibid.*, pp. 17-19. Beckwith cites Jubilees 2:19-21, 31; *Sanhedrin* 56b; *Mekilta*, Shabbata 1; and Bereshith Rabbah 11.

57. Beckwith, pp. 19-20.

58. Watson, pp. 95-96.

59. W. O. Carver, *Sabbath Observance: The Lord's Day in Our Day* (Nashville, Tenn.: Broadman Press, 1940), p. 25.

60. A. E. Waffle, *The Lord's Day: Its Universal and Perpetual Obligation* (Philadelphia: American Sunday-School Union, 1885), p. 358.

61. Beckwith, p. 24.

62. Love, p. 89.

63. *Ibid.*, p. 123. See also Beckwith, pp. 30-38.

64. Herbert S. Bird, *Theology of Seventh-day Adventism* (Grand Rapids, Mich.: Eerdmans, 1961), p. 109.

65. Martin, pp. 103-140.

66. Lee, pp. 30-37. Lee combines this insight with the "now-not yet" tension of fulfilling eschatological hope, using a diagram to show the overlap of the ages. See also Beckwith, p. 45.

67. E.g., Lee, pp. 219, 224-227, 237-238. Many of the writers in this position, however, do not mention the texts in Romans and Colossians.

68. Beckwith, p. 28.

69. *Ibid.*, pp. 140-141.

70. Willy Rordorf, *Sunday: The History of the Day of Rest and Worship in the Earliest Centuries of the Christian Church*, trans. A. A. K. Graham (Philadelphia: Westminster Press, 1968), p. 116.

71. Clarence Jordan, *The Substance of Faith; Cotton Patch Sermons* (New York: Association Press, 1972), p. 145.

72. H. M. Riggle, *The Sabbath and the Lord's Day*, 6th ed., rev. (Anderson, Ind.: Gospel Trumpet Company, 1928), p. 148.

73. *Ibid.*, p. 23.

74. *Ibid.*, pp. 16-17.

75. *Ibid.*, p. 17.

76. *Ibid.*, pp. 17-18.

77. *Ibid.*, p. 154.

78. *Ibid.*, p. 151.

79. *Ibid.*, pp. 172-173.

80. *Ibid.*, pp. 184-186.

81. *Ibid.,* pp. 192-226.
82. *Ibid.,* p. 227. The words in brackets are not in the sixth edition but are in the first edition (1918), p. 258.
83. Rordorf, p. 12. Rordorf regards Exodus 23:12 and 34:21 as the oldest statements of the Sabbath command, originating from a pre-Elohistic period.
84. This emphasis which dominated the priestly account of creation (Gen. 2:2-3) originated much earlier than the priestly document itself, according to Rordorf, and is found, therefore, in both these Elohistic and Deuteronomic formulations (p. 14).
85. As Rordorf puts it: "In Gen. 1—2:23 we are told that God created the world in six days and rested on the seventh day, but this motivation was added after the institution of a day of rest recurring after every six days had already been in existence for a long time" (p. 18). Rordorf holds that the seventh-day rest originated after the occupation of Canaan before the monarchial period, since the form of the command reflects an agricultural setting (p. 18).
86. Rordorf, p. 15.
87. *Ibid.,* p. 16.
88. *Ibid.,* pp. 51ff. The references are Ezekiel 20:11f.; the priestly material in Exodus 31:14f.; 35:2; Numbers 15:32-36; and the later writings such as Jubilees 2:25, 27; 50:8, 13 and the Damascus Document 12:3-6.
89. Rordorf, p. 63.
90. *Ibid.,* pp. 66-67.
91. *Ibid.,* p. 70.
92. Both John 9:4 and Luke 13:16 root Jesus' Sabbath activities in the *dei* of the divine necessity of the Father's will.
93. Rordorf regards this saying to be derived from the early church, which saw in Jesus' Sabbath activities his messianic claim over the Sabbath and therefore enunciated this theme more explicitly (p. 71).
94. Rordorf, p. 71.
95. *Ibid.,* pp. 67-68. Rordorf also notes that the statement in Matthew 24:20, "Pray that your flight may not be . . . on a sabbath," carries no weight in measuring Jesus' attitude since the scholarly views of the composition of this discourse in Matthew would regard this verse as deriving from Jewish Christian circles after Jesus (p. 68).
96. Rordorf, pp. 88-89.
97. *Ibid.,* pp. 89-90. Based on this Jewish view of the coming Sabbath of the last age, Jesus excused his Sabbath work in John 5:17, says Rordorf, because the Father is not yet resting! At the same time, Jesus implicitly claimed messianic authority in identifying himself with "God's activity and rest" (pp. 99-100).
98. Rordorf, p. 101.
99. *Ibid.,* p. 117.
100. *Ibid.,* p. 102.
101. *Ibid.,* p. 119.
102. *Ibid.,* p. 127.
103. *Ibid.,* pp. 127-139.
104. *Ibid.,* p. 140. Rordorf says that no further evidence regarding Christian Sabbath observance occurs again until the end of the second century. His reconstruction holds that Sabbath observance by Christians

ceased during the first two centuries, revived in the next two, especially the fourth, and disappeared again in the fifth, probably because Constantine's imperial edict made Sunday the official day of rest (pp. 142-153).

105. *Ibid.,* pp. 154-173.

106. *Ibid.,* pp. 215-256.

107. *Ibid.,* p. 218.

108. *Ibid.,* p. 215.

109. Paul K. Jewett, *The Lord's Day: A Theological Guide to the Christian Day of Worship* (Grand Rapids, Mich.: Eerdmans, 1971), pp. 16-18.

110. *Ibid.,* p. 18.

111. *Ibid.,* p. 24.

112. *Ibid.,* p. 25.

113. *Ibid.,* pp. 27-29.

114. *Ibid.,* p. 38.

115. *Ibid.,* p. 42.

116. *Ibid.,* p. 43.

117. *Ibid.,* p. 67.

118. *Ibid.,* pp. 59-60.

119. *Ibid.,* p. 73.

120. *Ibid.,* pp. 82.

121. *Ibid.,* pp. 80-81.

122. In Jewett's further theological treatment of the matter, including the Reformers and Karl Barth, he moves closer and closer to position 2 above; even though he states his disagreement with the English Puritans (pp. 115-122). Jewett disagrees with Rordorf, who advocates giving up all attempts to understand Sunday in terms of the fourth commandment (p. 89). In answer to the test question which distinguishes position 3 from 2—Is one day especially holy?—Jewett ends up by saying both "no, according to the New Testament," and "yes, according to the Old Testament," since he recognizes the continuing authority of both Testaments for Christian theology and living.

123. Harold H. P. Dressler, "The Sabbath in the Old Testament," pp. 29-31; and A. T. Lincoln, "From Sabbath to Lord's Day: A Biblical and Theological Perspective," pp. 348-358, both in *From Sabbath to Lord's Day: A Biblical, Historical, and Theological Investigation,* ed. D. A. Carson (Grand Rapids, Mich.: Zondervan, 1982).

124. D. A. Carson, "Jesus and the Sabbath in Four Gospels," in *From Sabbath to Lord's Day,* pp. 84-85; Lincoln pp. 345, 362.

125. Max M. B. Turner, "The Sabbath, Sunday and the Law in Luke/Acts," in *From Sabbath to Lord's Day,* pp. 124-127.

126. D. R. de Lacey, "The Sabbath/Sunday Question and the Law in the Pauline Corpus," in *From Sabbath to Lord's Day,* pp. 180-183; Lincoln, pp. 364-368.

127. Lincoln, pp. 401-402.

128. Lincoln, pp. 398-400. Another similarity which may have been noted, unfortunately underemphasized in this book, is that both stand for the justice and shalom of God's reign for humanity and all God's creation.

129. *Ibid.,* pp. 403-405.

130. The same logic applies to the third position, but with lesser force since celebrating the Lord's supper and resting on the same day would not necessarily be viewed as contradictory practices, as would the choice of a

specific day, Sunday versus Saturday, for observance.

131. If, however, one can show textual variants in early manuscripts that favor the later church's position and suppress textual evidence for Sabbath observance or identify other points of tension between the church and Scripture, evidence emerges that a wedge was driven somewhere, somehow, between the Scripture's teaching and the later church's practice. In that case, it is wrong for us not to recognize the wedge. Assuming as a Seventh-Day Adventist that such a wedge was driven on the matter of Sabbath/Sunday observance, George Edward Rice, New Testament professor at Andrews University, devoted his doctoral dissertation to a study of Luke-Acts in Codex Bezae (D), a Greek New Testament manuscript written in Rome in the fourth century. His study identifies anti-Sabbath bias in the manuscript in Luke's Gospel. This evidence, which Rice claims to show, testifies to the later church's discomfort with Luke's generally favorable view of the Sabbath. See George Edward Rice, "The Alteration of Luke's Tradition by the Textual Variants in Codex Bezae," Diss. Case Western Reserve University 1974 (available on microfilm from University Microfilms International, Ann Arbor, Mich.). But such evidence could just as well support the third position in this study, since it too recognizes that the later church (and specifically the fourth-century church) initiated emphases which put Sunday rest in direct competition with the Sabbath observance of rest.

132. To amass the evidence for such a difference is the goal of Bacciocchi's study. But he does not answer how or why the church could affirm that Scripture as authoritative, without altering it at crucial places.

133. In an extensive analysis of how seven recent theologians use Scripture, David Kelsey demonstrates that each theologian (from Warfield to Tillich) used Scripture differently to support their respective theological proposals. See David H. Kelsey, The Uses of Scripture in Recent Theology (Philadelphia: Fortress, 1975). But such a study does not conclusively answer the question posed here since it focuses on how theologians use Scripture; as such the study does not falsify, but rather supports the fact that Scripture may also produce and form distinctive theological understandings.

134. The Mennonite Church statement Biblical Interpretation in the Life of the Church (see Appendix 1) recognizes both sides of influence. Part I.B speaks of the Bible as the church's book, and Part I.C acknowledges certain theological perspectives which have developed from but also influence a denominational way of reading Scripture. Part II of the statement, on the other hand, sets forth a method which seeks to allow the Scripture to speak its own piece. To be sure, theological perspectives affect one's use of any method. Nonetheless, the method has the potential for allowing Scripture to influence, even change, a person's or a group's theology.

135. An excellent recent study which explains and demonstrates the historical-critical method allied fruitfully with the linguistic method is Perry B. Yoder's From Word to Life: A Guide to the Art of Bible Study (Scottdale, Pa.: Herald Press, 1982). For additional resources to understand the historical-critical method together with its usefulness and limitations, see George Eldon Ladd, The New Testament and Criticism (Grand Rapids, Mich.: Eerdmans, 1977); I. Howard Marshall, New Testament Interpretations: Essays on Principles and Methods (Grand Rapids, Mich.: Eerdmans, 1977). For a historical account of the rise of the historical method, see Edgar

296

Krentz, *The Historical-Critical Method* (Philadelphia: Fortress Press, 1975). Peter Stuhlmacher's *Historical-Criticism and Theological Interpretation of Scripture: Towards a Hermeneutics of Consent*, translated by Roy A. Harrisville (Philadelphia: Fortress Press, 1977), is also insightful and helpful.

136. Bacciocchi does recognize this connection and stresses that Jesus' deeds on the Sabbath were truly sabbatical acts. But to regard the Sabbath as a memorial of Jesus rather than seeing Jesus' and his followers' deeds as the fulfillment of the Sabbath is to put the lesser point into prominent position, a pattern with precedent in the priestly reinterpretation of the Sabbath in Old Testament times, according to Rordorf.

137. This is what Karl Barth called "discovering the strange New World of the Bible." Walter Wink's book *The Bible in Human Transformation* (Philadelphia: Fortress Press, 1977) calls this process "distantiation," a necessary prelude to "fusion" wherein the text and the interpreter "commune," with the text giving life, direction, and change to the interpreter.

138. I address this issue in an article, "The Historical-Critical Method: New Directions" in a forthcoming issue of *Occasional Papers*, Institute of Mennonite Studies, Elkhart, Ind.

CHAPTER 3

1. The six I wrote to were Loraine Boettner, Gordon H. Clark, V. R. Edman (then president of Wheaton College), General Wm. K. Harrison, who wrote in *Christianity Today* (Apr. 13, 1959), Carl F. H. Henry, and Wilbur Smith (professor at Fuller Theological Seminary). (Boettner, Clark, and Henry are introduced in the text.) Clark's comment reported in the text corresponds to his earlier, published statement: "If the Old Testament is clear on anything, it is clear that God positively commanded war. Since this cannot be denied, shall we accept pacifism with the implication that God commanded his people to sin?" "Is Pacifism Christian?" *United Evangelical Action* (Aug. 1, 1955), p. 5.

2. Historically, the Roman Catholic Church and many Protestants supported Christian participation in war by the just war theory, formulated as early as Augustine. For discussion of the development of this position, see Walter Klaassen, "The Just War: A Summary," *Peace Research Reviews*, 7, No. 6 (Sept. 1978), 1-70; Roubert G. Clouse, ed., *War: Four Christian Views* (Downers Grove, Ill.: InterVarsity Press, 1981), pp. 14-15; and Arthur F. Holmes' essay in the same book, pp. 117-135.

3. George W. Knight III, "Can A Christian Go To War?" *Christianity Today*, 20, No. 4 (Nov. 21, 1975), 4.

4. Loraine Boettner, *The Christian Attitude Toward War*, 2nd ed., rev. (Grand Rapids, Mich.: Eerdmans, 1942), p. 25.

5. Ex. 17:8-16; Num. 33:50-56; Josh. 1:1-9; 5:13—6:27; Judg. 4:1-23; 6:12; 1 Sam. 15:1-23; 17:1-54; 2 Sam. 5:19-20. Boettner also cites Psalms in which Yahweh is a warrior (35:1-2; 68:1-2, 12, 17; 83:2, 17; 108; 124; 136; 144:1). Further, when Israel fought against God's command, defeat occurred (Num. 14:39-45; Josh. 7:1—8:29; 1 Sam. 28:15-19; 2 Chron. 18:1-34). See Boettner, pp. 21-24.

6. Clark, p. 5.

7. Richard S. Taylor, "A Theology of War and Peace as Related to Perfect Love: A Case for Participation in War," in *Perfect Love and War*, ed.

Paul Hostetler (Nappanee, Ind.: Evangel Press, 1974), p. 30.

8. Arthur F. Holmes, ed., *War and Christian Ethics* (Grand Rapids, Mich.: Baker Book House, 1975), p. 144.

9. Harold Snider, *Does the Bible Sanction War? (Why I Am Not a Pacifist)* (Grand Rapids, Mich.: Zondervan, 1942), p. 62.

10. Clark, p. 23; Boettner, p. 32; Knight, p. 5; and W. G. Corliss, "Can a Christian Be a Fighting Man?" *Eternity*, 13 (Sept. 1962), 22-23.

11. Only Corliss makes this connection to 1 Corinthians 7:20. But see chap. 1, note 137.

12. *Ibid.*, pp. 22-23.

13. Knight, p. 5. The use of Acts 10 is in the other writers as well.

14. These are codified into ten major arguments as follows:

(i) Jesus justified war because he prophesied that there would be wars in the future.

Mt. 24:6-8. Parallel passages: Mk. 13:7-8; Lk. 21:9-11.

Lk. 19:41-44. Parallel passages: Mt. 24:2; Mk. 13:2.

Lk. 21:20-24.

Mt. 24:1-2. Parallel passages: Mk. 13:2; Lk. 21:6.

(ii) Jesus justified war because he recognized that his religion would bring dissension.

Mt. 10:34-36.

Lk. 12:49-53.

Lk. 14:25-26.

(iii) Jesus justified war because he recognized the value of being prepared.

Lk. 22:35-36.

Lk. 11:21-22. Parallel passages: Mt. 12:29; Mk. 3:27.

Lk. 14:31.

Lk. 12:37-40. Parallel passage: Mt. 24:42-44.

(iv) Jesus justified war by implying that war is justifiable under certain conditions.

Jn. 18:35-36.

Mk. 12:1-9. Parallel passages: Lk. 20:9-16; Mt. 21:33-41.

Mt. 18:6-7. Parallel passages: Mk. 9:42; Lk. 17:1-2.

(v) Jesus justified war in commending the Centurion, a man of war.

Mt. 8:5-10, 13. Parallel passage: Lk. 7:1-10.

(vi) Jesus justified war in advocating obedience to authority.

Mk. 12:13-17. Parallel passages: Mt. 22:15-22; Lk. 20:20-26.

(vii) Jesus justified war in advocating the paying of taxes, knowing that they might be used by the Roman war machine.

Mk. 12:13-17. Parallel passages: Mt. 22:15-22; Lk. 20:20-26.

(viii) Jesus justified war because he demanded self-sacrifice, even to the point of death, in defense of values that are more im-

portant than life.
Lk. 9:23-25. Parallel passages: Mt. 16:24-26; Mk. 8:34-37.
Mt. 20:25-28. Parallel passages: Mk. 10:42-45; Mk. 9:35b; Lk. 22:25-26.
Jn. 15:12-13.

(ix) Jesus justified war because he portrayed God as one who would use force in awarding punishment.
Mt. 18:23-35.
Mt. 13:40-42. Similar passage: Mt. 13:49-50.
Lk. 19:11-27. Parallel passage: Mt. 25:14-30.
Mt. 24:45-51. Parallel passage: Lk. 12:42-48.
Mt. 10:14-15.
Lk. 10:10-15.
Mt. 24:29-31. Parallel passages: Mk. 13:24-27; Lk. 21:27-28.

(x) Jesus justified war in using force to drive the moneychangers from the Temple.
Jn. 2:13-16. Parallel passages: Mt. 21:12-13; Mk. 11:15-17; Lk. 19:45-46. [From the FCC Commission, in Boettner, pp. 16-18.]

15. Boettner, pp. 30-31.
16. *Ibid.*, pp. 45-56.
17. Clark, p. 23.
18. *Ibid.*
19. Knight, p. 5.
20. *Ibid.*
21. Corliss, p. 23. Taylor argues that it is inconsistent to believe that God authorizes the functions of the state, and yet refuse to hold positions correlative to those functions. He says, "I believe the Christian may fill any legitimate role in the state—including that of soldier—without violating his primary allegiance to Christ" (p. 35).

Capt. W. G. Corliss, a naval aviator involved in Pentagon intelligence, thinks there is a point, however, beyond which Christians cannot go:

> I have come to the conclusion that a true Christian cannot serve his country today in a public position, past a certain point, without compromising and cooperating with evil. In all conscience he cannot propose courses of action he knows are hopeless and wrong and yet most actions he proposes as sound and Christian invariably get perverted or never find acceptance.

> He would appear to have three courses of action: (a) he can compromise and propose answers he knows won't work or answers which he knows are wrong, (b) he can produce the very best answers he knows, going to the heart of the matter and proposing Christian solutions, or (c) he can voluntarily remove himself from his position.

> In case (a), he assumes the sin of hypocrisy, opportunism, and cooperation with evil. In case (b), he is honest but he will be labeled as an idealist, impracticable and unrealistic; in this case I should

expect him either never to have arrived in a position of responsibility or rapidly to be demoted from it. In case (c), he retired from the conflict [p. 24].

22. Snider pp. 37-47; Knight, p. 4.
23. Peter C. Craigie, *The Problem of War in the Old Testament* (Grand Rapids, Mich.: Eerdmans, 1978), p. 58.
24. Taylor, p. 30.
25. Knight, p. 6; Boettner, pp. 29-30.
26. Carl F. H. Henry, *Christian Personal Ethics* (Grand Rapids, Mich.: Eerdmans, 1957), p. 323.
27. *Ibid.*, p. 322. This distinction between personal and social realms has been used widely in ascertaining the moral demands of the Sermon on the Mount. In my 1960 correspondence with Henry (see note 1 above), Henry illustrated this distinction by comment on Matthew 5:40, saying that if he owned a clothing store to which someone came and asked for a coat, he would not be obligated to give it; if, however, the person came to his home and asked for a coat, he would be morally obligated to give it.
28. Boettner, p. 28.
29. Snider, p. 84.
30. Knight, p. 5.
31. Holmes, p. 168.
32. Craigie (in report of Elbert W. Russell's study), p. 14.
33. Leslie Rumble, "The Pacifist and the Bible," *The Homiletical and Pastoral Review*, 59, No. 12 (Sept. 1959), 1086. Rumble quotes from essays from a Protestant symposium published as *Biblical Authority for Today* (1951), pp. 141-42.
34. Boettner, p. 21.
35. Gerhard von Rad's *Der Heilige Krieg im Alten Israel* (Vandenhoeck and Ruprecht, 1951) is an important, seminal study on this topic. Von Rad argues, however, that the emphasis upon miraculous victory coupled with Israel's "standing still" is a late theological readback upon the bloody history. For more recent scholarly treatments of the topic, see Patrick Miller, *The Divine Warrior in Early Israel* (Cambridge, Mass.: Harvard University Press, 1972), and "God the Warrior," *Interpretation*, 19 (1965), 35-46; Frank Cross, "The Divine Warrior in Israel's Early Cult," in Vol. III of *Biblical Motifs: Studies and Texts*, ed. Alexander Altmann (Cambridge, Mass.: Harvard University Press, 1966), pp. 11-30; Peter C. Craigie, "Yahweh Is a Man of War," *Scottish Journal of Theology*, 22 (1969), 183-188; A. Gelston, "The Wars of Israel," *Scottish Journal of Theology*, 17 (1964), 325-331.
36. G. Ernest Wright, *The Old Testament and Theology* (New York: Harper and Row, 1969), p. 130.
37. *Ibid.*, pp. 148-150. For a pacifist reply to Wright, see Waldemar Janzen, "God as Warrior and Lord: A Conversation with G. E. Wright," *Bulletin of American Society of Oriental Research*, 220 (Dec. 1975), 73-75.
38. Craigie, *Problem of War*, p. 33.
39. *Ibid.*, pp. 35-36.
40. This summarizes Craigie's argument in *Problem of War*, pp. 39-82; see also Craigie's summary, pp. 94ff. Craigie utilizes Jacques Ellul's analysis of the state and of violence (pp. 71-72), drawing on Ellul's books

Political Illusion (New York: Kropf, 1967) and *Violence: Reflections from a Christian Perspective* (New York: Seabury Press, 1969).

41. Craigie, *Problem of War*, p. 102.
42. *Ibid.*; these three quotations are from pp. 108, 62, 198, respectively. They represent the unresolved ethical dilemma of Craigie's position.
43. *Ibid.*, p. 110.
44. Rumble, p. 1090.
45. *Ibid.*
46. *Ibid.*, pp. 1090-1091.
47. Wright, p. 130.
48. Reinhold Niebuhr, *Christianity and Power Politics* (New York: Charles Scribner's Sons, 1940), pp. 8-10. In *Moral Man and Immoral Society* (New York: Charles Scribner's Sons, 1932), Niebuhr argues for the use of nonviolence as a political strategy, but one which involves coercion and conflict; it is not nonresisting love (pp. 248-256).
49. Reinhold Niebuhr, *An Interpretation of Christian Ethics* (New York: Harper & Brothers, 1935), p. 31.

50. *Ibid.*, p. 39.
51. Niebuhr, *Christianity and Politics*, p. xi.
52. *Ibid.*, pp. 1-5; Niebuhr, *Christian Ethics*, pp. 65, 110, 223. For a pacifist critique of Niebuhr, see John Howard Yoder, *Reinhold Niebuhr and Christian Pacifism* (Zeist, The Netherlands: The International Conference Center, 1954).
53. Paul Ramsey, *War and the Christian Conscience: How Shall Modern War Be Conducted Justly?* (Durham, N.C.: Duke University Press, 1961), pp. xvii-xviii.
54. This selection of themes is not exhaustive, and the literature cited can only be representative.
55. James H. Cone, *God of the Oppressed* (New York: Seabury Press, 1975), p. 63.
56. *Ibid.*, 217-219.
57. *Ibid.*, p. 219.
58. Rubem Alves, *A Theology of Human Hope* (Cleveland: Corpus Books, 1969), p. 125.
59. Bruce O. Boston, "How Are Revelation and Revolution Related?" *Theology Today*, 26 (July 1969), p. 146.
60. Richard Shaull, "Christian Faith as Scandal in a Technocratic World," *New Theology No. 6*, ed. Martin E. Marty and Dean G. Peerman (London: Macmillan, 1969), pp. 126, 130.
61. José Miranda, *Marx and the Bible: A Critique of the Philosophy of Oppression* (Maryknoll, N.Y.: Orbis Books, 1974), pp. 111ff.; *Communism in the Bible* (Maryknoll, NY: Orbis Books, 1982), pp. 74-78. Gustavo Gutierrez similarly regards salvation as essentially liberation and justice, but does not *explicitly* endorse violence. Instead, he argues for revolution because of the violence in the existing established structure; *A Theology of Liberation* (Maryknoll, N.Y.: Orbis Books, 1973), pp. 48, 89, 149-168, 194-208, 276. See also L. John Topel for an implicitly pacifist treatment of the liberation and justice themes, in *The Way to Peace: Liberation Through the Bible* (Maryknoll, N.Y.: Orbis Books, 1979), pp. 2-10, 42-68; and Allan Aubrey Boesak, *Farewell to Innocence: A Socio-Ethical Study on Black Theology and Black Power* (Maryknoll, N.Y.: Orbis Books, 1977), pp. 16-26.

62. George Celestin, "A Christian Looks at Revolution," *New Theology No. 6*, pp. 100-101.

63. *Ibid.*, pp. 101-102.

64. Cone, pp. 66-70.

65. José Miguez Bonino, *Doing Theology in a Revolutionary Situation* (Philadelphia: Fortress Press, 1975), p. 116.

66. *Ibid.*, pp. 117-118. See also Jon Sobrino, *Christology at the Crossroads: A Latin American Approach*, trans. John Drury (Maryknoll, N.Y.: Orbis Books, 1978), pp. 119, 122.

67. Boston, p. 150. See also Gutierrezz, pp. 167-168.

68. Celestin, p. 101.

69. Cone, p. 73.

70. Ernesto Cardenal, *The Gospel in Solentiname*, I, trans. Donald D. Walsh (Maryknoll, N.Y.: Orbis Books, 1978), 31.

71. *Ibid.*, p. 77.

72. *Ibid.*, p. 83.

73. Bonino, p. 118.

74. *Ibid.*, p. 122.

75. *Ibid.*, pp. 122-123.

76. Juan Luis Segundo, *The Liberation of Theology*, trans. John Drury (Maryknoll, N.Y.: Orbis Books, 1976), p. 164.

77. *Ibid.*,

78. *Ibid.*, pp. 164-165. Segundo then argues that "Thou shalt not kill" cannot be taken as an absolute rule (p. 165f.).

79. Boston, p. 152.

80. *Ibid.*

81. *Ibid.*

82. Shaull, p. 127; Celestin, p. 101.

83. Boston, p. 153.

84. Choan-Seng Song, *Third-Eye Theology: Theology in Formation in Asian Settings* (Maryknoll, N.Y.: Orbis Books, 1979), p. 182.

85. Cone, p. 80.

86. *Ibid.*, pp. 81-82. See also Rubem Alves' discussion regarding the resurrection and messianism as the core of Christian hope—based, on the one hand, upon liberation already experienced and, on the other, upon the expectation of God's continuing liberation from all bondage (pp. 125-132).

87. John Howard Yoder, *Nevertheless: Varieties of Christian Pacifism* (Scottdale, Pa.: Herald Press, 1971).

88. Vernard Eller, *War and Peace from Genesis to Revelation*, rev. ed. (Scottdale, Pa.: Herald Press, 1981), pp. 26-38.

89. Guy F. Hershberger, *War, Peace, and Nonresistance*, rev. ed. (Scottdale, Pa.: Herald Press, 1953), p. 16.

90. William Keeney, *Lordship and Servanthood* (Newton, Kan.: Faith and Life Press, 1975).

91. J. Irvin Lehman, *God and War* (Scottdale, Pa.: Herald Press, 1951), pp. 16-24, 30-31.

92. John L. Stauffer, *The Message of the Scriptures on Nonresistance* (Harrisonburg, Va.: *The Sword and Trumpet*, n.d.). See also Stauffer's "Was Nonresistance God's Plan for Old Testament Saints?" *The Sword and Trumpet*, 13 (May 1945), 377ff.; "The Error of Old Testament Nonresistance," *ST*, 6 (Qtr. 2, 1960), 6-16; "Can We Agree on Nonresistance?"

ST, 47 (June 1979), 1-3; and Amos W. Weaver, "Some Implications of Law and Grace," *ST,* 30 (Qtr. 3, 1962), 12-16.

93. Hershberger (*War, Peace,* p. 31) does, however, draw upon the writings of Edward Yoder for this view: "War in the Old Testament," *Gospel Herald,* 33 (Apr. 1940), 366.

94. Hershberger, *War, Peace,* p. 30. Hershberger says (on p. 31):

> [That God would drive out the nations by miracle] is altogether reasonable when we remember that God had only recently delivered Israel by supernatural means at the Red Sea. From the beginning Israel should have followed the principle: "Not by might, nor by power, but by my spirit, saith the Lord of hosts" [Zech. 4:6].

95. *Ibid.,* pp. 16-41 (quotation from p. 41).

96. Hershberger, *War, Peace,* pp. 31-32; Eller pp. 46ff.; John W. Miller, " 'Holy War' in the Old Testament," *Gospel Herald,* 48 (Mar. 15, 1955), 249-250; Waldemar Janzen, "War in the Old Testament," *MQR,* 46 (April, 1972), 155-162; and Richard McSorley, *New Testament Basis of Peacemaking* (Washington, D.C.: Center for Peace Studies, Georgetown University, 1979), pp. 52ff. Many biblical scholars who do not hold to an absolute pacifist position also agree, at least in part, with this interpretation; see note 35 above.

97. Millard C. Lind, *Yahweh Is a Warrior* (Scottdale, Pa.: Herald Press, 1980). While this is the thesis developed by the entire book, see especially pp. 23, 48ff., 160-174. See also his articles "Paradigm of Holy War in the New Testament," *Biblical Research,* 16 (1976), 1-16, and "The Concept of Political Power in Ancient Israel," *Annual of Swedish Theological Institute,* 7 (1970), 4-24.

Eller, writing in a more popular vein, cites numerous verses to support this view: Exodus 15:3, 6-7; Joshua 5:13-15; 23:8-11; Judg. 4:14-15; 7:2-3, 7, 20-22; 6:17-19, 21, 24; Is. 14:4-7; 2:2-5; 9:5-7; 10:5-7, 12-13; 13:3-5; 30:1-2; 31:1-3, etc. (pp. 39-87). Eller also makes the point that Israel misunderstood God's plan—for all families of earth to bless themselves through Abraham's seed—and wrongly considered people to be *the enemy.* Eller is not clear on the implications of this statement. He appears to infer that Israel's perception of a fighting God was due to Israel's error (pp. 58-60). This view is indicated more clearly by Jean Lasserre, *War and the Gospel* (Scottdale, Pa.: Herald Press, 1962), p. 61.

98. Lind has developed these points in unpublished class lectures. See also John Howard Yoder, *The Original Revolution* (Scottdale, Pa.: Herald Press, 1971), ch. 3.

99. Hershberger, *War, Peace,* p. 18.

100. Lind, *Yahweh,* pp. 45, 34-44.

101. *Ibid.,* pp. 46-89.

102. See notes 96 and 97 above.

103. Lind, *Yahweh,* pp. 109-112.

104. Eller, pp. 73ff.

105. From my own syllabus on "Biblical Theology of War and Peace"; and Gelston, pp. 329-330.

106. Janzen, "War in the Old Testament," pp. 162-165.

107. While the critique of kingship is present in *Yahweh Is a Warrior,* pp. 90-144, this interpretation of Jesus is only briefly referred to on p. 174.

Lind has developed this point in several unpublished papers.

108. Yoder, *Original Revolution*, p. 106.

109. Yoder sets this practice within the context of the moral views of the time by discussing Abraham's sacrifice of Isaac. To sacrifice one's son, an offense to our morality, was not morally abhorrent to Abraham. "All the neighbors did the same thing." But the real point of the story is God's call to faithful obedience; so in holy war, including *herem*, Israel was called to trust God (Yoder, *Original Revolution*, pp. 104-106).

110. Janzen, "War in the Old Testament," pp. 160, 165.

111. Lasserre, pp. 62-63.

112. Eller, p. 104.

113. Jacob J. Enz, *The Christian and Warfare: The Roots of Pacifism in the Old Testament* (Scottdale, Pa.: Herald Press, 1972), pp. 13-23.

114. *Ibid.*, p. 89. See also pp. 34ff., 58ff., and 69ff. for more images of continuity whereby the Old Testament prepares for the New.

115. John Howard Yoder, "Exodus 20:13—'Thou shalt not kill,'" *Interpretation*, 34, No. 4 (Oct. 1980), 398. See also Lasserre, pp. 165-168.

116. Yoder *ibid.*, p. 397.

117. Donald F. Durnbaugh, ed., *On Earth Peace: Discussions on War/Peace Issues Between Friends, Mennonites, Brethren, and European Churches, 1935-1975* (Elgin, Ill.: The Brethren Press, 1978).

118. *Ibid.*, pp. 86-87.

119. To my knowledge, no one has attempted such a synthesis before, despite the many endeavors to use the Bible in support of particular pacifist emphases. The excellent article by Jesuit scholar Juan Mateos, "The Message of Jesus," illustrates the interrelatedness of the first three points. The article, translated from the Spanish by Kathleen England, appeared in *Sojourners* (July 1977). It was written as an introduction to a new Spanish edition of the New Testament.

120. John Ferguson, *The Politics of Love: The New Testament and Non-violent Revolution* (Greenwood, S.C.: The Attic Press, n.d.), pp. 4-5. Clarence Bauman, Mennonite professor of theology and specialist in the Sermon on the Mount studies, also proposes "Do not resist by (with) evil" as the better translation of the Greek text. This alternate translation is most significant, for it eliminates the key textual basis supporting a passive response to evil.

121. Hershberger, *War, Peace*, pp. 50-60. John E. Lapp's study manual, *Studies in Nonresistance: An Outline for Study and Reference* (Peace Problems Committee of the Mennonite General Conference, 1948) also illustrates this point. See also the Mennonite statement in Durnbaugh, p. 50.

122. Henry A. Fast, *Jesus and Human Conflict* (Scottdale, Pa.: Herald Press, 1959), pp. 34-35. Fast's emphasis upon the personal religious sphere might be considered a variant position to John Howard Yoder's and Ronald Sider's presented later. But Fast does not limit the application of the teaching to a personal-sphere ethic.

123. *Ibid.*, pp. 25, 91.

124. G. H. C. Macgregor, *The New Testament Basis of Pacifism*, (Nyack, N.Y.: Fellowship Publications, 1954), pp. 32-37.

125. Topel, pp. 125, 136. Topel then discusses the "just war" ethic as a case in point (p. 136).

126. Culbert G. Rutenber, *The Dagger and the Cross: An Examination*

of Pacifism (Nyack, N.Y.: Fellowship Publications, 1958), pp. 26-27.

127. *Ibid.,* pp. 65-68.

128. Yoder, *Original Revolution,* pp. 48-49.

129. Durnbaugh, p. 82. For an attempt to make the case that "Love for the enemy" and "killing the enemy" are not incompatible, see pp. 101ff., where Angus Dun and Reinhold Niebuhr argue the point. For a more forthright statement of the case, see Taylor, pp. 28-35. For rebuttals see Durnbaugh, p. 113, and Taylor, pp. 41, 50, 54-57.

130. Durnbaugh, pp. 266-269. See also Lasserre's statement, pp. 270-271.

131. John Howard Yoder, "The Way of the Peacemaker," in *Peacemakers in a Broken World,* ed. John A. Lapp (Scottdale, Pa.: Herald Press, 1969), pp. 116-118. Ferguson says that the Greek word *teleios* may mean (1) "perfect," (2) "all-embracing," (3) "absolute," and (4) "mature." All shades of meaning should be included (pp. 5-6).

132. Ronald J. Sider, *Christ and Violence* (Scottdale, Pa.: Herald Press, 1979), p. 26.

133. *Ibid.,* pp. 27, 32ff.

134. Macgregor, pp. 32-33. See p. 108 for his collections of verses on the love ethic.

Rutenber similarly connects the love command to God's love in Christ, saying:

> This love can never be mere vague goodwill, or absence of a will-to-harm. It is always as positive and outgoing as the love of God himself....
>
> This is not a passive principle of supine submission, but the active effort to express the divine love by seeking the enemies' good [pp. 57-38].

135. Gordon D. Kaufman, "Nonresistance and Responsibility," in *Nonresistance and Responsibility and Other Mennonite Essays* (Newton, Kan.: Faith and Life Press, 1979), pp. 64-78 (quotation on p. 65). In his next essay, "Christian Decision Making," Kaufman proposes four considerations that inform how one decides on such a matter as participation in war. These are justice, promises, and commitments we have made, together with the role one plays in society, redemptive love for the sinner, and the knowledge of oneself as sinner (pp. 86-91). After observing that justice may conflict with redemptive love, Kaufman argues for the moral and religious right of Mennonites as a "believers' church" subcommunity to hold its position of nonparticipation in war (pp. 91-98).

136. William Klassen's two key essays are "Love Your Enemy: A Study of New Testament Teaching on Coping with the Enemy," in *Biblical Realism Confronts the Nation,* ed. Paul Peachey (Fellowship Publications, distributed by Herald Press, 1963), pp. 153-183, and "The Novel Element in the Love Commandment of Jesus," in *The New Way of Jesus,* ed. William Klassen (Newton, Kan.: Faith and Life Press, 1980), pp. 100-114.

137. Klassen, "The Novel Element," pp. 110-112. This, Klassen says, testifies to the "deepest union of Judaism and Christianity ... a view of God's love ... fundamental to both religions ... and a view of what God's people are called upon to be and to do to the stranger, the outsider, and the enemy" (p. 110).

138. *Ibid.* p. 111.
139. Klassen, "Love Your Enemy," pp. 162-168.
140. *Ibid.*, pp. 170-171. Another type of exposition, collections of peace stories showing nonresistant love, bears witness to Jesus' peace children living out their calling: Elizabeth Hershberger Bauman, *Coals of Fire* (Scottdale, Pa.: Herald Press, 1954); and Cornelia Lehn, *Peace Be With You* (Newton, Kan.: Faith and Life Press, 1980). Both collections of stories, written for children, are also instructive to adults.
141. Lasserre, pp. 65-66.
142. Jesus refused the third temptation; he refused Peter's view of messiahship (Mk. 8:27-33); he refused to call down fire upon the Samaritans (Lk. 9:51-55); he entered Jerusalem on a donkey (Mt. 21:1-9); and he commanded Peter to put up the sword (Rev. 13:10 makes the same point). See Ferguson, pp. 24-26.
143. Ferguson, p. 26.
144. Rutenber, p. 47.
145. Martin Hengel describes the similarities and differences between Jesus and the Zealots. While Jesus shared the Zealot commitment of exclusive loyalty to the sovereignty of God, unlike the Zealots he appeared as a wandering prophet, called *all* to repent, kept critical distance from political power, located evil in the human heart, and summed up the law in love for God and neighbor, including the enemy *(Victory Over Violence: Jesus and the Revolutionists,* trans. David E. Green [Philadelphia: Fortress, 1973], pp. 31-34, 46-55).

In his extensive treatment of Jesus' political standing *(The State in the New Testament* [New York: Charles Scribner's Sons, 1956] Oscar Cullmann uses Jesus' statement "the green wood and the dry wood" (Lk. 23:28-30) to indicate Jesus' similarity to the Zealots (the green wood) but also his difference (the dry wood). Cullmann sums up, saying:

1. Throughout his entire ministry Jesus had to come to terms with Zealotism;

2. He renounced Zealotism, although he assumed a critical attitude toward the Roman State;

3. He was condemned to death as a Zealot by the Romans [p. 48].

146. Klassen, "The Novel Element," p. 110.
147. Yoder, *Original Revolution,* pp. 18-30. See Donald B. Kraybill, *The Upside-Down Kingdom* (Scottdale, Pa.: Herald Press, 1978) for further exposition of this new way. Dale Brown also interprets Jesus' mission as an alternative to the prevailing political options; see *The Christian Revolutionary* (Grand Rapids, Mich.: Eerdmans, 1971) pp. 102-113.
148. André Trocmé, *Jesus and the Nonviolent Revolution,* trans. Michael H. Shank and Marlin E. Miller (Scottdale, Pa.: Herald Press, 1973), pp. 27-40.
149. John Howard Yoder, *The Politics of Jesus* (Grand Rapids, Mich.: Eerdmans, 1972), pp. 26-60.
150. *Ibid.*, pp. 62-63. See Sider's discussion in *Christ and Violence,* pp. 18ff., which follows and extends this emphasis.

151. Ferguson, p. 83.
152. *Ibid.*, pp. 84-87.
153. *Ibid.*, pp. 87-89.
154. Macgregor, p. 46. Rutenber identifies the issues in the temptations as lack of trust, seeking a good end in the wrong way, and avoiding the suffering of the cross (pp. 48-49). Fast proposes that Jesus, in the temptations, said "no" to the two predominant messianic images that flashed into his mind, "the popular picture of the Messiah coming in the clouds of heaven," thus asserting his kingship "by dazzling and overawing . . . 'signs' and displays of power," and coming as a conquering military hero. Fast says, "The kingdom of God would embrace the world, but the method of political revolution and of military conquest was not the way to achieve it" (pp. 124-126).
155. Yoder, *Politics*, p. 32.
156. *Ibid.*, pp. 30-34.
157. Kraybill, pp. 41-94. I have also proposed connecting the three temptations respectively (Matthean order) to feeding the multitudes, the dramatic Palm Sunday entrance, and calling twelve legions of angels as Jesus' opportunities to gain kingship via alternatives to the cross; see Willard M. Swartley, "Peacemakers: The Salt of the Earth," in *Peacemakers*, ed. Lapp, pp. 86-88.
158. Ferguson, p. 21. Unfortunately, most pacifist writers have failed to notice the significance of this text as well as the bearing of New Testament Christology upon the issue generally.
159. *Ibid.*
160. *Ibid.* For fuller treatment of this subject, see Willard M. Swartley, *Mark: The Way for All Nations* (Scottdale, Pa.: Herald Press, 1979), pp. 102, 138-144; and Ernest Best, *The Temptations and the Passion: The Markan Soteriology* (New York: Cambridge University Press, 1965).
161. Ferguson, p. 22.
162. Macgregor, pp. 42, 44.
163. Topel, pp. 94-95.
164. *Ibid.*, pp. 95-97. For fuller discussion of this, see Swartley, *Mark*, pp. 138-144, and "The Structural Function of the Term 'Way' (*Hodos*) in Mark's Gospel" in *New Way*, ed. Klassen, pp. 73-86.
165. Topel, pp. 97-100. This view has broad support in New Testament scholarship. See Oscar Cullmann, *The Christology of the New Testament* (Philadelphia: Westminster Press, 1981), especially pp. 51-82, 111-136; T. W. Manson, *The Servant Messiah* (New York: Cambridge University Press, 1961), especially ch. 5; and John Wick Bowman, *Which Jesus?* (Philadelphia: Westminster Press, 1970), ch. 7.
166. Eller, p. 129. See also Yoder, *Nevertheless*, p. 124.
167. Eller, p. 175.
168. T. Canby Jones, *George Fox's Attitude Toward War* (Annapolis, Md.: Academic Fellowship, 1972), pp. 12-13. This book presents an excellent view of pacifism as fervent witness to the gospel of truth and love.
169. *Ibid.*, pp. 98-99.
170. Yoder, *Politics*, pp. 238-239.
171. Sider, p. 38.
172. Yoder, *Politics*, chs. 7, 11, and 12.
173. Eller, chs. 5, 6, and 7.

174. Hershberger, *War, Peace,* pp. 58-60. See also Topel, pp. 98, 110-113.
175. Thomas N. Finger develops this idea in a manuscript on Christology, presently in the draft stage.
176. *Ibid.*
177. See H. Berkhof, *Christ and the Powers,* trans. John H. Yoder (Scottdale, Pa.: Herald Press, 1977), especially ch. 4; Cullmann, pp. 95-116; and G. B. Caird, *Principalities and Powers: A Study in Pauline Theology* (Oxford: Clarendon Press, 1956). For an evaluative discussion of this emphasis, including negative scholarly appraisal, see Clinton B. Morrison, *The Powers That Be: Earthly Rulers and Demonic Powers in Romans 13:1-7* (London: SCM Press, 1960). While Morrison agrees with the "new interpretation" of Cullmann, Berkhof, and Caird in showing that the interconnection of earthly rulers and spiritual powers was standard thought in both Judaism and the Greco-Roman world (thus to recipients of Paul's writing in Romans 13), he disagrees by restricting the locus of Christ's victory to the believers. Christ's victory effected no change upon the powers; they continue as before under God (pp. 114-130).
178. Yoder, *Politics,* pp. 149-150.
179. *Ibid.,* pp. 148, 150ff. See also Sider, pp. 49-63; Swartley, "Peacemakers," pp. 79-80, 92-93; and Jim Wallis, *Agenda for Biblical People* (New York: Harper & Row, 1976), pp. 66-77.
180. Durnbaugh, p. 274.
181. Compare Gustav Aulen, *Christus Victor: An Historical Study of the Three Main Types of the Idea of the Atonement,* trans. A. G. Hebert (New York: Macmillan, 1961), especially chs. 1-2, 6, and 8.
182. These emphases permeate John Howard Yoder's writings.
183. Markus Barth, "Jews and Gentiles: The Social Character of Justification in Paul," *Journal of Ecumenical Studies,* 5, No. 2 (Spring 1968), 241ff. This emphasis has since been developed by Krister Stendahl, *Paul Among Jew and Gentile* (Philadelphia: Fortress Press, 1976).
184. Yoder, *Politics,* pp. 226-229.
185. Marlin E. Miller, "The Gospel of Peace," in *Mission and the Peace Witness,* ed. Robert L. Ramseyer (Scottdale, Pa.: Herald Press, 1979), p. 16. To quote Miller further:

> Nothing less than the cross of the Messiah could overcome a hostility as profound and pervasive as that between Jew and Gentile.... "Through the cross" the hostility was defeated without reinforcing the kind of Jewish existence which necessarily implied enmity with the Gentiles or spiritual or political subjugation to the Jews [p. 18]. The crucifixion of Jesus as the representative of God's chosen people [therefore] ... destroy[ed] the barrier between His people and their enemies rather than compelling the outsiders to submit to the spiritual and social domination of His people.... In destroying the barrier of hostility, Jesus' purpose "was to create in Himself one new man out of the two, thus making peace" [p. 17].

186. Sider, pp. 33-34. See also Wallis, p. 94. Pacifist writings on atonement as reconciliation are numerous: see Macgregor, pp. 48-49, 65-78, 110; Eller, pp. 119ff.; Rutenber, pp. 66ff.; Topel, pp. 103ff.; Richard C. Detweiler, "Peace Is the Will of God," in *Peacemakers,* ed., Lapp, pp. 70-71; Sanford

Shetler, "God's Sons Are Peacemakers," p. 77; and Swartley, "Peacemakers,"
pp. 85-86, 88-89. Sider's further commentary is also pertinent:

> Jesus' vicarious death for sinful enemies of God lies at the very
> heart of our commitment to nonviolence. It was because the in-
> carnate One knew that God was loving and merciful even toward
> the worst of sinners that He associated with sinners, forgave their
> sins, and completed His mission of dying for the sins of the world.
> And it was precisely the same understanding of God that
> prompted Him to command His followers to love their enemies [pp.
> 33-34].

> It is a tragedy of our time that many of those who appropriate the
> biblical understanding of Christ's vicarious cross fail to see its
> direct implications for the problem of war and violence. And it is
> equally tragic that some of those who most emphasize pacifism
> and nonviolence fail to ground it in Christ's vicarious atonement.
> It is a serious heresy of the atonement to base one's nonviolence in
> the weak sentimentality of the lowly Nazarene viewed merely as a
> noble martyr to truth and peace rather than in the vicarious cross
> of the Word who became flesh. The cross is much more than
> "Christ's witness to the weakness and folly of the sword" although
> it certainly is that. In fact,.... death for our sins is the ultimate
> demonstration that the Sovereign of the universe is a merciful
> Father who reconciles His enemies through self-sacrifical love [pp.
> 34-35].

187. Sider, p. 95.
188. Yoder, *Politics*, pp. 123-130. Macgregor also lists numerous texts
under the discipleship theme (pp. 108-110).
189. Yoder, *Politics*, p. 134.
190. Eller, pp. 140-143.
191. *Ibid.*, 145-152.
192. *Ibid.*, pp. 168-172. Topel uses the same texts Mt. 5—7; Mk. 10:42-
45) and stresses Jesus' teaching on love, especially in its call to identify with
the poor (1 Jn. 3:17-18; Jas. 1:27; 2:1-4; 5:1-3 and parallel teaching in Lk.
6:24; 12:16-21; 16:19-31). He concludes:

> Our response to [Jesus'] love is to be converted to the neighbor so
> totally, beginning from the spontaneous desires of our heart, that
> we share all of this world's goods with those who are poor. In this
> way we incarnate the suffering Servant in our world and really
> enter into that community in poverty that makes us blessedly
> happy and brings justice to those less fortunate than we. This
> message . . . is the only salvation for our world [p. 131].

Ferguson's description of "The Way of Christ" for his followers focuses
similarly on love, the cross, and the Christian's life in Christ:

> Christ showed us a new way, a way of life, a way of changing the
> world. It was politically relevant. It was *in its own way* revolu-
> tionary. It was the way of love, the way of the Cross, the way of non-

violence, the way of Truth-force, Soul-force, Love-force. It is still the way. He seeks to fulfil it in us [p. 115].

193. McSorley, p. 18. For an evaluation of the scholarly discussion of the relationship between imitation and discipleship, see Willard M. Swartley, "The Imitatio Christi and the Ignatian Letters," *Vigiliae Christianae,* 27 (1973), 86-87.

194. McSorley, pp. 19, 21. Martin Hengel concludes his study of Jesus' *Victory Over Violence* by noting that the early Christians, even in the second and third centuries, followed the nonviolent, reconciling way of Jesus Christ (pp. 60-64). This point, going beyond the scope of this study, has been amply documented and argued well by Jean-Michel Hornus in *It Is Not Lawful for Me to Fight,* trans. Alan Kreider and Oliver Coburn (Scottdale, Pa.: Herald Press, 1980).

195. M. Miller, p. 19.

196. Yoder, *Original Revolution,* p. 130.

197. Swartley, "Peacemakers," p. 90; Ernest J. Bohn, *Christian Peace According to New Testament Peace Teaching Outside the Gospels* (Peace Committee of the General Conference Mennonite Church, 1938), pp. 20-23.

198. Myron Augsburger, "The Basis of Christian Opposition to War," *Gospel Herald,* 63 (Nov. 24, 1970), p. 990.

199. Myron Augsburger, "Beating Swords Into Plowshares," *Christianity Today,* Nov. 21, 1975, p. 196.

200. Myron Augsburger, "Facing the Problem," in *Perfect Love,* ed. Hostetler, p. 15.

201. Augsburger, "Beating Swords," p. 197.

202. Wallis, pp. 4-5.

203. C. Norman Kraus, *The Community of the Spirit* (Grand Rapids, Mich.: Eerdmans, 1974), p. 40. See also Kraus; *The Authentic Witness* (Grand Rapids, Mich.: Eerdmans, 1979).

204. *Ibid.,* pp. 76-77.

205. Yoder, *Politics,* pp. 150-151.

206. *Ibid.,* p. 153. Yoder quotes J. H. Oldham's statement to the 1948 WCC Amsterdam Assembly to illustrate the distinctive task of the church:

> The church is concerned with the primary task of recreating a true social life ... through ... its primary functions of preaching the Word and ... its life as a worshipping community....
>
> There is nothing greater that the church can do for society than to be a center in which small groups of persons are together entering into this experience of renewal and giving each other mutual support in Christian living and action in secular spheres [p. 155].

207. Yoder, *Politics,* p. 161.

208. James E. Metzler, "Shalom Is the Mission," in *Mission,* ed. Ramseyer, p. 44. Compare Robert L. Ramseyer's own article in the same volume, "Mennonite Missions and the Peace Witness," pp. 122-123.

209. Durnbaugh, pp. 332, 336.

210. Sjouke Voolstra, "The Search for a Biblical Peace Testimony," ed. Ramseyer, pp. 34-35. See also Sider, pp. 67-87.

211. John Howard Yoder, *The Christian Witness to the State* (Newton,

Kan.: Faith and Life Press, 1964), pp. 5, 8-10, 21. See also Durnbaugh, pp. 136-145.

212. Robert Friedmann, *The Theology of Anabaptism: An Interpretation* (Scottdale, Pa.: Herald Press, 1973), pp. 36ff.

213. Walter Klaassen, *Anabaptism in Outline: Selected Primary Resources* (Scottdale, Pa.: Herald Press, 1981), pp. 244-264.

214. *Ibid.*, p. 244.

215. Archie Penner, *The Christian, the State, and the New Testament* (Altona, Man.: D. W. Friesen & Sons, Ltd., 1959), pp. 216-217.

216. *Ibid.*, p. 97.

217. Yoder, *Politics*, pp. 195-207 (quotation on p. 207).

218. *Ibid.*, pp. 298-221.

219. *Ibid.*, pp. 212-213. Compare pp. 190-191. For further discussion see Durnbaugh, pp. 85ff., 132 ff., 281-284.

220. Sider, p. 60. See also Samuel Escobar and John Driver, *Christian Mission and Social Justice* (Scottdale, Pa.: Herald Press, 1978).

221. Numerous articles appearing in *The Sword and Trumpet* represent this stance. See Sanford G. Shetler's review and criticism of John H. Yoder's *The Politics of Jesus* in *ST*, 41 (May 1973), 33f., and Shetler's earlier article " 'The Triumphal Tactic,' " *ST*, 35 (Feb. 1967), 5-9. See also in the same periodical Clay Cooper, "The Church Is Found Meddling," *ST*, 34 (Qtr. 3, 1966), 34-39; J. Ward Shank, "Which Way to Peace?" *ST*, 38 (Aug. 1970), 5-6; "Anything and Everybody in the Name of Peace" and "What Is Political?" *ST*, 39 (June 1971), 5-7; "To the Streets," *ST*, 46 (Oct. 1978), 7-8; John M. Snyder, "Social Evils and Christian Action," *ST*, 38 (Apr. 1970), 16-19, and (May 1970), 11-15; J. Otis Yoder, "The Church and the 'New Left,' " *ST*, 39 (July 1971), 7-8; "Eschatology and Peace," *ST*, 34 (Apr. 1966), 29-32; and Herman R. Reitz, "Prayer and the Selective Conscience," *ST*, 47 (Nov. 1979), 6-7.

222. The publications and work of the American Friends Service Committee reflect this stance.

223. John Driver, *Community and Commitment* (Scottdale, Pa.: Herald Press, 1976), p. 71.

224. Macgregor, p. 107.

225. M. Miller, p. 12.

226. Driver, *Community*, and *Kingdom Citizens* (Scottdale, Pa.: Herald Press, 1980), p. 68ff. See also M. Miller, p. 15; and Hans-Werner Bartsch, "The Biblical Message of Peace: Summary," in *On Earth Peace*, ed. Durnbaugh, pp. 278-279.

227. Willard M. Swartley, "Politics and Peace (Eirēnē) in Luke's Gospel"; in *Political Issues in Luke-Acts*, ed. Richard J. Cassidy and Philip Scharper (Maryknoll, N.Y.: Orbis Press, 1983), ch. 2.

228. Eller, pp. 198-201.

229. *Ibid.*, pp. 200-205.

230. John Howard Yoder, *Peace Without Eschatology?* (Scottdale, Pa.: Herald Press, 1954), p. 25.

231. *Ibid.*, p. 5.

232. *Ibid.*, pp. 8-12.

233. Sider, p. 38.

234. David Lochhead, *The Liberation of the Bible* (Student Christian Movement of Canada, 1927), pp. 6-13.

235. *Ibid.,* pp. 13-14.
236. Holmes' essay in *War: Four Christian Views,* ed. Clouse, p. 124. The second issue, according to Holmes, "is disagreement over whether and to what extent the Christian should participate in government and its exercise of force" (p. 124).
237. Wright, pp. 122, 130, 148-150.
238. Clark, p. 5.
239. *Ibid.*
240. Boettner, p. 7.
241. Richard C. Detweiler, *Mennonite Statements on Peace 1915-1955: A Historical and Theological Review of Anabaptist-Mennonite Concepts of Peace Witness and Church-State Relations* (Scottdale, Pa.: Herald Press, 1968), p. 12.
242. Augsburger, "Facing the Problem," p. 12.
243. Enz, pp. 68-70. See his discussion of this presented above.
244. Waldemar Janzen, "Christian Perspectives on War and Peace in the Old Testament," *Occasional Papers of the Institute of Mennonite Studies,* No. 1 (1981), pp. 3-18 (quotation on p. 13). Also printed in *Still in the Image: Essays in Biblical Theology and Anthropology,* by Waldemar Janzen (Newton, Kan.: Faith and Life Press, 1982), pp. 193-211 (quotations on p. 204).
245. Yoder, *Original Revolution,* pp. 100-101.
246. These views permeate Lind's book *Yahweh Is a Warrior* and have been stated by him in oral discussion. Lasserre's treatment of the Old Testament disagrees with this viewpoint and places the major break between the Testaments, inferring that Old Testament writers attributed "to God orders which came from an incomplete, primitive revelation" (p. 61).
247. Eller, pp. 12-13.
248. Hershberger, *War, Peace,* p. 15.
249. William Klassen, *Covenant and Community: The Life, Writings and Hermeneutics of Pilgram Marpeck* (Grand Rapids, Mich.: Eerdmans, 1968), pp. 124-128.
250. *Ibid.,* pp. 126-127.
251. *Ibid.,* pp. 116-117.
252. *Ibid.,* pp. 118-120.
253. It has been pointed out by numerous Anabaptist scholars that humanistic learning significantly influenced some of the Anabaptist Reformers. In my judgment, their hermeneutical method supports this claim.
254. This was strongly evident in three of the responses in the 1960 correspondence I referred to at the beginning of the chapter. Quotations, however, will be limited to published sources.
255. Boettner, pp. 20-21.
256. Taylor, p. 31.
257. Guy F. Hershberger, "Biblical Nonresistance and Modern Pacifism." *MQR,* 17, No. 3 (July 1943), p. 116. Elsewhere Hershberger says he "accepts the Old and New Testaments as the inspired Word of God," regarding them as an integrated revelation of God's nature and of his divine will" ("War and Peace in the Old Testament," *MQR,* 17, No. 1 [Jan. 1943], pp. 5-6).
    So also Myron Augsburger says, "... we regard the total Bible as the inspired Word of God in which he unfolded a revelation of Himself" ("Facing the Problem," p. 12).

258. Durnbaugh, p. 50.

259. John Howard Yoder, "The Unique role of the Peace Churches," *Brethren Life and Thought,* 14 (Summer 1969), 139.

260. See Sider's quotation at the end of the pacifist section.

261. Eller, pp. 11-12.

262. This point may be disputed on the basis of pacifist developments within Mishnaic Judaism. But I would argue that those developments are confirmed as "truth" in the Old Testament partly by comparison to the teachings of Jesus. For Christians, their messianic belief provides the criterion for their moral discernment on this subject.

263. I do not mean to say or infer that the views allowing war do not recognize or accept this view of biblical revelation. Many, probably most writers, do espouse this view. Theoretically, however, the nonpacifist position could get along without it; pacifism cannot, unless its appeal to the Bible is arbitrarily selective.

264. This latter endeavor guided the anti-slavery argument, in my judgment. Similarly, it is this same concern that should guide the church's deliberation about the role relation of men and women. Also, as I have written in an unpublished paper, "The New Testament and the Payment of Taxes Used for War" (available from Mennonite Board of Congregational Ministries, Box 1245, Elkhart, IN 46515), this concern should guide nonresistant/pacifist Christians today when discussing the refusal to pay taxes used for nuclear weapons.

265. Niebuhr's arguments can be criticized on other grounds as well, both factual and conceptual. See Yoder, *Reinhold Niebuhr,* pp. 16-22.

266. Hengel, *Victory Over Violence,* and *Was Jesus a Revolutionist?* trans. William Klassen (Philadelphia: Fortress Press, 1971).

267. Hengel, *Victory Over Violence,* p. 49. See also *Was Jesus a Revolutionist?* p. 32. Richard J. Cassidy considers Hengel's portrait of Jesus' nonviolence as insufficiently political. He says that because Hengel does not contrast Jesus' nonviolence with the violence of the Romans and because he does not situate Jesus' nonviolence within the context of his overall social and political stance, he portrays Jesus as more complacent about the existing social and political conditions than Luke's account allows (*Jesus, Politics, and Society: A Study of Luke's Gospel* [Maryknoll, N.Y.: Orbis Books, 1978], p. 84). Cassidy evaluates Cullmann's works similarly.

268. Hengel, *Victory Over Violence,* pp. 26-27.

269. *Ibid.,* p. 34.

270. Martin Hengel, "Das Ende Aller Politik," Evangelische Kommentar, 12 (1981), 686-690, and "Die Stadt auf dem Berge" *Ev. Komm.,* 1 (1982), 19-22. Compare Hengel's treatment of this issue with Leander E. Keck's "The Church, the New Testament, and Violence," *Pastoral Psychology,* 22 (1971), 5-14.

271. Hengel, "Stadt," p. 22.

CHAPTER 4

1. Cited from a news report by Wesley G. Pippert, in *Christianity Today,* May 4, 1979, p. 48.

2. Writings from the early decades of this century, however, are most

instructive. One of the very best treatments of the total New Testament teaching is the book by T. B. Allworthy, *Women in the Apostolic Church: A Critical Study of the Evidence in the New Testament for the Prominence of Women in Early Christianity* (Cambridge: W. Heffer & Sons, Ltd., 1917). Other significant works, arguing also for a liberationist view, are Charles Ryder Smith, *The Bible Doctrine of Womanhood and Its Historical Evolution* (London: The Epworth Press, 1923); Lee Anna Starr, *The Bible Status of Women* (New York: Revell, 1926, republished in 1955 by the Pillar of Fire, Zarephath, N.J.); and Katherine C. Bushnell, *God's Word to Women* (Oakland, Calif.: privately printed, 1923; now available from Ray B. Munson, Box 52, North Collins, NY 14111). From the last century, B. T. Roberts' *Ordaining Women* (Rochester, N.Y.: Earnest Christian Publishing House, 1891) is an important contribution to the subject.

3. Stephen B. Clark, *Man and Woman in Christ: An Examination of the Roles of Men and Women in Light of Scripture and the Social Sciences* (Ann Arbor, Mich.: Servant Books, 1980), p. 14. In a footnote Clark states three arguments against Karl Barth's interpretation (reflected in the liberationist commentary by Paul Jewett): (1) its motive is theological rather than exegetical, (2) the New Testament use of "image of God" is ethical in nature, and (3) it is a modern notion; no one before the twentieth century proposed it (p. 14 note).

4. Paul K. Jewett, *Man as Male and Female: A Study in Sexual Relationships from a Theological Point of View* (Grand Rapids, Mich.: Eerdmans, 1974), pp. 33, 36.

5. *Ibid.*, p. 49.

6. Letha Scanzoni and Nancy Hardesty, *All We're Meant to Be: A Biblical Approach to Women's Liberation* (Waco, Tx.: Word, 1974), pp. 24-25.

7. World Council of Churches' *Study on Women*, p. 25.

8. Perry Yoder, "Woman's Place in the Creation Accounts," in *Study Guide on Women*, ed. Herta Funk (Newton, Kan.: Faith and Life Press, 1975), pp. 10-11.

9. Phyllis Trible, *God and the Rhetoric of Sexuality* (Philadelphia: Fortress Press, 1978), pp. 16-17.

10. *Ibid.*, pp. 18-19.

11. *Ibid.*, p. 20.

12. Georgia Harkness, in her liberationist commentary, explains at some length how the Pentateuch was formed, how those accounts present different perspectives, and how both may be harmoniously understood (*Women in Church and Society*, [Nashville, Tenn.: Abingdon Press, 1972], pp. 143-156).

13. Charles C. Ryrie, *The Place of Women in the Church* (New York: Macmillan, 1958), p. 79.

14. George Knight III, *The New Testament Teaching on the Role Relationship of Men and Women* (Grand Rapids, Mich.: Baker, 1977), p. 43.

15. Clark, pp. 24-25.

16. Clark (in p. 26 note) argues against Trible's exegesis which distinguishes between "naming the woman" (implying authority over) and "calling to the creature woman" (rejoicing in their mutuality). See also Knight, pp. 41-42.

17. Clark, p. 26.

18. *Ibid.*, p. 25.

19. *Ibid.*, p. 28.

20. *Op. cit.*, p. 30.

21. *Op. cit.*, p. 26. See also Stephen Sapp's excellent summary, *Sexuality, the Bible, and Science* (Philadelphia: Westminster Press, 1974), p. 13. Compare Lois Clemens, *Woman Liberated* (Scottdale, Pa.: Herald Press, 1971), pp. 149-150.

22. Yoder, pp. 12-13.

23. Trible, pp. 99-100.

24. Jewett, p. 128.

25. Fritz Zerbst, *The Office of Woman in the Church: A Study in Practical Theology*, trans. Albert G. Merkens (St. Louis, Mo.: Concordia Publishing House, 1955), pp. 54, 56.

26. Knight, pp. 43-44.

27. Clark, pp. 32, 35.

28. Jewett, p. 114. Jewett expresses his shock at Helen Andelin's use of this text: "The first commandment which God gave unto the woman was, 'Thy desire shall be to thy husband and he shall rule over thee.' . . . To find a *curse* on woman called a *commandment* is surprising; to find such a mistake in a book written for women, more surprising; to learn that the author is herself a woman, more surprising still" (p. 114, n. 82).

29. Phyllis Trible, "Depatriarchalizing in Biblical Interpretation," *Journal of the American Academy of Religion*, 40, No. 1 (Mar. 1973), p. 41. Trible also argues that Genesis 2—3 does not portray the woman to be weaker or more easily enticed. Instead, the initiative and decision are hers; the man is "passive, brutish, and inept." The woman "is the more intelligent one, the more aggressive one, and the one with greater sensibilities" (p. 40).

30. Yoder, p. 14.

31. Ryrie, p. 31.

32. Zerbst, p. 67.

33. John H. Otwell, *And Sarah Laughed: The Status of Women in the Old Testament* (Philadelphia: Westminster Press, 1977), p. 66. I have not classified Otwell among the liberationist writers because he does not argue for hierarchy or subordination.

34. *Ibid.*, pp. 176-177.

35. *Ibid.*, p. 194.

36. One of the best treatments is by Evelyn and Frank Stagg, *Woman in the World of Jesus* (Philadelphia: Westminster Press, 1978, pp. 15-32. This source also considers Jewish literature after the Old Testament period, plus the Greek and Roman literature, and therefore portrays well the status of women at the time of Jesus. Compare Scanzoni and Hardesty, pp. 42-47, in this regard.

37. Phyllis Bird, "Images of Women in the Old Testament," in *Religion and Sexism: Images of Women in the Jewish and Christian Traditions*, ed. Rosemary Radford Ruether (New York: Simon and Schuster, 1974), p. 70.

38. Dorothy Yoder Nyce, "Factors to Consider in Studying Old Testament Women," in *Study Guide*, ed. Funk, p. 21.

39. Trible, "Depatriarchalizing," pp. 32-33. See also Leonard Swidler's extensive citation of feminine imagery regarding God in *Biblical Affirmations of Women* (Philadelphia: Westminster Press, 1979), pp. 21-36 especially, also pp. 357-359 to see the scope of discussion.

40. Trible, p. 34.

41. *Ibid.*, pp. 34-35.
42. *Ibid.*, pp 42-48 (quotation on p. 48). See also Trible, *Rhetoric*, pp. 144-165.
43. Trible, *Rhetoric*, pp. 35-56 (quotation on p. 56).
44. *Ibid.*, pp. 166-196 (quotation on p. 196).
45. Ryrie, pp. 21, 23.
46. *Ibid.*, pp. 31-32.
47. *Ibid.*, p. 38.
48. Zerbst, pp. 60-61. It is noteworthy that Knight does not discuss Jesus and women in his New Testament study. His only reference to Jesus is an innuendo against liberationists: if Paul and Peter were wrong in restricting women, then Jesus, by selecting only twelve men, "perpetuated this supposedly horrendous, male-chauvinist approach" (p. 57).
49. Jesus healed women (Mk. 5:25-34), touched them (Mt. 8:14-15), discoursed publicly with them (Jn. 11:17-44), talked to a woman alone (Jn. 4:7-26), taught women along with men (Lk. 10:38-42), used women for parable characters (Lk. 15:3-10), had women traveling with him to serve him (Lk. 8:1-3), called women "daughters of Abraham" (Lk. 13:16), and appeared to women first after his resurrection, having them bear the news to the men (Jn. 20:11-18; Mt. 28:9-10). See Clark, pp. 241-242.
50. Clark, pp. 245-249.
51. *Ibid.*, p. 251.
52. Leonard Swidler, "Jesus Was A Feminist," *Catholic World*, 212 (Jan. 1971), 177-183.
53. *Ibid.*, pp. 180-81. The rabbinic literature abounds with male prejudice against women, e.g., "Without both male and female children the world could not exist, but blessed is he whose children are male and woe to him whose children are female" (from T. B. Baba Bathra 16b, in *Compendia Rerum Iudicarum ad Novum Testamentum*: Section One: *The Jewish People in the First Century*, Vol. II [Philadelphia: Fortress Press, 1976], p. 750).

In Danby's edition of the Mishnah, seven pages of case laws are devoted to the suspected adulteress (Division Three, *Sotah*, chs. 1-6), with only one paragraph mentioning the "man" (3:8; N.B., he is not designated "adulterer," but "the man"). Two sentences mention the paramour, but gloss over his penalty by specifying that the suspected adulteress is "forbidden to the paramours" as she is also to her husband (*The Mishnah*, trans. H. Danby [New York: Oxford University Press, 1922], pp. 297-298.

Against the stream of evidence (see Leonard Swidler's extensive documentation in *Women in Judaism: The Status of Women in Formative Judaism* [Metuchen, N.J.: Scarecrow Press, 1976]), Judith Hauptman argues for a more positive interpretation of women in the Talmud. See Hauptman, "Images of Women in the Talmud," in *Religion and Sexism*, ed. Ruether, pp. 184-212.
54. Swidler, "Jesus," p. 181.
55. *Ibid.*, pp. 181-182.
56. *Ibid.*, p. 182.
57. *Ibid.*, p. 183. Not all liberationist writers interpret the data as positively as Swidler does. Elizabeth Clark and Herbert Richardson argue that little advance in women's rights (for the majority, at least) occurred before recent years:

The Gospels, as far as we know, were all composed by men, or groups of men, and the new faith to which they testified was one of which had arisen from the male-oriented religion of Judaism. The readers and hearers of the Gospels, although they were not living in environments as oppressive of women as postexilic Palestinian Judaism, still were not part of a world in which females had equal rights and responsibilities with men. Yet the Gospels give us a picture of Jesus as a man who mingled and talked with women, was not afraid of becoming ritually defiled by them, and did not think that their only function lay in kitchen and childbearing duties. All of the Gospels mention the female followers of Jesus and stress their roles in the resurrection events. The Gospel of Luke, in particular, written to a primarily Gentile audience, stresses Jesus' friendship with Mary and Martha (Luke 10:38-42), mentions Jesus' female traveling companions (Luke 8:1-3), and even compares God to a woman in the parable of the lost coin (Luke 15:8-10).

To what extent does such evidence suggest that Jesus was a feminist, as Leonard Swidler has argued? The gospel portrayals of Jesus can be assessed from different viewpoints. Although Jesus is represented as dealing with women in a kindly fashion, he is also shown treating other kinds of outcasts—lepers, tax collectors, the poor—with similar good will and benevolence. Whether or not the depiction of Jesus in the Bible gives us the right to claim that he would favor modern feminism is a dubious matter. No doubt this topic will be much debated in the years to come.

See *Women and Religion: A Feminist Sourcebook of Christian Thought*, ed. Elizabeth Clark and Herbert Richardson (New York: Harper and Row, 1977), p. 32.

58. Swidler, *Biblical Affirmations*, pp. 161-281.

59. Staggs, p. 129.

60. *Ibid.*, p. 255, see also pp. 123-125.

61. Hamerton-Kelly, Robert. *God the Father: Theology and Patriarchy in the Teaching of Jesus* (Philadelphia: Fortress Press, 1979), pp. 102-103.

62. Ryrie, p. 71.

63. Zerbst, p. 35.

64. Knight, p. 39.

65. While observing that the 1 Corinthians 12 text speaks of the gifts of the Spirit, Clark does not address the issue of whether the Spirit makes male and female gift distinctions, a point necessary to his view (pp. 143-144).

66. Clark, pp. 140-157.

67. *Ibid.*, pp. 149-155, 157-160. Clark does note, however, that the church's teaching on celibacy was based in part on foregoing sexual roles (p. 160).

68. *Ibid.*, p. 150.

69. Richard and Joyce Boldrey, *Chauvinist or Feminist? Paul's View of Women* (Grand Rapids, Mich.: Baker, 1976), p. 33.

70. Don Williams, *The Apostle Paul and Women in the Church*, (Van

Nuys, Cal.: BIM Publishing Co., 1977), p. 70.
71. John Neufeld, "Paul's Teaching on the Status of Men and Women," in *Study Guide*, ed. Funk, pp. 28-32.
72. Jewett, pp. 142-145.
73. Virginia Ramey Mollenkott, *Women, Men, and the Bible* (Nashville, Tenn.: Abingdon Press, 1977), pp. 102-103.
74. Ryrie, pp. 76-77.
75. Zerbst, p. 49.
76. Knight, pp. 32-33.
77. *Ibid.*, p. 34.
78. *Ibid.*, pp. 34-35.
79. *Ibid.*, p. 38.
80. *Ibid.*, p. 34.
81. Clark, pp. 167-173.
82. *Ibid.*, pp. 175, 183.
83. *Ibid.*, p. 179.
84. *Ibid.*, pp. 179, 185.
85. Russell C. Prohl, *Woman in the Church* (Grand Rapids, Mich.: Eerdmans, 1957), p. 80. Prohl supports his interpretation by citing Near Eastern customs and biblical practices:

An Ancient Assyrian Text
If a man would veil his concubine (captive woman) five or six of his companions he shall cause to sit down: before them he shall veil her. He shall say, "She is my wife." She is his wife. But the captive woman who was not veiled in front of the men, whose husband did not say, "She is my wife," she is not a wife.

The harlot is not to veil herself, her head is to be uncovered. The one who sees a veiled harlot is to seize her, secure witness, and bring her for the judgment of the palace [p. 27].

The Talmud
The following married women are to be divorced without the marriage portion: Such as go out with their heads uncovered. . . . It is a godless man who sees his wife go out with her head uncovered. He is duty bound to divorce her [p. 28].

Numbers 5:18
And the priest shall set the woman before the Lord, and unbind the hair of the woman's head, and place in her hands the cereal offering of remembrance, which is the cereal offering of jealousy. And in his hand the priest shall have the water of bitterness that brings the curse [p. 28].

86. Morna D. Hooker, "Authority on Her Head: An Examination of 1 Cor. 11:10," *New Testament Studies*, 10 (1963-64), 410-416; Boldreys, pp. 36-37; C. K. Barrett, *A Commentary on the First Epistle to the Corinthians* (New York: Harper & Row, 1968), pp. 254-255.
In support of the liberating power of the veil, one might also cite the related view that it gives the woman dignity and freedom to be in public.

In the Tyndale New Testament Commentary on 1 Corinthians, Leon Morris cites Robertson and Plummer for this view:

> In Oriental lands the veil is the power and honour and dignity of the woman. With the veil on her head she can go anywhere in security and profound respect. She is not seen; it is a mark of thoroughly bad manners to observe a veiled woman in the street. She is alone. The rest of the people around are non-existent to her, as she is to them. She is supreme in the crowd.... But without the veil the woman is a thing of nought, whom any one may insult.... A woman's authority and dignity vanish along with the all-covering veil that she discards.

Morris himself holds that the veil secures the woman's "place of dignity and authority" and, disagreeing with Ramsay, says it also expresses her subordination (*The First Epistle of Paul to the Corinthians: An Introduction and Commentary* [Grand Rapids, Mich.: Eerdmans, 1958], p. 154).

87. Although numerous scholars have long held that 14:34-35 is a post-Pauline interpolation (since it occurs after verse 40 in manuscripts D F G 88* and numerous early Itala manuscripts), only recently has anyone proposed that 11:2(3)-16 is an interpolation. William O. Walker, Jr., initiated the view in "1 Corinthians 11:2-16 and Paul's View Regarding Women," *Journal of Biblical Literature*, 94, No. 1 (Mar. 1975), 94-110. Jerome Murphy O'Connor replied, arguing against Walker and for the text's authenticity ("The Non-Pauline Character of 1 Corinthians 11:2-16?" *JBL*, 95, No. 4 [Dec. 1976], 615-621). Lamar Cope's counterresponse defends Walker's views but argues that the interpolation begins with verse 3, not 2 ("1 Cor. 11:2-16: One Step Further," *JBL*, 97, No. 3 [Sept. 1978], 435-436).

This exegesis, while nicely showing Paul, like Jesus, to be radically liberationist for women, makes the later post-Pauline church the male-chauvinist culprit, rewriting Paul to make him support the emerging conservative cultural traditions permeating the church. Such interpretation is not totally convincing, for why then didn't the post-Pauline revisionists further modify the liberationist perspective in Paul? And the problem remains with us since the church seeks to take the whole canon seriously.

88. Robin Scroggs, "Paul: Chauvinist or Liberationist," *The Christian Century*, 89 (1972), 309.

89. *Ibid*. See also Scroggs, "Paul and the Eschatological Woman," *Journal of the American Academy of Religion*, 40 (1972), 283-303; "Paul and the Eschatological Woman Revisited," *JAAR*, 42 (1974), 532-537; and Elaine Pagel's response, "Paul and Women: A Response to Recent Discussion," *JAAR*, 42 (1974), 538-549.

90. Barrett, p. 248; Boldreys, p. 34; Scanzoni and Hardesty, pp. 30-31. See also J. Massyngberde Ford, who argues that man as *kephalē* signifies woman's participation in his being, thus teaching essential complementarity, not domination. Man is not lord *(kurios)* over woman, and man does not have authority *(exousia)* over woman. Only in marriage does each have authority *(exousiazō)* over the other's body (1 Corinthians 7:4), and this is reciprocal ("Biblical Material Relevant to the Ordination of Women," *Journal of Ecumenical Studies*, 10 (1973), 679-680.

91. Pagels, pp. 543-544.

92. *Ibid.*, pp. 544-546.
93. Jewett, p. 54.
94. *Ibid.*, p. 119.
95. *Ibid.*, p. 134.
96. *Ibid.*, p. 131.
97. Virginia Mollenkott, "Women and the Bible: A Challenge to Male Interpretations," in *Mission Trends No. 4: Liberation Theologies in North America and Europe*, ed. Gerald H. Anderson and Thomas F. Stransky (Grand Rapids, Mich.: Eerdmans, 1979), pp. 224-225.
98. Constance F. Parvey, "The Theology and Leadership of Women in the New Testament," in *Religion and Sexism*, ed. Ruether, p. 124.
99. *Ibid.*, p. 125.
100. *Ibid.*, pp. 125-126. Parvey argues that Jewish apocalyptic had developed the view, found in Genesis 6:4, that evil spirits might attack women sexually (p. 126). This "watcher's myth," as it is called, holds that angels who were intended to watch over creation were seduced by feminine immodesty. The Staggs support this interpretation (p. 176), but Hooker, Barrett, and Morris disagree, holding that these angels are "present as the guardians of the natural order,... seeing that the worship of God is conducted in a fitting matter" (Hooker, pp. 414-415; compare Barrett, p. 254; and Morris, p. 154.
101. Parvey, pp. 127-128. This view concurs with Krister Stendahl's that 1 Corinthians 11:11-12 and Galatians 3:28 point to the new order of freedom in Christ; but Paul did not achieve the full social implementation of this vision (*The Bible and the Role of Women* [Philadeliphia: Fortress Press, 1966]).
102. *Ibid.*, pp. 130-131. Barrett also basically supports this view (pp. 331-333).
103. Catherine Clark Kroeger, "Pandemonium and Silence at Corinth," *Free Indeed* (April-May 1979), p. 5, and *The Reformed Journal*, 28, No. 6 (June 1978), 6-11. Among Kroeger's citations are Euripedes' description of the Dionysic religion at Corinth:

> This city, first in Hellas, now shrills and echoes to my women's cries, their ecstasy of joy.

Also the Neoplatonist Iamblichus' description of the frenzy of the mystery cults:

> The frenzy causes words to let fall that are not uttered with the understanding of those who speak them; but it is declared, on the contrary, that they are sounded with a frenzied mouth, the speakers being all of them subservient and entirely controlled by the energy of a dominant intelligence [*Free Indeed*, p. 6].

Kroeger also suggests that "the law" mentioned in 14:35 may be the well-known law of ancient Corinth which "forbade any woman to participate in the orgies of the Great Mother, in an attempt to control improprieties" (*Free Indeed*, p. 7). This offers an attractive solution since commentators agree that no Old Testament law specifically required women to be silent. Most commentators relate the comment to Genesis 3:16, but Prohl settled on the sixth commandment. Both, however, are possible only by theological inference or rabbinic commentary upon these texts.

In another article, Richard and Catherine Kroeger cite additional documentation of pandemonium in Corinth, including the 1964-65 archeological excavations at Corinth, which confirm the prominence of the Dionysic and Eleusinian cults in the city ("An Inquiry into Evidence of Maenadism in the Corinthian Congregation," in *Society of Biblical Literature 1978 Seminar Papers*, Vol. II, ed. Paul J. Achtemeier [Missoula, Mont.: Scholars Press, 1978], pp. 331-336).

104. *Ibid.*, pp. 7-8; Boldreys, pp. 61-62.

105. A helpful survey and analysis of various interpretations of 1 Corinthians 11:2-16 from John Calvin to the present has been done by Linda Mercadante *(From Hierarchy to Equality: A Comparison of Past and Present Interpretations of 1 Corinthians 11:2-16 In Relation to the Changing Status of Women in Society* (Vancouver, B.C.: Regent College, 1978]).

Katherine C. Bushnell, writing over a half century ago, argues that 1 Corinthians 11:2-16 has been badly misunderstood. Citing Dr. John Lightfoot, she argues that the main point of the text is to forbid men to veil, but *permit* women to veil. She says:

> The Jewish man veiled as a sign of reverence before God, and of condemnation for sin. This sort of head covering was called a *tallith*, and is worn, to this day, "by all male worshipers." The Romans also veiled in worship, and the Corinthian church was made up in large part of Roman converts. The testimony disagrees as to whether Greeks veiled in worship, or did not. The question therefore arose, were women to be *forbidden* veiling, as the Christian men, or not? Paul, in the passage, (1) forbids men to veil (since *"There is now no condemnation to them which are in Christ Jesus"*); (2) permits women to veil; (3) but guards against this permission being construed as a command to veil, by showing that *ideally* the woman should unveil, before God, man, and angels; (4) shows that there is special propriety in women unveiling when addressing God in prayer; (5) declares that (contrary to the teaching of the Jews) there is nothing for a woman to be ashamed of in showing her hair, for it is a "glory" to her; (6) and disavows veiling as a church custom [Section 240].

Taking issue with the English translations of this text (the Greek does not include punctuation), Bushnell argues that verse 13b is a declarative sentence, not a question: "It is comely that a woman pray unto God uncovered." Likewise, verse 14 should read: "Nor doth nature teach you that if a man has long hair it is a shame." Bushnell (many years a missionary in China) says:

> It is not nature, but the barber who keeps man's hair short. In China, millions of men wear long hair, and nature has never taught them that it is a shame. Furthermore, the last time the Corinthians saw the apostle Paul before he wrote this Epistle, he himself had long hair (Acts 18:18); and to the Jew, accustomed to

religious vows (Num. 6:1-21), long hair ... was more of a "glory" than a "shame" [Section 230].

Finally, Bushnell argues that "no such custom" in verse 16 refers to veiling. Thus, Paul is generally arguing against veiling, rather than for it (Section 231). See Bushnell, *God's Word to Women*.

Although modern commentators have not accepted (and probably not considered) Bushnell's view, one of its strengths is that it fits well with Paul's comments about the veil in 2 Corinthians 3:12-18: in Christ we behold the Lord's glory with *unveiled* face!

106. Other events from the early church add to this portrait:

> Acts 2:16-17: Women prophesy at Pentecost, a mark of the new age.
> Acts 5:1-11: Sapphira, like Ananias, is equally culpable.
> Acts 6:1ff.: The needs of the widows are of major importance.
> Acts 9:1-2: Women, as well as men, are martyred.
> Acts 9:36-43: Dorcas functions in an outstanding role.
> Acts 12:12: The apostles meet in Mary's home.
> Acts 13:50; 17:4, 11-12, 34: "Women of standing" respond to Paul's missionary message.
> Acts 21:9: Four daughters of Philip prophesy.

107. Ryrie, p. 90.
108. *Ibid.*
109. *Ibid.*
110. Zerbst, p. 62.
111. *Ibid.*, p. 63.
112. Knight, p. 50.
113. *Ibid.*, pp. 51-52.
114. *Ibid.*, p. 52.
115. Clark, pp. 118-120.
116. *Ibid.*, p. 130.
117. Mollenkott, *Women, Men*, p. 97.
118. With Junia (verse 7), eight are named: Phoebe, Prisca, Mary, Junia, Tryphoena, Tryphosa, Persis, and Julia. In addition, Paul greets the mother of Rufus, whom he calls also "his mother" and Nereus' sister. This totals ten females.
119. Williams, p. 43.
120. *Ibid.*, p. 43.
121. *Ibid.*, p. 45.
122. Bernadette J. Brooten, "'Junia ... outstanding among the Apostles' (Romans 16:7)," in *Women Priests: A Catholic Commentary on the Vatican Declaration*, ed. Leonard and Arlene Swidler (New York: Paulist Press, 1977), pp. 141-143.
123. *Ibid.*, p. 143. In another article, Brooten presents inscriptional evidence that women held various leadership positions in the Jewish synagogues during the Roman and Byzantine periods. She cites evidence of women identified as "President of the Synagogue," "leader," "elder," "mother of the synagogue," and "priestess." She argues that the modern male bias has influenced the scholarly commentary which regards these as honorific titles and refuses to recognize functioning female leaders. See Bernadette J. Brooten, "Inscriptional Evidence for Women as Leaders in the Ancient Syna-

gogue," in *Society of Biblical Literature 1981 Seminar Papers*, ed. Kent H. Richards (Chico, Calif.: Scholars Press, 1981), pp. 1-12.

124. Elisabeth Schüssler Fiorenza, "Women in the Pre-Pauline and Pauline Communities," *Union Seminary Quarterly Review*, 33, Nos. 3-4 (Spring-Summer, 1978), 157-58, and "The Apostleship of Women in. Early Christianity," in *Women Priests*, ed. Swidler, p. 137.

125. Fiorenza, "Pauline Communities," p. 158. Much of the same perspective is presented by J. Massyngberde Ford in "Women Leaders in the New Testament," in *Women Priests*, ed. Swidler, pp. 132-134, and "Biblical Material Relevant to the Ordination of Women," *Journal of Ecumenical Studies*, 10 (1973), pp. 670-678. See also the more cautious, but basically supportive reconstruction by Roger Gryson, *The Ministry of Women in the Early Church*, trans. Jean Laporte and Mary Louise Hall (Collegeville, Minn.: The Liturgical Press, 1976), pp. 1-6.

126. Boldreys, pp. 19-21; Parvey, pp. 132, 143-146; and Dennis R. Kuhns, *Women in the Church* (Scottdale, Pa.: Herald Press, 1978), pp. 36-38.

127. Ryrie, p. 79.

128. *Ibid.*, pp. 85, 90.

129. *Ibid.*, p. 90.

130. Zerbst, pp. 73, 80. Similar viewpoint and phraseology is found in Peter Brunner, *The Ministry and the Ministry of Women* (St. Louis, Mo.: Concordia Publishing House, 1971), p. 20.

131. Zerbst, pp. 88-89. Zerbst also argues that in the second and third centuries the deaconesses remained subordinate to the authority of the deacons and bishops.

132. Knight, p. 30.

133. *Ibid.*, p. 31.

134. *Ibid.*, p. 48.

135. Clark, p. 191.

136. *Ibid.*, p. 193.

137. *Ibid.*, pp. 195-199.

138. *Ibid.*, pp. 204-207.

139. The four possible meanings: (1) having children is the means of salvation or belongs to her salvation call; (2) she will be saved even though she is bearing children (since the difficulty of childbearing is rooted in the curse of the fall); (3) she will be saved during the experience (the Lord will help her through it); (4) she will be saved by the birth of the child, the Messiah, Jesus Christ.

140. Clark, pp. 205-208.

141. This issue (June 1975) was occasioned by the public response (some negative—see Harold Lindsell's *Battle for the Bible*) to Jewett's book *Man as Male and Female*.

142. A. J. Gordon, "The Ministry of Women," *Theology, News, and Notes* (June 1975), p. 6.

143. *Ibid.*, p. 142. Gordon's article then cites the ministries of various New Testament worr en as deacons, prophetesses, and possibly even Junia as apostle. Gordon's view combines the liberationist and hierarchical approaches. His final emphasis calls us to go beyond the grammar and lexicography, be open to the Spirit's way of using women, and quench not the Spirit's gifts (p. 23).

144. Williams, p. 111.

145. *Ibid.*, pp. 113-114.
146. *Ibid.*, pp. 114-115. The Boldreys take a view similar to Williams' but note additionally that the verb *authentein* means "domineer," and suggest a connection between it and Eve's taking advantage of power derived from her new knowledge in the fall (pp. 42-43).
147. Jewett, p. 119. See also pp. 60, 116, 126, 131.
148. *Ibid.*, p. 60.
149. Mollenkott, *Women, Men*, p. 103.
150. *Ibid.*, p. 102. Neufeld (p. 29) and the Staggs (p. 202) generally follow this same approach.
151. Staggs, pp. 232-233.
152. *Ibid.*, p. 235.
153. *Ibid.*
154. Parvey, pp. 137-138.
155. *Ibid.*, pp. 140-146.
156. Granted, by reserving the domestic codes (Ephesians 5:21-33 and parallels) for discussion in an appendix, the subordinationist texts are bracketed out. But clearly these do address the marriage relationship, as does 1 Corinthians 7:1-7. For this reason, it is instructive to examine the remaining texts apart from the domestic codes in order to see the difference in focus.
157. Robert McAfee Brown, *Theology in A New Key* (Philadelphia: Westminster Press, 1978), pp. 78-80. Brown rightly calls every biblical interpreter to acknowledge his/her ideology; he notes that liberation theology makes "ideological suspicion" a foundational principle for hermeneutics.
158. For example, Harold Lindsell, *The Battle for the Bible* (Grand Rapids, Mich.: Zondervan, 1976). For definitive research that shows such a view of Scripture to be a departure from both the early church's and the Reformers' views of Scripture, see Jack B. Rogers and Donald K. McKim, *The Authority and Interpretation of the Bible: An Historical Approach* (San Francisco: Harper & Row, 1979) and the shorter essay by Jack Rogers on the same topic, "The Church Doctrine of Biblical Authority," in *Biblical Authority*, ed. Jack Rogers (Waco, Tex.: Word, 1977), pp. 15-46.
159. Paul D. Hanson, *The Diversity of Scripture: A Theological Interpretation* (Philadelphia: Fortress Press, 1982), p. xv.
160. *Ibid.*, pp. 4 and 113 respectively.
161. Hanson's work in *The Diversity of Scripture* is addressed specifically to the diversity between the form/reform polarity in the Old Testament royal and prophetic traditions and the visionary/pragmatic polarity in the later apocalyptic and priestly traditions (pp. 14-62). He then demonstrates how these differing traditions, despite their diversity, were utilized and transformed in serving as a *"Praeparatio* for the Messianic Interpretation of Jesus' Mission" (pp. 63-82). Finally, Hanson focuses on the basic affirmations of the biblical revelation which guide the church in its faithful response to this diversity of tradition (pp. 83-135).
Hanson's earlier study, *The Dawn of Apocalyptic*, rev. ed. (Philadelphia: Fortress Press, 1979), focusing on the similarities and differences between the prophetic and apocalyptic writings, argued for the essential eschatological continuity between the prophetic and the apocalyptic.
162. J. Christiaan Beker, *Paul the Apostle: The Triumph of God in Life*

and Thought (Philadelphia: Fortress Press, 1980), especially pp. 11-18, 351ff.

163. Compare this statement with James Barr's discussion in Old and New in Interpretation: A Study of the Two Testaments (New York: Harper & Row, 1966), especially chs. 1 and 5; and Millard C. Lind, "The Hermeneutics of the Old Testament," Mennonite Quarterly Review, 40, No. 3 (July 1966), 227-237.

164. For emphasis on this point from another context see Leander Keck, A Future for the Historical Jesus (Nashville, Tenn.: Abingdon Press, 1971), pp. 26ff. Keck says it is necessary to study the extracanonical Gospels in order to understand the Gospels. For three complementary essays on the significance of diversity, on the one hand, and the need to exclude some interpretations, on the other, see Charles H. Talbert, "The Gospel and Gospels;" Jack Dean Kingsbury, "The Gospel in Four Editions"; and Robert Morgan, "The Hermeneutical Significance of Four Gospels" (these three essays are chs. 2-4 in Interpreting the Gospels, ed. James Luther Mays [Philadelphia: Fortress Press, 1981]). For a descriptive analysis of the variety of the theological traditions included in the New Testament and an attempt to identify the unity among these viewpoints see James D. G. Dunn, Unity and Diversity in the New Testament (Philadelphia: Westminster, 1977).

165. See, e.g., George Eldon Ladd, The New Testament and Criticism (Grand Rapids, Mich.: Eerdmans, 1967), pp. 19-33; and J. C. Wenger, God's Word Written (Scottdale, Pa.: Herald Press, 1966), pp. 32-33.

166. S. Scott Bartchy has classified the pertinent New Testament texts into three groups: normative texts which show mutuality between men and women (Acts 2:17-18; 5:7-10, 14; 8:3; 9:2; 16:13-15; 21:9; Gal. 3:28; 1 Cor. 7:4-5, 7; 11:11-12); descriptive texts which portray women in leadership roles (Mt. 28:9-10; Mk. 16:7, 9-11; Lk. 24:10-11; Jn. 20:14-18; 1 Cor. 11:4-5; Acts 21:8-9; Phil. 4:2-3; Rom. 16:1-4); and problematic texts which restrict women (1 Cor. 14:34-35; 1 Tim. 2:11-15). He concludes by pointing to the teaching in Mark 10:42-45 as a Christian way to solve the problem of relationships. See Bartchy's essay "Power, Submission, and Sexual Identity Among the Early Christians," in Essays on New Testament Christianity: A Festschrift in Honor of Dean E. Walker, ed. C. Robert Wetzel (Cincinnati, Ohio: Standard Publishing, 1978), pp. 50-80.

This approach together with the accent upon the new way of life in the kingdom and using the gifts of all God's children points in the right direction, in my judgment. Also, the book by Erhard S. Gerstenberger and Wolfgang Schrage, Woman and Man (trans. Douglas W. Stott; Nashville, Tenn.: Abingdon, 1981) helpfully develops a biblical and theological view of mutuality, partnership, and interdependence for male-female relationships. Note also the generally helpful work of Philip Siddons, Speaking Out for Women—A Biblical View (Valley Forge, Pa.: Judson Press, 1980).

CHAPTER 5

1. The same point can be made for war from the pacifist position, but the appeal to a primeval mandate plays no particular significance in the nonpacifist use of the Bible.

2. One might say the same thing about war and subordination of

women. However, it is *more* difficult to see in the Old Testament the bud of liberation that flowers in the New on these two issues.

3. For a recent and scholarly study of this topic, see Jean-Michel Hornus, *It Is Not Lawful For Me To Fight: Early Christian Attitudes Toward War, Violence, and the State* trans. Alan Kreider and Oliver Coburn (Scottdale, Pa.: Herald Press, 1980).
See also C. J. Cadoux, *The Early Church and the World* (New York: Charles Scribner's Sons, 1925). For a more popular statement, see John C. Wenger, *Pacifism and Nonresistance* (Scottdale, Pa.: Herald Press, 1971).

4. A stimulating discussion of this occurs in *Theology, News, and Notes,* published for the Fuller Theological Seminary Alumni (1976 Special Issue). The title of the issue is "The Authority of Scripture at Fuller."

5. George Knight III, *The New Testament Teaching on the Role Relation of Man and Woman* (Grand Rapids, Mich.: Baker, 1977), pp. 21-27.

6. Perry B. Yoder's helpful study *From Word to Life: A Guide to the Art of Bible Study* (Scottdale, Pa.: Herald Press, 1982) explains and illustrates such a method, incorporating both the linguistic and historical approaches to Bible study.

7. Mildred Bangs Wynkoop helpfully describes the nature of *agape* love in *A Theology of Love* (Kansas City, Mo.: Beacon Hill Press, 1972).

8. Jack T. Sanders, *Ethics in the New Testament* (Philadelphia: Fortress Press, 1975), especially pp. 28-29, 46-47, 80-91, 98-99, 114-115, 128-130.

9. *Ibid.,* p. 130.

10. Rudolf Schnackenburg, *The Moral Teaching of the New Testament* (New York: Herder and Herder, 1965).

11. *Ibid.,* p. 82.

12. *Ibid.,* pp. 82, 88.

13. *Ibid.,* pp. 122-123

14. John Howard Yoder, *The Politics of Jesus* (Grand Rapids, Mich.: Eerdmans, 1972).

15. *Ibid.,* pp. 12-13.

16. *Ibid.,* pp. 62-63.

17. John Howard Yoder, *The Original Revolution* (Scottdale, Pa.: Herald Press, 1971), and *The Christian Witness to the State* (Newton, Kan.: Faith and Life Press, 1964).

18. Yoder, *Original Revolution,* pp. 112-182.

19. Yoder, *Christian Witness,* especially pp. 8-11, 22-25, 35-44.

20. Bruce C. Birch and Larry L. Rasmussen, *Bible and Ethics in the Christian Life* (Minneapolis, Minn.: Augsburg, 1976).

21. *Ibid.,* p. 202.

22. *Eschatologie und Friedenshandeln: Exegetische Beiträge zur Frage christlicher Friedensverantwortung* (with contributions by Ulrich Luz, Jürgen Kegler, Peter Lampe, Paul Hoffmann), Stuttgarter Bibelstudien 101 (Stuttgart: Verlag Katholisches Bibelwerk GmbH, 1981).

23. *Ibid.,* pp. 207-208. Compare pp. 92-93, 161-162.

24. *Ibid.,* pp. 198-199, 213, also 191.

25. *Ibid.,* pp. 197-198. In my judgment, the responsibility of God's people to do justice, especially in the prophets, does not receive sufficient attention. Further, the pentateuchal and historical materials of the Old Testament have been neglected.

26. *Ibid.*, pp. 193, 213. This point, prominent in the book's conclusions, merits quotation:

Der Hinweis auf die *Kirche als Handlungsraum. Dadurch, daß sie Liebe in ihrer eigenen Gestalt verwirklicht, dadurch also, daß sie Kirche wird, wird sie zum Friedensfaktor in der Welt.* Konkret bedeutete das: Reformation der Kirche an Haupt und Gliedern, auf daß sie wirklich das Kreuz Christi in der Welt repräsentiere; das wäre der entscheidende kirchliche Beitrag zum Frieden.

It is unfortunate that Luz' study says nothing about the Pauline emphasis on Christ's victory over, and the church's freedom from, the powers. This dimension of thought may have altered, or at least amplified, this conclusion.

That the ethic of the gospel, especially the Sermon on the Mount, is addressed to the church and not to world politics, is also Martin Hengel's conclusion in two articles published in *Evangelische Kommentar:* "Das Ende aller Politik" (Dec. 1981), pp. 686-690, and "Die Stadt auf dem Berge" (Jan. 1982), pp. 19-22.

27. Anthony J. Tambasco, *The Bible for Ethics: Juan Luis Segundo and First-World Ethics* (Washington, D.C.: University Press of America, 1981). For a helpful survey of liberation theology's hermeneutical emphasis, see Anthony C. Thiselton, *The Two Horizons: New Testament Hermeneutics and Philosophical Description* (Grand Rapids, Mich.: Eerdmans, 1980), pp. 110-13.

28. Tambasco, pp. 56-57.

29. *Ibid.*, p. 136.

30. Victor Paul Furnish, *The Moral Teaching of Paul* (Nashville, Tenn.: Abingdon Press, 1979), p. 14.

31. *Ibid.*, p. 27.

32. *Ibid.*, pp. 24-28. Furnish then discusses four major issues in Paul: marriage and divorce, homosexuality, women in the church, and Christians and the governing authorities.

33. I do not see how one can read Mark's Gospel and fail to see that Jesus' condemnation of the misuse of the Sabbath and the temple led to his death. See Willard M. Swartley, *Mark: The Way for All Nations,* rev. ed. (Scottdale, Pa.: Herald Press, 1981), chs. 2, 9-10.

34. Yoder's most helpful contributions to the way the Christian social ethic addresses society are *The Christian Witness to the State* (see note 17 above), and *The Christian and Capital Punishment* (Newton, Kan.: Faith and Life Press, 1961). Stephen Charles Mott's recent book is helpful to this discussion (*Biblical Ethics and Social Change* [New York/Oxford: Oxford University Press, 1982]). See also the historically descriptive work edited by Ernest Sandeen, *The Bible and Social Reform* (Chico, Cal.: Scholar Press and Philadelphia: Fortress Press, 1982).

35. Birch and Rasmussen, p. 150.

36. *Ibid.*

37. *Ibid.*, pp. 152-153.

38. This point of view leads me to disagree with Elouise Renich and David A. Fraser in saying that "Scripture does not and cannot settle 99 percent of the questions that might be raised about roles of female and male

within our society." To innoculate Scripture against our social problems is an unnecessary reaction to the "sacred cow" use of the Bible. See Renich and Fraser, "Merrily We Role Along," *Free Indeed* (April-May 1979), p. 12.
   39. See notes 25 and 26 above.
   40. I deliberately avoid these phrases because they carry along a history of almost hopeless philosophical baggage, involving precommitments to a variety of philosophical positions which seek to explain unconscious forces at work upon the interpreter. I see no reason why one first has to espouse Freudian, Nietzchian, existentialist (Bultmann), or Marxist philosophy before one rightly interprets the Bible. See Thiselton's review of this matter (pp.107-114).Certainly I agree, however, with Thiselton when he says that *"the modern interpreter, no less than the text, stands in a given historical context and tradition"* (p. 11), and with his quotation from the Church of England's Doctrine Communion Report, *Christian Believing:* " 'No one expounds the Bible to himself or to anyone else without bringing to the task his own prior frame of reference, his own pattern of assumptions which derives from sources outside the Bible' " (p. 114). Only if one is a Freudian or Marxist, etc. (including capitalist, if capitalism's value commitments are determinative) is such philosophical prolegomenon a prerequisite for his/her hermeneutics. Indeed, it is important for every interpreter to own the philosophical, political, economic, social and religious factors that affect her/his understanding of the text. But this is the opposite of making those perspectives preconditions for understanding the text.
   41. Quoted from Larry R. Morrison, "The Religious Defense of American Slavery Before 1830," *The Journal of Religious Thought,* 37, No. 2 (Fall-Winter 1980-81), 16-17.
   42. Grant R. Osborne, "Hermeneutics and Women in the Church," *Journal of the Evangelical Theological Society,* 20, No. 4 (Dec. 1977), 337-340.
   43. *Ibid.,* p. 351.
   44. William E. Hull, "Woman in Her Place: Biblical Perspectives," *Review and Expositor,* 72, No. 1 (Winter 1975), 5-9.
   45. *Ibid.,* p. 17.
   46. Elisabeth Schüssler Fiorenza, "Women in the Pre-Pauline and Pauline Churches," *Union Seminary Quarterly Review,* 33, Nos. 3-4 (Spring-Summer 1978), 154-155.
   47. *Ibid.,* p. 162.
   48. *Ibid.* What is striking about these models of approach to the biblical text is that each of the models themselves is shaped very much by the interpreter's position on the issue that prompted the model. Critiques of these models further demonstrate the same point. See especially A. Duane Litfin, "Evangelical Feminism: Why Traditionalists Reject It," *Bibliotheca Sacra,* 136 (July-Sept. 1979), 258-271; and H. Wayne Houser, "Paul, Women, and Contemporary Evangelical Feminism," *Bibliotheca Sacra,* 136 (Jan.-Mar. 1979), 40-53.
   49. Elisabeth Schüssler Fiorenza, " 'For the Sake of Our Salvation' . . . Biblical Interpretation as Theological Task," in *Sin, Salvation and the Spirit,* ed. D. Durksen (Collegeville, Minn.: Liturgical Press, 1979), pp. 21-39.
   50. *Ibid.,* p. 28.
   51. *Ibid.,* pp. 29-30.
   52. Peter Stuhlmacher, *Vom Verstehen des Neuen Testament: Eine*

Hermeneutik (Göttingen, Germany: Vandenhoeck & Ruprecht, 1979). In partial form, Stuhlmacher's contribution is accessible in English: *Historical Criticism and Theological Interpretation of Scripture: Toward a Hermeneutic of Consent,* trans. Roy A. Harrisville (Philadelphia: Fortress Press, 1977).

    53. Stuhlmacher, *Vom Verstehen,* pp. 219-224. A fuller analysis of Stuhlmacher's and other scholars' contributions may be found in my article "The Historical Critical Method: New Directions" in a forthcoming issue of *Occasional Papers,* Institute of Mennonite Studies, Elkhart, Ind. Martin Hengel has also advanced critique of the historical-critical method; see his *Acts and the History of Earliest Christianity,* trans. John Bowden (Philadelphia: Fortress Press, 1980), pp. 50-58, 129-136.

    54. See Appendix 1 p. 236, in this book.

    55. James Barr's article has been published in *The Bible as a Document of the University,* ed. Hans Dieter Betz (Chico, Calif.: Scholars Press, 1981); it appears also as ch. 7 in James Barr, *The Scope and Authority of the Bible* (Philadelphia: Westminster Press, 1980). The quotation here is found on pp. 25 and 111 respectively.

    56. *Ibid.,* pp. 28-29 and 114-115 respectively.

    57. Compare Barr's discussion, pp. 30ff. and 116ff. respectively and John H. Yoder, "The Authority of the Canon" in a forthcoming issue of *Occasional Papers* (see note 53 above). See also Appendix 1 in this book, pp. 236-237; and Willard M. Swartley, "The Bible: Of the Church and over the Church," *Gospel Herald,* 69 (Apr. 6, 1976), 282-283.

    58. See Appendix 1, p. 236.

    59. For this reason, option 2 in the "Supplement to the Slavery Debate" deserves to be underscored (see pp. 54-56 above).

    60. Barr, pp. 28 and 115 respectively.

    61. Brevard Childs, *Biblical Theology in Crisis* (Philadelphia: Westminster Press, 1970), pp. 99ff. Note his three exegetical examples (pp. 151-200) and his discussion on diversity and unity (pp. 201-219).

    62. See Swartley, *Mark,* pp. 187, 142-145.

    63. A helpful demonstration of such a method is Perry B. Yoder's description of method correlated with the study of four biblical texts *(From Word to Life).*

    64. The 1970's may well go down in the history of hermeneutics as the "decade of doubt" (some "disgust") about the historical-critical method. Walter Wink opened his book by saying, "Historical biblical criticism is bankrupt" (*The Bible in Human Transformation: Toward a New Paradigm for Biblical Study* [Philadelphia: Fortress Press, 1973], p. 1). Gerhard Maier entitled his book *Das Ende der Historisch-Kritischen Methode* (1974), translated by Edwin W. Leverenz and Rudolph F. Norden and published as *The End of the Historical-Critical Method* (St. Louis, Mo.: Concordia, 1977). While disagreeing with Maier's virtual dismissal of the method, Martin Hengel and Peter Stuhlmacher call for the freeing of the method from the nineteenth-century naturalistic view of history and for allowing historical research to assist interpreters to better grasp the claims and testimonies of the texts (see note 53 above).

    Edgar Krentz helpfully assesses both the strengths and weaknesses of the method in *The Historical Critical Method* (Philadelphia: Fortress Press, 1975), pp. 63-72. For other important critical analyses, see Marlin E.

Miller, "Criticism and Analogy in Historical Interpretation," in a forthcoming issue of *Occasional Papers* (see note 53 on page 328), and Christian Hartlich, "Is Historical Criticism out of Date?" in *Conflicting Ways of Interpreting the Bible,* ed. Hans Küng and Jürgen Moltmann (New York: Seabury Press, 1980), pp. 3-8. For directions beyond the crisis, see Paul Ricoeur, *Essays on Biblical Interpretation,* (Philadelphia: Fortress Press, 1980), especially editor Lewis S. Mudge's Introduction; Bernhard W. Anderson, "Tradition and Scripture in the Community of Faith," *Journal of Biblical Literature,* 100, No. 1 (Mar. 1981), 5-21; and George T. Montague, "Hermeneutics and the Teaching of Scripture," *Catholic Biblical Quarterly,* 41 (Jan., 1979), 1-17.

    65. See Swartley, "New Directions."

    66. For a description of how various aspects of the historical-critical method work in interpreting the text, see I. Howard Marshall, *New Testament Interpretation: Essays on Principles and Methods* (Grand Rapids, Mich.: Eerdmans, 1977); and George Eldon Ladd, *The New Testament and Criticism* (Grand Rapids, Mich.: Eerdmans, 1967).

    67. An illustration of the usual features of the method is demonstrated by George R. Brunk III, in "Journey to Emmaus: A Study in Critical Methodology," in a forthcoming issue of *Occasional Papers* (see note 53 on page 328).

    68. P. Yoder, *From Word to Life;* Henry A. Virkler, *Hermeneutical Principles and Processes of Biblical Interpretation* (Grand Rapids, Mich.: Baker Book House, 1980).

    69. Hans Rudi Weber, *Experiments in Bible Study* (Geneva, Switzerland: World Council of Churches, 1972).

    70. One might expand this point by considering the historical role of pneumatic exegesis. See, for example, Earle E. Ellis' discussion of pneumatic exegesis in early Christianity: *Prophecy and Hermeneutic in Early Christianity* (Grand Rapids, Mich.: Eerdmans, 1978). Points 1 and 7 in my model call for testing the word of the prophet in the community through the variety of charismatic gifts God gives to the community (1 Cor. 12-14).

    71. Ricoeur, *Essays.* The "new hermeneutic" with its emphasis on the role of language and liberation hermeneutics have also informed my work. Karl Barth's contribution, asking us to *listen* to the biblical text and enter its "strange new world," has also been significant: *The Word of God and the Word of Man,* trans. Douglas Horton (New York: Harper and Row, 1957), pp. 28-96; *Church Dogmatics: A Selection,* trans. G. W. Bromiley (New York: Harper, 1962), pp. 65-80; *Church Dogmatics* I, 2 trans. G. T. Thompson and Harold Knight (Edinburg: T. & T. Clark, 1956), pp. 457-660.

    72. Ricoeur, pp. 231-239.

    73. P. Yoder, *From Word to Life.*

    74. For a fuller outline of the structural factors, see Swartley, *Mark,* 235-236.

APPENDIX 2

    1. This book, written by the son of the founders of The Salvation Army, General William and Catherine Booth, is an eloquent testimony to the historic pacifist position of The Salvation Army.

330 Slavery, Sabbath, War, and Women

2. Lasserre has written a major exegetical article on this text. Published originally in *Cahiers de la Reconciliation* (Oct. 1967), it has been translated by John H. Yoder and published under the title "A Tenacious Misinterpretation: John 2:15," in *Occasional Papers*, 1 (1981), 35-49, available from the Institute of Mennonite Studies of the Associated Mennonite Biblical Seminaries, Elkhart, Ind.

3. This point is of special significance to Mark's Gospel. See Willard M. Swartley, *Mark: The Way for All Nations*, rev. ed. (Scottdale, Pa.: Herald Press, 1981), pp. 169-171, 188-189.

4. Lasserre, *War and the Gospel* (Scottdale, Pa.: Herald Press, 1962), p. 88.

APPENDIX 3

1. Charles C. Ryrie, *The Place of Women in the Church* (New York: Macmillan, 1958), pp. 65-66.

2. Fritz Zerbst, *The Office of Women in the Church: A Study in Practical Theology*, trans. Albert G. Merkens (St. Louis, Mo.: Concordia Publishing House, 1955), p. 74; George Knight III, *The New Testament Teaching on the Role Relationship of Men and Women* (Grand Rapids, Mich.: Baker Book House, 1977), pp. 48-49.

3. Stephen B. Clark, *Man and Woman in Christ: An Examination of the Roles of Men and Women in Light of Scripture and the Social Sciences* (Ann Arbor, Mich.: Servant Books, 1980), pp. 71-100. 1 Corinthians 7:1-6 is not even listed in the Scripture index! Clark apparently has omitted this text because it did not fit his criterion. He defines a "key text" as "a text which contains explicit teaching on the roles of men and women. A 'key' text is one which directly addresses the subject of this book and offers authoritative teachings" (pp. 71-72). Clark regards other texts as background texts that illumine the key texts, which in this chapter on the family are Ephesians 5:22-33; Colossians 3:18-19; and 1 Peter 3:1-7. This illustrates the serious weakness and bias of Clark's book: he knows what he wants the Scriptures to say, and texts which don't say exactly that or would even alter his desired emphasis are neglected. And as the discussion below on Ephesians 5 will show, even his selected texts *are made to support* his emphasis.

4. Richard and Joyce Boldrey, *Chauvinist or Feminist? Paul's View of Women* (Grand Rapids, Mich.: Baker Book House, 1977), p. 51.

5. Don Williams, *The Apostle Paul and Women in the Church* (Van Nuys, Calif.: BIM Publishing Co., 1977), p. 54.

6. Robin Scroggs, "Paul and the Eschatological Woman," *Journal of the American Academy of Religion*, 42 (1974), 294-295. While supporting this liberationist emphasis, Frank and Evelyn Stagg note that the discussion, however, is introduced from a male perspective: "It is not good for a man *(kalon)* to touch a woman" (verse 1). See *Woman in the World of Jesus* (Philadelphia: Westminster Press, 1978), p. 170.

7. Ryrie, pp. 66-67.

8. *Ibid.*, pp. 67-68.

9. Zerbst says that Sarah's obedience to Abraham is an illustration, not a command (p. 77).

10. *Ibid.*

11. *Ibid.,* p. 77-78.
12. *Ibid.,* p. 81.
13. Knight, p. 44.
14. *Ibid.,* p. 58.
15. *Ibid.*
16. Clark, p. 73.
17. *Ibid.,* pp. 74, 78.
18. *Ibid.,* pp. 74-76. This latter point is a strange twist to the natural meaning of mutuality inherent in *allēlois* (to one another); nor does James 5:16 necessarily assume the hierarchical (Roman Catholic) pattern for confession of sins (likely confession is to be made directly to the one wronged). The vast majority of the New Testament uses of the word *allēlois* simply do not support this point.
19. *Ibid.,* pp. 75-77.
20. *Ibid.,* p. 78.
21. *Ibid.,* pp. 78-85 (quotation on p. 85).
22. *Ibid.,* pp. 86-87.
23. *Ibid.,* pp. 89-94.
24. *Ibid.,* p. 95.
25. *Ibid.,* p. 96.
26. Markus Barth, *Ephesians* (Anchor Bible), Vol. II (Garden City, N.Y.: Doubleday, 1974), p. 605.
28. *Ibid.,* p. 652.
29. *Ibid.,* p. 618.
30. *Ibid.,* pp. 618-621.
31. *Ibid.,* pp. 700-701.
32. *Ibid.,* p. 667.
33. *Ibid.,* p. 713.
34. *Ibid.,* pp. 709-710.
35. *Ibid.,* p. 712.
36. David and Elouise Fraser, "A Biblical View of Women: Demythologizing Sexegesis," *Theology, News and Notes* (Fuller Theological Seminary, June 1975), p. 18.
37. *Ibid.*
38. *Ibid.*
39. Letha Scanzoni and Nancy Hardesty, *All We're Meant to Be: A Biblical Approach to Women's Liberation* (Waco, Tex.: Word, 1974), pp. 98-100.
40. Boldreys, pp. 50-53.
41. These are as follows:

(1) Christian marriage presupposes and mirrors the functioning Christian community; (2) Christian marriage is always Christologically defined—that is, the relationship between husbands and wives is always determined by Jesus Christ and the church; (3) Christian marriage is egalitarian and a partnership in that husbands and wives are to live in mutual submission to Christ and to each other; (4) Wives express their submission by surrendering themselves to the love of Christ given them through their husbands; (5) Husbands express their submission by loving their wives as Christ loved the church and gave Himself for her; (6) Husbands' love for their wives is to be no less than their love for

themselves. The standard, again, is the love of Christ for His body, the church; and (7) Marriage is to reflect the union of man and woman in the "one flesh" which is now realized first in the spiritual union of Christ and the church and then reflected in the marriage union [Williams, pp. 91-92].

42. *Ibid.*, p. 92.
43. John Howard Yoder, *The Politics of Jesus* (Grand Rapids, Mich.: Eerdmans, 1972), p. 175.
44. *Ibid.*, p. 174.
45. *Ibid.*, pp. 176-179.
46. *Ibid.*, p. 192.
47. *Ibid.*, p. 180.
48. *Ibid.*, p. 181. Yoder applies this same perspective to the parent-child, master-slave, and government-subject relationships, but notes a striking difference in the latter. The authorities are not called to subordinate themselves because they are not the recipients of the Christian ethic, nor are they models for Christians to follow, as Jesus expressly noted (Mk. 10:42-45) [p. 188].
49. *Ibid.*, pp. 190-191.
50. Krister Stendahl, *The Bible and the Role of Women: A Case Study in Hermeneutics,* trans. Emilie T. Sander (Philadelphia: Fortress Press, 1966).
51. Yoder, pp. 176-177, notes 22-23.
52. Dennis R. Kuhns, *Women in the Church* (Scottdale, Pa.: Herald Press, 1978), p. 45.
53. *Ibid.*, pp. 64-65.
54. Paul K. Jewett, *Man as Male and Female* (Grand Rapids, Mich.: Eerdmans, 1975), p. 138.
55. *Ibid.*, p. 139.
56. *Ibid.*, p. 147.
57. Virginia Ramey Mollenkott, *Women, Men and the Bible* (Nashville, Tenn.: Abingdon Press, 1977), pp. 102-103.
58. John Neufeld, "Paul's Teaching on the Status of Men and Women," in *Study Guide on Women,* ed. Herta Funk (Newton, Kan.: Faith and Life Press, 1975), p. 31.
59. Frasers, p. 18.
60. *The Origin and Intention of the Colossian Haustafel* (Göttingen, Germany: Vandenhoeck & Ruprecht, 1972).
61. The Staggs acknowledge that such codes were found in Aristotle and Philo (p. 187). For a convincing scholarly analysis of the Greco-Roman origin of the domestic codes, see David L. Balch, *Let Wives Be Submissive: The Domestic Code in 1 Peter* (Chico, Calif.: Scholars Press, 1981), pp. 21-64. In his doctoral dissertation, however, David Schroeder argues that literary dependence cannot be demonstrated ("Die Haustafeln des Neuen Testaments, Ihre Herkunft und ihr theologischer Sinn" [University of Hamburg, 1959]).
62. Staggs, pp. 190-191.
63. *Ibid.*, pp. 203-204.

APPENDIX 4

1. Some of the best early Greek manuscripts lack "in Ephesus" in Ephesians 1:1; this has led to the view that the letter was written for several churches in Asia Minor: it was circulated from one congregation to another (see Col. 4:16).

2. Bruce C. Birch and Larry L. Rasmussen emphasize this point. (*Bible and Ethics in the Christian Life* [Minneapolis, Minn.: Augsburg, 1976]).

3. See Appendix 3 for commentary on this text.

4. The pacifist use of the New Testament, presented in chapter 3, has made some good contributions to this emphasis, but more needs to be done.

5. These are the hello greetings in Greek and Hebrew speaking societies respectively.

BIBLIOGRAPHY OF SOURCES CITED

1. Slavery

Allen, Isaac. *Is Slavery Sanctioned by the Bible?* Boston: American Tract Society, 1860.

Armstrong, George D. *The Christian Doctrine of Slavery.* New York: Negro Universities Press, 1969.

Barnes, Albert. *An Inquiry into the Scriptural Views of Slavery.* New York: Negro Universities Press, 1969 (orig. pub. 1857).

Barnes, Gilbert Hobbs. *The Antislavery Impulse: 1830-1844.* New York-Chicago-Burlingame: Harcourt, Brace, 1933.

Bartchy, S. Scott. ΜΑΛΛΟΝ ΧΡΗΣΑΙ *First-Century Slavery and the Interpretation of 1 Corinthians 7:21.* Missoula, Mont.: Scholars Press, 1973.

Bibb, Henry. *The Narrative of Henry Bibb.* New York: by the author, 1849.

Blassingame, John W. *The Slave Community.* New York et al.: Oxford University Press, 1975.

Bledsoe, Albert Taylor. See Elliott, ed.

Bourne, George. *The Book and Slavery Irreconcilable.* Philadelphia: J. M. Sanderson & Co., 1816. Reprinted in Christie and Dumond, eds.

_____. *A Condensed Anti-Slavery Bible Argument: By a Citizen of Virginia.* New York: S. W. Benedict, 1845. Reprinted in *Essays and Pamphlets.*

_____. *Picture of Slavery in the United States of America.* Middletown, Conn.: Edwin Hunt, 1834.

Brown, William Wells. *The Anti-Slavery Harp.* Boston: Bela Marsh, 1848.

Burkholder, Peter. *The Confession of Faith of the Christians Known by the Names of Mennonites, in Thirty-three Articles, with a Short Extract from Their Catechism . . . also, Nine Reflections . . . Illustrative of Their Confession, Faith & Practice.* Translated by Joseph Funk. Winchester, Va.: Robinson & Hollis, 1837.

Channing, William Ellery. *Slavery.* New York: Negro Universities Press, 1968 (orig. pub. 1836).

Christie, John W. and Dumond, Dwight L. *George Bourne and The Book and Slavery Irreconcilable.* Wilmington, Del., The Historical Society of Delaware and Philadelphia and The Presbyterian Historical Society, 1969.

Clark, James Freeman. See *Essays and Pamphlets.*

Coleman, Charles L. "The Emergence of Black Religion in Pennsylvania, 1776-

1850." *Pennsylvania Heritage*, 4 (December 1977), 24-28.

Dabney, Robert L. *A Defence of Virginia [and through her, of the South]: Recent and Pending Contests Against the Sectional Party*. E. J. Hale & Son, 1867, republished by Negro Universities Press, 1969.

Dew, Professor. See *The Pro-Slavery Arguments*.

Discussion Between Rev. Joel Parker and Rev. A. Rood on the Question of Slavery, The. New York: S. W. Benedict, 1852.

Douglass, Frederick. *My Bondage and Freedom*. New York: Miller, Orton & Mulligan, 1855.

Elliott, E. W., ed. *Cotton Is King, and Proslavery Arguments Comprising the Writings of Hammond, Harper, Christy, Stringfellow, Hodge, Bledsoe, and Cartwright on This Important Subject*. New York: Negro Universities Press, 1969 (orig. pub. 1860). Essays by: Bledsoe, Albert Taylor, "Liberty and Slavery, or Slavery in the Light of Moral and Political Philosophy."
Hodge, Charles. "The Bible Argument on Slavery."
Stringfellow, Thornton. "The Bible Argument: or Slavery in the Light of Divine Revelation."

Essays and Pamphlets on Antislavery. Westport, Conn.: Negro Universities Press, 1970 (orig. pub. 1833-1898). Articles by:
Bourne, George. *A Condensed Anti-Slavery Bible Argument*.
Clark, James Freeman. "Sermon: delivered in Amory Hall, Thanksgiving Day, Nov. 24, 1842."

Fretz, Herbert, "The Germantown Antislavery Petition of 1688." *Mennonite Quarterly Review*, 23 (Jan. 1959),42-59.

Goodell, William. *Slavery and Antislavery; A History of the Great Struggle in Both Hemispheres; with a View of the Slavery Question in United States*. New York: Negro Universities Press, 1968.

Hammond, Governor. See *The Pro-Slavery Argument*.

Harshberger, Emmett Leroy. "African

Slave Trade in Anglo-American Diplomacy." PhD Diss.: Ohio State University, 1933.

Hertzler, James R. "Slavery in the Yearly Sermons Before the Georgia Trustees." *The Georgia Historical Quarterly*, 59, 1975 Supplement, 118-125.

Hodge, Charles. See Elliott, ed.

Hopkins, John Henry. *A Scriptural, Ecclesiastical, and Historical View of Slavery, from the Days of the Patriarch Abraham, to the Nineteenth Century*. New York: W. I. Polley & Co., 1864.

Hosmer, William. *The Church and Slavery*. New York: W. J. Moses, 1853.

Jenkins, William Sumner. *Pro-slavery Thought in the Old South*. Chapel Hill: The University of North Carolina Press, 1935.

Lovell, John, Jr. "The Social Implications of the Negro Spiritual." *The Journal of Negro Education*, 18 (October 1929), 634-643.

McKitrick, Eric L. *Slavery Defended: the Views of the Old South*. Englewood Cliffs, New Jersey: Prentice-Hall, Inc., 1963.

Mannhardt, Hermann G. "Die Sklaverei in Afrika und die Nothwendigkeit ihrer Beseitigung." *Mennonitische Blätter*, 36 (1889), 27-29.

Minutes of the Virginia Mennonite Conference. . . . First Edition, 1939. Virginia Mennonite Conference, second edition, 1950.

Morrison, Larry R. "The Religious Defense of American Slavery Before 1830." *The Journal of Religious Thought*, 37 (Fall-Winter 1980-81), 16-17.

Neff, Christian. "Die erste Ansiedlung unserer Glaubensbrüder in Amerika und ihr Protest gegen die Sklaverei." *Christliche Gemeinde Kalendar*, 12 (1903), 86-94. Reprinted in *Mennonitische Volkswarte*, 1 (Aug. 1935), 299-304.

Proctor, H. H. "The Theology of the Songs of the Southern Slave." *Southern Workman*, 15 (December 1907), 652-656.

Pro-Slavery Arguments: Several Essays,

The. New York: Negro Universities Press, 1968 (orig. pub. 1852). Essays: "Professor Dew on Slavery"; "Hammond's Letters on Slavery."

Risser, Johannes. "Enthält das alte Testament, das heilige Wort Gottes eine Lehre oder nur einen entfernten Grund, welcher zu Gunsten unserer Sklaverei im Süden spricht?" *Christliche Volksblatt* 3 (Sept. 4, 1861), 12-16. "Abschaffung der Sklaverei." *Chr. Volks,* 6 (Oct. 2, 1861), 20.

Simms, David McD. "The Negro Spiritual: Origin and Themes." *The Journal of Negro Education,* 35 (Winter 1966), 35-41.
Steward, Austin. *Twenty-Two Years a Slave.* Rochester: William Alling, 1857.
Stowe, Harriet Beecher. *Uncle Tom's Cabin.* Boston: J. P. Jewett & Co., 1852.
Stringfellow, Thornton. See Elliott, ed.
Sunderland, LaRoy. *The Testimony of God Against Slavery.* N.Y.: American Anti-Slavery Society, 1839.

Taylor, Stephen. *Relation of Master and Servant, as Exhibited in the New Testament; Together with a Review of Dr. Wayland's Elements of Moral Science on the Subject of Slavery.* Richmond, Va.: T. W. White, 1836.
Thompson, Joseph P. *Teachings of the New Testament on Slavery.* New York: Joseph H. Ladd, 1856.

Vos, Willem de. *Over den slaaven-stand. Door Philalethes Eleutherus.* Met eenige aanteekeningen en een voorbericht van den uitgever J. van Geuns. Leyden: van Genuns, 1797.

Wayland, Francis. *The Elements of Moral Science.* Edited by Joseph L. Blau, Cambridge, Mass.: The Belknap Press of Harvard University Press, 1963 (orig. pub. 1835).
Weld, Theodore Dwight. *American Slavery as It Is: Testimony of a Thousand Witnesses.* New York: The American Anti-Slavery Society, 1839. Reprinted by ed. William Loren Katz; New York: Arno Press and the New York Times, 1968.
_____ . *The Bible Against Slavery:* or, *An Inquiry into the Genius of the Mosaic System, and the Teachings of the Old Testament on the Subject of Human Rights.* Detroit, Mich.: Negro-Press, 1970 (orig. pub. 1865).
Wenger, J. C. *History of the Franconia Mennonites.* Scottdale, Pa.: Herald Press, 1937.
Woolman, John. *Journal of John Woolman.* New York: Corinth Books, 1961.

2. Sabbath

Andreasen, M. L. *The Sabbath: Which Day and Why?* Washington, D.C.: Review and Herald Publishing Association, 1942.
Andreasen, Niels-Erik A. *The Old Testament Sabbath: A Tradition-Historical Investigation.* Society of Biblical Literature, Dissertation Series, Number Seven, 1972.

Bacchiocchi, Samuele. *From Sabbath to Sunday: A Historical Investigation of the Rise of Sunday Observance in Early Christianity.* Rome: The Pontifical Gregorian University Press, 1977.
Beckwith, Roger T. and Stott, Wilfrid. *This Is the Day: The Biblical Doctrine of the Christian Sunday in its Jewish and Early Church Setting.* London: Marshall, Morgan & Scott, 1978.
Bird, Herbert S. *Theology of Seventh-day Adventism.* Grand Rapids, Mich.: Eerdmans, Publishing Co., 1961.
Bonar, Andrew A. *Memoir and Remains of Robert Murray M'Cheyne.* London: Cox and Wyman, Ltd., 1966 (orig. pub. 1844).
Butter, George Ide. *The Change of the Sabbath: Was It by Divine or Human Authority?* Title page missing.

Carson, D. A., ed. *From Sabbath to Lord's Day: A Biblical, Historical, and Theological Investigation.* Grand Rapids, Mich.: Zondervan, 1982. Articles by:
Carson, D. A. "Jesus and the Sabbath in the Four Gospels," pp. 57-98.
Dressler, Harold H. P. "The Sabbath in the Old Testament," pp. 21-42.
Lacey, D. R. de "The Sabbath/Sunday Question and the Law in the Pauline Corpus," pp. 159-198.

Lincoln, A. T. "From Sabbath to Lord's Day: A Biblical and Theological Perspective," pp. 343-412.

Turner, Max M. B. "The Sabbath, Sunday and the Law in Luke/Acts," pp. 99-158.

Carver, W. O. Sabbath Observance: The Lord's Day in Our Day. Nashville, Tenn.: Broadman Press, 1940.

Day, Dan. Why I'm an Adventist: A Christian Invites You to Examine His Faith. Mountain View, Calif., et al.: Pacific Press Publishing Association, 1947.

Dressler, Harold H. P. See Carson, ed.

Hasel, Gerhard F. "Capito, Schwenkfeld, and Crautwald on Sabbatarian Anabaptist Theology." Mennonite Quarterly Review, 46 (Jan. 1972) 41-57.

——————. "Sabbatarian Anabaptists." Mennonite Encyclopedia Vol. 4, p. 396.

Haynes, Carlyle B. From Sabbath to Sunday. Washington, D.C.: Review and Herald Publishing Association, 1942.

Heschel, Abraham. The Sabbath: Its Meaning for Modern Man. New York: Farrar, Straus, and Giroux, 1951.

Jewett, Paul K. The Lord's Day: A Theological Guide to the Christian Day of Worship. Grand Rapids, Mich.: Eerdmans, 1971.

Jordan, Clarence. The Substance of Faith: Cotton Patch Sermons. New York: Association Press, 1972.

Junkin, George. Sabbatismos; a Discussion and Defense of the Lord's Day of Sacred Rest. Philadelphia, Pa.: James B. Rodgers, 1866.

Klassen, William. Covenant and Community: The Life, Writings, and Hermeneutics of Pilgrim Marpeck. Grand Rapids, Mich.: Eerdmans, 1968.

——————. "Pilgram Marpeck's Theology." Mennonite Quarterly Review, 40 (April 1966), 97-111.

Lacey, D. R. de. See Carson, ed.

Lee, Francis Nigel. The Covenantal Sabbath. London: The Lord's Day Observance Society 1966.

Lincoln, A. T. See Carson, ed.

Love, William DeLoss. Sabbath and Sunday. New York: Fleming H. Revell Co., 1896.

Martin, R. H. The Day: A Manual for the Christian Sabbath. Pittsburgh, Pa.: Office of the National Reform Association, 1933.

Murray, John. Collected Writings of John Murray; Vol. 1: The Claims of Truth. Chatham, Great Britain: W. and J. Mackay, Ltd., 1976.

Rice, George Edward. "The Alteration of Luke's Tradition by the Textual Variants in Codex Bezae." PhD Diss.: Case Western Reserve University, 1974.

Riggle, H. M. The Sabbath and the Lord's Day. Anderson, Ind.: Gospel Trumpet Company, sixth edition, revised 1928.

Rordorf, Willy. Sunday: The History of the Day of Rest and Worship in the Earliest Centuries of the Christian Church. Trans. by A. A. K. Graham. Philadelphia, Pa.: The Westminster Press, 1968.

Seventh-day Adventists Answer Questions on Doctrine (SAAQD). Washington, D.C.: Review and Herald Publishing Co., 1957.

Turner, Max M. B. See Carson, ed.

Waffle, A. E. The Lord's Day: Its Universal and Perpetual Obligation. Philadelphia: American Sunday School Union, 1885.

Watson, Thomas. The Ten Commandments. Guildford, Great Britain: Billings and Sons, Ltd., rev. ed., 1965 (orig. pub. 1692).

3. War

Alves, Rubem. A Theology of Human Hope. Cleveland: Corpus Books, 1969.

Augsburger, Myron. "The Basis of Christian Opposition to War." Gospel Herald, 63 (November 24, 1970), 990.

——————. "Beating Swords into Plowshares." Christianity Today, 21 (November 21, 1975), 195-197. See Clouse, ed.

Aulén, Gustav. Christus Victor: An Historical Study of the Three Main Types of the Idea of the Atonement. Trans.

by A. G. Hebert. New York: Macmillan, 1961.

Barclay, Oliver, ed. *When Christians Disagree: War and Pacifism.* London: InterVarsity Press, forthcoming.

Barth, Markus. "Jews and Gentiles: the Social Character of Justification in Paul." *Journal of Ecumenical Studies,* 5 (Spring 1968), 241-267.

Bartsch, Hans-Werner. "The Biblical Message of Peace: Summary," pp. 278-279. See Durnbaugh, ed.

Bauman, Elizabeth Hershberger. *Coals of Fire.* Scottdale, Pa.: Herald Press, 1954.

Berkhof, H. *Christ and the Powers.* Trans. by John H. Yoder. Scottdale, Pa.: Herald Press, 1962.

Best, Ernest. *The Temptation and the Passion: The Markan Soteriology.* Cambridge: University Press, 1965.

Boesak, Allan Aubrey. *Farewell to Innocence: A Socio-Ethical Study on Black Theology and Black Power.* Maryknoll, N.Y.: Orbis Books, 1977.

Boettner, Loraine. *The Christian Attitude Toward War.* Grand Rapids, Mich.: Eerdmans, 1942.

Bohn, Ernest J. *Christian Peace According to New Testament Peace Teaching Outside the Gospels.* Peace Committee of the General Conference Mennonite Church, 1938.

Booth, Herbert. *The Saint and the Sword.* New York: George H. Doran Company, 1923.

Boston, Bruce O. "How Are Revelation and Revolution Related?" *Theology Today,* 26 (July 1969), 142-155.

Bowman, John Wick. *Which Jesus?* Philadelphia: The Westminster Press, 1970.

Brown, Dale. *The Christian Revolutionary.* Grand Rapids, Mich.: Eerdmans, 1971.

Brown, Robert McAfee. Theology in a New Key: Responding to Liberation Themes. Philadelphia: Westminster Press, 1978.

Caird, G. B. *Principalities and Powers: A Study in Pauline Theology.* Oxford: Clarendon Press, 1956.

Cadoux, C. J. *The Early Church and the World.* Edinburgh: T. & T. Clark and New York: Charles Scribner's Sons, 1925.

Cardenal, Ernesto. *The Gospel in* Solentiname. Vol. I. Trans. by Donald D. Walsh. Maryknoll, N.Y.: Orbis Books, 1978.

Cassidy, Richard J. *Jesus, Politics, and Society: A Study of Luke's Gospel.* Maryknoll, N.Y.: Orbis Books, 1978.

Celestin, George. See Marty and Peerman, eds.

Clark, Gordon H. "Is Pacifism Christian?" *United Evangelical Action,* 14 August 1, 1955), 5, 23.

Clouse, Robert G., ed. *War: Four Christian Views.* Downers Grove, Ill.: InterVarsity Press, 1981. Articles by:
Augsburger, Myron S., "Christian Pacificism," pp. 79-97.
Holmes, Arthur F. "The Just War," pp. 115-135.

Cooper, Clay. "The Church Is Found Meddling." *The Sword and Trumpet,* 34 (Qtr 3, 1966), 34-39.

Cone, James H. *God of the Oppressed.* New York: Seabury Press, 1975.

Corliss, W. G. "Can a Christian Be a Fighting Man?" *Eternity,* 13 (September 1962), 22-25, 38.

Craigie, Peter C. *The Problem of War in the Old Testament.* Grand Rapids, Mich.: Eerdmans, 1978.

——————. "Yahweh Is a Man of War." *Scottish Journal of Theology,* 22 (June 1969), 183-188.

Cullmann, Oscar. *The Christology of the New Testament.* London: Bloomsbury Press, 1959 and Philadelphia: Westminster, 1981.

——————. *Jesus and the Revolutionaries.* New York: Harper, 1970.

——————. *The State in the New Testament.* New York: Scribners, 1956.

Detweiler, Richard C. *Mennonite Statements on Peace 1915-1966: A Historical and Theological Review of Anabaptist-Mennonite Concepts of Peace Witness and Church-State Relations.* Scottdale, Pa.: Herald Press, 1968.

Driver, John. *Community and Commitment.* Scottdale, Pa.: Herald Pr. 1976.

——————. *Kingdom Citizens.* Scottdale, Pa.: Herald Press, 1980.

Durnbaugh, Donald F. ed. *On Earth Peace: Discussions on War/Peace Issues, Between Friends, Mennonites, Brethren, and European Churches 1935-1975.* Elgin, Ill.: The Brethren Press, 1978.

Eller, Vernard. *War and Peace from Genesis to Revelation.* Scottdale, Pa.: Herald Press, 1981.

Ellul, Jacques. *Political Illusion.* New York: A. Kropf, 1967.

_____. *Violence: Reflections from a Christian Perspective.* New York: Seabury Press, 1969.

Enz, Jacob J. *The Christian and Warfare: The Roots of Pacifism in the Old Testament.* Scottdale, Pa.: Herald Press, 1972.

Escobar, Samuel and John Driver. *Christian Mission and Social Justice.* Scottdale, Pa.: Herald Press, 1978.

Fast, Henry A. *Jesus and Human Conflict.* Scottdale, Pa.: Herald Press, 1959.

Ferguson, John. *The Politics of Love: The New Testament and Non-Violent Revolution.* Greenwood, S.C.: The Attic Press. Inc. n.d.

Friedmann, Robert. *The Theology of Anabaptism: An Interpretation.* Scottdale, Pa.: Herald Press, 1973.

Gelston, A. "The Wars of Israel." *Scottish Journal of Theology* 17 (Sept. 1964), 325-331.

Gutierrez, Gustavo. *A Theology of Liberation: History, Politics and Salvation.* Trans./ed. Caridad Inda and John Eagleson. Maryknoll, N.Y.: Orbis Books, 1973.

Hengel, Martin. "Das Ende aller Politik" and "Die Stadt auf dem Berge." *Evangelische Kommentar,* Dec. 1981, 686-690; Jan. 1982, 19-22.

_____. *Victory Over Violence: Jesus and the Revolutionists.* Trans. by David E. Green. Philadelphia, Pa.: Fortress Press, 1973.

_____. *Was Jesus a Revolutionist?* Trans. by William Klassen. Philadelphia, Pa.: Fortress Press, 1971.

Henry, Carl F. H. *Christian Personal Ethics.* Grand Rapids, Mich.: Eerdmans, 1957.

Hershberger, Guy F. "Biblical Nonresistance and Modern Pacifism." *Mennonite Quarterly Review* 17, 3 (July 1943), 5-22.

_____. *War, Peace, and Nonresistance.* Scottdale, Pa.: Herald Press, rev. ed. 1953.

Holmes, Arthur F. ed. *War and Christian Ethics* Grand Rapids, Mich.: Baker Book House, 1975.

_____. See Clouse, ed.

Hornus, Jean-Michel. *It Is Not Lawful for Me to Fight.* Trans. by Alan Kreider and Oliver Coburn. Scottdale, Pa.: Herald Press, 1980.

Hostetler, Paul, ed. *Perfect Love and War: A Dialogue on Christian Holiness and the Issues of War and Peace.* Nappanee, Ind.: Evangel Press, 1974. Articles by:

Augsburger, Myron. "Facing the Problem," pp. 11-20.

Taylor, Richard S. "A Theology of War and Peace as Related to Perfect Love: A Case for Participation in War," pp. 28-35.

Janzen, Waldemar. "Christian Perspectives on War and Peace in the Old Testament." *Still in the Image: Essays in Biblical Theology and Anthropology* by W. Janzen. Newton, Kan.: Faith and Life Press, 1982, pp. 193-211.

_____. "God as Warrior and Lord: A Conversation with G. E. Wright." *Bulletin of American Schools of Oriental Research,* 220 (Dec. 1975), 73-75. Also in *Still in the Image,* pp. 187-192.

_____. "War in the Old Testament." *Mennonite Quarterly Review,* 46 (April 1972), 155-166. Also in *Still in the Image,* pp. 173-186.

Jones T. Canby. *George Fox's Attitude Toward War.* Annapolis, Md.: Academic Fellowship, 1972.

Kaufman, Gordon D. *Nonresistance and Responsibility and Other Mennonite Essays.* Newton, Kan.: Faith and Life Press, 1979,

Keeney, William. *Lordship and Servanthood.* Newton, Kan.: Faith and Life Press, 1975.

Klaassen, Walter. *Anabaptism in Outline: Selected Primary Resources.* Kitchener, Ont. and Scottdale, Pa.: Herald Press, 1981.

_____. "The Just War: A Summary." *Peace Research Reviews,* 7, 6. (Sept. 1978), 1-70.

Klassen, William. *Covenant and Community: The Life, Writings, and Hermeneutics of Pilgram Marpeck.* Grand Rapids, Mich.: Eerdmans, 1968.

_____. "Love Your Enemy: A

Study of New Testament Teaching on Coping with the Enemy." *Biblical Realism Confronts the Nation.* Edited by Paul Peachey. Fellowship Publications, distributed by Herald Press, 1963, pp. 153-183.

—————, ed. *The New Way of Jesus.* Newton, Kan.: Faith and Life Press, 1980. Articles by:
Klassen, William. "The Novel Element in the Love Commandment of Jesus," pp. 100-114.
Swartley, Willard M. "The Structural Function of the Term 'Way' *(Hodos)* in Mark's Gospel," pp. 73-86.
Knight, George W. III. "Can a Christian Go to War?" *Christianity Today,* 20 (Nov. 21, 1975), 4-5.
Kraus, C. Norman. *The Authentic Witness.* Grand Rapids, Mich.: Eerdmans, 1979.

—————. *The Community of the Spirit.* Grand Rapids, Mich.: Eerdmans, 1974.
Kraybill, Donald B. *The Upside-Down Kingdom.* Scottdale, Pa.: Herald Press, 1978.

Lapp, John A., ed. *Peacemakers in a Broken World.* Scottdale, Pa.: Herald Press, 1969. Articles by:
Shetler, Sanford G. "God's Sons Are Peacemakers," pp. 75-84.
Swartley, Willard M. "Peacemakers: The Salt of the Earth," pp. 85-100.
Yoder, John H. "The Way of the Peacemaker," pp. 111-125.
Lapp, John E. *Studies in Nonresistance: An Outline for Study and Reference.* Peace Problems Committee, 1948.
Lasserre, Jean. *War and the Gospel.* Scottdale, Pa.: Herald Press, 1962.
Lehman, J. Irvin. *God and War.* Scottdale, Pa.: Herald Press, 1951.
Lehn, Cornelia. *Peace Be with You.* Newton, Kan.: Faith and Life Press, 1980.
Lind, Millard C. "The Concept of Political Power in Ancient Israel." *Annual of the Swedish Theological Institute,* 7 (1970), 2-24.
—————. "Paradigm of Holy War in the New Testament." *Biblical Research,* 16 (1976), 1-16.
—————. *Yahweh Is a Warrior.* Scottdale, Pa.: Herald Press, 1980.
Lochhead, David. *The Liberation of the Bible.* Student Christian Movement of Canada, 1977.

Macgregor, G. H. C. *The New Testament Basis of Pacifism.* Nyack, N.Y.: Fellowship Publications, 1954.
McSorley, Richard. *New Testament Basis of Peacemaking.* Georgetown University, Washington, D.C.: Center for Peace Studies, 1979.
Manson, T. W. *The Servant Messiah.* Cambridge: University Press, 1961.
Marty, Martin E., and Peerman, Dean. *New Theology No. 6.* London: Macmillan, 1969. Articles by:
Celestin, George. "A Christian Looks at Revolution," pp. 93-102.
Shaull, Richard. "Christian Faith as Scandal in a Technocratic World," pp. 123-134.
Mateos, Juan. "The Message of Jesus." Trans. by Kathleen England. *Sojourners,* 6 (July 1977), 8-16.
Metzler, James E. See Ramseyer, ed.
Miguez-Bonino, José. *Doing Theology in a Revolutionary Situation.* Philadelphia: Fortress Press, 1975.
Miller, John W. "Holy War in the Old Testament." *Gospel Herald,* 48 (March 15, 1955), 249-250.
Miller, Marlin E. See Ramseyer, ed.
Miller, Patrick. *The Divine Warrior in Early Israel.* Cambridge, Mass.: Harvard University Press, 1972.
—————. "God the Warrior." *Interpretation,* 19 (Jan. 1965), 35-46.
Miranda, José. *Marx and the Bible: A Critique of the Philosophy of Oppression.* Maryknoll, N.Y.: Orbis Books, 1974.
—————. *Communism in the Bible.* Maryknoll, N.Y.: Orbis Books, 1982.
Morrison, Clinton B. *The Powers That Be: Earthly Rulers and Demonic Powers in Romans 13:1-7.* London: SCM Press, 1960.

Niebuhr, Reinhold. *Christianity and Power Politics.* New York: Charles Scribner's Sons, 1940.
—————. *Moral Man and Immoral Society.* New York: Scribner's Sons, 1932.
—————. *An Interpretation of Christian Ethics.* New York: Harper & Brothers, 1935.

Penner, Archie. *The Christian, the State, and the New Testament.* Altona, Man.: D. W. Friesen & Sons Ltd., 1959.

Rad, Gerhard von. *Der Heilige Krieg im Alten Israel.* Göttingen: Vandenhoeck and Ruprecht, 1951.

Ramsey, Paul. *War and the Christian Conscience. How Shall Modern War Be Conducted Justly?* Durham, N.C.: Duke University Press, 1961.

Ramseyer, Robert L. ed. *Mission and the Peace Witness.* Scottdale, Pa.: Herald Press, 1979. Articles by:
Metzler, James E. "Shalom Is the Mission," pp. 36-51.
Miller, Marlin E. "The Gospel of Peace," pp. 9-23.
Ramseyer, Robert L. "Mennonite Missions and the Christian Peace Witness," pp. 114-134.
Voolstra, Sjouke. "The Search for a Biblical Peace Testimony," pp. 24-35.

Reitz, Herman R. "Prayer and the Selective Conscience." *The Sword and Trumpet,* 47 (Nov. 1979), 6-7.

Ruether, Rosemary Radford. *Liberation Theology: Human Hope Confronts Christian History and American Power.* New York: Paulist Press, 1972.

Rumble, Leslie. "The Pacifist and the Bible." *The Homiletical and Pastoral Review,* 59 (Sept. 1959), 1083-1092.

Rutenber, Culbert G. *The Dagger and the Cross: An Examination of Pacifism.* Nyack, N.Y.: Fellowship Publications, 1958.

Segundo, Juan Luis. *The Liberation of Theology.* Trans. by John Drury. Maryknoll, N.Y.: Orbis Books, 1976.

Shank, J. Ward. "Anything and Everybody in the Name of Peace," and "What Is Political?" *The Sword and Trumpet,* 39 (June 1971), 5-7.
_____. "Which Way to Peace?" *The Sword and Trumpet,* 38 (Aug. 1970), 5-6.
_____. "To the Streets," *The Sword and Trumpet,* 46 (Oct. 1978), 7-8.

Shaull, Richard. See Marty and Peerman, eds.

Shetler, Sanford G. " 'The Triumphal Tactic.' " *The Sword and Trumpet,* 35 (Feb. 1967), 5-9.
_____. See Lapp, ed.

Sider, Ronald J. *Christ and Violence.* Scottdale, Pa.: Herald Press, 1979.

Snider, Harold. *Does the Bible Sanction War? (Why I Am Not a Pacifist).* Grand Rapids, Mich.: Zondervan, 1942.

Snyder, John M. "Social Evils and Christian Action." *The Sword and Trumpet,* 38 (Apr. 1970) 16-19, and (May 1970), 11-15.

Sobrino, Jon. *Christology at the Crossroads: A Latin American Approach.* Trans. by John Drury. Maryknoll, N.Y.: Orbis Books, 1978.

Song, Choan-Seng. *Third-Eye Theology: Theology in Formation in Asian Settings.* Maryknoll, N.Y.: Orbis Books, 1979.

Stauffer, John L. "Can We Agree on Nonresistance?" *The Sword and Trumpet,* 47 (June 1979), 1-3.
_____. "The Error of Old Testament Nonresistance." *The Sword and Trumpet,* 6 (Qtr. 2, 1960), 6-16.
_____. "Was Nonresistance God's Plan for Old Testament Saints?" *The Sword and Trumpet,* 13 (May 1945), 377ff.

Stendahl, Krister. *Paul Among Jews and Gentiles.* Philadelphia: Fortress Press, 1976.

Swartley, Willard M. "The Imitatio Christi in the Ignatian Letters." *Vigiliae Christianae,* 27 (1973), 81-103.
_____. *Mark: The Way for All Nations.* Scottdale, Pa.: Herald Press, rev. ed. 1981.
_____. "Politics and Peace (*Eirēnē*) in Luke's Gospel." *Political Issues in Luke-Acts.* Edited by Richard J. Cassidy and Philip Scharper. Maryknoll, N.Y.: Orbis Press, 1983.
_____. See Klassen, ed.
_____. See Lapp, ed.

Taylor, Richard S. See Hostetler, ed.

Topel, John L. *The Way to Peace: Liberation Through the Bible.* Maryknoll, N.Y.: Orbis Books, 1979.

Trocmé, André. *Jesus and the Nonviolent Revolution.* Trans. by Michael H. Shank and Marlin E. Miller. Scottdale, Pa.: Herald Press, 1973.

Voolstra, Sjouke. "See Ramseyer, ed.

Wallace, Jim. *Agenda for Biblical People.* New York: Harper and Row, 1976.

Weaver, Amos W. "Some Implications of Law and Grace." *The Sword and Trumpet,* 30 (Qtr. 3, 1962), 12-16.

Wenger, J. C. *Pacifism and Nonresistance.* Scottdale, Pa.: Herald Press, 1971.

Wright, G. Ernest. *The Old Testament*

and Theology. New York: Harper and Row, 1969.

Yoder, Edward. "War in the Old Testament." Gospel Herald, 33 (April 1940), 366.
Yoder, John H. The Christian and Capital Punishment. Newton, Kan.: Faith and Life Press, 1961.
_____. The Christian Witness to the State. Newton, Kan.: Faith and Life Press, 1964.
_____. "Exodus 20:13—'Thou Shalt Not Kill.'" Interpretation, 34 (October 1980), 394-99.
_____. Nevertheless. Scottdale, Pa.: Herald Press, 1971.
_____. The Original Revolution. Scottdale, Pa.: Herald Press, 1971.
_____. Peace Without Eschatology? Scottdale, Pa.: Herald Press, 1954.
_____. The Politics of Jesus. Grand Rapids, Mich.: Eerdmans, 1972.
_____. Reinhold Niebuhr and Christian Pacifism. Zeist, Netherlands: The International Conference Center, 1954.
_____. See Lapp, ed.
_____. "The Unique Role of the Peace Churches." Brethren Life and Thought, 14 (Summer 1969), 132-149.
Yoder, J. Otis. "Eschatology and Peace." The Sword and Trumpet, 34 (Apr. 1966), 29-32.
_____. "The Church and the 'New Left.'" The Sword and Trumpet, 39 (July 1971), 7-8.

4. Women.

Allworthy, T. B. Women in the Apostolic Church: A Critical Study of the Evidence in the New Testament for the Prominence of Women in Early Christianity. Cambridge: W. Heffer & Sons, Ltd., 1917.

Balch, David L. Let Wives Be Submissive: the Domestic Code in 1 Peter. Chico, Calif.: Scholars Press, 1981.
Barrett, C. K. A Commentary on the First Epistle to the Corinthians. New York and Evanston: Harper & Row, 1968.
Bartchy, S. Scott. "Power, Submission and Sexual Identity Among the Early Christians. Essays on New Testament

Christianity: A Festschrift in Honor of Dean E. Walker. Edited by C. Robert Wetzel. Cincinnati, Ohio: Standard Publishing, 1978, pp. 50-80.
Bird, Phyllis. See Ruether, ed.
Boldrey, Richard and Joyce. Chauvinist or Feminist? Paul's View of Women. Grand Rapids, Mich.: Baker, 1976.
Brooten, Bernadette. "Inscriptional Evidence for Women as Leaders in the Ancient Synagogue." Society of Biblical Literature 1981 Seminar Papers. Editor Kent H. Richards, Chico, Calif.: Scholars Press, 1981, pp. 1-12.
_____. See Swidler, eds.
Brunner, Peter. The Ministry and the Ministry of Women. St. Louis, Mo.: Concordia Publishing House, 1971.
Bushnell, Katherine C. God's Word to Women. Oakland, Calif.: K. C. Bushnell, 1923. Available now from Ray B. Munson, Box 52, North Collins, N.Y. 14111.

Clark, Elizabeth and Herbert Richardson. Women and Religion: A Feminist Sourcebook of Christian Thought. New York et al.: Harper and Row, 1977.
Clark, Stephen B. Man and Woman in Christ: An Examination of the Roles of Men and Women in Light of Scripture and the Social Sciences. Ann Arbor, Mich.: Servant Books, 1980.
Clemens, Lois. Woman Liberated. Scottdale, Pa.: Herald Press, 1971.
Cope, Lamar. "1 Corinthians 11:2-16: One Step Further." Journal of Biblical Literature, 97 (Sept. 1978), 435-436.
Crouch, James E. The Origin and Intention of the Colossian Haustafel. Göttingen: Vandenhoeck & Ruprecht, 1972.

Danby, H. The Mishnah. Oxford: University Press, 1922.

Fiorenza, Elisabeth Schüssler. "Women in the Pre-Pauline and Pauline Communities." Union Seminary Quarterly Review, 33 (Spring-Summer 1978), 153-166.
_____. See Swidler, eds.
Ford, J. Massyngberde. "Biblical Material Relevant to the Ordination of Women." Journal of Ecumenical Studies, 10 (1973), 669-700.
_____. See Swidler, eds.

Frazer, David and Elouise. "A Biblical View of Women: Demythologizing Sexegesis." *Theology, News, and Notes,* Fuller Theological Seminary, June 1975, 14-18.

Funk, Herta, ed. *Study Guide on Women.* Newton, Kan.: Faith and Life Press, 1975. Essays by:
Neufeld, John. "Paul's Teaching on the Status of Men and Women," pp. 28-32.
Nyce, Dorothy Yoder. "Factors to Consider in Studying Old Testament Women," pp. 16-22.
Yoder, Perry. "Woman's Place in the Creation Accounts," pp. 7-15.

Gerstenberger, Erhard S. and Schrage, Wolfgang. *Woman and Man* (Biblical Encounter Series). Trans. by Douglas W. Stott. Nashville, Tenn.: Abingdon, 1981.

Gordon, A. J. "The Ministry of Women." *Theology, News, and Notes,* Fuller Theological Seminary, June 1975, 5-8.

Gryson, Roger. *The Ministry of Women in the Early Church.* Trans. by Jean Laporte and Mary Louise Hall. Collegeville, Minn.: The Liturgical Press, 1976.

Hamerton-Kelly, Robert. *God the Father: Theology and Patriarchy in the Teaching of Jesus.* Philadelphia: Fortress Press, 1979.

Harkness, Georgia. *Women in Church and Society.* Nashville, Tenn.: Abingdon, 1972.

Hauptman, Judith. See Ruether, ed.

Hooker, Morna D. "Authority on Her Head: An Examination of 1 Corinthians 11:10." *New Testament Studies,* 10 (1963-64), 410-416.

Houser, H. Wayne. "Paul, Women, and Contemporary Evangelical Feminism." *Bibliotheca Sacra,* 136 (Jan.-Mar. 1979), 40-53.

Hull, William E. "Woman in Her Place: Biblical Perspectives." *Review and Expositor,* 72 (Winter 1975), 5-9.

Hurley, James B. *Man and Woman in Biblical Perspective.* Grand Rapids, Mich.: Zondervan, 1981.

Jewett, Paul K. *Man as Male and Female: A Study in Sexual Relationships from a Theological Point of View.* Grand Rapids, Mich.: Eerdmans, 1974.

Knight, George III. *The New New Testament Teaching on the Role Relationship of Men and Women.* Grand Rapids, Mich.: Baker, 1977.

Kroeger, Catherine Clark. "Pandemonium and Silence at Corinth." *Free Indeed* (April-May, 1979), 5-8. Also in *The Reformed Journal* 28 (June 1978), 6-11.

Kroeger, Catherine and Richard. "An Inquiry into Evidence of Maenadism in the Corinthian Congregation." *Society of Biblical Literature 1978 Seminar Papers,* Vol. II. Edited by Paul J. Achtemeier. Missoula, Mont.: Scholars Press, 1978, pp. 331-336.

Kuhns, Dennis R. *Women in the Church.* Scottdale, Pa.: Herald Press, 1978.

Litfin, A. Duane. "Evangelical Feminism: Why Traditionalists Reject It." *Bibliotheca Sacra,* 136 (July-Sept. 1979), 258-271.

Mercadante, Linda. *From Hierarchy to Equality. A Comparison of Past and Present Interpretations of 1 Corinthians 11:2-16 in Relation to the Changing Status of Women in Society.* Vancouver, B.C.: Regent College, 1978.

Mollenkott, Virginia Ramey. *Women, Men, and the Bible.* Nashville, Tenn.: Abingdon, 1977.

_____. "Women and the Bible: A Challenge to Male Interpretations." *Mission Trends* No. 4: *Liberation Theologies in North America and Europe.* Edited by Gerald H. Anderson and Thomas F. Stransky. New York: Paulist Press and Grand Rapids: Eerdmans, 1979, pp. 221-233.

Morris, Leon. *The First Epistle of Paul to the Corinthians: An Introduction and Commentary.* Grand Rapids, Mich.: Eerdmans, 1958.

Neufeld, John. See Funk, ed.

Nyce, Dorothy Yoder. See Funk, ed.

O'Connor, Jerome Murphy. "The Non-Pauline Character of 1 Corinthians 11:2-16." *Journal of Biblical Literature,* 95 (Dec. 1976), 615-621.

O'Neill, William. *Everyone Was Brave: A History of Feminism in America.* Chicago: Quadrangle Books, 1969.

Osborne, Grant R. "Hermeneutics and

Women in the Church." *Journal of the Evangelical Theological Society,* 20 (December 1977), 337-340.

Otwell, John H. *And Sarah Laughed: The Status of Women in the Old Testament.* Philadelphia: Westminster, 1977.

Pagels, Elaine H. "Paul and Women: A Response to Recent Discussion." *Journal of the American Academy of Religion,* 42 (1974), 538-549.

Parvey, Constance F. See Reuther, ed.

Prohl, Russell C. *Woman in the Church.* Grand Rapids: Eerdmans, 1957.

Renich, Elouise and David A. Fraser. "Merrily We Role Along." *Free Indeed.* (April/May 1979), 12.

Roberts, B. T. *Ordaining Women.* Rochester, N.Y.: Earnest Christian Publishing House, 1891.

Ruether, Rosemary Radford. *Religion and Sexism: Images of Women in the Jewish and Christian Traditions.* New York: Simon and Schuster, 1974. Essays by:
Bird, Phyllis. "Factors to Consider in Studying Old Testament Women," pp. 41-88.
Hauptman, Judith. "Images of Women in the Talmud," pp. 184-212.
Parvey, Constance F. "The Theology and Leadership of Women in the New Testament," pp. 117-149.

Ryrie, Charles C. *The Place of Women in the Church.* New York: Macmillan, 1958.

Safrai, S. and Stern, M. eds. *Compendia Rerum Iudaicarum ad Novum Testamentum;* Section One: *The Jewish People in the First Century,* Vol. II. Philadelphia: Fortress Press, 1976.

Sapp, Stephen. *Sexuality, the Bible, and Science.* Philadelphia: Westminster Press, 1974.

Scanzoni, Letha and Hardesty, Nancy. *All We're Meant to Be: A Biblical Approach to Women's Liberation.* Waco, Tex.: Word, 1974.

Schroeder, David. "Die Haustafeln des Neuen Testaments, Ihre Herkunft and ihr Theologischer Sinn." DrTh Diss.: University of Hamburg, 1959.

Scroggs, Robin. "Paul: Chauvinist or Liberationist." *The Christian Century,* 89 (1972), 307-309.

_____. "Paul and the Eschatological Woman." *Journal of the American Academy of Religion,* 40 (1972), 283-303.

_____. "Paul and the Eschatological Woman Revisited." *Journal of the American Academy of Religion,* 42 (1974), 532-537.

Siddons, Philip. *Speaking Out for Women—A Biblical View.* Valley Forge, Pa.: Judson Press, 1980.

Smith, Charles Ryder. *The Bible Doctrine of Womanhood and Its Historical Evolution.* London: The Epworth Press, 1923.

Stagg, Evelyn and Frank. *Woman in the World of Jesus.* Philadelphia: Westminster, 1978.

Starr, Lee Anna. *The Bible Status of Women.* New York: Revell, 1926. Republished in 1955 by the Pillar of Fire, Zarephath, N.J.

Stendahl, Krister. *The Bible and the Role of Women: A Case Study in Hermeneutics.* Philadelphia: Fortress Press, 1966.

Swidler, Leonard. *Biblical Affirmations of Women.* Philadelphia: Westminster Press, 1979.

_____. "Jesus was a Feminist." *Catholic World,* 212 (January 1971), 177-183.

_____. *Women in Judaism: The Status of Women in Formative Judaism.* Metuchen, N.J.: Scarecrow Press, 1976.

Swidler, Leonard and Arlene, eds. *Women Priests: A Catholic Commentary on the Vatican Declaration.* New York: Paulist Press, 1977. Essays by:
Brooten, Bernadette. "Junia . . . Outstanding Among the Apostles' (Romans 16:7)." pp. 141-144.
Fiorenza, Elisabeth Schüssler. "The Apostleship of Women in Early Christianity," pp. 135-140.
Ford, J. Massyngberde. "Women Leaders in the New Testament," pp. 132-134.

Trible, Phyllis. "Depatriarchalizing in Biblical Interpretation." *Journal of the American Academy of Religion,* 4 (March 1973), 30-48.

_____. *God and the Rhetoric of Sexuality.* Philadelphia: Fortress Press, 1978.

Walker, William O. Jr. "1 Corinthians 11:2-16 and Paul's View Regarding Women." *Journal of Biblical Literature*, 94 (March 1975), 94-100.

Williams, Don. *The Apostle Paul and Women in the Church.* Van Nuys, Calif.: BIM Publishing Co., 1977.

World Council of Churches. *Study on Women.* Geneva: WCC, 1964.

Yoder, Perry. See Funk, ed.

Zerbst, Fritz. *The Office of Woman in the Church: A Study in Practical Theology.* Trans. by Albert G. Merkens. St. Louis, Mo.: Concordia Publishing House, 1955.

5. Biblical Interpretation and General (not in 1-4)

Achtemier, Paul J. *An Introduction to the New Hermeneutic.* Philadelphia: Westminster Press, 1969.

_____. *The Inspiration of Scripture: Problems and Proposals.* Philadelphia: Westminster Press, 1980.

Anderson, Bernhard W. "Tradition and Scripture in the Community of Faith." *Journal of Biblical Literature,* 100 (March 1981), 5-21.

Barr, James. *Old and New in Interpretation: A Study of the Two Testaments.* New York: Harper & Row, 1966.

Barth, Karl. *Church Dogmatics: A Selection.* Trans. by G. W. Bromiley. New York: Harper, 1962.

_____. *Church Dogmatics I/2.* Trans. by G. T. Thompson and Harold Knight. Edinburgh: T. & T. Clark, 1956.

_____. *The Word of God and the Word of Man.* Trans. by Douglas Horton. New York: Harper and Row, 1957.

Beardslee, William A. *Literary Criticism of the New Testament.* Philadelphia: Fortress Press, 1970.

Beker, J. Christiaan. *Paul the Apostle: The Triumph of God in Life and Thought.* Philadelphia: Fortress Press, 1980.

Birch, Bruce C. and Larry L. Rasmussen. *Bible and Ethics in the Christian Life.* Minneapolis, Minn.: Augsburg, 1976.

Brunk, George R. III. See Swartley, ed.

Childs, Brevard. *Biblical Theology in Crisis.* Philadelphia, Pa.: Westminster Press, 1970.

Dunn, James D. G. *Unity and Diversity in the New Testament.* Philadelphia: Fortress Press, 1977.

Ellis, Earle E. *Prophecy and Hermeneutic in Early Christianity.* Grand Rapids, Mich.: Eerdmans, 1978.

Fiorenza, Elisabeth Schüssler. " 'For the Sake of Our Salvation' ... Biblical Interpretation as Theological Task." *Sin, Salvation and the Spirit.* Edited by D. Durksen. Collegeville, Minn.: Liturgical Press, 1979, pp. 21-39.

Grant, Robert. *A Short History of the Interpretation of the Bible.* New York: Macmillan, rev. ed., 1963.

Hanson, Paul D. *The Dawn of Apocalyptic.* Philadelphia: Fortress Press, revised edition, 1979.

_____. *The Diversity of Scripture: A Theological Interpretation.* Philadelphia: Fortress Press, 1982.

Hartlich, Christian. "Is Historical Criticism Out of Date?" *Conflicting Ways of Interpreting the Bible.* Edited by Hans Küng and Jürgen Moltmann. New York: The Seabury Press and Edinburgh: T. & T. Clark, 1980, pp. 3-8.

Hengel, Martin. *Acts and the History of Earliest Christianity.* Trans. by John Bowden. Philadelphia: Fortress Press, 1980.

Keck, Leander. *A Future for the Historical Jesus.* Nashville and New York: Abingdon, 1971.

Kelsey, David H. *The Uses of Scripture in Recent Theology.* Philadelphia: Fortress, 1975.

Kingsbury, Jack Dean. See Mays, ed.

Krentz, Edgar. *The Historical Critical Method.* Philadelphia: Fortress Press, 1975.

Ladd, George Eldon. *The New Testament and Criticism.* Grand Rapids, Mich.: Eerdmans, 1967.

Lind, Millard C. "The Hermeneutics of the Old Testament." *Mennonite Quarterly Review,* 40 (July 1966), 227-237.

Lindsell, Harold. *The Battle for the Bible*. Grand Rapids, Mich.: Zondervan, 1976.

Luz, Ulrich, et al. *Eschatologie und Friedenshandeln: Exegetische Beiträge zur Frage Christlicher Friedensverantwortung*. Stuttgart: Katholisches Bibelwerk GmbH, 1981.

Maier, Gerhard. *The End of the Historical-Critical Method*. Trans. by Edwin W. Leverenz and Rudolph F. Norden. St. Louis, Mo.: Concordia, 1977.

Mays, James Luther, ed. *Interpreting the Gospels*. Philadelphia: Fortress Press, 1981. Articles by:
Kingsbury, Jack Dean. "The Gospel in Four Editions," pp. 21-40.
Morgan, Robert. "The Hermeneutical Significance of Four Gospels," pp. 41-54.
Talbert, Charles H. "The Gospel and the Gospels," pp. 14-26.

Marshall, I. Howard. *New Testament Interpretation: Essays on Principles and Methods*. Grand Rapids, Mich.: Eerdmans, 1977.

Miller, Marlin E. See Swartley, ed.

Morgan, Robert. See Mays, ed.

Montague, George T. "Hermeneutics and the Teaching of Scripture." *Catholic Biblical Quarterly*, 41 (Jan. 1979), 1-17.

Mott, Stephen Charles. *Biblical Ethics and Social Change*. New York/Oxford: Oxford University Press, 1982.

Peterson, Norman R. *Literary Criticism for the New Testament Critic*. Philadelphia: Fortress Press, 1978.

Ricoeur, Paul. *Essays on Biblical Interpretation*. Philadelphia: Fortress Press, 1980.

Rogers, Jack. "The Church Doctrine of Biblical Authority." *Biblical Authority*. Edited by Jack Rogers. Waco, Tex.: Word, 1977, pp. 15-46.

Rogers, Jack B., and Donald K. McKim. *The Authority and Interpretation of the Bible: An Historical Approach*. San Francisco: Harper & Row, 1979.

Sandeen, Ernest, ed. *The Bible and Social Reform*, Chico, Calif.: Scholars Press and Philadelphia: Fortress Press, 1982.

Sanders, Jack T. *Ethics in the New Testament*. Philadelphia, Pa.: Fortress Press, 1975.

Schnackenburg, Rudolf. *The Moral Teaching of the New Testament*. New York: Herder and Herder, 1965.

Smalley, Beryl. *The Bible in the Middle Ages*. Oxford: Clarendon Press, 1941.

Stuhlmacher, Peter. *Historical Criticism and Theological Interpretation of Scripture: Toward a Hermeneutics of Consent*. Trans. by Roy A. Harrisville. Philadelphia: Fortress Press, 1977.

_____. *Vom Verstehen des Neuen Testament: Eine Hermeneutik*. Göttingen: Vandenhoeck & Ruprecht, 1979.

Swartley, Willard M., "The Bible: Of the Church and over the Church" *Gospel Herald*, 69 (April 6, 1976), 282-283.

_____, ed. *Essays on Biblical Interpretation. Occasional Papers*. Elkhart, Ind.: Institute of Mennonite Studies, forthcoming. Articles by:
Brunk, George R. III. "Journey to Emmaus: A Study in Critical Methodology."
Miller, Marlin E. "Criticism and Analogy in Historical Interpretation."
Swartley, Willard M. "The Historical-Critical Method: New Directions."

_____. *Mark: The Way for All Nations*. Scottdale, Pa.: Herald Press, 1981.

Talbert, Charles H. See Mays, ed.

Tambasco, Anthony J. *The Bible for Ethics: Juan Luis Segundo and First-World Ethics*. Washington, D.C.: University Press of America, 1981.

Tannehill, Robert C. *The Sword of His Mouth*. Missoula, Mont.: Scholars Press and Philadelphia: Fortress Press, 1975.

Thiselton, Anthony. *The Two Horizons: New Testament Hermeneutics and Philosophical Description with Special Reference to Heidegger, Bultmann, Gadamer, and Wittgenstein*. Grand Rapids, Mich.: Eerdmans, 1980.

Virkler, Henry A. *Hermeneutical Principles and Processes of Biblical Interpretation*. Grand Rapids, Mich.: Baker Book House, 1980.

Weber, Hans Rudi. *Experiments in Bible Study.* Geneva: World Council of Churches, 1972.

Wenger, J. C. *God's Word Written.* Scottdale, Pa.: Herald Press, 1966.

Wink, Walter. *The Bible in Human Transformation: Toward a New Paradigm for Biblical Study.* Philadelphia, Pa.: Fortress Press, 1973.

Wynkoop, Mildred Bangs. *A Theology of Love.* Kansas City, Mo.: Beacon Hill Press, 1972.

Yoder, Perry B. *From Word to Life: A Guide to the Art of Bible Study.* Scottdale, Pa.: Herald Press, 1982.

INDEX OF SCRIPTURES

GENESIS 80, 152
1 .... 22, 117, 153, 154,
  155, 166, 224
1—2 .... 186, 193
1 & 2 154
1—3 261
1—11 .... 193, 194
1—2:23 ...... 293 n85
1:26 .... 153, 154
1:26-27 .... 152, 184
1:26b 153
1:27 ..... 153, 165, 171
1:27a 152
1:27b 152
1:28a 154
1:28b 153, 154
2 .... 74, 89, 154,
  155, 156, 157, 169,
  181, 182, 184, 186,
  190
2—3 ..... 159, 166, 293
  n85, 314 n29
2:1-4 .... 89, 194
2:2-3 .... 67, 68, 71,
  80, 82, 90, 293 n84
2:18 198
2:18-23 171
2:18-25 ...... 154, 168
2:19, 23 156
2:20 156
2:24 ..... 155, 156, 244,
  264

3 .... 157, 171
3—4 113
3:9, 22 155
3:16 ..... 156, 157, 181,
  265, 319 n103
3:20 .... 155, 157
5:1 .... 152, 153
6 173
6:4 .... 319 n100
6:11 .... 285 n130
9:6 .... 101, 107
9:24-27 33
9:25 .... 39, 46, 50
9:26 50
10:15-19 39
12 193
12—50 196
12:1-3 .... 197, 238
12:5 33
12:10-20 .... 289 n172
12:16 33
13 40
14:14 33
16:1-9 33
17:9-14 42
17:12 42
17:23 42
17:27 42
20:14 33
24:35-36 33
26:13-14 33
37:27-28, 36 .. 283 n66

40:15 .... 283 n66
42:21-22 ..... 283 n66
47:15-25 33
47:19-23 ..... 283 n66

EXODUS 60, 106,
  138
Exodus-Joshua ... 196
3:9 .... 285 n130
6:6 106
12:2 80
12:29 .... 285 n130
12:44 42
12:44-45 46
14:14 .... 114, 115, 197
14:28 .... 285 n130
15:1-2 106
15:1-21 115
15:3-4 102-103
15:3, 6-7 ...... 302 n97
16—20 74
16:4-5 68
16:20-30 68
16:23-30 80
16:29 81
17:4 107
17:8-16 .... 296 n5
19—20 114
19:5, 6 238
20:1-17 68
20:8 81
20:8-11 69

20:9-10a 82
20:10 . . . . .42, 81
20:11 87
20:12 58
20:13 . . . . . . .303 n115
20:17 40
20:21 40
21 34
21—23 61
21:2-4 34
21:2-6 . . . . . .41, 42, 83
21:4 . . . . .283 n69
21:12 107
21:15 107
21:16 . . . . .38, 47, 107,
  283 n66
21:17 107
21:20-21 . . . . .34, 41
21:26-27 . . . . .34, 41
22:21 41
23:9 41
23:11 83
23:12 . . . . . .42, 82, 293
  n83
23:20-23 114
31:13 81
31:14f. 293 n88
31:16-17 69
34:21 . .82, 87, 293 n83
35:2 . . . . .293 n88

LEVITICUS 60
19:9-10 83
19:15 42
19:18 . . .41, 42, 48, 204
19:20 . . . . .283 n69
19:34 41
20:2 107
20:27 107
24:14 107
24:17 . . . . .283 n66
24:22 42
24:23 107
25 . . . . .34, 47
25:2-7 87
25:4-6 42
25:6f. 83
25:8ff. 83
25:10 42
25:20-22 87
25:39 50
25:39-43 41
25:42-43 41
25:44-45 62
25:44-46 . . . .34, 47, 48
25:47-52 41
26:34ff. 87

26:43 87

NUMBERS
5:18 . . . . .317 n85
6:1-21 . . . . . .321 n105
9:14 42
14:39-45 . .115, 296 n5
15:15 42
15:16 42
15:29 42
15:32-35 69
15:32-36 . .82, 293 n88
33:50-56 . . . . . .296 n5
35 117
35:30-31 . . . . .283 n66

DEUTERONOMY . . .60
1:16-17 42
5:12-15 69
5:13-14a 82
5:14 81
5:14c-15 83
5:15 . . . . .80, 87
6:4 204
12:11-12 42
15:1ff. 83
15:12 41
15:12-18 83
16:9-14 42
20 196
20:10-18 . . . . .40, 50
20:10-20 42
23:15-16 . . . . . . .42, 51
24:7 . . . . .283 n66
24:19-22 83
26:5-9 270
26:6-8 41
27:19 41
29:10-13 42
31:10-13 42
32 115

JOSHUA
Joshua-Kings 196
1:1-9 . . . . .296 n5
5:13-15 . . . . . .302 n97
5:13—6:27 . . . . .296 n5
7 115
7:1—8:29 . . . . . .296 n5
9 42
23:8-11 . . . . . .302 n97
24 270
24:13 196
3:22, 23 238
4:1-23 . . . . .296 n5
4:14-15 . . . . . .302 n97

7:2, 3, 7, 20-22 302
  n97
6:12 . . . . .296 n5
6:17-19, 21, 24 302
  n97

RUTH 117, 160

1 SAMUEL
4 115
8:1ff. 114
8:7 238
15:1-23 . . . . .296 n5
17:1-54 . . . . .296 n5
24:6 100
26:9 100
28:15-19 . . . . . . .296 n5

2 SAMUEL
5:19-20 . . . . .296 n5
7:13 100

1 KINGS
3:26 160
10:22 43

2 KINGS
4:1 . . . . .283 n66

2 CHRONICLES
9:21 43
18:1-34 . . . . .296 n5
28:8-15 43

NEHEMIAH
5:5-13 . . . . .283 n66
9 . . . . .270, 271
9:12-24 87
13:15-22 70

JOB
20:19 . . . . .285 n130
27:13, 23 . . . .285 n130

PSALMS . .274, 296 n5
2 117
24:8 103
33:6 . . . . .22, 224
35:1, 2 . . . . .296 n5
42—43 271
68:1, 2, 12, 17 . .296 n5
78 115
83:2, 17 . . . . .296 n5
85 109
105 270
108 . . . . .296 n5

118:24 76
124 ....296 n5
135...............270
136 ......270, 296 n5
144:1 ....296 n5

PROVERBS
1:11 ....285 n130
8:15, 16 100

SONG OF SOLOMON
159

ISAIAH 114, 126
1:15-24......285 n130
1:16-17 108
1:25-27 115
2:1-4 ....114, 116
2:2-5 ....302 n97
3:1 115
3:13-15 108
3:25-26 115
9:5-7 ....302 n97
10 137
10:1-4 ....285 n130
10:5-7, 12, 13 115,
   302 n97
13:3-5....115, 302 n97
14:2 ....285 n130
14:4-7 ....302 n97
16:4 ....285 n130
19:20........285 n130
28:21-22 115
30:1-2 ....302 n97
30:15 116
31:1-3 ....302 n97
32:17 109

40—55 ..116, 123, 126
41:22-23a 136
42:9 136
43:18-19 111
43:19 142
43:19a 136
46:3-4 160
49:13-15 160
52:7 136
53 127
58:6 ....280 n38
58:6-7 ......285 n130
61:1-2 ....87, 117
63:15-16 160
66:22-23 67

JEREMIAH
1:10 ....107, 108
5:26-28 108
7:13-15 115
17:21-27 69
21:4-5 115
27:6, 12 100
31:15-22 160
31:31 237
31:31-34 238
34:8-17 ......283 n66
34:8-20 43
44:11ff. 115

EZEKIEL 247
7:23, 27 .....285 n130
9:9 ....285 n130
18:10-13 ....285 n130
20:10, 12 80
20.11f.......293 n88
20:11-12 87
20:13 69

20:16 69
20:21 69
20:24 69
22:29, 31 ....285 n130
27:13 43
37:22........289 n163

DANIEL 240, 247
3:12-18 101
7 72
7:13 126
7:24-25 72

HOSEA
12:6 108
13:5-8 108

AMOS
2:10 108
3:2 108
4:1 ....285 n130
4:2 108
6:1-9.............115
6:12 108
8:4-8....108, 285 n130
9:7-8.............108

JONAH 117

MICAH
6:8 108

ZEPHANIAH
3:1-8 ....285 n130

ZECHARIAH
4:6 ....302 n94
7:9, 14 ......285 n130

MATTHEW 85, 94,
   293 n95
4:8-10 122
4:8-11 124
5, 6, 7 ...101, 131, 239,
   308 n192
5:5 197
5:6 133
5:9 ....121, 136,
   137
5:17 238
5:17-18 81
5:17-20 70
5:21-22 122
5:21-48 147

5:22, 23 242
5:28 163
5:38-40 101
5:38-42......120, 121
5:39..........119, 121
5:39-41 118
5:40 ....299 n27
5:43-48 121
5:44 ....104, 120
5:46-47 121
8:5ff. 284 n82
8:5-10.......251, 297
   n14
8:10 99
8:13 ....297 n14

8:14-15......315 n49
10:5-6 111
10:14-15......298 n14
10:34 108
10:34-35 .....251, 255
10:34-36......297 n14
10:34-39 131
10:37ff. 130
10:38 137
11:12 253
11:19 121
11:28—12:14......197
11:28, 29 81
11:28-30 85
12:1-14 85

12:6 .... .84
12:9-14 70
12:11ff. .... .84
12:12-17 .... .251
12:29 ... .252, 297 n14
13:40-42 ...... .298 n14
13:47-50 .... .252
13:49-50 ...... .298 n14
15:3-6 107
15:7 .... .99
15:18-19 .... .122
16:24-26 ...... .298 n14
17:24-27 .... .251
17:27 100
18:6-7 .... 253, 297 n14
18:15-18 .... .273
18:18 236
18:23-35 ...... .298 n14
18:32-35 .... .252
19:1-9 .... .244
19:6 .... .244
19:7-9 .... .47
20:25-28 ..... 130, 298
  n14
21:1-9 ...... .305 n142
21:12-13 ...... .298 n14
21:33-41 ...... .297 n14
21:41 .... .99
22:7 .... .252
22:15-22 ..... 251, 297
  n14
22:21 100
22:37-39 .... .70
22:39b .... .120
23 .... 108, 253
23:14 .... .285 n130
23:24 130
23:33 .... .99
24:1-2 .... 297 n14
24:2 .... 297 n14
24:6-7 .... .252
24:6-8 .... .297 n14
24:20 ...... 71, 94, 293
  n95
24:29-31 ...... .298 n14
24:42-44 ...... .297 n14
24:43-44 .... .253
24:45-51 ..... 252, 298
  n14
25 100
25:14-30 ..... 252, 298
  n14
25:41 100
26:52 ... 104, 122, 253,
  254
26:53 122
27:57-60 .... .71

28:1 76
28:9-10 . . 315 n49, 324
  n166

MARK ... 218, 224, 326
  n33
1:15 .... .238
1:27-28 .... .70
1:32ff. .... .83
2:25ff. par. .... .84
2:28 .... .84
2:28—3:6 .... .81
3:1ff. .... .83
3:4 .... .84
3:6 .... .84
3:27 .... 252, 297
  n14
5:25-34 ...... .314 n49
6:1-2 .... .70
7:1-13 .... .70
7:9-11 107
7:9-13 .... .147
7:27 111
8:27-33 ...... .305 n142
8:27-38 .... .125
8:29 .... .125
8:34-35 .... .253
8:34-37 ...... .298 n14
8:34ff. 130
8:34—9:1 .... .239
8:35 .... .239
9:35b .... .298 n14
9:42 ..... 253, 297 n14
10:2-9 .... .114
10:34ff. .... .137
10:42-45 ..... 130, 298
  n14, 308 n192, 324
  n166, 333 n48
10:45 .... 126, 263
11:1-10 .... .122
11:15ff. 111
11:15-17 ...... .298 n14
11:15-19 .... .251
11:17 .... .254
12:1-9 ... 130, 252, 297
  n14
12:13-17 ..... 251, 254,
  297 n14
12:38-40 .... .253
13:2 .... .297 n14
13:7 .... .147
13:7-8 .... .297 n14
13:7-13 .... .252
13:24-27 ..... 252, 298
  n14
14:24 .... .237
14:61 .... .125

15:2 .... .125
15:37-39 .... .218
15:39 .... .99
15:40f. .... .162
15:42 .... .71
15:46 .... .71
16:2 .... .76
16:9 .... .76
16:7, 9-11 .... 324 n166

LUKE 85, 123, 183
  295 n131, 312 n267,
  316 n57
Luke-Acts 136, 183,
  295 n131
1:46ff. .... .123
1:49-53 109
1:50-53 108
1:51-52 109
1:74, 75 .... .81
1:79 .... .136
2:14 .... .136
2:14, 29 136
3:7ff. .... .123
3:14 ...... 99, 195, 252
3:21—4:14 123
4:13 125
4:14ff. .... .123
4:16 .... .70
4:16ff. .... .126
4:16-19 .... .123
4:16-21 .... .85, 87
4:18-19 .... .71, 117
4:31 .... .70
6:12ff. .... .123
6:24 .... .308 n192
6:27b-36 .... .120
7 .... .162
7:1-10 .... .297 n14
7:5-10 .... .251
7:9 .... .99
7:34 121
8:1-3 ..... 315 n49, 316
  n57
8:3 .... .162
9:23-25 ...... .298 n14
9:51-55 ...... .305 n142
10:5-6 .... 122, 136
10:10-15 ...... .298 n14
10:13-15 .... .252
10:38-42 ..... .315 n49,
  316 n57
11:20 .... .238
11:21-22 . 252, 297 n14
11:27 .... .163
11:37-52 .... .253
12:16-21 .... .308 n192

12:33 248
12:37-40 . . . . . .297 n14
12:39-40 253
12:42-48 . . . . . .298 n14
12:49-53 . . . . . .297 n14
12:49—13:9 123
12:51 . . . . .251, 255
13:10ff. 83
13:14 83
13:15 84
13:16 . . . . .71, 293 n92,
  315 n49
14:1ff. 83
14:5 84
14:25-26 . . . . .123, 297
  n14
14:27 137
14:27-33 130
14:31 . . . . .297 n14
14:31-32 252
14:33 248
15:3-10 . . . . . .315 n49
15:8-10 . . . . . .316 n57
16:16 253
16:19-31 . . . .308 n192
17:1-2 . . . .253, 297 n14
17:7-10 48
19:11-27 . . . . . .298 n14
19:27 99
19:36-46 123
19:38, 42 136
19:41-44 . . . . .124, 297
  n14
19:45-46 . . . . . .298 n14
19:45-48 251
20:9-16 . . . .48, 297 n14
20:20-26 .251, 297 n14
21:6 . . . . .297 n14
21:9-11 . .252, 297 n14
21:20-24 . . . . . .297 n14
21:27-28 . . . . . .298 n14
22:24-53 123
22:25-26 . . . . . .298 n14
22:25, 26 239
22:35, 36 . . . . .297 n14
22:36 108
22:36-38 . . . . .251, 254
22:37 254
22:38 254
22:49-53 254
23—24 123
23:2 255
23:28-30 . . . .305 n145
23:35 122
23:47 99
23:53-54 71
24:1 76

24:10-11 . . . .324 n166
24:20 130
24:25 239
24:26, 46 125
24:44 235

JOHN 183
1 117
1:3 70
1:18 245
2:13ff. 111
2:13-16 . . . . . .298 n14
2:13-17 . . . . . .251, 254
2:14-22 108
2:15 . . . . .330 n2
4:7-26 . . . . . . .315 n49
4:25-26 125
4:39 183
4:46-53 251
5:1ff. 83
5:17 . . .71, 84, 293 n97
5:18 84
5:38-39 218
5:38-40 236
5:39, 40 245
6 124
6:15 122
7:17 237
7:25 84
8 162
8:31ff. 242
8:44, 45 99
9:1ff. 83
9:4 . . . . .71, 84, 293 n92
11:17-44 . . . . . .315 n49
11:45 183
13:1-13 130
13:34-35 . . . .289 n163
14:15-24 237
14:27 136
15:10 70
15:12-13 . . . . . .298 n14
15:13 252
15:20 137
15:20f. 130
15:26 245
16:7-11 242
16:13 242
17:18 239
17:25 245
18:23 101
18:35-36 . . . . . .297 n14
18:36 . . .104, 122, 239,
  252
19:30 71
20:1 76
20:11-18 . . . . . .315 n49

20:14-18 . . . .324 n166
20:18 183
20:19 . . . . . . .76, 82, 91
20:26 . . . . .76, 82, 91

ACTS . . . 182, 298 n163
2:1 82
2:16-17 . . . . . .321 n106
2:17 180
2:17-18 . . . . . .324 n166
2:36 . . . . .130, 238
4:10 130
5:1-11 . . . . . . .321 n106
5:7-10, 14 . . . .324 n166
5:29 101
6:1ff. 321 n106
6:14 86
7 270
7:26 136
7:42-49 86
7:52 130
8:3 . . . . .324 n166
9:1-2 . . . . .321 n106
9:2 . . . . .324 n166
9:31 136
9:36-43 . . . . . .321 n106
10 . . . . . . .99, 297 n13
10—11 253
10:36 136
12:12 . . . . .321 n106
13:13ff. 270
13:50 . . . . .321 n106
14:4, 14 177
14:23 77
15 223
15:28 223
15:33 136
16 174
16:13-15 . . . .324 n166
17:4, 11-12, 13, 34 . .321
  n106
17:26 57
18 174
18:18 . . . . .320 n105
18:26 175
20:6, 7 82
20:7 . . . . .77, 86, 88
20:7a 86
20:7-12 71
21:8-9 . . . . . .324 n166
21:9 . . . .180, 321 n106,
  324 n166
23:3 101
23:24 130

ROMANS 174, 269,
  292 n67

1:1 48
1:19-21 253
2:14-15 253
4:13-16 197
4:25 130
5:1 129
5:8 129
5:8, 10 130
5:10 121
5:10f. 129
5:12, 15, 17-19 180
6:1, 2 118
6:1-11 129
6:5 131
6:10-11 131
6:17f. 129
7:22f. 129
8:1-17 129
8:17 239
8:19-23 129
8:29 222
10:4 81
10:12 131
10:15 136
11:33 245
12—13 . . . . . . .122, 134
12:3-8 273
12:9 . . . . .120, 122
12:17 118
12:17-21 . . . . .104, 120
12:19-21 118
12:21 119
13 . . .96, 100, 134, 263,
    307 n177
13:1-7 . . .122, 134, 135,
    251, 307 n177
13:3 195
13:3, 6, 7 135
13:6 135
13:8-10 120
14:2-3 77
14:5 . . . . .89, 94
14:5ff. 91
14:5, 6 81
16 . . . . . .164, 166, 167,
    174, 175, 176, 186
16:1 . . . . .174, 176
16:1-2 175
16:1-4 . . . . . . .324 n166
16:2 . . . . .174, 214
16:3 175
16:7 . . . . .175, 176, 177,
    214, 321 n122
16:20 136

1 CORINTHIANS . .182,
    183, 269, 318 n86

Corinthians 172
1:22-24 131
3:5 176
3:16 237
4:9-13 131
5:4 77
6:20 48
7 . . .164, 197, 256, 257,
    286 n137
7:1-6 . . . . . .257, 330 n3
7:1-7 . . . . .323 n156
7:3 257
7:3-4 256
7:4 . . . . . .257, 318 n90
7:4-5, 7 . . . . . .324 n166
7:5 257
7:12-16 261
7:17-24 . . . . .286 n137
7:19 . . . . .286 n137
7:20 . . . . . .99, 297 n11
7:20-22 35
7:20-24 36
7:21 . . . . .52, 284 n80,
    286 n137
7:23 48
7:24 . . . . .286 n137
7:31 . . . . .239, 266
8:6 70
9:1 177
9:7 252
10:33f. 130
11 . . . . . .154, 167, 169,
    171, 172, 179, 181,
    186, 197, 202
11—14 . . . . . . .190, 191
11 & 14 . .164, 175, 214
11:1, 2ff. 169
11:1, 17ff. 169
11:2-10 189
11:2-16 . .165, 166, 169,
    188, 200, 201, 318
    n87, 320 n105
11:3 . . . . .154, 171, 318
    n87
11:4-5 . . . . . . .324 n166
11:5 180
11:6, 13 167
11:8, 9 168
11:8-9 155
11:9 154
11:10 . . . . .317 n86
11:10-11 267
11:11, 12 . . . . .168, 173,
    324 n166
11:11-12 . . . . .169, 189,
    319 n101
11:12 168

11:13-16 189
11:13b 320 n105
11:14 . . . . . . .320 n105
11:15 169
11:16 . . .169, 321 n105
11:17, 18 77
11:20 . . . . .77, 88
11:25 238
12 . . . . .316 n65
12—14 . . . . . .286 n137,
    329 n70
12, 14 . . . . . . .286 n137
12:12-13 165
12:13 . . . . . .35, 57, 131,
    289 n163
12:17ff. 273
13 . . . . .286 n137
13:12 245
14 . . . . .165, 167
14:19, 26, 28 77
14:23 202
14:29 236
14:33b-36 171
14:34 . . .167, 168, 173,
    183
14:34-35 . . . . .170, 173,
    318 n87, 324 n166
14:34-36 . . . . . .166, 169
14:35 . . .167, 319 n103
14:40 . . . . .264, 318
15:20-28 133
15:24 . . . . .137, 238
15:24-26 197
15:24-28 264
16:1-2 82
16:1-3 71
16:2 . . . . .77, 86, 88

2 CORINTHIANS . .188
1:5 137
3:2 236
3:6 238
3:12-18 . . . . . .321 n105
3:18 222
4:10 . . . . .130, 137, 208
5:17 . . . . .111, 118, 129,
    136
5:21 121
10:4 . . . . .122, 127, 239
10:5 237
11:13, 15 177
13:11 136

GALATIANS . .172, 188,
    269
1:1, 11f. 177
2:14ff. 129

2:20 129
3:23 ....81, 161
3:26-28.....289 n163
3:28 ......35, 131, 164,
    165, 166, 167, 189,
    191, 201, 266, 267,
    268, 286 n137, 319
    n101, 324 n166
4 128
4:8-11..............86
4:10 ....89, 91
4:10, 11 81
5:14 120
5:24 130

EPHESIANS..164, 182,
    262, 269, 270, 271
1.............270, 271
1:1 ....333 n1
1:2 275
1:3-14 271
1:11-14 271
1:15-23 271
1:19-23 206
2 271
2:1-10 271
2:5-7.............271
2:11f.............129
2:11-22 271
2:12 238
2:14-17......129, 271
2:15 129
3:1 133
3:10 207
3:2-13 272
3:8-11 133
3:14-21 271
3:14f.............131
4:1 272
4:1-3 ....136, 264
4:1-16 272
4:4-6.............274
4:7-16 273
4:17-32 272
4:17—5:18 273
4:24 272
4:25 131
4:31-32 273
5 ....179, 265, 330 n3
5:1f. 130
5:1-2 ....272, 274
5:3-14 272
5:4 273
5:15-20 272
5:18b-20 274
5:21 ....260, 261, 263,
    264, 269, 275

5:21-22 262
5:21-33 .....186, 258,
    262, 323 n156
5:21—6:9 .....44, 274
5:22 275
5:22-24......171, 263
5:22-33....260, 330 n3
5:22—6:9 ....260, 261,
    268
5:23ff. 201
5:25a 263
5:25, 21 264
5:28-30 263
5:31-33 264
5:33 263
6:5-9 .....35, 195, 280
    n38
6:10-17.......252, 275
6:10-18.......196, 197
6:10-20 100
6:11-12 197
6:15 136
6:18-20 271
6:21 176
6:23-24 275

PHILIPPIANS
1:29 130
2:3-14 130
2:5-11 ....127, 135
3:10f. 130
4:2-3....174, 324 n166
4:7 136

COLOSSIANS.....164,
    182, 292 n67
1:13 197
1:16 70
1:24 130
2:10, 15 133
2:12 131
2:13-15 128
2:14 131
2:14-16 ....77, 82
2:15 ....128, 197, 206
2:16 ....81, 89, 91, 94
2:16f.............85, 91
2:16, 20 194
3:9-11 165
3:11 .....35, 132, 268,
    289 n163
3:18 171
3:18ff. 261
3:18-19 .....260, 261,
    330 n3
3:18—4:1 ....258, 268
3:20 58

3:22-25 35
4:1 35
4:7 176
4:15 ....174, 176
4:16 ....333 n1

1 THESSALONIANS
1:6 130
2:15ff. 130
4:9-12 202
5:15 118

2 THESSALONIANS
2:3-8..............72

1 TIMOTHY...182, 268
1:6-7.............180
1:8-10............38
1:9-10............47
1:18 252
2 ....154, 156, 165
2:1ff..............268
2:1-4.............134
2:8 180
2:8-11 180
2:8-15 179
2:8ff.............268
2:9 180
2:11 180
2:11-12 178
2:11-15 ......180, 200,
    324 n166
2:12 .....167, 168, 181
2:12ff. 171
2:12-13 155
2:12-14 182
2:13-14 181
2:13-15 181
2:15 181
3:1ff..............268
3:2, 12........178, 181
3:8ff.............268
3:11 .....174, 175, 178,
    181
4:1 180
4:6 176
5:2 178
5:17ff. 268
6:1 202
6:1f. 268
6:1-2.............35
6:1-6 ....34, 36, 48, 61,
    200, 201
6:2................53
6:4-5.............37
6:20 180

2 TIMOTHY
2:3 252
2:3-4 100
3:2 130
3:15-17 . . . . . . 242, 249
4:3-4 72
4:7 . . . . 196, 252

TITUS 182
2:3 178
2:3-4 179
2:5 202
2:9-10 . . . . 35, 202
3:1-2 134

PHILEMON 46, 174,
289
2:5-11, 14-15 119

HEBREWS 85, 243
1:1-2 70
1:2 142
3—4 . . . 77, 89, 196, 197
3:7—4:11 84
4:1-11 . . . . 81, 82
4:10 81
7:22 237
8:5 85
8:8-13 238
11:1—12:4 137
11:1—12:5 130
12:1-4 137
12:14 136

JAMES
1:15 82
1:27 . . . . 308 n192
2:1-4 . . . . 308 n192
2:8 120
3:18 136
4:1-3 113
5:1-3 . . . . 308 n192
5:4 . . . . 285 n130
5:16 . . . . . 261, 331 n18

1 PETER 182
2:13-17 251
2:13—3:7 268
2:17ff. 100
2:18-19 . . . . 35, 52
2:18—3:7 258
2:20f. 130
2:21-23 119
2:21-24 127
2:21 133
2:21f. 137
3:1-7 . . . . 260, 261, 330
n3
3:6 261
3:7 265
3:9 . . . . . . 118, 120, 133
3:14-18 130
4:1f. 130
4:12-16 130
4:13 130

2 PETER
1:1 48
1:20, 21 236

1 JOHN
2:3-11 237
2:4-6 242
3:1-3 . . . . 137, 222
3:8 82
3:15 122
3:16 130
3:17-18 . . . . . . 308 n192
4:10, 19 121
4:17 137

JUDE
1 48

REVELATION 126,
131, 240, 247, 274,
275
1:10 . . . . 71, 73, 76,

77, 82, 86, 88
5 239
5:9ff. 131
6:9-11 137
11:15 . . . . 149, 238
12:7-9 253
12:10ff. 131
12:11 137
13:10 . . . 137, 305 n142
14:12 137
17:14 131
19:11, 15 100
19:15 253

OTHER SOURCES
Intertestamental
  Damascus Document
    12:3-6 . . . 293 n88
  Jubilees 2:19-21, 31
    292 n56
  Jubilees 2:25 . . . 293
    n88
  Jubilees 2:27 . . . 293
    n88
  Jubilees 50:8 . . . 293
    n88
  Jubilees 50:13 . . 293
    n88
Rabbinic Literature
Babylonian Talmud
  Baba Bathra 16b
    315 n53
  Sanhedrin 56b   292
    n56
Midrash, The
  Bereshith (Genesis)
  Rabbah 11 292
  n56
Mishnah
  Division III *(Nashim),*
  Sotah 1-6 315
  n53
Mekilta, Shabbata 1
  292 n56

INDEX OF PERSONS

Abelard, Peter, 176
Achtemeier, Paul J., 277 n3, 278 n5, 320 n103
Adams, John Quincy, 281 n40
Aegidius of Rome, 176
Allen, Isaac, 289 n163, n166
Allworthy, T. B., 313 n2
Alves, Rubem, 106, 300 n58, 301 n86
Andelin, Helen, 314 n28
Anderson, Bernhard W., 329 n64
Anderson, Gerald H., 319 n97
Andreasen, M. L., 67, 290 n7, n10, 291 n13, n22, n27
Andreasen, Niels-Erik A., 290 n11
Archelaus, 110
Aristobulus, 74
Aristotle, 332 n61
Armstrong, George D., 32, 37, 278 n10, 279 n25, n26, 280 n28, n30, n33, n35, 285 n106, n112, n116
Athanasius, 76
Augsburger, Myron, 132, 140, 309 n198, n199, n200, n201, 311 n242, n257
Augustine, 76, 105, 254, 296 n2
Aulén, Gustav, 307 n181

Bacchiocchi, Samuele, 70, 71, 72, 89, 291 n23, n29, n30, n32, n36, 295 n132, 296 n136
Bacchus, 44, 173

Balch, David L., 332 n61
Barclay, Oliver, 96
Barnes, Albert, 37, 38, 40, 41, 42, 43, 44, 46, 280 n38, 282 n52, 283 n59, n60, n62, n63, n64, n65, n70-75, n77, 284 n79, n80, n81, n82, n84, n86-94, n97, 285 n121, n125, 286 n134, n135, n136, n137, n138
Barnes, Gilbert Hobbs, 280 n39, n40, 281 n40
Barr, James, 216, 217, 324 n163, 328 n55, n57, n60
Barrett, C. K., 170, 317 n86, 318 n90, 319 n100, n102
Barth, Karl, 152, 294 n122, 296 n137, 313 n3, 329 n71
Barth, Markus, 129, 262, 263, 264, 269, 307 n183, 331 n26
Bartsch, Hans-Werner, 120, 310 n226
Bartchy, S. Scott, 284 n80, 286 n137, 324 n166
Bauman, Clarence, 303 n120
Bauman, Elizabeth Hershberger, 305 n140
Bear, Jacob, 287 n151
Beardslee, William A., 289 n171
Beckwith, Roger T., 74, 75, 89, 91, 291 n44, 292 n55, n56, n57, n61, n63, n66, n68
Begin, Menachem, 65

Beker, J. Christiaan, 188, 323 n162
Berkhof, H., 128, 133, 307 n177
Best, Ernest, 306 n160
Betz, Hans Deiter, 328 n55
Bibb, Henry, 288 n159
Birch, Bruce, 207, 209, 210, 325
    n20, 326 n35, 333 n2
Bird, Herbert S., 292 n64
Bird, Phyllis, 159, 314 n37
Blassingame, John W., 288 n159
Blau, Joseph L., 282 n48
Bledsoe, Albert Taylor, 32, 34, 36,
    278 n6, n9, 279 n17, n19, 280
    n30, n31, 283 n60, 285 n104,
    n117, n119, n126
Boesak, Allen Aubrey, 300 n61
Boettner, Loraine, 98, 99, 100, 140,
    144, 296 n1, n4, n5, 297 n10, 298
    n14, n15, 299 n25, n28, n34, 311
    n240, n255
Bohn, Ernest J., 309 n197
Boldrey, Richard & Joyce, 165, 170,
    171, 173, 257, 265, 316 n69, 317
    n86, 318, 320 n104, 322 n126,
    323 n145, 330 n4, 331 n40
Bonar, Andrew A., 291 n39
Bonino, José Miguez, 108, 110, 301
    n65, n73
Booth, Gen. Wm. and Catherine, 329
    n1
Booth, Herbert, 250, 251, 252, 254
Boston, Bruce, 107, 109, 111, 300
    n59, 301 n67, n79, n83
Bourne, George, 38, 39, 40, 41, 42,
    44, 46, 60, 63, 211, 281 n41, n42,
    n43, 282 n49, n55, 283 n58, n65,
    n66, n68, n70, n75, n76, n78, 284
    n83, n85, 285 n100, n122, n130-
    132, 286 n133, n134, n140
Bowman, John Wick, 306 n165
Brandon, S. G. F., 254
Brooten, Bernadette, 176, 177, 321
    n122, n123
Brown, Dale, 305 n147
Brown, Rap, 106
Brown, Robert McAfee, 185, 323
    n157
Brown, Wm. Wells, 58
Brunk, George R. III, 329 n67
Brunner, Emil, 119
Brunner, Peter, 322 n130
Bultmann, R., 327 n40
Burkholder, Peter, 55, 287 n148
Bushnell, Katherine C., 313 n2, 320
    n105, 321 n105
Butler, George Ide, 71, 291 n14, n29,
    n31

Cadoux, C. J., 325 n3
Caird, G. B., 128, 307 n177
Calvin, John, 102, 156, 320 n105
Cardenal, Ernesto, 109, 301 n70
Carson, D. A., 79, 89
Carter, Jimmy, 65, 150, 151
Cartwright, S. A., 33
Carson, D. A., 89, 294 n124
Carver, W. O., 292 n59
Cassidy, Richard J., 310 n227, 312
    n267
Celestin, George, 108, 109, 111, 301
    n62, n68, n82
Channing, Wm. Ellery, 38, 282 n50,
    284 n84, n88, 286 n134
Childs, Brevard, 218, 328 n61
Christie, John W., 281 n41, n42,
    n43, 282 n44
Chrysostom, 176
Clark, Elizabeth, 315 n57, 316 n57
Clark, Gordon H., 96, 98, 100, 140,
    296 n1, n6, 297 n10, 298 n17,
    311 n238
Clark, Stephen B., 152, 154, 155,
    157, 161, 165, 168, 175, 179, 180,
    184, 257, 260, 269, 313 n3, n15,
    n16, n17, 314 n27, n50, 315 n49,
    n50, 316 n65, n66, n67, 317 n81,
    321 n115, 322 n135, n140, 330
    n3, 331 n16
Clarke, James Freeman, 38, 282
    n46, 285 n132, 286 n134
Clemens, Lois, 314 n21
Clouse, Robert G., 96, 296 n2, 311
    n236
Coleman, Charles L., 289 n163
Cone, James H., 106, 108, 109, 112,
    300 n55, 301 n64, n69, n85
Constantine, 78, 294 n104
Cooper, Clay, 310 n221
Cope, Lamar, 318 n87
Corliss, W. G., 99, 101, 297 n10, n11,
    298 n21
Craigie, Peter, 101, 102, 103, 104,
    143, 299 n23, n32, n35, n38, n40,
    300 n41, n42
Cranfield, C. E. B., 135
Cross, Frank, 299 n 35
Crouch, James E., 268
Cullman, Oscar, 128, 305 n145, 306
    n165, 307 n177, 312 n267

Dabney, Robert L., 278 n9
Danby, H., 315 n53
Day, Dan, 291 n12
Detweiler, Richard C., 140, 307
    n186, 311 n241

Dew, Professor, 32, 35
Dibelius, M., 255
Dionysus, 173, 319 n103, 320 n103
Douglass, Frederick, 56, 288 n157
Dressler, Harold H. P., 294 n123
Driver, John, 136, 310 n220, n223,
    n226
Dumond, Dwight L., 281 n41, 282
Dun, Angus, 304 n129
Dunn, James D. G., 324 n164
Durksen, D., 327 n49
Durnbaugh, Donald F., 303 n117,
    n121, 304 n129, n130, 307 n180,
    309 n209, 310 n211, n219, n226,
    312 n258

Edman, V. R., 296 n1
Eller, Vernard, 113, 114, 115, 116,
    126, 127, 131, 136, 138, 141, 145,
    301 n88, 302 n96, n97, n104, 303
    n112, 306 n166, n167, n173, 307
    n186, 308 n190, 310 n228, 311
    n247, 312 n261
Elliot, E. N., 278 n6
Ellis, Earle E., 329 n70
Ellul, Jacques, 103, 299 n40
Enz, Jacob, 117, 140, 145, 303 n113,
    311 n243
Escobar, Samuel, 310 n220
Euripedes, 319 n103
Eusebius, 78, 82
Ewert, David, 59

Fast, Henry A., 119, 250, 251, 252,
    254, 255, 303 n122, 306 n154
Ferguson, John, 118, 122, 124, 125,
    145, 147, 250, 251, 252, 254, 255,
    303 n120, 304 n131, 305 n142,
    n143, 306 n151, n158, n161, 308
    n192
Finger, Thomas N., 127, 307 n175
Finney, Charles, 281 n40
Fiorenza, Elisabeth Schüssler, 177,
    213, 214, 277 n1, 322 n124,
    n125, 327 n46, n49
Fisk, Dr., 53
Ford, J. Massyngberde, 318 n90, 322
    n125
Fox, George, 126, 127
Fraser, David A., 326-327 n38
Fraser, David A. and Elouise, 264,
    268, 331 n36, 332 n59
Fretz, Herbert, 287 n146
Friedmann, Robert, 134, 310 n212
Funk, Herta, 313 n8, 314 n38, 317
    n71, 332 n58
Funk, Joseph, 287 n148, n151

Furnish, Victor Paul, 209, 326 n30,
    n32

Garrison, Wm. Lloyd, 38
Gelston, A., 299 n35, 302 n105
Gerstenberger, Erhard S., 324 n166
Girardi, Guilio, 110
Glait, Oswald, 72
Goodell, Wm., 53, 54, 286 n141,
    n142, n143
Gordon, A. J., 180, 322 n142
Grant, Robert, 289 n170
Gryson, Robert, 322 n125
Gutierrez, Gustavo, 300 n61, 301
    n67

Hamerton-Kelly, Robert, 164, 316
    n61
Hammond, Gov., 32, 34, 50, 283 n61
Hanson, Paul D., 187, 188, 323
    n159, n161
Hardesty, Nancy, 152, 155, 265, 313
    n6, 314 n36, 318 n90, 331 n39
Harkness, Georgia, 313 n12
Harrison, Wm. K., Gen., 296 n1
Harshberger, Emmett Leroy, 287
    n150
Hartlich, Christian, 320 n64
Hasel, Gerhard F., 72, 290 n2, 291
    n38
Hatto of Vercelli, 176
Hauptman, Judith, 315 n53
Haynes, Carlyle B., 290 n12, 291 n26
Hengel, Martin, 148, 305 n145, 309
    n194, 312 n266, n267, n268,
    n270, n271, 326 n26, 328 n53,
    n64
Henry, Carl F. H., 101, 104, 143, 296
    n1, 299 n26, n27
Hershberger, Guy F., 113, 114, 115,
    119, 127, 141, 145, 250, 251, 252,
    254, 255, 288 n152, 301 n89, 302
    n93, n94, n95, n96, n99, 303
    n121, 307 n174, 311 n248, n257
Hertzler, James R., 287 n150
Heschel, Abraham Joshua, 290 n9
Hillel, Rabbi, 244
Hodge, Charles B., 32, 37, 48, 278
    n9, 279 n25, 280 n37, 285 n107,
    n110, n114, n115, n117, n118
Hoffmann, Paul, 207, 325 n22
Holmes, Arthur F., 98, 139, 296 n2,
    297 n8, 299 n31, 311 n236
Hooker, Morna D., 170, 171, 317
    n86, 319 n100
Hopkins, John Henry, 31, 32, 33, 35,
    37, 278 n1, n3, n5, n12, 279 n15,

n22, n24, 280 n35, 285 n101,
  n102, n125
Hornus, Jean-Michel, 309 n194, 325
  n3
Hosmer, William, 38, 41, 45, 63, 283
  n69, 284 n96, n98, 285 n123,
  n124
Hostetler, Paul, 297 n7, 309 n200
Houser, H. Wayne, 327 n48
Hull, Wm. E., 213, 327 n44
Hurley, James B., 169

Iamblichus, 319 n103
Ignatius, 76, 86
Innocentius, 76
Isidore, 76

Janzen, Waldemar, 115, 140, 299
  n37, 302 n96, n106, 303 n110,
  311 n244
Jenkins, William Sumner, 278 n11,
  279 n14
Jeremias, Joachim, 284 n80
Jerome, 72, 176
Jewett, Paul K., 79, 87, 88, 89, 93,
  152, 156, 157, 166, 171, 172, 181,
  184, 186, 189, 190, 199, 267, 269,
  294 n109, n122, 313 n3, n 4, 314
  n24, n28, 317 n72, 319 n93, 322
  n141, 323 n147, 332 n54
Jones, T. Canby, 126, 127, 306 n168
Jordan, Clarence, 289 n173, n174,
  292 n71
Josephus, 285 n131, 286 n137
Junkin, George, 292 n53

Katz, William Loren, 282 n51
Kaufman, Gordon D., 121, 304 n135
Keck, Leander E., 312 n270, 324
  n164
Keeney, William, 113, 145, 301 n90
Kegler, Jürgen, 207, 325 n22
Kelsey, David, 295 n133
Kingsbury, Jack Dean, 324 n164
Klaassen, Walter, 134, 296 n2, 310
  n213
Klassen, William, 121, 122, 123, 290
  n6, 304 n136, n137, 305 n139,
  n146, 306 n164, 311 n249
Knight, George W. III, 97, 100, 102,
  152, 154, 157, 165, 167, 168, 175,
  179, 184, 200, 257, 260, 296 n3,
  297 n10, n13, 298 n19, 299 n22,
  n25, n30, 313 n14, n16, 314 n26,
  315 n48, 316 n64, 317 n76, 321
  n112, 322 n132, 325 n5, 330 n2,
  331 n13

Kraus C. Norman, 132, 309 n203
Kraybill, Donald B., 124, 305 n147,
  306 n157
Krentz, Edgar, 289 n171, 296 n135,
  328 n64
Kroeger, Catherine Clark, 173, 188,
  319 n103
Kroeger, Richard & Catherine, 320
  n103
Kuhns, Dennis, 266, 322 n126, 332
  n52
Küng, Hans, 329 n64

Lacey, D. R. de, 294 n126
Ladd, George Eldon, 289 n171, 295
  n135, 324 n165, 329 n66
Lampe, Peter, 207, 325 n22
Lapp, John A., 304 n131, 307 n157,
  n186
Lapp, John E., 303 n121
Lasserre, Jean, 116, 122, 145, 146,
  250, 251, 252, 254, 255, 302 n97,
  303 n111, n115, 304 n130, 305
  n141, 311 n246, 330 n2, n4
Lee, Francis Nigel, 74, 75, 77, 88, 90,
  91, 290 n4, 292 n46, n48, n54,
  n66, n67
Lehman, J. Irvin, 113, 301 n91
Lehman, James O., 287 n151
Lehn, Cornelia, 305 n140
Lightfoot, J. B., 178
Lightfoot, Dr. John, 320 n105
Lincoln, A. T., 90, 294 n123, n124,
  n126, n127, n128
Lind, Millard C., 114, 115, 138, 141,
  145, 146, 302 n97, n98, n100,
  n103, 303 n107, 311 n246, 324
  n163
Lindsell, Harold, 199, 322 n141, 323
  n158
Litfin, A. Duane, 327 n48
Lochhead, David, 138, 139, 310
  n234
Love, Wm. DeLoss, 292 n51, n62
Lovell, John Jr., 288 n155, n156,
  n158
Luther, Martin, 59, 98, 142, 176, 292
  n48
Luz, Ulrich, 207, 325 n22, 326 n26

Macgregor, G. H. C., 119, 121, 124,
  125, 131, 136, 145, 250, 251, 252,
  254, 255, 303 n124, 304 n134,
  306 n154, n162, 307 n186, 308
  n188, 310 n224
McKim, Donald K., 323 n158
McKitrick, Eric L., 278 n7

McSorley, Richard, 131, 145, 146,
   250, 251, 252, 254, 255, 302 n96,
   309 n193, n194
Maier, Gerhard, 328 n64
Mannhardt, Hermann G., 287 n150
Manson, T. W., 306 n150
Marcion, 141
Marpeck, Pilgram, 141, 142, 144,
   145, 146, 290 n6
Marshall, I. Howard, 289 n171, 295
   n135, 329 n66
Martin, R. H., 90, 291 n43, 202 n65
Marty, Martin E., 300 n60
Mateos, Juan, 303 n119
Mays, James Luther, 324 n164
Mercadante, Linda, 320 n105
Metzler, James, 133, 309 n208
Miller, John W., 302 n96
Miller, Marlin E., 129, 131, 136, 307
   n185, 309 n195, 310 n225, n226,
   328-329 n64
Miller, Patrick, 299 n35
Miranda, José, 107, 300 n61
Mollenkott, Virginia Ramey, 166,
   172, 175, 176, 182, 186, 189, 190,
   267, 317 n73, 319 n97, 321 n117,
   323 n149, 332 n57
Moltmann, Jürgen, 329 n64
Montague, George T., 329 n64
Morgan, Robert, 324 n164
Morris, Leon, 318 n86, 319 n100
Morrison, Clinton B., 307 n177
Morrison, Larry R., 327 n41
Mott, Charles, 326 n34
Mudge, Lewis S., 277 n3, 329 n64
Murray, John, 291 n41, 292 n50

Neff, Christian, 287 n146
Neufeld, John, 166, 267, 317 n71,
   323 n150, 332 n58
Niebuhr, Reinhold, 105, 119, 139,
   143, 147, 300 n48, n49, n51, n52,
   304 n129, 312 n265
Nyce, Dorothy Yoder, 159, 314 n38

O'Connor, Jerome Murphy, 318 n87
O'Neill, William, 277 n3
Oldham, J. H., 309 n206
Origen, 176, 286 n137
Osborne, Grant R., 212, 213, 327
   n42
Otwell, John, 158, 314 n33

Pagels, Elaine, 171, 187, 318 n89,
   n91
Parker, Joel, Rev., 289 n167
Parvey, Constance F., 172, 173, 183,

188, 319 n98, n100, n101, 322
   n126, 323 n154
Peachey, Paul, 304 n136
Peerman, Dean, 300 n60
Penner, Archie, 134, 310 n215
Petersen, Norman R., 289 n171
Philo, 74, 332 n61
Pippert, Wesley G., 312 n1
Pitt, William, 286 n140
Pliny, 82
Potter, Alonzo, 278 n4
Proctor, H. H., 288 n158
Prohl, Russell C., 170, 317 n85, 319
   n103

Rad, Gerhard von, 229 n35
Rahner, Karl, 108
Ramsey, Paul, 105, 139, 300 n53,
   318 n86
Ramseyer, Robert L., 133, 307 n185,
   309 n208, n210
Rasmussen, Larry, 207, 209, 210,
   325 n20, 326 n35, 333 n2
Reitz, Herman R., 310 n221
Renich, Elouise, 326-327 n38
Rice, George Edward, 295 n131
Richards, Kent H., 322 n123
Richardson, Herbert, 315 n57, 316
   n57
Ricoeur, Paul, 277 n3, 329 n64, n71
Riggle, H. M., 79, 80, 81, 82, 90, 93,
   292 n72
Risser, Johannes, 55, 287 n150
Roberts, B. T., 313 n2
Robertson & Plummer, 318 n86
Rogers, Jack B., 323 n158
Rood, Rev. A., 289 n167
Rordorf, Willy, 79, 82, 83, 84, 85, 86,
   88, 89, 90, 91, 93, 94, 292 n70,
   293 *passim*, 294 n122, 296 n136
Ruether, Rosemary Radford, 277 n1,
   314 n37, 315 n53
Rumble, Leslie, 102, 104, 299 n33,
   300 n44
Russell, Elbert W., 299 n32
Russell, Letty M., 277 n1
Rutenber, Culbert, 119, 122, 145,
   250, 251, 252, 254, 255, 303
   n126, 304 n134, 305 n144, 306
   n154, 307 n186
Ryrie, Charles C., 152, 154, 157, 160,
   161, 164, 167, 174, 178, 256, 258,
   259, 313 n13, 314 n31, 315 n45,
   316 n62, 317 n74, 321 n107, 322
   n127, 330 n1, n7

Sadat, Anwar, 65

Sandeen, Ernest, 326 n34
Sanders, Jack T., 205, 209, 325 n8
Sapp, Stephen, 314 n21
Scanzoni, Letha, 152, 155, 265, 313
    n6, 314 n36, 318 n90, 331 n39
Scharper, Philip, 310 n227
Schnackenburg, Rudolf, 205, 209,
    325 n10
Schrage, Wolfgang, 324 n166
Schroeder, David, 332 n61
Schweitzer, Albert, 205
Scroggs, Robin, 170, 171, 257, 318
    n88, 330 n6
Segundo, Juan Luis, 111, 208, 209,
    210, 220, 301 n76, n78
Shammai, Rabbi, 244
Shank, J. Ward, 310 n221
Shaull, Richard, 107, 111, 300 n60,
    301 n82
Shetler, Sanford, 308 n186, 310
    n221
Showalter, Grace I., 287 n151
Siddons, Philip, 324 n166
Sider, Ronald, 120, 127, 130, 135,
    137, 145, 148, 303 n122, 304
    n132, 305 n150, 306 n171, 307
    n179, n186, 308 n186, n187, 309
    n210, 310 n220, n233, 312 n260
Simms, David McD., 58, 288 n154,
    n160, 289 n168
Smalley, Beryl, 289 n170
Smith, Charles Ryder, 313 n2
Smith, Wilbur, 296 n1
Snider, Harold, 98, 297 n9, 299 n22,
    n29
Snyder, John M., 310 n221
Sobrino, Jon, 301 n66
Song, Choan-Seng, 112, 301 n84
Stapulensis, 176
Starr, Lee Anna, 313 n2
Stagg, Evelyn & Frank, 163, 182,
    183, 268, 269, 314 n36, 316 n59,
    319 n100, 323 n150, n151, 330
    n6, 332 n61, n62
Stauffer, John L., 301 n92
Stendahl, Krister, 266, 267, 307
    n183, 319 n101, 332 n50
Steward, Austin, 58, 289 n164
Stott, Wilfrid, 78, 89, 291 n44
Stowe, Harriet Beecher, 289 n167
Stransky, Thomas F., 319 n97
Stringfellow, Thornton, 32, 33, 34,
    36, 278 n7, n9, n13, 279 n16, n18,
    n20, 280 n31, n32, n36, 285
    passim
Stuart, Moses, 53, 54, 60, 286 n132
Stuhlmacher, Peter, 215, 223, 295

n135, 327 n52, 328 n53, n64
Sunderland, Rev. LaRoy, 289 n166
Swartley, Willard M., 235, 296 n138,
    302 n105, 306 n157, n160, n164,
    307 n179, 308 n186, 309 n193,
    n197, 310 n227, 312 n264, 326
    n33, 328 n53, n57, n62, 329 n62,
    n74, 330 n3
Swidler, Leonard, 161, 162, 163, 314
    n39, n52, 315 n53, n54, n57, 316
    n58, 322 n124, n125
Swidler, Leonard & Arlene, 321
    n122

Talbert, Charles H., 324 n164
Tambasco, Anthony, 208, 326 n27,
    n28
Tannehill, Robert C., 277 n3
Taylor, Richard S., 98, 101, 144, 296
    n7, 298 n21, 299 n24, 304 n129,
    311 n256
Taylor, Stephen, 282 n48
Theophylact, 176
Thiselton, Anthony C., 22, 277 n2,
    326 n27, 327 n40
Thomas of Aquinas, 291 n37
Thompson, Joseph P., 289 n166
Tillich, Paul, 295 n133
Topel, L. John, 106, 119, 125, 126,
    131, 145, 300 n61, 303 n125, 306
    n163, n165, 307 n174, n186, 308
    n192
Tostatus, 292 n48
Trible, Phyllis, 153, 154, 156, 157,
    159, 160, 184, 313 n9, n16, 314
    n23, n29, n39, n40, 315 n42, n43
Trocmé, André, 123, 145, 305 n148
Turner, Max M. B., 294 n125

Urbach, E. E., 284 n80

Virkler, Henry A., 220, 329 n68
Voolstra, Sjouke, 133, 309 n210
Vos, Willem de, 287 n150

Waffle, A. E., 290 n3, 292 n60
Walker, William O., 318 n87
Walpole, 160
Wallis, Jim, 132, 307 n179, n186,
    309 n202
Warfield, B. B., 295 n133
Watson, Thomas, 75, 76, 291 n40,
    292 n52, n58
Wayland, Francis, 38, 40, 45, 282
    n48, n56, 283 n78, 284 n84, n95,
    286 n134
Weaver, Amos W., 302 n92

Weber, Hans Rudi, 220, 329 n69
Weld, Theodore Dwight, 31, 38, 39,
    41, 44, 278 n2, 280 n40, 281 n40,
    282 n51, n53, n54, 283 n57, n65,
    n66, n67, 284 n85, 285 n127,
    n128-129, 286 n134, n139, n140,
    289 n166
Wenger, John C., 287 n146, n147,
    288 n153, 324 n165, 325 n3
Wetzel, C. Robert, 324 n166
Wiesinger, 180
Williams, Don, 165, 176, 180, 181,
    257, 265, 316 n70, 321 n119, 322
    n144, 323 n145, 330 n5, 332 n41
Wink, Walter, 296 n137, 328 n64
Woolman, John, 27, 54, 55, 56, 63,
    287 n144, n145
Wright, George Ernest, 103, 105,
    140, 143, 299 n36, n37, 300 n47,
    311 n237
Wynkoop, Mildred Bangs, 325 n7

Yoder, Edward, 302 n93
Yoder, J. Otis, 310 n221

Yoder, John H., 112, 116, 117, 120,
    123, 124, 127-137, 139, 141, 145,
    146, 148, 206, 207, 209, 210, 265,
    266, 269, 300 n52, 301 n87, 302
    n98, 303 n108, n109, n115, n116,
    n122, 304 n128, n131, 305 n147,
    n149, 306 n155, n166, n170,
    n172, 307 n178, n182, n184, 308
    n188, n189, 309 n196, n205,
    n206, n207, n211, 310 n217,
    n221, 230, 312 n259, n265, 325
    n14, n17, n18, n19, 326 n34, 328
    n57, 332 n43, n48, n51
Yoder, Perry B., 153, 155, 157, 184,
    220, 224, 225, 289 n171, n172,
    295 n135, 313 n8, 314 n22, n30,
    325 n6, 328 n63, 329 n68, n73

Zeitlin, Solomon, 284 n80
Zerbst, Fritz, 152, 156, 157, 158,
    161, 164, 167, 174, 179, 257, 259,
    314 n25, n32, 315 n48, 316 n63,
    317 n75, 321 n110, 322 n130,
    n131, 330 n2, n9

THE CONRAD GREBEL
LECTURES

The Conrad Grebel Lectureship was set up in 1950 to make possible an annual study by a Mennonite scholar of some topic of interest and value to the Mennonite Church and to other Christian people. It is administered by the Conrad Grebel Projects Committee appointed by and responsible to the Mennonite Board of Education. The committee appoints the lecturers, approves their subjects, counsels them during their studies, and arranges for the delivery of the lectures at one or more places.

Conrad Grebel was an influential leader in the sixteenth-century Swiss Anabaptist movement and is honored as one of the founders of the Mennonite Church.

The lectures are published by Herald Press, Scottdale, Pa. 15683, and Kitchener, Ont. N2G 4M5, as soon as feasible after the delivery of the lectures. The date of publication by Herald Press is indicated by parenthesis.

Lectures thus far delivered are as follows:

1952—*Foundations of Christian Education,*
　　by Paul Mininger

1953—*The Challenge of Christian Stewardship* (1955),
　　by Milo Kauffman

1954—*The Way of the Cross in Human Relations* (1958),
　　by Guy F. Hershberger

1955—*The Alpha and the Omega* (1955),
　　by Paul Erb

1956—*The Nurture and Evangelism of Children* (1959),
　　by Gideon G. Yoder

1957—*The Holy Spirit and the Holy Life* (1959),
by Chester K. Lehman

1959—*The Church Apostolic* (1960),
by J. D. Graber

1960—*These Are My People* (1962),
by Harold S. Bender

1963—*Servant of God's Servants* (1964).
by Paul M. Miller

1964—*The Resurrected Life* (1965),
by John R. Mumaw

1965—*Creating Christian Personality* (1966),
by A. Don Augsburger

1966—*God's Word Written* (1966),
by J. C. Wenger

1967—*The Christian and Revolution* (1968),
by Melvin Gingerich

1968-1969—*The Discerning Community: Church Renewal*,
by J. Lawrence Burkholder

1970—*Woman Liberated* (1971),
by Lois Gunden Clemens

1971—*Christianity and Culture: An African Context*,
by Donald R. Jacobs

1973—*In Praise of Leisure* (1974),
by Harold D. Lehman

1977—*Integrity: Let Your Yea Be Yea* (1978),
by J. Daniel Hess

1979—*The Christian Entrepreneur* (1980),
by Carl Kreider

1980—*From Word to Life* (1982),
by Perry Yoder

1980—*Slavery, Sabbath, War, and Women* (1983),
by Willard M. Swartley

1981—*Christians in Families* (1982),
by Ross T. Bender

Willard M. Swartley is director of the Institute of Mennonite Studies and professor of New Testament at the Associated Mennonite Biblical Seminaries, Elkhart, Indiana. He teaches courses in biblical interpretation, New Testament theology and ethics, and war and peace in the Bible.

He holds the PhD degree from Princeton Theological Seminary and has studied at Garrett Theological Seminary. He received the BD degree from Goshen Biblical Seminary and earned his BA degree at Eastern Mennonite College.

Swartley has published numerous articles, among which are "The Biblical Basis of Stewardship" in *The Earth Is the Lord's* (Paulist Press, 1978); "Politics and Peace (*Eirēnē*) in Luke's Gospel" in *Political Issues in Luke-Acts*, Orbis Press, 1983; "The Structural Function of the Term 'Way' *(Hodos)* in Mark's Gospel" in *The New Way of Jesus* (Faith and Life Press, 1980); and a scholarly essay on Ignatius in *Vigiliae Christianae* (1973).

Swartley served on the Mennonite Publication Board from 1971 to 1980 and was executive secretary for the Conrad Grebel Projects Committee, 1973-1980. He taught at Goshen College, Eastern Mennonite College and Seminary, and Conrad Grebel College.

Willard and Mary (Lapp) Swartley are the parents of Louisa Renee and Kenton Eugene. They are members of Belmont Mennonite Church in Elkhart.